# HUSKISSON AND HIS AGE

THE STATUE OF WILLIAM HUSKISSON
IN PIMLICO GARDENS

# HUSKISSON
## AND HIS AGE

by
### C. R. FAY

LONGMANS GREEN AND CO
LONDON    NEW YORK ✦ TORONTO

LONGMANS, GREEN AND CO LTD
6 & 7 CLIFFORD STREET LONDON W 1

ALSO AT MELBOURNE AND CAPE TOWN

LONGMANS, GREEN AND CO INC
55 FIFTH AVENUE NEW YORK 3

LONGMANS, GREEN AND CO
215 VICTORIA STREET TORONTO 1

ORIENT LONGMANS LTD
BOMBAY CALCUTTA MADRAS

FIRST PUBLISHED 1951

PRINTED IN GREAT BRITAIN BY ROBERT MACLEHOSE AND CO. LTD.
THE UNIVERSITY PRESS, GLASGOW

# MOTTO

*ἐγὼ δὲ ὀφείλω λέγειν τὰ λεγόμενα, πείθεσθαί γε μὴν οὐ πανταπᾶσι ὀφείλω.*—Herodotus

# PREFACE

EDUCATED at Merchant Taylors' School, Crosby, I had a natural interest in the growth of Liverpool, and also a family interest in railways. This combination of circumstances first focussed my attention on William Huskisson, and my interest in the statesman grew as I came to the study of Imperial Economy at Toronto and Cambridge.

I have drawn heavily on the Huskisson Papers in the British Museum and the Public Reference Library, Liverpool, as well as on the Board of Trade material in the Public Record Office. And I desire to express my special obligation to Lord Hatherton for permitting me to consult at Teddesley (Staffs.) the valuable records (correspondence, diaries, etc.) inherited by him from his ancestor Edward John Littleton, the first Lord Hatherton.

References in numbered thousands are to the Additional Manuscripts in the British Museum.

C. R. FAY

*Cambridge*, 1950

# ACKNOWLEDGMENTS

ACKNOWLEDGMENTS for permission to include copyright material are due to Messrs. Gerald Duckworth & Co. Ltd., for part of the poem *The South Country* by Hilaire Belloc; and The Editor of the *Leek Post & Times* for two extracts from the issue of February 11th 1899.

# CONTENTS

# PLATES

# MAPS

# INTRODUCTION
## 15 September 1830

### The Date

'HUSKISSON, isn't he the man that was run over . . .?'

Yes, he was. It is the fact about him which everyone knows, and usually the only one. So we may begin by knowing it once again, this time with some local colour. Birtsmorton Court, seven miles south-east of Malvern, is one of the oldest and most beautiful moated houses in England. It sheltered the Lollard, Sir John Oldcastle, after his escape from the Tower: Queen Margaret of Anjou and her son Edward, Prince of Wales, took refuge here during the Wars of the Roses: next it was the home of the youth who became Cardinal Wolsey: 'lastly', says our Guide to the Malvern Country, 'it was the birthplace of William Huskisson, the statesman who was killed by Stephenson's famous *Rocket*,[1] at the opening of the Liverpool and Manchester Railway in 1830.'

The strange thing was that of the numerous engines assembled for the occasion it should be the *Rocket* which struck him down. Nor was George Stephenson driving it, his engine was the *Northumbrian*.

### 1830

It is convenient when kings, governments and great men terminate at an 'o'—George II, 1760: George III, 1820:

---

[1] The Science Museum, South Kensington, exhibits:

1. The *Rocket*, in its final much altered condition. Recent scraping of the painted buffer has disclosed 'No. I'.

2. A replica of the *Rocket* by Messrs. Ro. Stephenson & Co., makers of the original engine—in form and material as at the Rainhill trials in October 1829. No buffer at this stage.

3. List of distinguished guests in the Ducal train, with fanciful drawing of it. The band waggon has tiers on it.

4. List of guests invited to the Mayoral Dinner on 16 September, and invitation card of C. Lawrence, Chairman of the Railway.

5. Maps, Committee Report of 1825 and Annual Reports of the Liverpool and Manchester Railway.

6. The 'Order of the Day', with engines, drivers and colours, and in particular 'The Engines will stop at Parkside (a little beyond Newton) to take in a supply of water, during which the company are requested not to leave their carriages'.

B

I

George IV, 1830. 1830 also saw the end of the long Tory reign and of Huskisson its most liberal representative. Economic periods are only marked by o's, because we elect that it shall be so. But 1760-1830 is as real an economic period as there is, and it is denominated by a most appropriate title *The Industrial Revolution*—not so called nor in inverted commas but italicised to signal the one and only Industrial Revolution in our national story. Precursors and consummations of course there were in this and other lands, otherwise history would make nonsense; but the historian who baulks at this title for this period merely advertises an academic whim. There was not merely a difference of quantity, an intensification of what had gone before, but a fundamental reshaping, welded at the centre by a generation of war, which itself was heralded by the French Revolution of 1789. Before 1760 there were, indeed, significant signs of the transition both in England and South Wales, but in Scotland, the magnetic north of the new industrial compass, next to none—unless we are to argue that a tobacco lord in scarlet cloak must one day end in something solid. After 1830 comes the railway age, when machinery, harnessed to locomotion, mechanised itself on a kind of Severn bore, which rolled along the decades to break into world war, when the new century was young. Of these seventy crucial years, 1760 to 1830, Huskisson saw sixty. For he was born on 11 March 1770 and died on 15 September 1830.

### SEPTEMBER

David Ricardo (1772-1823) and William Huskisson (1770-1830) were the two greatest financial brains of their day. Between them they fixed the status of sterling for a century. 'Il commence l'âge d'or'—to adapt Castlereagh's after-dinner *mot* at Vienna. Ricardo, Huskisson's junior by two years, died seven years before him: and both in their exits were 'Septembrists'. Ricardo died on 11 September and was buried on 18 September:

This day the remains of David Ricardo Esq. were removed from Gatcombe Park, and interred in a vault in the Parish Church of Harnish, about one and a half miles from this place [*Chippenham, Wilts.*].

Huskisson died on Wednesday 15 September and was buried on Friday 24 September in St. James's Cemetery, Liverpool (adjoining the Liverpool Cathedral of to-day), before a gathering of 15,000 mourners. To see the Mausoleum as it is now—desolate and dirty, with rubbish on the floor, and to crane through the grill at the bottom up to the cracked face of Gibson's statue makes one sick at heart for the memory of the statesman and dubious of the civic pride of Liverpool.

### THE 15TH OF SEPTEMBER

I had watched the fly-past from the Club Terrace, with the open page of *Rasselas* before me:

But what would be the security of the good if the bad could at pleasure invade them from the sky? Against an army sailing through the clouds neither walls nor mountains nor seas could afford any security. A flight of northern savages might hover in the wind, and light at once with irresistible violence upon the capital of a fruitful region that was rolling under them.

But the good on this occasion had Spitfires to help them: the day (for us) of the Battle of Britain: the day Dizzy lost his Mary Anne: the day and round about it that Moscow burned—the fingers of Napoleon: the day that death claimed Huskisson.

If you don't know it, 'you don't know much,' said the Duchess, 'and that's a fact.' I ask pardon for the seeming inconsequence, but Daresbury is seven miles south of Warrington, and Parkside, Newton, is five miles north of it; and Newton, alias Newton-le-Willows, alias Newton-in-Makerfield, Lancs, contained the abode from which on 11 July 1832 Charles Lutwidge Dodgson was taken to be baptised at the parochial chapelry of Daresbury. And though you may not have been to Parkside, which is a couple of signal boxes half a mile east of Newton Station, you almost must have been to see the Lewis Carroll window in Daresbury Church, with the Tenniel panels of the Duchess, the Cheshire Cat, the Mad Hatter and others in that glorious company.

The tablet to Huskisson is between the signal boxes and is becoming soiled. The only traces of the station are two small houses adapted from its premises, a horse ramp leading down to the old platform, and a disused pump well, where the engines watered. The tablet is white, on a black background framed in marble, and reads:

### THIS TABLET

A tribute of personal respect and affection has been placed here to mark the spot where on the 15th of September 1830, the day of the opening of this Railroad, the Right Honourable William Huskisson M.P., singled out by the decree of an inscrutable Providence from the midst of the distinguished multitude that surrounded him, in the full pride of his talents and the perfection of his usefulness, met with the accident that occasioned his death and which deprived England of an illustrious statesman and Liverpool of its most honoured representative: which changed a moment of the noblest exaltation and triumph that science and genius achieved, into one of desolation and mourning, and striking terror into the hearts of assembled thousands brought home to every bosom the forgotten truth that

IN THE MIDST OF LIFE WE ARE IN DEATH

This is early nineteenth-century style, as sorry as the college buildings of the time, and makes one regret that the epitapher had been freed from the discipline of Latin. Said Dr Parr to Dr Butler, 'It's all very well, Sammy, to say that so-and-so is a good scholar, but can he write an inscription?' However, it is a consolation that William Hayley had been ten years in his grave.

### The Accident
The letter which follows is definitive:

To the Marquess of Anglesey.[1]

Teddesley Sept. 19, 1830

Having attended poor H. to Eccles where he died, I was so occupied that

---

[1] Huskisson's time-table, as given by Mrs H., 20 July-15 September 1830:

July 20—Operation in London.

Aug 9—By Godalming to Cowes, to stay with *Lord Anglesey*, 'for whom Mr H. entertained a high attachment' (weather bad).

Aug 15—Eartham.

Sept 4-6—Weekend at Testwood (Hants) with Sturges Bourne. *Palmerston* came over from Broadlands to see him.

Sept 7—Via Woodstock to Teddesley.

Sept 8—Trentham (confined to his room).

Sept 9—Liverpool.

I was unable to write today, as I had wished. The Papers give substantially accurate accounts of his accident and death. We were waiting on the rail-road to take in water. It was in a large stone quarry through which a dam is raised for the railroad. This dam is very narrow, only allowing room for the double railroad—but no standing room on the sides: Huskisson was speaking to the D. of W., who was standing at the head of the car inside—when the Duke observing the people re-entering the car said 'Well, we seem to be preparing to go on—I think you had better get in'. I was stand-ing close to Huskisson at the time, and on hearing the Duke say this, I turned round and saw an engine on the opposite railway coming up at great speed—then about 200 yards distant. I got up on the side of one of the cars through the wicket, but not without difficulty, for it was very high, and there were no steps. I turned round and pulled in Esterhazy after me—I then saw Huskisson in great trepidation seize the wicket, which was open, and try to get round it. He even lifted up his leg to try to enter, but it was too late. He had lost his head entirely—the engine had come up, and in trying to fling himself out of the way the engine knocked him down on his back in the centre of its road, but with his left leg bent in this way[1] on the Rail so that the leg and thigh were crushed to a pulp, the bones being quite comminuted. He was perfectly sensible from the moment of his accident to that of his death and bore his suffering with surprising fortitude and drawing the ear of those he wished to speak to down to his lips and giving directions about his Will etc.

Mrs. Huskisson has reluctantly consented to part with his remains and that he should be buried with public honours at Liverpool. The corpse went from Eccles to Liverpool yesterday. I mean to go there on Wed. Mrs. H. has come here for the moment. She is in the profoundest afflic-tion, but I hope her health will not suffer.

I have a letter from Palmerston[2] full of grief on the occasion on public and private grounds. What a sad loss to the country at this moment.

Ever my dear Lord
Faithfully yrs.

The Marquess of Anglesey.                    E. J. Littleton.

A second letter carries the story forward. It was given to me in type-script by Mr G. R. Smith of the L.M.S. I do not know who Arabella is. There are three Egertons on the Railway Dinner list for the evening of the 15th—Sir Philip Egerton,

[1] In the original a drawing of the leg was inserted here.
[2] Palmerston had just been to Testwood to see him.

W. Egerton, M.P., and Col. Egerton; is R. Egerton of the letter the Colonel?

Park Field
Near Liverpool.
16th September, 1830

My dear Arabella,

I have declined accompanying Lord Hill[1] to Childwall this morning that he is gone to see the Duke that I might have time to write you a few lines before the post goes out. We did not return from the Railroad expedition before 11 o'clock last night. A terrible damper was thrown upon the proceedings by an accident that occurred to poor Mr. Huskisson which has terminated in his death! The Duke of Wellington's party in suitable carriages fitted up for the purpose and drawn by the best steam engine was to proceed alone on the right hand railroad so as to have perfect view of all the other trains which were drawn up on the left hand road running of course parallel with the former. The Duke had shot ahead some distance and had halted for the purpose of seeing the procession pass when some of their party, contrary to express instructions, left their carriage to look about them, amongst others Lord Delamere, General Gascoyne, Mr. Huskisson, and as the trains on the other line approached, there not being much space between, everyone endeavoured to resume his place, and in the hurry a little confusion ensued when poor Mr. H., being nervous and rather infirm, missed his footing and fell forward, his left leg and thigh protruding over the parallel line on which the other trains were rapidly advancing when shocking to relate the wheel instantly went over that part and lacerated it to such a degree that the limb was almost severed from the body! Poor Mrs. H. was in the carriage and witnessed the sad occurrence. A medical man was in attendance and the sufferer was placed upon a door in the Musicians Car and conveyed by steam with the utmost rapidity to Eccles where he was accommodated at the Blackburne's.[2] From his exhausted state amputation was not resorted to and the poor man breathed his last between nine and ten o'clock in the evening. Lord Hill, who was of course in the carriage with the great people, had witnessed the meeting between the Duke and Mr. H. not two minutes before the accident, and an apparently cordial shake by the hand with his Grace may almost be termed the last act of this poor man's existence. It is needless to

[1] Rowland Hill, 1772-1842, Baron Hill of Almarez and of Hardwicke. His seat was Hardwicke Grange, nr. Shrewsbury.

[2] Rev. Thomas Blackburne, Vicar of Eccles and a friend of Huskisson. Mrs Huskisson remembered his widow in her Will.

say such an accident occasioned doubt, hesitation and delay. A considerable time elapsed before it was decided whether we should go on to Manchester or return. The former was at length resolved upon, which indeed was due to the Directors of this spirited and stupendous undertaking. The arrangements for the day had been admirable, though this catastrophe of course prevented all enjoyment. The presentation of the Freedom, which was to have taken place to-day, and a Ball this evening are both put off, as well as a public Dinner which the Duke had promised to attend on Saturday, and as Mr. H. was the most intimate friend of Lord Stafford I have no doubt the visit there will be put off and that Lord Hill will return to Hardwick tomorrow. . . .

God bless you.

R. Egerton

P.S. The Directors of the Railroad appear to have surmounted every difficulty and there is no doubt of its coming into general use and answering perfectly.

R. E.

At the Inquest held next day (16 September) at Flixton and repeated at Manchester later in the afternoon, the jury viewed the body but did not examine the wounds. The principal witnesses were Lords Wilton and Granville.

The Earl of Wilton stated:

Mr. Huskisson with several other gentlemen were standing outside of the ducal car, of which the door was open. On the alarm being given that the *Rocket* engine was advancing upon them, he endeavoured to come round the edge of the door, and in doing so, became in some measure entangled with it. His movements then became confused, and whilst in that state, the *Rocket* passed him, and knocked him down, and the consequence was that his left leg and thigh were crooked into an angle, so that two parts of the whole limb rested on the rail, one part about the middle of the thigh, and the other just above the calf of the leg. At this moment the wheel went over him.

Lord Granville said that Mr Huskisson was affected by a numbness in the limb in consequence of an operation he had lately undergone: a circumstance which might account for the slowness and irresolution of his motion.[1]

---

[1] Perhaps this confuses the weakness caused by the recent operation for strangury with the numbness from which he suffered through previous accidents (note the plural). But the operation

This is the accident as seen by those who were in the ducal party. Let us now take the best of the Press accounts. (All the papers, provincial and London, contained columns about it during the next few days—sometimes by an eye-witness of the scene.)

Shortly we passed the boro' of Newton, crossed a fine bridge over the Warrington Road and reached Parkside 16 miles from Liverpool, in about 4 minutes under the hour (the start having been at 10.40). . . . During the watering many of the noblemen and gentlemen alighted, walking or standing in the road close to the ducal car. Among the group was Mr. Huskisson whom Mr. Holmes[1] M.P. of the Treasury joined and with a view of bringing him and the Duke of Wellington together . . . he [Huskisson] walked up to the part of the car in which the noble duke had taken up his station. His Grace perceiving Mr. Huskisson by the side of the car extended his hand over to the Rt. Hon. gentleman, who shook it most cordially. A few words of mutual compliment had passed, when the Duke and other personages in his car, perceiving an engine, which turned out to be the *Rocket*, rapidly approaching on the other line, called out to the passengers on the road 'Get in, get in'. Several did . . . but Mr. Huskisson, who was in a weak state of health . . . became flurried, and after making two attempts to cross the road upon which the *Rocket* was moving, he ran back in a state of great agitation to the side of the Duke's carriage. White, the engineer, saw the unfortunate gentleman, as the engine approached, in a position of the most imminent danger, and he immediately threw the machine aback; but it and its train moved onwards several yards by the impetus before the operation of stopping it could be performed. Mr. Holmes, M.P., who had not succeeded in getting into the carriage, stood next to Mr. Huskisson, and perceiving that he had altogether lost his presence of mind, seeming like a man bewildered, he cried out 'For God's sake, Mr. Huskisson be firm'.

The space between the two lines of rail is just 4 feet, but the ducal car being 8 feet wide, it extended 2 feet beyond the rail on which it moved, thus diminishing the space to 2 feet between its side and the rail on which the *Rocket* was moving and on which Mr. H. and several other gentlemen were standing. Then the engine *itself* projected somewhat over the railroad on which it ran, still further diminishing the standing room to not

may have brought back old trouble. In driving from Eartham to Testwood, their carriage was damaged in passing a gate, but there is no suggestion of any injury to the occupants.

[1] William Holmes, Treasurer of the Ordnance and Tory Whip. He was conversant, doubtless, with the Ordnance Passage imbroglio of Ch. VII, p. 234 below.

more perhaps than 1 foot and a half when the vehicles were side by side on the opposite rails—a space scarcely sufficient to allow a man of ordinary bulk to escape contact by placing himself sideways between the carriages. The door of the ducal car happened most unfortunately to be 3 feet broad, and upon the full swing extended one foot beyond the rail on which the *Rocket* moved;[1] so that it was impossible for that engine to pass without striking and throwing it back with a violent concussion in the direction in which the machine was moving.

Of this door Mr. Huskisson had grasped hold, when he slipped back after his vain attempts to cross the road, when warned of the approach of the *Rocket*. Mr. Littleton, M.P. for Staffs, who had sprung, we believe, into the ducal car, which was ascended by a step ladder broad enough to permit only one person on it at a time, had just 'pulled in' Prince Esterhazy, when he saw Mr. H. alarmed and agitated with his hand on the door, which he seemed to grasp with a kind of trembling or convulsive hold. . . .

At this moment the *Rocket* struck the door of which Mr. H. had a hold, fractured the edge, peeling off nearly 2 feet of the red baize with which it was lined, and pushed it back with violence, squeezing a gentleman against the side of the car: Mr. H. being weak and agitated and having lost all presence of mind, fell as soon as the door was struck by which he had supported himself: and the space between the engine and the car being less than 2 feet, scarcely indeed more than 1 foot and a half, the whole of the *Rocket* caught his left leg, which had been placed on the rail and smashed the limb to mummy, passing over it in an oblique direction halfway up the thigh. The unfortunate gentleman uttered a faint scream, and the blood gushed from the wound. The whole was the work of a moment. The sufferer was with difficulty raised by Mr. Joseph Parkes of Birmingham and the Earl of Wilton, and he immediately exclaimed, 'This is the end of me.'

To visualise the scene correctly we must have three things firmly in our mind:

1. The ducal train and the *Rocket* were travelling in the *same* direction: namely, towards Manchester, the former on the south side (down line) the latter on the north side (up line). George Stephenson on the *Northumbrian* drove the ducal train. It was made up of

[1] i.e. 2 feet of bulge and 3 feet of door = 5 feet: clear space 4 feet: so that the tip of the open door extended 1 foot over the *Rocket*'s near rail.

(*a*)  the band waggon in front, with the musicians,

(*b*)  the Duke's decorated saloon car,

(*c*)  on either side of it smaller cars divided into compartments for the directors and distinguished guests. In one of these were Mr and Mrs Huskisson in the company (I presume) of General Isaac Gascoyne, with whom he had shared the representation of Liverpool since 1823. On the other line were the seven trains, containing shareholders and citizenry. The procession of trains constituted a 'cavalcade' in the language of the Press; and before the start from Edgehill the engines puffed up and down trying out their paces.

Train 1 was drawn by the *Phoenix:* Train 2 by the *North Star:* Train 3 by the *Rocket* (with White as engineer).

The ducal train had stopped under Rainhill Bridge (Rainhill, where the trials of 1829 were held) for the edification of the spectators, and the trains of the cavalcade passed, and were repassed by, it. It was 'sometimes in advance of the other cars, sometimes behind and sometimes abreast of them'. Mr Huskisson was seen by a passing train 'standing with his face towards us'. And that was for many their last glimpse of him, both for those in the trains and the thousands who lined the Olive Mount Cutting outside Edge Hill.

> 'The wave of the hand and the smile of the eye
> We ne'er shall encounter again.'

At Parkside there was a general halt—the ducal train taking in water here, and the seven trains in the procession proceeding to other watering points on their side of the line. Two had passed and the third, drawn by the *Rocket*, was following when the accident occurred. It was in disobedience of the regulations that any passengers had descended. But to the quality a train was a private equipage, and such regulations were for the many.

2. The second point emerges from Littleton's letter—the narrow causeway or 'dam' carrying the rail across the quarry. As the track is to-day, even a lame man could step across the vacant line into safety. I conjecture that he had walked along the causeway, and could neither get back to his own carriage

because of the overtaking train nor across and clear of the vacant line because of the broken quarry edge. He therefore returned to the ducal car to try and mount that.

3. Whether he lost his hold before the *Rocket* struck the tip of the door, or whether, as it struck, it flung him to the ground, we do not know. (The one independent fact is that the door was forced back on its hinges, so as to press the other man against the side of the car—it was not slammed to.) At any rate he fell into the posture described by the journalist and sketched by Littleton—his body on the ground this side of the *Rocket* and short of it and his left leg and thigh on the *Rocket*'s rail.

### The Sequel

The accident having occurred, Lord Wilton[1] took charge. Two Liverpool doctors checked the flow of blood by a tourniquet. The band waggon was emptied and detached and Huskisson was carried into it, Wilton, Granville and Wainewright going with him. George Stephenson on the *Northumbrian* took them full speed to Eccles. A Quaker girl, stationed at a viewing point on Chat Moss, saw the train pass. She thought that the engine had run away, so swiftly was it travelling and so set were the faces of those standing in the car.

At Eccles he was taken to the Vicarage, while Stephenson hurried on to Manchester for medical aid, bringing back four surgeons. A ligature was put around the thigh with a view to amputation, but they dared not operate, and as he was in great pain they gave him laudanum to deaden it. When he was told he had but a few hours to live, he added codicils to his will, himself signing Codicil I but too weak to sign Codicil II. He then took the sacraments, said good-bye to his wife and shortly after expired.

I append the will.

The Codicils added on 15 September begin after the words 'Freeland Solicitors Chichester': 'I WILLIAM HUSKISSON', etc. Note in the penultimate paragraph—'was then in so much pain

---

[1] 1799-1882, brother of the 2nd Marquis of Westminster. He was a great hunter and died at Egerton Lodge near Melton Mowbray. The family name was Grosvenor—hence the Wilton St., Grosvenor Road, and Grosvenor Road Embankment, of Chapter I.

and so near his end'; and the formalities involved by the insertion '*and be hers*', and by the method of appending Codicil II.

*The Right
Honble*
WILLIAM
HUSKISSON
*One of his
Majesty's
Most Honble
Privy
Council*

THIS IS THE LAST WILL and Testament of me The Right Honorable William Huskisson one of His Majesty's Most Honorable Privy Council that is to say first I direct that all my just debts funeral and Testamentary Expenses be fully paid and satisfied as soon as conveniently may be after my decease I give to my Brother Charles Huskisson Esquire the legacy or sum of one thousand pounds to be paid to him within six calendar months after my decease I give to each of my domestic Servants whom my dear wife may not have occasion to retain in her service after my decease in case such Servants shall have lived with me not less than a year and shall continue to conduct themselves to the satisfaction of my said wife until the time of their being discharged one years wages over and above what shall be then due to them I give the sum of one hundred pounds unto or for the benefit of the West Sussex East Hampshire and Chichester General Infirmary and Dispensary to be paid within six calendar Months after my decease I give and devise all and singular my freehold Lands Tenements and Heredits called Fockbury and all other my real estate situate lying and being in or near the parish of Bromsgrove in the County of Worcester with their and every of their rights members and appurts unto and to the use of my Brother Major General Edward Samuel Huskisson his heirs and assigns for ever but charged with the payment of an annuity or yearly sum of one hundred pounds unto John Huskisson[1] of West Lodge near Wickham in the County of Hants Esquire or his assigns for and during the term of his natural life without any deduction for any present or future taxes whatsoever and to be paid to the said John Huskisson or his assigns by two equal half yearly payments the first of such payments to be made at the Expiration of six calendar months next after my decease and my will is that in case the said annuity or yearly sum or any part thereof shall be unpaid for the space of twenty one days next after the same ought to be paid then and so often it shall be lawful for the said John Huskisson and his assigns to enter into and upon all and every or any part of the said heredits charged with the said annuity or yearly sum and to distrain for the same or for so much thereof as shall be so in arrear and all costs and charges occasioned by the nonpayment thereof and such distress to sell in like manner as for rent reserved by a Lease or common demise all the REST RESIDUE and REMAINDER of my freehold Leasehold and Copyhold Messuages Lands Tenements Tithes—Heredits and Real Estate whatsoever and

[1] His half-brother, 1781-1842, Deputy Surveyor of Bere Forest.

wheresoever and all my Monies Securities for money Household Goods
and furniture wines Horses Carriages and all and singular other my personal Estate whatsoever and wheresoever I give devise and bequeath unto
and to and for the sole use and benefit of my dear wife Emily Huskisson
her heirs Executors admors and assigns according to the different natures
and qualities of such real and personal Estates respectively and I constitute
and appoint my friends the Reverend Richard Cockburn[1] Vicar of Boxley
in the County of Kent Alexander Milne of the Office of Works Whitehall London Esquire and James Bennett Freeland of the city of Chichester
Esquire Executors of this my Will and I give to the said Alexander Milne
and James Bennett Freeland the legacy or sum of one hundred pounds
each as some compensation for the trouble they will have in the Execution
of this my Will and lastly I revoke all former Wills by me made and do
declare this only to be my last will and Testament In Witness whereof I
the said William Huskisson the Testator have to this my last Will and
Testament set my hand and Seal this thirteenth day of July in the year of
our Lord one thousand eight hundred and twenty seven—W. Huskisson

L. S.

Signed sealed published and declared by the above named William Huskisson the Testator as and for his last Will and Testament in the presence of us
who in his presence at his request and in the presence of each other have hereunto subscribed our names as witnesses. B. Binstead—P. Binstead—Emy
Churcher—Clerks to Messrs Price and Freeland Solicitors Chichester.

I WILLIAM HUSKISSON do hereby declare that it is my wish and desire
that all property of every description which I may have become possessed
of since the date of my last Will or any and all—property whereby that
will I may not have already bequeathed to Mrs Huskisson may be placed
at her disposal *and be hers* subject to the conditions of my last Will Signed *Interlined*
by me this fifteenth day of September in the year 1830—W. Huskisson *in the*
(signed)—Signed Sealed—and delivered in the presence of us we being in *original*
the presence of each other—Wm. Wainewright—Wilton—Granville—
Wm. Wainewright. (*Codicil I.*)

I William Huskisson do hereby confirm the appointment of the Executors already named in my aforesaid last Will and Testament. The
above written wish was expressed in the presence of us this fifteenth day of
September 1830. Wilton—Granville—Wm. Wainewright. (*Codicil II.*)

In the Prerogative Court of Canterbury In the Goods of the Right
Honorable William Huskisson deceased.    10 November 1830

[1] The husband I think, of Harriet Cockburn, *née* Tilghman, Mrs Huskisson's niece.

APPEARED PERSONALLY William *Wainewright* of Fludyer Street Westminster in County of Middlesex Esquire and made oath that he is one of
the subscribing witnesses and is the writer of the two Codicils to the last
Will and Testament of the Right Honorable William Huskisson one of
His Majestys Most Honorable privy Council deceased bearing date respectively the fifteenth day of September 1830 and contained in one sheet
of paper now hereunto annexed signed at the top 'J. Addams' and refer-
ring to the words 'and be hers' written over the first line of the second side
of the said paper and being part of the first Codicil the Deponent saith
that the said words were written and inserted in the said Codicil by Directions of the said deceased prior to the Execution of the said Codicil and he
further saith that the second Codicil contained in the words following 'I
William Huskisson do hereby confirm the appointment of the Executors
already named in my aforesaid last Will and Testament' was written by
this Deponent by directions of the said deceased and in his presence on the
day aforesaid and after the execution of the said first Codicil that after
writing the said second Codicil the Deponent read the same over to the
deceased in the presence of the Right Honorable Thomas Earl of Wilton
and Granville Lord Viscount Granville who have together with the Deponent subscribed their names as witnesses thereto and he the said deceased
approved of the same but was then in so much pain and so near his end
that this Deponent did not think himself justified in putting the deceased
to the trouble and distress which must necessarily have been occasioned
to him by any attempt to sign or execute the said second Codicil.
Wm. Wainewright—Same day the said William Wainewright Esquire was
duly sworn to the truth of this Affidavit Before me—J. Phillimore Srgt.
—Bt. John Bayford Not. Pub.

PROVED at London with two Codicils 13th Novr 1830 before the
worshipful Jesse Addams doctor of Laws and Surrogate by the oaths of
The Revd Richard Cockburn Clerk Alexander Milne and James Bennett
Freeland Esquires the Executors to whom admon was granted having
been first sworn and sworn duly to administer.

I have seen the original will with the trembling signature of
the dying man attached to Codicil I. On the margin of the will
is a subsequent note by the Revenue Authority 'Estate under
£60,000'.

But what of the desolate company at Parkside and the expectant thousands at Manchester? The first idea was to cancel everything, but when Mr Hulton, J.P., objected that there would be a riot if the procession did not reach Manchester, the Duke said 'There is something in that'. Sir Robert Peel asked 'Where are those Directors?' and after debate with them, it was agreed to carry on.

The day turned wet and cold. On the way back the Duke stopped at Eccles to enquire after the injured man, and was told there was no hope. In the dinner that evening at the Wellington Rooms by Mr Radley of the Liverpool Adelphi only forty-seven out of 230 appeared. Mr Huskisson's health was drunk, for it was not yet known that the accident was fatal.

Thus in tragedy was opened the Railway Age, and beyond doubt the luckless Huskisson stole its thunder. It is, as I began by saying, the one thing the ordinary man knows about him; and from time to time new evidence, even at this late day, comes forward of the way in which the tragedy fixed itself on people's minds. I read, for example, in the *Manchester Guardian* of 25 February 1947 the following in an article entitled 'Sailor's Weather' by G. Ridstill Smith. The writer's great-grandfather, a sailor, reached Liverpool on 10 September 1830. During his stay there, he records that Huskisson was killed—'long a member of Parliament for Liverpool and one of its principal supporters in trade with the Western World, though we on the East coast of England have severely to lament the Reciprocity Act, which originated from the able abilities of this statesman'. He witnessed the great funeral procession of mourners six abreast. 'If Mr Huskisson had been a king, he could not have had more respect shown him by the town of Liverpool. Every shop in the principal streets was closed, and all the ships in the different docks had colours half-mast.'

*The Liverpool and Manchester Railway*

Soon shall thy arm, Unconquer'd Steam! afar
Drag the slow barge, or drive the rapid car.
　　　　　　　　　　　　—Erasmus Darwin

It was Liverpool's response to two calls—the call of Puffing Billy snorting along a Durham coalfield, and the call of the steam ferry hooting its way through a fog-bound Mersey. It was, in fact, a steam-driven land ferry—Liverpool to Manchester, 1st *return* (Canada hardly knows the word—there it is 'two-way' or 'round trip', the presumption being 'Go west young man', never to come back). No engine-hauled coal trucks, with a horse coach on rails for the passengers, as on the Stockton and Darlington, but a locomotive railway train with compartment seats for the passengers and guards perched above their coach.

Curiosity is the salt of the earth, and Huskisson's friend, Littleton, had it in full measure. I quote first from his Diary for the winter of 1819-20, when he was in Vienna:

In England a few years ago the boiler of a steam boat (one of the first in England) burst and killed some passengers, and various other accidents happened about the same time. Luckily we had no police—a free press published the details, and through the same means the remedies were found. Steam boats became numerous and safe, and now proved a cheap commodious conveyance for the public, as they will in a few years a source of taxation for the government.

*Laissez-mourir*, with a vengeance!

I quote next from his Diary for 10 October 1821, when he was on tour in the North of England:

We entered a larger coal waggon which was covered with a carpet and which was with several others full of coal all linked together and drawn along a Railroad by a locomotive Steam Engine about 3 tons in weight, which carried us as fast as a horse trot. This to us was wonderful—this Steam Engine being the first in use in this country. It drew about 5 times its own weight with facility on a perfect flat. A little further towards the River Wear we saw a fine specimen of an inclined plane—Lord Stewart's coal rolling along rapidly to the river with its own weight and drawing up the empty returning waggons at the same time, while Lambton's were being led down both ways at much labour by horses.

And then of course, in 1825, the Peases and George Stephenson between them showed what could be done with a colliery railroad on the grand scale—from Shildon, by Bishop Auckland, to the ports of Yarm and Stockton-on-Tees, on no account missing Darlington. 'We brought thee to Darlington. Do thee bring the railway to Darlington.' I have sat at the desk in the original office of the Worsted Mills of Henry Pease & Co., Darlington, at which the prospectus of the Stockton and Darlington Railway was drawn up—Edward Pease on one side and young Joseph on the other. For the next five years its performance was front page news, of interest not only to the merchants of Liverpool and Manchester, but to those numerous landlords who had coal properties of their own. One of these, J. E. Denison, wrote to Huskisson from Leeds, 10 September 1830:

I write from this emporium of trade to you at your emporium of commerce. You will attend, I presume, the opening of the railroad, I have just been in Durham travelling on one railroad and inspecting the progress of another, which passes through coal property of mine there. I have been astonished at the fruits which spring from planting these iron rails on the ground. Liverpool is not a greater lesson of the results of free trade than the Darlington railroad is of the effects of free and cheap communication. Darlington and Stockton are two unimportant country towns—a few years ago a three horse coach dragged along between the two places and starved in the operation (two active verbs in a neuter sense!). Now these coaches run every day on the railroad from each place, and are loaded with passengers—as about 100 people from each place find they want to go to the other, or part of the way, as they can go for a penny a mile. Locomotive engines are used for dragging the coal wagons but not for coaches —but so little power is wanted that one horse canters along drawing a coach and 30 or 40 passengers and luggage at the rate of 10 miles an hour. There is every prospect of the coal trade being in some considerable amount diverted from Newcastle to the Tees. I shall be happy to contract for your annual ship load to London.

It was this sort of news which made the mouths of hungry Irish landlords water. But they had no coal, and their horizon was limited to a horse-drawn tramway for their slate and lime. 'All we want' (writes Palmerston to William Temple in Berlin, 2 December 1825) 'is a railroad to the sea, as at present the

c

slates are sent 12 miles along an infamously bad road, but some other slate owners, whose quarries are near ours, are equally interested in this, and a survey has been made of a line for a railway and in the course of this next year it is probable that such will be made.'

'Results of free trade.' 'Railroad to the sea.' Huskisson spent his life trying to find what free trade was; and free trade for him meant something to do with the sea. His last pleasure outing was on a steamboat. 'Monday Sept. 13' (says Mrs Huskisson in her *aide mémoire* to the last days) 'we embarked early in one of the steamboats on the Mersey in order that I might have the opportunity of seeing to the best advantage those magnificent docks and quays of Liverpool, those wonderful emporiums of her wealth and industry.'

Steamboats had been plying on the Mersey for some time. Touzeau in his *Liverpool*, p. 772, gives 1817 as the date when they were started there. In 1818 William Denny's *Rob Roy*, engined by David Napier, shewed the way from the Clyde to the open sea by plying between Greenock and Belfast, and by 1821 there were river and cross-channel steam services on both sides of the English coast. But what of a coastal steam service, plying daily with the regularity of a steam train over twenty miles or so, carrying passengers and miscellaneous produce? The idea occurred to some people, but the customs bogey stood in the way.

The story is given in full in the Out-port Letter Books of the Custom House[1]:

23 Sept. 1820
The Collector to the Board.

On application made by Mr. Samuel Parkes 18 Sept. Parkes states it is proposed to run a daily steam packet between Liverpool and Bagillt, Flints. Intended to be a vessel of from 80 to 100 tons, 'to carry the numerous passengers who at present cross the Dee to Parkgate (the navigation of which is much obstructed by sand banks) and from thence across the peninsula of Cheshire to the ferries on the South of the Mersey, by

---

[1] Selections from Outport Letter Books 1675-1862, edited in ink—in the Customs House Library, London.

which at present they are conveyed to Liverpool'. The distance at present travelled is 17 or 18 miles. The steamboat would make a passage of 25 miles, going from Bagillt around Hilbre Island past Hoylake, (calling at the Hotel). The course will be practicable at any time 'except $1\frac{1}{2}$ hours before and after the ebb of the highest spring tides'. The passage across the Dee to Parkgate at present occupies 3 hours owing to the sand banks. Many passengers travel around by Chester for Holywell to avoid this—a journey of 33 miles.

States there are expectations of a good trade by this route in market stuffs, groceries, etc. which in their present course of transit across 'the peninsula' [*i.e. Wirral*] are often damaged. Desires to know whether the Customs Regulations as regards to coast despatches etc. will apply to the projected traffic. It would be impracticable on account of the variety and nature of the goods proposed to be carried, to enter them coastwise at the Customs House.

Collector reports that he is not aware that there would be any objections to the transport of live cattle, fowls, butter, eggs, vegetables etc. by steam boat for market purposes without coast despatches, but the privilege will not extend to livestock (which are prohibited by open sea without a licence) or corn or other merchandise. Thinks it might be proper to allow the farmers on their return from Liverpool to carry small quantities of goods, for the supply of their families, but not to permit them 'whole packages' or articles for shops or sale.

7. Nov 1820. It appears the Board informed Parkes that the vessel would be subject to the Coasting Regulations. On 26 Oct 1820 he approached the Treasury. Collector reports he does not think revenue will be endangered, if the coasting regulations be dispensed with. Altho' the vessel may during part of her voyage traverse the open sea, she will have to pass Hoylake in view of the Hoylake officers and of the crew of the Viper cruiser.

*Compiler's Comment:* This is a good example of the manner in which the old Coasting Laws crippled trade. 30 years earlier they had been more oppressive, and the fees levied by the officers often stopped trade altogether.

With fees and dues and duties which throttled trade, Huskisson had to struggle all his Board of Trade life. For the truth was, the moment the sea became open sea it was no longer open to trade. Inland there was more freedom in one way, less in another, complete freedom from customs barriers, a threat to freedom from the monopolist. It was this second struggle in which the merchants of Liverpool and Manchester engaged in their fight for the railway to break the canal monopoly.

I do not propose to attempt here the story of the Liverpool and Manchester Railway. It has been twice told, by C. F. Dendy Marshall in his Centenary History and by G. S. Veitch in his *Struggle for the Liverpool and Manchester Railway*. Suffice it to say, after surveys and re-surveys, the railroad bill was introduced on 11 February 1825. Huskisson spoke in support: 'In this project there was no appearance of a desire to further private interests. The great object seemed to be to confer a benefit on the commerce of the country.' And he supported it, as he wrote to John Gladstone, 16 February, not as minister, but as member for Liverpool. He sought only improved transport facilities of *some* kind, and the reduction of canal tolls. But the bill was lost in Committee—'this devil of a railway is strangled at last' (Creevey).

After a new survey the bill was reintroduced and passed both Houses, and on 5 May 1826 received the royal assent. That is the line that we used to know as the London and North Western from Liverpool Lime St. to Manchester Exchange. Two others were built later, on the north side the Lancashire and York-shire,[1] skirting Wigan, from Liverpool Exchange to Manchester Victoria: on the south the line of the Cheshire Lines Committee through Warrington, Liverpool Central to Manchester Central, the line by which in my youth you set your watch, so good was its time-keeping.

Lime St. station was not opened till 1836. The terminus was at Crown St. (now a coal yard), from which by a cable the train

---

[1] My grandfather, Charles Fay, 1812-1900, was superintendent of the Wagon Department of the Lancashire and Yorkshire (formerly Manchester and Leeds) Railway. Coming as a lad from Dublin he apprenticed himself to a coachbuilder in premises on the site of St George's Hall. There he helped to build the 1st class coaches for the Liverpool and Manchester Railway which were Road Coaches, bolted on to logs of wood. Joining the L. & Y. he became Carriage Superintendent of the Carriage Works, attached to the Locomotive Department before transferring to the Wagon Department. In 1857 he patented his chain brake, which gripped simultaneously all the wheels of the train (see Sherrington, *A Hundred Years of Inland Transport*, pp. 184-5). In a competition held on the Oldham incline into Manchester Victoria, with Sir William Fairbairn as judge, his brake won. On his death we sent the large drawings which hung in my home at Waterloo, Liverpool, to Sir Jno Aspinall for the L. & Y. Museum together with his photograph. After a run of some twenty years his brake was ousted by the Westinghouse Air Brake.

was wound up to Edgehill, through a tunnel carrying the date
1829. The procession of 15 September 1830 started from the
old Edgehill station, where one may still see traces of the steps
leading down to it, and the foundations of the engine cable
house and of the Moorish arch which spanned the track.

The hopes entertained are well set out in a Memorial noted
on the Minutes of the Board of Trade for 9 March 1825, the
Memorial itself being in the related Bundle (both in the Public
Record Office):

To the Rt. Hon. the President of the Board of Trade the Memorial of
the Chamber of Commerce of Belfast showeth That important benefits
will be conferred on this part of the United Kingdom by the adoption of
any means, which may have the effect of lessening the time and expense
at present required to bring its produce to the English markets. That the
formation of the projected Rail-ways between Liverpool and Manchester
promises to afford means of conveyance for agricultural produce and
manufactures to the interior of the North of England hitherto unparalleled
for cheapness and despatch; and of supplying the most populous inland
town in that part of the Kingdom [sc. *Manchester*] with the necessaries of
life, disburthened of a large proportion of the present charge of transport.

That the formation of the projected Railways by developing the advantages to be derived from this species of internal communication may
lead to their extension throughout the Kingdom, to the aggrandisement
of the Nation and the promotion of its wealth and prosperity. Your
memorialists therefore pray that you may be pleased to support and encourage the projectors of the Liverpool and Manchester Railway in the
execution of their undertaking.

Belfast is looking at it from the Irish point of view, but
points to the two main things. (1) The railway was pressed from
Liverpool for the supply of the inland market with foodstuffs
and raw material rather than from Manchester for the export of
Manchester goods, less in bulk and greater in value. (2) It
would be the beginning of a railway network. This existed in
programme even before the Liverpool and Manchester was
opened. John Moss, the projector of the Liverpool and Manchester Railway, projected and brought into being the much
larger Railway, the Grand Junction, from Liverpool to Birming-

ham, and was for many years its Chairman. The opposition of
the canal interest to the Liverpool and Manchester Railway
was not prolonged; for it involved no threat to the coal trade
and was likely to be supplementary rather than rival. In any
case, opposition was neutralised by getting Lord Stafford to
take 1000 shares, with the appointment of three directors.[1] But
it was otherwise with the Grand Junction, which would take
the railway into the heart of the canal zone. The age of the railway network, the real railway age, began when the railway
reached Birmingham from Lancashire in the north (1837) and
a year later (say 17 September 1838) from Euston, London.
The politics, as well as the results of Moss's life work, have to
be told around the Grand Junction Railway.

I have before me the Reports of its Annual General Meeting
from 1833 to 1845 inclusive. In much fascinating matter four
things stand out:

1. The birth and growth of Crewe: foreshadowed in 1836
when, with the Manchester and Chester Junction Line, it was
projected to bring Manchester traffic directly to Crewe. By
1843 the locomotive carriage and waggon departments had
been transferred there from Liverpool, and each ensuing step
in the formation of the L. & N.W. Ry. enhanced the importance of Crewe as a junction and works centre.

2. The inception of Sunday trains, necessary to the fulfilment of the mail contract. A bye-law of the Liverpool and Manchester Railway forbad it at first on their line. The Sunday
receipts came to about 10/- per share per year: the precise
figure being calculated annually, so that tender consciences
might refuse it.

3. The initial predominance of passenger over goods traffic.
In 1838, after six months operation, receipts were drawn only
from the coaching business. Next year waggons were put on
the railway, but the initial overwhelming predominance of passenger traffic only slowly disappeared. However, in 1845

---

[1] One of these being James Loch of the Railway Correspondence and another James Bradshaw,
not to be confused with Robert Haldane Bradshaw, the dictatorial manager of the Bridgewater
Trust, or with the Quaker George Bradshaw, the originator of the Railway Guide.

£18,700 of the *increase* for the previous year had come from goods and livestock: £12,000 from passengers.

4. The linking up of companies by amalgamation, culminating in the amalgamation in 1846 of the Grand Junction Railway with the Liverpool and Manchester, London and Birmingham, Manchester and Birmingham Railways, to produce England's senior line, the London and North Western Railway.

*Railway Correspondence*

The politics of the story, in the initial stage, in so far as Huskisson was concerned in it, are contained in the numerous letters to him from John Moss and John Gladstone on the railway side, and from James Loch, M.P., Lord Stafford's confidential adviser, on the canal side. There are some dozens of them, and some are long. Huskisson's purpose throughout is to find a middle way and keep the peace between them. I have space only for extracts from a few. But the whole, together with the Reports aforesaid, would make a noble start for a Ph.D. thesis. The two central letters, viz. 4 and 5(i), I give in full, omitting only two unimportant paragraphs in 4.

1. Gladstone to Huskisson     14 October 1824
2. Moss to Huskisson     16 April 1826
3. Loch to Huskisson     1 October 1829
4. Moss to Huskisson     14 December 1829
5. Loch to Huskisson     (i) 25 December 1829
        (ii) 31 December 1829
6. Huskisson to Loch     7 January 1830
7. Loch to Huskisson     8 January 1830
9. Wainewright to Huskisson     12 August 1830
10. Lord to Lady Hatherton     August 1833

*(1) Gladstone to Huskisson*

Additional means are greatly wanted for the conveyance of goods from Liverpool to Manchester, which accumulate in quantity before they can be forwarded by the canals; their charge is enormous for carriage, for which there is no remedy; the supply of water is ingrossed by the existing canals and therefore no means could be found for feeding another, was permission given to make it. Such are the beneficial effects of this indirect but effective monopoly that the shares of the Mersey and Irwell, commonly called the Old Navigation, which cost £70, have been sold at £1,250— though I understand from the apprehension of this railroad scheme the price has since fallen to £1,000—can it be reasonable that the public should be *so* laid under contribution for such purposes, or to such an extent? Surely it is the bounden duty of the Government to support, of the Legislature to protect, every fair and honest application that will afford the means for relief.

### (2)  *Moss to Huskisson*

What chance can we, a few Liverpool merchants, have against Lord Derby? Please help, as you have done already in the House of Commons.

### (3)  *Loch to Huskisson*

A scheme to make a new harbour at Dalpool on the Dee and to convert it by a ship canal with a set of new docks at Walazee Pool, opposite Liverpool with a side canal to Chester and joining the Duke's Canal at Preston Brook: the promoters of the scheme are Sir John Tobin, the proprietor of the land, and they say Sir Henry Parnell on behalf of Ireland and the Clives on behalf of Ellesmere and Chester (and Telford is the engineer and a Mr. Gillespie Graham from Edinburgh the architect).

### (4)  *Moss to Huskisson*

I beg to thank you for the kindness of your communications through Mr. Wainewright respecting our proposed Rail Road to Birmingham. . . .

In proposing the new scheme I must admit that pecuniary advantages form no inconsiderable part of our expectations. The Liverpool and Manchester Railroad was a struggle for the public, the few shares taken by those who fought the battle ill paid us for the time we gave to it. We must now take care of ourselves.

The very decided success which has attended that measure (for Lords Derby and Sefton, Mr. Creevy [*sic*], Mr. Birch, Mr. Blackburn and others admit their surprise and admiration) has so opened the eyes of the canal people, the land-owners and public that almost everyone is desirous to get into a railroad. No less than 4 new schemes are announced to come into the Liverpool and Manchester Line: I am one of those who fear that we shall have more to do than we can do well.

It occurred to myself and some others that by proposing a line by Runcorn, and declaring our intentions of conciliating all parties, we should keep the public from joining any wild adventurer, who might propose a new line to Manchester and one also to Birmingham.

The gentlemen whose names are attached to the above paper have given their confidence to Mr. Lawrence, Mr. Sandars and myself, and when I add that Mr. Loch, M.P. gives us his best judgement and that Mr. Buck, the engineer to the Birmingham and Ellesmere Canal, has been here for some time sent by Lord Clive to report to him what can be done on railroads, I trust you will allow that we have not a bad foundation to commence upon.

To secure the ground and the public, both of whom were in danger of being taken possession of by persons who have not the same prudence and experience as ourselves, we have given notice of a line to Runcorn only and we have pledged ourselves not to go on with the next session of Parliament without the approbation of the Marquis of Stafford.

Provided our Liverpool and Manchester Railroad answers our expectations, that is, if goods and passengers *can* be carried at less than half the present prices—no one can doubt but a railroad will be made between Liverpool and London; our work is to injure as little as possible and to protect as much as lies in our power the canal interest, we feel that before we can expect them to give up their opposition and come into our views, they must be perfectly satisfied that a canal cannot exist where there is a railroad. A railroad to Runcorn interferes with no canal. We propose to cross the river above the entrance into the Duke of Bridgewater's and Old Quay Locks. Lord Francis Gower[1] should consider the importance of a railroad to him. From the point we join that canal to Manchester is a level line. I think we could prove to him and to Mr. Bradshaw that the canal cannot compete with the railroad, to convert their canal into a railroad and to come over the river at Runcorn would be only four miles more in distance than the present railroad, it would prevent any application for a new railroad to Manchester and secure to that canal as much profit as it ever had; for any loss of goods would be more than repaid by the traffic and passengers to Wales, Liverpool, etc. If Lord Francis Gower could once see the real state of the case, I am sure he would feel no one has so much cause to give his heart and hand to our scheme to Runcorn as he has, even if we go no further than Runcorn and his canal is never altered. The River Navigation is a more formidable obstacle to Lord F's canal than he is aware of. . . .

The new line of the Birmingham and Liverpool Canal is very nearly

[1] Lord Francis Gower, the Marquis of Stafford's second son, to inherit the Bridgewater estate took the Canal Duke's name of Egerton. He became 1st Earl of Ellesmere.

what was proposed for the railway to Liverpool in 1826, and it has occurred to us that it might form a very principal part of the line to Birmingham for the railroad.

Our appointment is one of conciliation, and as I think we can prove to each person whom we call upon, that it is for their interest to go with us, I hope we shall be prevented any contest similar to 1826. If we fail in negotiation, some other gentlemen must be found to conduct the Parliamentary warfare.

Besides, the railroad to Runcorn would bring the Mail at all events $1\frac{1}{2}$ hours sooner to Liverpool, and enable the steam packets to take the Irish letters.

## (5) *Loch to Huskisson*

(i)

Wimbledon Common
25 December 1829

My dear Sir,

I understand from Moss that he has written to you on a subject, that has lately occasioned a good deal of our attention, and he is desirous that I should likewise communicate with you before doing it. It relates to the position in which Canal and R.R. property now stands—a subject of infinite importance to Lord Stafford and his family.

The late experiments at Liverpool have given rise to a vast variety of projects, many of them ill-imagined, all got up in extreme haste—adopted on little rational principle—promoted by scheming attorneys and prepared by young and rash engineers, and entered into by people impatient of low interest for their money, quite ready to run the course of 1825 over again.

Such projects would be alike hurtful to the undertakers themselves—injurious to the immense capital invested in Canals, and vexatious to the Land Owners who would be affected by their schemes, without a sufficient case being made, for such interference.

But these experiments tho' very striking and wonderful are by no means conclusive—In regard to the carriage of light goods and passengers, the probability is that R.R. will have no competitor but it is still a matter of serious investigation, and of doubtful result whether they will carry heavy and bulky goods cheaper than Canals, and especially unless speed is to form an item in the calculation. Experience has still to prove this point —but be the result be as it may, still the profits of Canals must be materially affected by such a rivalry.

In this state of things a proposition was made to me, by some of our

Liverpool friends, for Lord Stafford's consideration, in order to ascertain whether the Canal and R.R. interest might not unite, giving the public the accomodation they require in point of celerity—enabling those who had capital to embark in such works—the means of employing it, and affording those who had capital vested in navigations an opportunity of saving part of it. Their plan being, that a R.R. should be constructed from the Liverpool and Manchester R.R.[1] to Runcorn Gap to cross the Mersey there, to assume the Duke's Canal or towing path to Preston Brook, thence to proceed by a new line to Namptwich, and there taking advantage of the Birmingham & Liverpool junction Canal works, advancing by Birmingham to London.

My reply was that it was impossible to decide on such a complicated and important question in a hurry, that experience was still wanting in order to see how a R.R. would work, when actually called into practice, and asking for the delay of a session.

Their answer was admitting generally the correctness of what I had stated, but urging as a reason for being permitted to take certain steps in advance, the necessity for securing the line and preventing the unemployed capital of the neighbourhood being fixed in rival projects. This was acceded to on condition that they should not proceed in Parliament without Lord Stafford's approbation, and that he was at full liberty to decide against the project as well as in favor of it.

It was suggested to me, that some communication might be fitly made to Government in order to state to them the propriety of recommending in Parliament the postponement of all these projects for one session—until the experience of the L & M R.R. had proved what this mode of conveyance was equal to, and that if such a recommendation was followed by the promoters of these schemes, much good would be obtained. Such as were undertaken on insufficient grounds would be abandoned and those that rested on more solid foundations would come forward better matured so that neither the capital embarked in existing establishments nor the comfort of the country would be unnecessarily, perhaps wantonly, interfered with.

You will no doubt observe that all this reasoning is founded on the assumption that a R.R. to Birmingham must be made by one party or another—either by more or less friendly competitors.

I have accordingly seen Mr Peel on the subject—he has desired me to send him a statement in writing with a copy of our correspondence—

[1] I think, from a point near Warrington: and thus by keeping north of Mersey, interfering with no canal. Cf. Moss, Letter 4.

which I have done—he asked me if I had communicated with you. I said not yet, for I was only authorised to do so by that morning's post (the 21st) and that besides, I thought it was right, to mention the matter to him in the first instance.

May I beg your particular attention to this subject, both as a person likely to be affected by the question and on account of the stakes our friends at Liverpool have in it—by the time you come to town I shall have a vast quantity of information on the subject which I will show you.

I have not conveyed the above proposal to Government without much consideration, and I was supported in the opinion of its reasonableness by my brother and Adam, whom I have advised with throughout—it can never be advantageous to a country, that much of its capital should be unnecessarily anihilated and a vast number of persons dependent on the existence of that capital reduced to poverty, except such a sacrifice is demanded on the clearest public necessity, founded on incontrovertible general principles.

What is asked for is no preference—no interference with the employment of private capital—but simply delay—and that this should be done by the legislature saying to all parties—we are of opinion that the data on which you proceed are not so well founded or so sure, as to induce us to give you powers which you have not, and cannot obtain without our sanction—of occupying the property of third parties in order to convert it to your use.

I have mentioned what has been communicated to me to Lord Clive and Bradshaw and when they come to town the question must be considered and as far as possible our future line of conduct determined on.

Pritt feels desirous that some person connected with Canals, should insert a paper such as I have enclosed (which is from him) in the newspapers. I felt that it could not be done by me, but Adam says that he thinks it so fair a statement of the case, that it is calculated to bring the question so fitting before the consideration of Parliament if it was circulated among the members of both Houses, that he suggests whether it might not be done thro' Mr Littleton as a person of influence and having much property in Canals—How does this strike you? and if you think it fit to be done could you suggest it to Mr Littleton. Some of his agents perhaps might do it. But I will add no more.

The Mersey and Irwell shares have fallen from £1250 which they were, three years ago—to £650.

I enclose you a list of the names connected with the above proposal—
and who have determined to form a company.

I am

Yours very sincerely

James Loch

The Right Hon.
Wm. Huskisson
M.P.

| | | |
|---|---|---|
| John Gladstone | W. W. Currie | T. Littledale |
| John Ashton Case | B. Rathbone | C. Horsfall |
| Charles Lawrence | D. Brandreth | S. Sandbach |
| John Moss | David Hodgson | W. Brown |
| Joseph Sandars | James Cropper | P. Bourne |
| Charles Tayleur | Joseph Ewart | Sir J. Tobin |
| Adam Hodgson | Richard Harrison | W. S. Roscoe |
| T. B. Birch | Henry Booth | W. Maxwell |
| Robt Gladstone | W. Rotheram | J. A. Yates |
| Hardman Earle | N. Robinson | J. N. Walker |
| T. Headlam | T. Forsyth | R. Bickersteth |
| T. Booth Jr | B. Wilson | T. Leathern |
| J. Hornby | H. Ashton | T. B. Barclay |
| C. Heyworth | G. A. Pritt | C. M. Clay |

(ii)

There is one ingredient in the case as it affects the desire to promote
the Railroad that has considerable influence and that is the low price of
iron. . . . You are aware that a new canal is projected from Birmingham
to the Oxford Canal—as injurious a measure to the [sc. *Bridgewater*]
Trustees and Duke as any railway can be. I suspect more so—but on the
other hand it is advantageous to Birmingham, Staffs. and Shropshire. You
see how variously and differently we are affected—meaning Lord Stafford
and the family.

(6) *Huskisson to Loch*

(*Reporting an exchange of views with Moss.*) It would appear that I
betrayed my great ignorance of the local bearings and relations of their
several interests. . . . Pray give me a little insight into the merits of R.R.
adverted to in the enclosed. . . . You see how I am pestered on these
subjects.

### (7) *Loch to Huskisson*

I return to you Mr. Watson's letter. The R.R. he alludes to we consider one of the most detrimental to the interests of the Bridgewater Canal than has been or can be devised. It is connected with a proposed extension to London. . . . The Directors of the Liverpool-Manchester R.R. staid pledged through Moss to Bradshaw not to promote this scheme, and acting up to that pledge they prevented Stephenson from having anything to do with the Survey, and parted with his best sub-engineer, who had.

### (8) *Loch to Huskisson*

Upon coming home I wrote to Pritt lamenting your illness and expressing my doubts whether you would be permitted to go to Liverpool though I thought you were exerting yourself too much to say so. . . . I saw them (*Moss & Co.*) on my way home from Stafford House and heard all they had to urge.

### (9) *Wainewright to Huskisson*

12 August 1830

You are, I suppose, aware that the Railway Dinner is fixed for the 15th and the Corporation Dinner for the 16th Sept. . . .

I have been so strongly urged to accompany Moss Lawrence Brooks and Sandars in an excursion to Manchester and back by the railroad to-morrow that I am induced to defer my departure from London till Saturday. P.S. Railway shares are at £195.

### (10) *Lord to Lady Hatherton*

King's Arms, Liverpool
Sunday 2 o'c. Aug. 1833

Dearest,

I arrived at Manchester last night at 11 o'c. This morning at 7 I rose, and at 8 had the carriage mounted on the Ry. (the work of one minute) and at ½ past 9 was at Liverpool—32 miles in 90 minutes!!! I then breakfasted, took my place in the packet—got the carriage and my 2 saddle horses, which I found here, on board, then went to the Cemetery where poor Huskisson was buried. You would have laughed to have seen Thompson and James on the box of the carriage, while we were some-times flying on the rly. a mile in 2 minutes. Thompson trying to grin with his tongue out and his fingers all on end, and James quite as usual, only losing his hat now and then. . . .

*'If only'*

If only the *Rocket* had been stopped in time (as it would have been if the train had been fitted with my grandfather's brake), how greatly the course of history might have been altered! The might-have-been of history is a veritable Grimpen Mire, tread we ever so warily, but we may plant a guiding wand or two to keep us on firm ground.

Huskisson was a born servant and could never have held with success the highest office. On Canning's death the *élan* went out of him: he was no more fitted than Goody Goderich to fill the Canning void. Would he in 1832 have joined the Whigs, as Palmerston and Goderich did? I think not. I think that by 1834 he would have been close enough to Peel to take the Colonial Office under him; and that his universal prestige with the commercial world might have induced Peel to make the accommodations in the matter of the Bedchamber which would have brought the Tories back in 1839 instead of 1841. Then I see him offered high office for the last time, but declining it, following the way of Sturges Bourne, his closest friend after the death of Canning. Stanley and Graham having joined Peel, the great ministry has seven years to run instead of five, and Huskisson rejoices to watch the rise of William Ewart Gladstone. Stanley carries his Canada Act in 1843, 6 and 7 Vic., c. 29. In 1844 the greatest speech in support of the Bank Charter Act comes from the veteran member for Liverpool. In 1845 his voice is heard in the House for the last time. His spiritual child, so near him in name, William Hutt, pleads for an extension to Australia of the free entry now accorded to Canadian wheat. Cobden and Bright demand total repeal. Cobden leads off with one of his 'short statistical statements', Bright draws on the armoury of Holy Writ. Both make little of William Hutt. Then Huskisson rises in his place. The House is silent in expectation as he unrolls the map of empire, and calls for the retention of a small fixed duty of 5/- per quarter, never to be suspended in good seasons or bad, the proceeds whereof shall be devoted to Empire Settlement, with a view to assuring that plenty for the consumer of wheat and decent livelihood for the grower of it, which was the dual purpose of the corn laws from 1688 onwards. A sentence of this length had no terrors for Huskisson.

You might have heard a pin drop as the Rt. Hon. Gentleman came to his final word, 'she must be the Mother Country of an Empire, or she is nothing.' And when he sat down, the cheers broke out on both sides, as the country gentlemen realised to their delight that they were good imperialists after all. I picture certain lords, commoners of an earlier day, looking down from their gallery on the scene—Bexley (Old Van) with silver locks, aloof, long since pensioned for his country's good and dreaming of a loan from Kingdom-come: Ripon (alias Goderich) enviously effusive and forgetting for the moment the tribulation of his wife: Stanley (newly summoned) bowing applause to his old chief, and wondering how in the Canada Act he had managed to miss the imperial boat: Brougham loudly asseverating that the best parts were lifted from his own two volumes on Colonial Policy: Melbourne lazily memorising fragments on the off-chance of an interview with the Empress Queen.

'Damme,' said the Duke to Gosh, as the pair re-entered Apsley House, 'that fellow Huskisson has done it again.'

# PART I
# THE HISTORICAL APPROACH

# CHAPTER ONE

# MR HUSKISSON REVISITS HIS CONSTITUENTS

*The Westminster Statue*

WILLIAM HUSKISSON

Statesman

Born 1770    Died 1830

so reads the inscription on the pedestal of the statue in Pimlico Gardens in the City of Westminster.

To those of the Empire who are outside England there is but one constituency: namely Westminster, after which the Statute of Westminster is named. There is Westminster Abbey, Westminster School, and Westminster, which signifies two things; a City with assigned limits, west of the City of London —with this Westminster Huskisson was not concerned; and Westminster in the larger sense of the seat of the Imperial Parliament. With this Westminster he was intimately concerned, as a member of the Lower House for over thirty years and as a leading Minister of State in a great quinquennium, 1823-8. If his statue was not to be in Parliament Square beside Peel and facing Canning, its present location on Thames Embankment is appropriate, though one could wish that it was not on just that stretch of it where no one, not even a bus or tram, goes. It was not always there. Intended originally for the Custom House at Liverpool, it passed later to Lloyd's, who placed it half-way up the stairs in their old Building at the back of the Royal Exchange. When they moved, they offered him round the town, among others to Euston, who bashfully declined the man they had run over, so that finally he came via the L.C.C. into the good keeping of the Westminster City Council.

There are three ways of getting to Pimlico Gardens. The first is for the élite. You summon a taxi and say '123, St. George's Square, S.W.1., last house on the left, corner of Grosvenor Road'. Alighting under the TOC H sign on Talbot

House and standing on the kerb, you see a few yards away by the river side the statue of the statesman. As you are of the élite, you should not climb the railings, and in any case there is a custodian to see you don't. You cross the road and walk to the entrance some paces to the west.

And so *you* go through the garden gate.

The second is for the multitude, who possess an affection for sight-seeing and an interest in lurid detail. You think of him as Huskinson, and remembering Lord Wilton at the Inquest, start from Wilton Street by Victoria Station on a No. 24 Bus— 'Chalk Farm to Pimlico Green all on a summer's day'. You thus make a circuit through the most uninteresting streets in all London till you can go no further: which is Pimlico. There you get out and proceed on foot past Dolphin Square, that great conurbation of flat-bound humanity, with half a dozen 'dolphin-ettes' springing up around it, till you reach the spot aforesaid, coming at it from the west.

And so *you* go through the garden gate.

The third is for the economic historian. You, too, start from Victoria Station, but by tram to Vauxhall Bridge. At the approach to the bridge you descend, to find Millbank on your left and Imperial House HOVIS on your right. Declining Emily and opting for the Corn Laws, with Huskisson's corn preferences from 1815 to 1827 on the tablets of your mind, you proceed at leisure along the Grosvenor Road Embankment. Shortly you find yourself along the considerable length of the Thames Wharves and Warehouses Limited, Somerset Wharf, with ample time to reflect upon the Warehousing Act of 1803, 43 Geo. 3, c. 132,[1] from which the Dock Acts which Huskisson licked into shape start off. In a brown study you almost go too far, lured on by the sight of Chelsea Bridge, but observing the railings you realise where you are, and recognise the figure within.

And so *you* go through the garden gate.

---

[1] The Act, on the good old enumeration principle, assigns certain produce to the West India Docks; certain to the London docks: timber, iron and the like to approved places anywhere: cotton, oils, etc. to approved warehouses anywhere.

Now all is set for the viewing. You cannot walk straight up to the statue because the Westminster Council has decreed that the garden shall be a model allotment. You therefore walk under the smokeproof plane trees till by a right angle turn you reach the pedestal. He is in Roman toga looking down upon the tomatoes and onions. I have asked these two questions of different custodians:

1. Do people come to see the statue? 2. Who is it?
*A.* 1. Yes. Teachers sometimes bring the children in the afternoons and I have to keep them off the beds.
   2. I am sure I don't know, sir.
*B.* 1. I've never seen anyone but I've only been here a few months.
   2. Wasn't he some Italian or other?

I gave *B* a 1/- for Answer 2. But it wasn't the Roman toga that earned it for him, it was the small side lettering which he had noticed on the statue:

OPUS JOHANES GIBSON
ROMÆ

We talked tomatoes for a while, and then he went back to his work while I stood brooding for a short half-hour. What does one get from a statue? Whether as sculpture it should be rated high or low, I liked it. It seemed to give the idea of the man, eloquent, sagacious and wistful, and, if one could think the allotment away, to be in the right setting—with the Thames traffic on the one side and a great population on the other. The statue is clean; and it is the face of an elder statesman. I had to fancy him saying something. And so I introduced to him a deputation of country gentlemen, who had come to ask for a rise in the duty on imported garden foodstuffs. The statesman listened with patient gravity; and when Mr Western, their spokesman, had finished, he changed from stone to living flesh, and, eyeing with disgust a cluster of diminutive tomatoes, exclaimed:

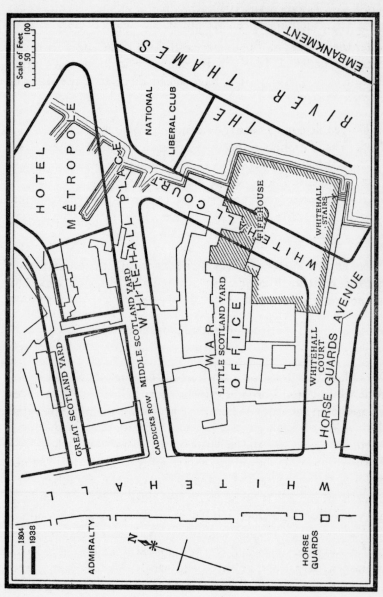

Whitehall in 1804 and 1938

So that, gentlemen, is the kind of produce on which you propose to nourish the inhabitants of this great emporium of commerce. It is a delusion greater than was entertained ever by the madman Buonaparte himself. I can hold out no hope that My Lords will consider favourably of your proposal either now or at any future date.

But it was time to go home. For a simple scholar that sleeps quietly in his chair, I had had a rather lengthy afternoon.

## The Stables in Whitehall Place

I had lived with my hero for weeks, nay months, in the Record Office and British Museum, and kept encountering him in strange places of which the strangest undoubtedly was within a few yards of where I slept in the National Liberal Club, Whitehall Place. In the Liverpool papers (British Museum) I came across the following:

*Mr. Burton Morice to Lord L. Complaining of proposed buildings in Scotland Yard.*                                                        8 *May* 1819

My Lord . . . I have the honour to hold the office of Steward of the Marshalsea of the King's House and of one of the Judges of his Palace Court, to which I was appointed in 1811. At that time the Court was in such a dangerous and decayed state that it was necessary that a new one should be found, and before my appointment many plans had been offered and one of them rejected as improper because it proposed a stable yard for the site of the Court. Soon after my appointment a spot was fixed upon in Gt. Scotland Yard and Mr. Perceval directed that the Surveyor of the Office of Woods should ascertain whether the space alloted and the spot had my approbation: there being then no stabling, but decent houses, with small gardens, opposite to that spot, and only some wretched wooden sheds near to it, but which I was told would be removed if I would only wait 6 months, till the notices to quit given to the tenants of them had expired. I gave my approbation. Very soon after the houses were pulled down and stables erected in their place. The wooden sheds, tho' I made frequent representations to the Treasury and the Office of Woods to have them removed, were suffered to remain until within the last month, when they were pulled down. This, I soon found, had not been done from any regard to the convenience of the Court, or the promise made to me, but to my astonishment, in order to create—fresh stables and the more easily to open a way from the wharf at the end of Whitehall Place *for the passage*

*of coal waggons and carts* thro' Gt. Scotland Yard, notwithstanding representations had been made some time ago by the Order of the Court to the
Board of Treasury to stop the passage, if it could be done, of those which
then passed thro' Gt. Scotland Yard, as producing from their noises great
inconvenience to the carrying on of the business of the Court.

On Thursday last I wrote to Mr. Huskisson to ascertain the accuracy
of this information, who returned me for answer that the measure had the
sanction of the Board of Treasury, and that the Board of Woods etc., had
been directed to carry it into execution. Under these circumstances I am
compelled to address your Lordship on the subject, which I am sure must
have received your sanction from not having the facts I now state brought
to your notice. For I would put it to your Lordship to decide whether
you think a *Stable Yard* with all its attendant consequences of Noise and
Filth, be a proper situation for one of H.M.'s Courts of Justice and
whether you think it unreasonable in the Judge of that Court, whose duty
it is to administer justice between suitors not only conscientiously, but
properly, to oppose, as far as he can, the evils I have complained of.

Should your Lordship think the business of the Court too trifling to be
inconvenienced by these Nuisances, I beg to inform to you, to remove
that impression, that its jurisdiction extends 12 miles around Westminster
where causes to any amount may be, and are tried, and that the average
amount of causes tried, of all descriptions in a year, is about 1,000. If also
your L'ship be led to suppose or it should be suggested to you that my
opposition comes more from the personal inconveniences I shall feel rather
than on public grounds, tho' I do honestly confess to you that I do feel
strongly the annoyance that such a measure will produce to my personal
comfort, and I shall always think that I have been hardly treated, yet to
that, I assure you, I should have submitted in silence.

I hope these reasons will be satisfactory to put a stop to the projected
measure, but if I have been unsuccessful in convincing you of the justice
of my remonstrance, I would entreat your L'ship to refer my letter to all
or any of the Judges in Westminster Hall for their opinion. If they think
my objections trifling I will rest satisfied, and be anxious to give you every
apology for the trouble I have given to you.          Burton Morice

Having copied out this long document, I retired to an early
rest, and had hardly put my head on the pillow when (so I
thought or dreamed) the night porter tapped on the door and
handed in a letter marked Urgent and Highly Confidential.
The letter ran:

My Dear Sir,

Having received leave of absence for 48 hours, I take the liberty of informing you that at 9 o'c tomorrow morning I shall venture to call upon you in the hope that after I shall have discharged a small matter of business in Whitehall you will be able to give me the pleasure of your company on a journey by railroad to my old constituents.

I am, My Dear Sir,

Ever yours most faithfully,

Wm. Huskisson

'He's come', I said, 'about the stables. But which constituents?' My mind started running through a pamphlet I had just perused, filling out here and contracting there, as is the way of dreamland.

## Morpeth

Professor Veitch in his *Electoral Wanderings of William Huskisson* (G. S. Veitch and R. Smith) reminds us that he was first elected to Parliament in 1796 as a member for Morpeth, a nomination borough in the gift of the Earl of Carlisle, for which he sat till 1802 in company with 'George Howard, commonly called Lord Viscount Morpeth'. It is not certain that he ever went there. We know, however, that he was made a steward for the races, in order, perhaps, that he should be ready with a subscription. But Carlisle was a tiresome person, his letters endlessly boring, and he was for ever pestering Huskisson for more news.

Why should a promising young Under-Secretary of State for the Colonies enter Parliament in this way? His patron, Henry Dundas (than whom no man in the kingdom knew more of constituency-mongering), was in favour of it. 'Better to come in' (wrote Dundas to Huskisson) 'this way, than on Pitt's ministerial list. But tell Carlisle you may one day differ from him in the "jumble of general politics".'

The young Under-Secretary gave his patron good value for the seat in the latest political gossip. Here is one of the best, written in 1798, the year of Pitt's income tax:

Enclosed is the Income Bill, which contrary to all expectations has hitherto made as little noise in the world, at least in the world of the Metropolis, as any of the Duke of Bridgewater's Canal Bills ever did, and not near so much as some of them. Whether it will go through its subsequent stages with equal facility is not quite certain, for I really think it open in two or three leading points to attack. These weaknesses are too obvious to have escaped the opposition. But feeble and disjointed as they are, I do not believe they can take advantage of them or that the minister will be compelled to any material modification, and I know that without a violent resistance very few and those unimportant will be conceded, and that in their first great measure of the session we have every prospect of success. The [*sc Irish*] Union, whenever it is brought forward, will not meet with so smooth a reception.

There speaks one of Pitt's coming men, who moreover, knew his canals at first hand; for his first patron, the Marquis of Stafford, was heavily interested in them, as were most men of property in Staffs., to some extent at least.

But though he might not have set foot in Morpeth, he had to have a qualification, which is duly filed in his Papers:

The qualification of William Huskisson of Parliament Street in the Parish of St. Margaret's, Westminster in the county of Middlesex esquire, one of the members returned to serve in Parliament for the Borough of Morpeth in the County of Northumberland being an annual clear rent charge of £300 granted by Alexander Davison . . . of Middlesex, issuing out of his freehold lands and tenements in the parish of Felton in the County of Northumberland unto the said William Huskisson during his life.

Felton is eight miles south of Alnwick.

It was not Huskisson's way to have anything to do with a place without knowing all about it, by the aid of book and map. He was not a great traveller, except when he was on forestry business or making the round of the country houses—which took him more than once to the Carlisles at Castle Howard, five miles south-west of Malton in the North Riding of Yorkshire. But whether he knew the ground or not, big things were working themselves out in Northumberland County. Thomas Bates, at Wark Eals on the North Tyne in 1796 and Halton

Castle 1800 on, was breeding 'in and in' and making Short-horn history. Coals were pouring out of the Newcastle coal field and running by gravity to the water side. Above all the Union with Scotland was yielding a rich economic harvest. The barrier of the Border had broken down. Students from England were flocking to Edinburgh to take Political Economy from Dugald Stewart, Palmerston for one, the said Thomas Bates (1809) for another. And this contact along the east coast route was about to be paralleled by a west coast contact, a water route, not a land route, binding Liverpool with Glasgow— John Gladstone with Kirkman Finlay, and both with the member for Morpeth, who was to become eventually the member for Liverpool.

Cattle were the textiles of English agriculture and Durham Shorthorns the cotton of the agricultural revolution. With them English and Scottish breeders captured the world's export trade in pedigree livestock: and Huskisson lived to see the start of it. Away out in the Argentine Republic, which he and Canning were prompt to welcome, at Kilometre Post 61, on the great highway from Buenos Ayres to Bahia Blanca, stands a tall obelisk:

On this very spot John Miller, Rancher, started his work of advancement. Born in Elgin, Scotland, 1787. Died at 'La Caledonia' Canuelas, 1843. He introduced to the Country the First Pedigree Bull 'Tarquin' of the Shorthorn Breed. Tribute of the Argentine Rural Society, 20th of May 1943.

Tarquin, purchased in England by Messrs. Hullet of London, reached the port of Buenos Ayres in 1823, the year in which Huskisson became President of the Board of Trade. By this time the Booths at Killerby and Warlaby, and Bates at Kirklevington were turning Teesdale into a mecca of stock farmers for all Britain and for America North and South.

Thus Teesdale, and the Scottish Lowlands to which they were taken to be improved, became the livestock complement of the Lancashire and Paisley-Glasgow tie-in. It could not rival the cattle trail of Professor Dobie's Texas Longhorns, for there was not the open range; but the vales of Northumberland and Cumberland were good grazing lands, and intensive stock farming with choice beasts flourished. In Cumberland were John Christian Curwen and Sir James Graham of Workington and Netherby respectively: in Northumberland the Duke of Northumberland, and the Earl of Tankerville with his famous Chillingham herd of native white cattle. How enviously must Huskisson, when struggling with deflation in corn-growing Sussex, have thought of those northern parts which he once represented, which were all but exempt from agricultural depression, because they were in essence factories of meat and milk. It never, I fancy, occurred to Edward West or Ricardo or Malthus to enumerate their beloved Law of Diminishing Returns in terms of animal husbandry; yet which showed the greater relative increase between, say, 1800 and 1830?—human beings on the one hand: cattle and pigs on the other? The latter surely; and how does this square with the Classical Law of Diminishing Returns?

In this way England and Scotland were now pulling together all along the line. Each gave to the other. England contributed spindles, locomotive engines and shorthorns: Scotland contributed hot blast, steam boats and joint stock banks. Thomas Joplin, in the name of Scotland, staged and won at Newcastle-on-Tyne the fight for the emancipation of England from Bank of England monopoly: which broadened the integration. England equipped Scotland with capital and culture, which Scotland repaid in enterprise and education.

### Liskeard

County of Cornwall: borough of Liskeard.[1]

1804, William Huskisson Esq. of Eartham Co. Sussex *vice* John Eliot Esq. called to the Upper House as Baron Eliot, 9 March 1804.

Double returns. By Order of the House, dated 16 May 1804, that by which Thomas Sheridan Esq. was returned was taken off the file.

1806. William Eliot  
William Huskisson $\Big\}$ 3 Nov. 1806.

[1] Parliamentary details in this and next section from Parliamentary Papers 1878 LXII. Members of Parliament, Pt. 2.

Yes, Liskeard was more likely for our visit than Morpeth. For he had no scores to settle with Morpeth; and with Liskeard he had. His representation of this little pocket borough cost him a packet. He had to pay the expenses of a disputed return and foot a monstrous drink bill. So heigh-ho for Wallop in the West to broach a hogshead or two. If I found him in the right mood, I could venture on that Electoral Lampoon:

*Addressed to the Independent Inhabitants of Liskeard*

> See H——ss——n advanced, that Gallic Rover,
> He lost alas! both Coat and Seat at Dover,
> And hunting on the Borough Scent so hard
> Smells out the rotten Junto of Liskeard.

For he had come electorally from Morpeth to Liskeard by way of the Cinque Port of Dover. But at Dover, so the story went, he lost both coat and seat.[1] Though he was supposed to be the Treasury nominee, his rival was the brother of an admiral, who helpfully blockaded the port, so that Huskisson's friends could not come to the poll. And so he moved on to Liskeard in Cornwall, a day's march beyond Plymouth.

Mr J. Carthew, his agent, informed him (6 April 1804) that he had paid the drink bill 'monstrous though it seemed at first sight'. It is to be remembered in excuse that a former M.P. had presented to the corporation a cup bearing the motto:

QUI FALLIT IN POCULIS FALLIT IN OMNIBUS

The bill was for

|  | £ |
|---|---|
| 563 Port at 4/6d | 126 |
| Dinners | 32 |
| Negus | 16 |
| Breakages | 5 |

[1] Cf. Dundas to Huskisson, after reporting on the success of his men in the General Election of 1802: 'I shall not be at rest till you are in Parliament . . . I suppose if there be an opening in England, the Treasury would at least assist you to the extent of the £1500 which you saved to them [*sc. by earning in office a salary which debarred him from drawing his Colonial Office pension of £1500*]. I have some little hold of the Borough of Gatton, but it would be too dear for you without very material assistance. What you have spent at Dover would have gone far to have done the business, and there is that advantage in such a place as Gatton that your re-election costs you no trouble'.

with incidentals, which brought it to £258 in all. But there was a heavier item to come:

1807—Expenses incurred in opposing the petition presented against my
  return  -  £738.

This was the end of a five year wrangle, to the intermediate stage of which Mrs Huskisson refers in a letter of 1804 to William Hayley: 'William has at length overcome all the difficulties of his three committees and took his seat in the House yesterday' (18 May 1804).

It was not to Huskisson as a man that the independent electors objected. He came in during the course of a local effort to enlarge the franchise of this pocket borough which belonged to the Eliots of Port Eliot (the seat of the Earl of St. Germans, near St. Germans, another Cornish pocket borough). Parliament determined in 1802 that the election was vested in the Mayor and Freemen alone, and not in the Scot and Lot inhabitants. But the petitioners persisted, and when John Eliot was elevated to the peerage in 1804, they engineered a false return which was quashed and the returning officer punished. In the 1806 election another Eliot and Mr Huskisson were returned, and the petition against them (which cost Huskisson so dear), was voted 'frivolous and vexatious', after which Liskeard disappeared from electoral history till it did itself the honour of electing in 1832 the great colonial reformer, Charles Buller, who sat for it till 1848.

These pocket boroughs, historically, were a survival of the days when the maritime county of Cornwall had numerous little ports and inland towns. With the narrowing of the franchise in a variety of ways, they became the instrument by which the Government of the day maintained its majority. The consideration which the Government paid might be in cash, but more often it was political advancement for the owner, culminating perhaps in the peerage, and jobs in the Customs or other public services for the owner's relatives and dependents. In return the owner promised on behalf of his nominees to support the administration in Parliament. In this form the pocket borough was a facet of government under capitalism. Their value rose, as the wealth of England rose; West Indian planters and Indian nabobs bought themselves thus into political influence and social standing. As with the slave trade and slavery, it was a case of property where there should have been no property, an immoral way of getting things done—of governing the country on parliamentary lines, or cultivating the tropics. The Reform Bill of 1832 was in a sense the abolition of Electoral Slavery. Moreover, the administrative reforms in the public services—the curtailment of sinecures, promotion by merit and the like, introduced by Pitt and continued by his successors—reduced the 'considerations' which Government could offer to borough owners and the prospective property value of a borough.

When a nominee of Government was in this way seated in Parliament, the last thing expected of him was that he should dwell among his constituents; for this threatened the patron's hold. And if we are to accompany Mr Huskisson to Liskeard, we may find that he is a stranger to the place.[1] So let us be ready to guide him to the Liskeard of 1804.

We shall cross the estuary of Hamoaze from Plymouth to Torpoint, escaping, let us hope, the soaking and the cold which Celia Fiennes caught a century ago, and proceed by the new road to Liskeard—a short and easy journey. The road after a few miles leaves the river and ascends to the hilly country where Liskeard lies. The husbandry is indifferent, but near the town the land is well tilled; and the labourers are well fed. They have meat in their pasties and plenty of fish. At Liskeard there is a large selection of inns, but we shall be asked to stay with friends. For Cornish hospitality is proverbial. In the old days

---

[1] But no stranger to Cornish interests, as a Board of Trade Minute of 29 March 1807 proves to the hilt. He supported then a memorial for an increase of duty on foreign copper, presented by Earl of Mt. Edgcumbe, Lord de Dunstanville, Sir Wm. Lemon and Mr Tremayne. 'William Huskisson Esq., agent for the Island of Ceylon, stated that a supply of about 44 tons of copper coin had been sent out to Ceylon in the year 1802; but that the coinage for that island had been suspended in consequence of the high price of copper, and [of] accounts having been received from the Island that the necessity of a Copper Coinage was no longer so pressing there. But that he was of opinion that a further supply of copper coin in the same amount would be highly acceptable to the Island.' He was now in his 2nd term at the Treasury.

Liskeard had a good yarn market. The Devon serge makers bought the yarn from local jobbers, or merchants, who gave out the work to the cottagers for their boys and womenfolk. But the introduction of machinery is robbing hand carders and spinners of their work, and causing local distress. The war, too, has brought suffering. For the price of provisions has risen steeply, and there has been rioting among the tinners. Risings among them are not uncommon; and they have marched into Liskeard, threatening bakers and corn dealers and trying to stop the carriage of corn to Plymouth and to force the bakers to sell at lower prices. Such invasions reduce the town to a state of siege, and the cry 'the tinners are rising' causes as much terror as rumours of a French raid.

It is a pity that we are not here at Whitsun for the famous sports, held at that season from time immemorial. Publicans and private patrons put up the money; and there are all manner of games, wrestling, cudgel-playing, donkey racing and what not. On the market days before the sports, urchins with poles parade the town, exhibiting the prizes to be awarded. On Monday the sports begin. An old man, famous for his wit and potations, is chosen as judge. He processes round the town, two pages holding his train, accompanied by thirty horsemen, decorated with ribbons and flowers. Next day the proceedings are repeated, and now the 'judge' travels in a carriage. On Wednesday, the last day, after a tour of the town, a mock trial is held, some disreputable characters are tried and sentenced to facetious punishments. The festivity ends in an ocean of intemperance. How much better than three boring days at Holkham or Woburn or Workington, admiring at a respectful distance the experiments of improving landlords!

It is all gone, of course; for it is 1950. But between us, I fancy, we shall make believe.

*Harwich*
1806     John Hiley Addington       }31 October 1806
        William Henry Freemantle

1807  John Hiley Addington
      William Huskisson    } 7 May 1807

1812  John Hiley Addington
      Nicholas Vansittart  } 6 October 1812

Harwich was a safer seat than Liskeard. For Harwich was a straight Treasury borough. Huskisson was now a secretary of the Treasury; and so, at the instance of the Treasury, Mr Huskisson in effect elected himself. There would be no disputed return. There were certain outgoings: bills for £248 for election expenses, 7 May 1807: also under the same date Admission to the Freedom of the Borough £25: Usual Donation to the Poor £10 10/-. And there were occasional subscriptions and services. Mayor Hopkins writes to him in 1812: 'We are endeavouring to establish a school upon Mr. Bell's system', etc.; and the Town Clerk begs his support of a Petition for denying English Registry to East India built ships. But he had only one term; for in 1812 he was no longer in the Treasury, which assigned Harwich to its higher self, Nicholas Vansittart, the new Chancellor of the Exchequer, dispenser-in-chief of Treasury patronage. Huskisson had to move on; and to his joy his home town of Chichester called him. 'I have been invited by the Electors of this city to represent them. I am now engaged in my canvas and with every prospect of success' (30 September 1812). He was M.P. for Chichester 1812 to 1823, and for Liverpool 1823 to 1830, without a single serious struggle and at no serious personal expense.

But what exactly was a Treasury borough? In the last 100 years of the unreformed Parliament, there were a few boroughs, such as the Cinque Ports, Queenborough (Isle of Sheppey) and Harwich, where the Government was able to control the elections by reason of the money expended in these places by the Post Office, the Customs and the Admiralty. As Porritt explains,[1] these places returned 'at election after election Commissioners of Treasury, of Admiralty, of Ordnance, of Trade and Plantations: and Parliamentary Secretaries to these Boards'. 'These elections cost the holders little because the electors, the

[1] E. Porritt, *The Unreformed House of Commons*, 'Treasury Boroughs', I, 340-8.

members of the corporation or freemen, received their bribes not from the members whom they returned, nor from patrons in the ordinary sense of the term, but from the Government in the form of local offices, many of them sinecures, in the Customs Department or Admiralty.' Re-election was much easier in the treasury-controlled boroughs. 'If a member representing a treasury borough was appointed to a new office, the notice in the *London Gazette* was almost a sufficient intimation to the local agent of the Government to arrange for a re-election.' The Government was an exacting patron, and treated its nominees rather like ministers on a Wesleyan circuit, moving them on, so that they should not become too attached to one seat.[1]

As a naval yard, a customs out-port and the headquarters of the postal packet service to the continent, Harwich was a Treasury borough *par excellence*.

But would any one on short leave wish to revisit it? Surely not, unless indeed it was Mr Huskisson's intention to hire a revenue cutter and slip across to Orford. He could not have received the invitation from Sudbourne bearing the date 15 September 1830, which forever remained unanswered.

My Dear Huskisson,

I hope you will do me the honour of shooting here before parliament meets and the earlier the better. Lay me at Mrs. Huskisson's feet and say that although Pye is like his master quite a cripple, he has one or two equally quiet successors.

Partridges scanty in places, plenty of hares, and I believe a very good breed of pheasants, but they are very small and backward. Copeland told me my warm sea baths would suit you and do you a great deal of good.

If you fix any time I will try for Warrender and Croker. The Duke and the great Government people won't come before Parliament meets—I want to do a great deal of havoc early this year as my knees ask for a little warm climate and so we can have a good battue every day—unless the revolution comes here meanwhile.

Ever yours most truly,
Hertford

---

[1] Oddly enough J. C. Herries, the Tory, was the first to defy the system. He held Harwich for eleven years against the Whig Government, and only lost the seat in 1841 when his chief supporter was driven from the borough by the collapse of his ship-building business.

P.S. Lord Dudley has promised me and I have no doubt that Farquhar would come to meet you.

This is one of several letters from the Marquis of Hertford to Huskisson, all written in the same excellent hand and with the same gracious friendliness. Huskisson and Mrs Huskisson were regular visitors at Sudbourne (Mrs Huskisson,[1] said the censorious Peel on one occasion, was the only decent lady present), and they enjoyed not only the sport and the sea-baths, but the society and the talk, with politics strictly barred. Huskisson writes to Littleton from Eartham, 12 November 1829:

What most amuses me, however is to find that some of the Whigs think my visit to Sudbourne extraordinary and that I ought not to have gone. Why not? I have been there every year for the last fifteen except when absent from England. I was again invited, Lord Hertford adding, good humouredly, that he never allowed politics to interfere with his private friendships, and that he hoped it would not keep me away from the usual party. The meeting was fixed for the 18th. I postponed going to the 21st, that I might not be considered one of the Duke's reunion—and for the same reason, I staid on four days after he and his tail were gone . . .

The usual courtesies and habits of private life have long been restored between the Duke and myself. . . . He appeared to be very well but not in good spirits at Sudbourne. But I judge only by appearances. We shot together in the morning and I beat him at whist in the evening, with perfect good humour on both sides. . . .

Who, then, was Lord Hertford and where is Sudbourne?

Francis Charles Seymour Conway, 3rd Marquis of Hertford, 1777-1842, figures in the *Dictionary of National Biography* only as an appendage to his father, the 2nd Marquis, 1743-1822, his courtesy title to 1822 being Earl of Yarmouth. The family was one of the richest in the kingdom. The 2nd Marquis was a Lord of the Treasury and had Court appointments: furthermore he married two heiresses. The 3rd Marquis, a favourite of the Regent, married another heiress, Maria

---

[1] Mrs Huskisson (*née* Emily Milbanke) was a distant relation of the Mark Milbank of Thorpe Hall, North Riding of York, who sat for Camelford along with the Earl of Yarmouth in 1820. This Mark Milbank (1795-1881), high Sheriff of Co. York 1837, married 2 June 1817 Lady Augusta Henrietta Vane, second daughter of William Henry, 1st Duke of Cleveland.

Fagnani, 'Old Q's[1] daughter "Mie-mie" '—George Selwyn's petted ward. He inherited 'entailed estates considered to be worth £90,000 a year, the annual value of the Irish estates being computed in 1797 at £15,000' (Vicary Gibbs in G.E.C.);[2] he had a private fortune of some £20,000 a year, and he could expect a further goodly sum from his father-in-law. In return he rendered occasional diplomatic service, but more important he had a son, the 4th Marquis, Richard Seymour Conway, 1800-70, who spent most of his life in Paris and who had a natural son, Richard Wallace. The 3rd Marquis ('no such thing as foisting sham Vandykes or copies from Rubens on Lord Hertford,' wrote Harriette Wilson), the 4th Marquis (the leading spirit in its formation) and Sir Richard Wallace amassed the splendid collection of pictures and articles of vertu which eventually Lady Wallace presented to the nation: to house them the Government bought Hertford House in Manchester Square, London. (Originally Manchester House, because built by the Duke of Manchester, it passed into the hands of the 2nd Marquis of Hertford and so became Hertford House.) All three had high artistic sense, yet for the economist the interest of the story lies in the extraordinary command which this family, never directly engaged in commerce, had over liquid capital. They anticipated the Rothschilds and Pierpont Morgans. When Europe was in the flux of war and revolution, they had the pick of its art market. There was no crushing income tax or death duties to frustrate their programme. Private property was sufficiently respected to allow of the transfer of art treasures from one country to another. But there had to be a beginning, and the beginning was in marriage dowries and farm lands. 'Poor Ireland maketh many rich,' Dean Swift had written in his *Drapier's Letters*; it is, indeed, a strange world which enriches out of peasant poverty the artistic wealth of a metropolis.

But the 3rd Marquis is more famous in fiction than in biography. For he is the Marquis of Steyne in Thackeray's *Vanity*

---

[1] 4th Duke of Queensberry, 1724-1810. His portrait by Reynolds is in the Founders' Room of the Wallace Collection.

[2] G. E. Cokayne, *Complete Peerage*.

*Fair*, and the Marquis of Monmouth in Disraeli's *Coningsby*. These figures live in fiction not because they have a prototype, but because as fiction they are alive. Yet we should be discarding a main source of economic history if we did not see how they translate into fiction. For fiction is the medium by which the novelist portrays real life. With great novelists such as these two, the atmosphere, background and general effect are unerring, and it is the picture as a whole that we need to understand without worrying whether Lord Hertford was as cynical a blackguard as Lord Steyne, or whether the author of *Coningsby* dealt too severely with the foibles of J. W. Croker.

And where is Sudbourne? Postal-wise, it is Sudbourne, near Orford, Suffolk; and Orford, together with Camelford, Cornwall and Lisburn, County Antrim, was one of the pocket boroughs of the Hertford family, for which in turn as Lord Yarmouth the 3rd Marquis sat.[1] Sudbourne Hall, with the estate, was in the possession of successive Marquises of Hertford from 1754 to 1871, and in 1884 Sir Richard Wallace sold it, since when it has passed through numerous hands. In World War II it was the headquarters of a battle area, where invasion operations were rehearsed, and now it lacks a tenant (unless indeed the ghost of Rebecca Sharp wanders round its rush-grown lake). If it could be pulled down brick by brick, like Trentham Abbey, it would be no loss to the district. It was never more than the headquarters of a sporting estate—the Dormy House of a fine shoot. The land has passed into good hands. There was a risk that this part of Suffolk might be condemned as sub-marginal and afforested, but modern technique has transformed the situation. Stagnant water has been cleared, and the land has been strengthened by the planting of suitable grasses. Under this treatment the last state promises to be better than the first.

Sudbourne Village lies inland and Orford is on the sea, and there is one rector for the twin parishes of Sudbourne cum Orford. In Sudbourne, the mother church, there is a monu-

---

[1] Orford 1797-1802; Lisburn 1802-1812; Antrim County 1812-1818; Camelford 1820-1822. By a misprint in the *D.N.B.* which has been carried over into modern literature, e.g. Bernard Falk, '*Old Q's' Daughter* (1937), Orford is written as Oxford.

ment to the Elizabethan Sir Michael Stanhope, who acquired
the manors of Sudbourne and Orford and built the first Sudbourne Hall. In Orford Church there is the organ case from
the organ given by the 1st Marquis of Hertford, 1719-94, who
incidentally was Walpole's nephew, and the parish registers
show John Wilson Croker as an Overseer in 1831. The two
churches tell us what they ought to tell us about the Hertford
family—namely, nearly nothing. But Orford has a famous land-
mark in its twelfth-century castle, recalling the days when it was
a pivotal point in the coastal defences of East Anglia. It is now
a national monument on the benefaction of Churchman's Cigar-
ettes. In a capitalist society the way in which a nation becomes
possessed of its own (or other nations') treasures is intriguing.[1]

### A Visit to the Bank of England

Morpeth, Liskeard, Harwich: with Chichester and Liverpool still to come. At this point I did what anyone in the
National Liberal Club should have done at the outset. I said to
myself 'wait and see'; and fell asleep (as I thought) till morning. I was up betimes and Mr Huskisson was punctual. It was
to be Liverpool after all; and he had dispatched his Whitehall
business, which had nothing to do with stables but was simply
a matter of recommending Wainewright's son (Wainewright
was his Liverpool agent, and the boy had got into some trouble)
for a free passage to Australia—which he had already secured
from the Colonial Secretary. We had thus nearly three hours to
spare before our train left Euston. Where should I take him?
To see himself in the National Portrait Gallery or in the corridor
of Church House, Westminster, or in Pimlico Gardens? Perhaps he would prefer to visit the Board of Trade or Stafford
House.[2] But you cannot visit the Board of Trade to-day; for it

[1] Cf. obituary of 4 February 1949, 'Lord Woodbridge (Sir Arthur Churchman), 81. Presented
to the town of Orford the 800-year-old Norman Castle at Orford Ness.'

[2] Lord Stafford, 1st Duke of Sutherland, settled Stafford House on his son and heir. Intended
for the Duke of York, second son of George III, who died 1827, Lord S., who had advanced the
money for its construction, took it over, spending on it £100,000, and his son a further £150,000.
In 1913 the lease was purchased by Lord Leverhulme and it was renamed Lancaster House. He
presented it to the nation to house historical relics of London originally lodged in Kensington
Palace.

is an anonymous ubiquity. And Stafford House, which under its new name of Lancaster House, ought to be the London Museum, is in fact a precinct of the Foreign Office, to which not even Mr Huskisson would gain instant admission. I thought of the docks, but there is no overhead railway in London from which you can get a bird's-eye view, and it might be difficult to secure at a moment's notice a Custom House launch. But the City—obviously I must take him to the City, and in the City, obviously, to the Bank.

So we went by taxi along the Embankment; and after peeps first at Bazalgette, the drainage man ('President of the Institution of Civil Engineers in 1884', I said to him, 'they have your bust in their corridor'), and W. S. Gilbert opposite Charing Cross Underground, and then at J. S. Mill and I. K. Brunel in the garden by the Temple Station, we drove up Norfolk Street past the offices of the West India Committee ('established by Royal Charter *circa* 1750'), and leaving our taxi to make the circuit of Aldwych Island inspected the diminutive figure of Dr Johnson in St. Clement Danes and the more ambitious statue of Mr Gladstone with Aspiration, Education, Brotherhood and Courage around him. Then rejoining our taxi, we went up Chancery Lane (I told Mr Huskisson of the many hours I had spent with him at the Record Office among the Treasury Papers, Board of Trade Minutes, Colonial Office Letters, and so forth), and into Lincoln's Inn Fields to the Soane Museum.

The Secretary was waiting for us and had laid out the necessary documents.

No. 50, Set 2. Drawing of the Old Board of Trade.

No. 49, Set 3. Designs of the new building as of November 1826.

Sir John Soane's commentary on the work we conned together:

The original directions of the Lords Commissioners of H.M. Treasury were to prepare designs of a building for the suitable accommodation of the Privy Council and the Board of Trade; confining the extent of the Front to the space between Downing St. and the Treasury Passage. . .

The 1st Lord of the Treasury and the Chancellor of the Exchequer having approved of this Design, the works were begun. . . . In these Designs the extent of the Front was confined to the space between Downing St. and the Treasury Passage. I was afterwards directed to continue the front of the Privy Council office and Board of Trade to the extremity of the Official Residence of the Secretary of State for the Home Department. This extension of the front in an unbroken line produced a monotonous effect. . . .

In the new Board of Trade Huskisson never worked; nor does his name appear in more than one of the numerous conferences between the architect and the Treasury. The old Board of Trade was an irregular patchwork building to the south of the new one; and he showed me the room where he had accommodated the grateful Frenchman.

A short run brought us to the Bank of England, to that institution of which, in his day, Huskisson said some harsh things. First we looked at the Bank's collection of Silver Tokens of the Suspension period: then at the famous £1000 Bank of England Note with which on 3 July 1815 Cochrane bought his freedom, endorsing it with these words:

My health having suffered by long and close confinement and my oppressors being resolved to deprive me of property or life, I submit to robbery to protect myself from murder in the hope that I shall live to bring the delinquents to justice.

If he had not given way, and so had not gone out to be Admiral of Chile and Brazil, there might have been no chance for Canning to call a new world into existence to redress the balance of the old.

Next we went into the basement for a look at the deposed busts of himself and Francis Horner, which formerly graced the Directors' Library. Perhaps they had seemed too intimate a reminder of the days when there was a gold standard.

Back in the Secretary's office I showed him some of the entries in the Committee of Treasury Minutes—in 1806, the Rules for Cash Accounts of Public Balances lodged at the Bank of England (Huskisson had a share in this salutary centralisation): in 1807, the squabble between the Bank and Joseph Bramah, whose bill for note printing machines the Committee thought 'enormous and highly unreasonable': in 1809, the Chief Cashier's urgent call for three additional assistants to sign Bank Notes under £25: on 5 December 1810, a Report from the Chair that they had seen the Chancellor of the Exchequer on Friday last and found that he had no expectation that Parliament would be likely to adopt any hasty measures upon the Report of the Bullion Committee.

Mr Huskisson, having helped to write the Report, smiled grimly, and as there was worse to come, I closed the volume and directed his attention to the noble history, on the side table, of the Bank of England by Sir John Clapham. He blanched a little at the frontispiece to Volume I. William Lowndes—'And pray what is become of William Paterson?' Then he turned nervously to Volume II, fearing (I suspect) to see Nicholas Vansittart: as, of course, it ought to have been, and as Gillray would have done it—St. Nicholas on a pedestal of paper credit, in a halo of exchequer bills, two million upon two million intertwined, in each corner cornucopias of depreciated bank notes and from the lips issuing the legend 'It will be an essential accommodation to the public service if . . .'

But it wasn't Van. It was only an innocuous Norman.

However, it was time now to go and I had reserved a minute or two to show him the view from the Bank steps—the multitudes disgorging from the Tube station, on one side of us the vacant Royal Exchange, now so meaningless, with its ironical motto in these sparse times 'The earth is the Lord's and the fulness thereof', on the other side the rather lowly Mansion House, and all round us taller buildings, many of them new, the head offices of Banks and Insurance Companies, of British Banks, Dominion Banks and Foreign Banks. At Number 1, Cornhill, he gazed with especial intentness. Was it at the gilt lettering 'Liverpool and London and Globe'? I thought it must be, but I was wrong. His eye was on the statue on horseback, just below it. 'It is the Duke' he cried and stepped on to the road. There was a shout of 'Look out there' and a grinding of brakes as a Number 6 bus all but flattened him, but I was ready for it. Grasping him by the undamaged shoulder, I literally flung him back on to the pavement and into our cab. 'For Heaven's sake, not a second time!' I gasped. 'Mrs Huskisson will be grateful to you,' he murmured. We were both too upset to say another word until we reached Euston station, where we made our bow to the Stephenson statue in the Great Hall, to which 3150 working men subscribed 2/- apiece.

### The Journey to Liverpool

We caught the Liverpool Express and I tried to divert his thoughts from mishaps by explaining things as we went along —the pull out of Euston station, which once had needed a cable engine at Camden Town, past Kilburn ('there is a spa here called Kilburn Wells, the water of which acts aperiently,' says an old Railway Guide), and so due west to Willesden. Here Herbert Spencer came in; for he was an engineer on the London-Watford section of the line, and in his Autobiography (I, 134-7) describes his adventure in the runaway truck which all but crashed him into the gates of the level crossing at Willesden Green. (Mr Huskisson was intrigued to know that Spencer's father as a youth taught Wilmot Horton's half brothers at Chaddesden Hall, Co. Derby, and that the Spencers once lived in Wilmot St., Derby). Harrow on the Hill, of course, he recognised. 'We wish' I said, 'that you had gone to Harrow and afterwards to Edinburgh and Cambridge—like Palmerston; for surely then you and not he would have been offered the Exchequer in 1809, and England might have escaped Vansittart and his Loan Finance.'

At Bletchley after making the standard joke—'equidistant from Oxford and Cambridge and no mails (males) stop there', I asked 'to which of the two had you rather gone—to Oxford with Liverpool, Canning and Peel or to Cambridge with Wilberforce, Castlereagh and Palmerston?' He inclined to Oxford, till I added unfairly to the Cambridge list 'and Mr Pitt': which settled it.

After Rugby came our first disquietude. He wanted to stop

off at Tamworth, but I had to explain that Peel's Drayton Manor was no more and we did not even know where the Lawrence of himself was. Then he said that he hoped for a view of the great metropolis of Birmingham, but I had to tell him that the main line no longer went that way, and as I did so, I found myself, with the inconsequence born of dreamland, humming the foolish ditty:

Oh, Mr Porter, what shall I do?
I wanted to go to Birmingham and you've taken me on to Crewe,
Send me back to London, as quickly as you can,
Oh Mr Porter, what a silly girl I am.

The great man was perplexed. I explained the persiflage: whereupon he smiled playfully and said 'It was a misunderstanding—I had supposed you were alluding to Mr G. R. Porter of the Board of Trade'.

But from that moment we were friends, and the sight of Lichfield Spires reminded him that he was in his own country. As we flashed through Great Bridgeford, he looked out for Shallowford Brook, sacred to Izaak Walton (what a pity we could not stop to see the Cottage), and very soon we were on the outskirts of Crewe. The converging maze of lines impressed him greatly and from Crewe on we were transport-minded. I showed him on the map how the main line ran north through Warrington (I said nothing of Parkside), how another line led to Manchester, and how we would cross the Mersey at Runcorn over the noble bridge of 1869. We ticked off the water navigations as we passed them one by one, the Shropshire Union (Middlewich in his day), the Weaver Navigation (Vale Royal and Dutton Locks), the descending locks of the Bridgewater Canal, the Manchester Ship Canal and the Mersey, and then after some minutes of smoke and smell we approached the suburbs of Liverpool. Edgehill was familiar ground, but not the last five minutes into Lime St.

A small group of friends awaited us on the platform. Sir John Tobin, (our host), John Moss, Robertson Gladstone (deputising for his father), George Holt, William Rathbone and James Cropper, with William Wainewright in attendance. We walked past the site of the pro-cathedral, where William Ewart Gladstone was baptised—now it carries a Woolworth Store—and so along Lord Street to the Exchange News Room, where he spoke a few words to the company assembled there. He was distressed (who would not be) to see the blitzed ruin of the old Custom House and the bust of himself boxed up during the demolitions which were in progress, but he welcomed a visit to the Riverside. We went, of course, on the Overhead Railway, first out to Seaforth and then back to the Dingle. (At Seaforth we ran over to Balliol Rd. to see the Huskisson Building Society.) He was pleased to find Canada Dock and Huskisson Dock in juxtaposition, and if our host had been advised in time, we might have found his *George Canning* and his *William Huskisson* unloading timber there. Going out we looked at the docks and the panorama of the river: coming back we fixed our attention on the transit sheds and the rail communications that emerge by tunnels at the dock side. It was dark before we had finished, and I had supposed work was over for the day, but not for Mr Huskisson. He worked on the notes (which his widow has preserved) of the speech he was to make at the banquet next day in honour of James Watt. He was dusting the last page as the hour of midnight struck, when Cinderella-like he vanished. This time I really was awake—to find that in two brief hours I had raced through a lifetime.

# CHAPTER TWO

# THE DISCIPLE AND HIS FRIENDS

*Huskisson and Canning*

> He stood the inheritor of the talents and fame of Canning. A lofty landmark in the moral and political horizon. And men loved him as much as they honoured him. (Mrs Lawrence of Liverpool to Mrs Huskisson, 19 September 1830.)

As Pitt was the child of his great father and also of the Wealth of Nations, so he had two great disciples, George Canning and William Huskisson, each of them masters in one half of the field—the former in politics and foreign policy, the latter in economics and public finance. It is after Canning that Oxford's first chair of politics should have been named: it is after Huskisson that a Cambridge chair of public finance might have been named, if someone in that University had supported Mrs Huskisson's desire to perpetuate her husband's memory by the creation of a professorship.[1] For nearly five years, namely from February 1823, when Huskisson entered the Board of Trade, to August 1827, when Canning died, the two were colleagues in high office, bound by a triple tie. They were absolute friends, a second David and Jonathan, and on Huskisson's part the friendship touched adoration. They were complementary not only in a professional, but in a temperamental sense. Canning had no aptitude for figures, but could manage men. Huskisson was a master of financial detail, but too shy and hesitant to lead a party. Finally, they were bound by a common veneration for the memory of Mr Pitt, under whom they had served their apprenticeship. It is arguable that Castlereagh was as great a foreign secretary as Canning, and J. C. Herries as clever a financier as Huskisson. But Castlereagh and Huskisson, Canning and Herries could not have paired for many reasons— differences of outlook, differences of disposition and differences in the interpretation of the heritage of Pitt.

[1] Cf. *Hatherton Correspondence* 1831. Letter of Mrs Huskisson to Littleton, August 1831.

Both Canning and Huskisson were born in 1770. Pitt died at 4 a.m. on Thursday 23 January 1806.

'God's will is done. Mr. Pitt's life is fast hastening to a close. . . . This seems to be like the end of all things.'

(Huskisson to Dundas (Lord Melville), 24 January 1806)

Dundas in reply makes proposals for the discharge of Pitt's debts. Himself in poor health and spirits, and with the shadow of impeachment hanging over him, he thinks of others first. Corrupt he may have been, financially careless he certainly was, but he had a great heart and unflinching spirit and to the youthful Huskisson he was a respected chief.

Miss Dorothy Marshall in her *Rise of George Canning* carries the story to the same date, her concluding words being: 'His love of his wife he took with him to his own grave, his political allegiance was buried in Pitt's.'

Canning had married Miss Scott, a considerable heiress, on 15 May 1800: and Huskisson married Emily Milbanke, who also had means, on 6 April 1799.[1] What Miss Marshall writes of Canning could with equal truth be written of Huskisson. How Huskisson and Canning first met is not recorded by either of them precisely, but it must have been in, or before, 1793, by which time Canning was on intimate terms with Lord and Lady Gower (later Marquis of Stafford and Lady Stafford, later Duke and Duchess of Sutherland). Canning was very fond of Lady Gower, and would meet Huskisson at Wimbledon. One of his first speeches was on the Emigrants Bill, and this was Huskisson's department, but it was not till Pitt's second Ministry, 1804-6, when Huskisson was a Secretary to the Treasury and

---

[1] The Register of St. Mary le bone Church (p. 21, of 1799) reads:

N. 62. William Huskisson Esquire of the Parish of Saint George Hanover Square in the County of Middlesex Bachelor and Eliza Emily Milbanke of this Parish Spinster

Married in this Church by Licence this sixth Day of April in the year One thousand seven hundred and ninetynine By me Roger Frankland Rector of Yarlington

This marriage was solemnised between US

|  |  |  |
|---|---|---|
|  | (Signed) | { William Huskisson<br>{ Eliza Emily Milbanke |
| In the presence of<br>(Signed) |  | { Mark Milbanke<br>{ Henry Dundas |

62. William Huskisson Esquire _____ of the Parish
of Saint George Hanover Square in the County of Middlesex
Bachelor and Eliza Emily Milbanke of this Parish Spinster were
Married in this Church by Licence _____ _____ _____
this Sixth Day of April in the Year One Thousand seven Hundred
Ninety Nine By me Roger Frankland Rector of
Darlington.

This Marriage was solemnized between Us { William Huskisson
                                          Eliza Emily Milbanke.

Presence of { W. Milbanke
             { Henry Dundas _____

Entry in Marylebone Parish Church Register, 1799,

of the marriage between William Huskisson and Elizabeth Milbanke

Canning Treasurer of the Navy, that the relations between them were of public importance, so that they stood out as Pitt's prize pupils.

Such was Phase I—the rise, independently, of Canning and Huskisson.

Phase II sees the rise of the Canningites to whom, from the first, Huskisson attached himself, and it terminated with Canning's mission to Portugal in 1814. In Phase III they are both back in office—Huskisson in Woods and Forests, Canning at the India Board of Control. Though not in the Cabinet, Huskisson was its financial brain. Currency and the Corn Laws brought him to the front, and here Canning took his cue from Huskisson, who had looked after his interest in Liverpool when he was abroad, and upon his return became his financial adviser both in personal and public matters. When the death of Castlereagh opened the Foreign Office to Canning, 16 September 1822, he set in motion the negotiations which brought Huskisson to the Board of Trade in February 1823, with a seat in the Cabinet as from November 1823. Then comes Phase IV—The Great Partnership, which will furnish the core of Volume II.

*Pitt's Disciple*

Phase I starts in the Paris Embassy; and we can have no better introduction than the note contributed by Lady Stafford at the request of Mrs Huskisson:

When Lord Gower (now Lord Stafford) was appointed to the Embassy at Paris in 1790, he was directed to proceed there immediately, he consequently had no time previously to procure a private secretary. Dr. Warner was recommended to him by Mr. Geo. Selwyn, and some others, as Chaplain, and accompanied him there. Soon after his arrival at Paris, he mentioned to him that a friend of his Dr. Gemm [*sic*], who was also known to Lord Gower, as being settled for many years at Paris (having gone there in 1763 as physician to the Duke of Bedford) had 2 nephews, promising young men, one of which, tho' very young, had distinguished himself by making a speech on financial subjects at the Club de Quatre Vingt-neuf. Ld. G. desired Dr. Warner to introduce him to him. I remember his bringing him to the Hotel de L'Université. Ld. G. was pleased with his sensible and unaffected manners and proposed to him to be his private secretary, which he willingly accepted, and came to live first in the Rue de l'Université and afterwards in the Hotel de Monaco with us, inhabiting an appartement on one side of the gate of that Hotel, similar to one on the other side, which had been the appartement of the Cte. de Valentinois while Princesse de Monaco lived there.

Dr. Gemm had intended, as I then heard, to educate him to his own profession. His air and countenance and manner were then very much the same I have always known them since. I think with less alteration than in most persons I have known during the same period. He had the mornings to himself. Excepting on the days of the Courier (Friday) he had not much occupation with Ld. G., who wrote the dispatches himself. He dined with us and did the honors at one end of the table. He had many previous acquaintances and made many more of our society. He was very much esteemed by the English who came to Paris and who had not the political prejudices which some entertained from his having belonged to the Club de 89. Party prejudices then ran high, but in this case the impression had no effect of importance against him. I regret we have no copy of the speech he made. I remember reading it. It is to be found among the printed papers circulated in that period and also in some of Cobbett's publications of that time. He had many friends and among the more intimate of those I recollect Mr. Boyd the Banker who has since behaved so honorably in the vicissitudes of his own fortunes—Mr. Ferguson of Craigdorroch, then very young, and I think he was frequently at Ld. Cholmondeley's.[1] He was acquainted with those who came to us. We generally had society and little suppers in the evenings at which he frequently was. He employed (I believe) in reading a considerable portion of his time. He gained a great deal of information, but without secluding himself from society, which he always liked. We never had the least fault to find with him. We were always good friends. He was kind and obliging, but never with an over-complacency. I used frequently to teize him and to make him read Chesterfield's Letters. He used frequently to walk out with me. I mention these trifles as the least likely to be remembered by others, though most of them unworthy of being written. His brother I think soon left Paris. I believe it is to him that an inscription is dedicated in the Church of Byshbury, and which is inserted in Stowe's Staffordshire. Vol. 2. p. 179. Dr. Gemm was a very fine looking old man, and with agreeable manners. His nephew was very dutiful to him, but I think he did not agree in some of his

---

[1] George James, 4th Earl and 1st Marquis (1749-1827), a gaming libertine immortalised by Reynolds, *vide Illustrated London News* of 5 February 1949. 'Chŭmlĭ' is in Cheshire.

opinions, which were singular and which he had adopted by living much in the society of the Baron d'Holbach, and some of the *Philosophers* whom he used frequently to quote, while Mr. H. tried to change the subject. We had a very sincere esteem for Mr. Huskisson and a real friendship for him. He continued in the way of society gaining many friends and acquaintances till Ld. Stafford was recalled in 1792, when he accompanied us on our return to England and lived with us in London and afterwards at Wimbledon, going I think to his own friends in Staffordshire (Mr. and Mrs. Swinfen and others) while we made a visit at Trentham where the late Ld. Stafford[1] then was. He resided with us, when we returned, and lived at Wimbledon. Ld. Stafford[2] was then very weak from the consequences of a fever he had on returning from Paris, which settled on his eyes. He regretted that Mr. H. had no certain occupation, so being frequently in society when at Wimbledon with Mr. Pitt and Mr. Dundas he introduced Mr. H. to them. Mr. Arbuthnot a few days ago mentioned his recollecting meeting Mr. Pitt and Mr. Dundas at dinner with Ld. Stafford then and that Mr. Dundas said he wished to find a man of ability who understood French well as he was in want of such a person to be placed in the Alien Office which was then forming or about to be formed. Ld. Stafford recommended Mr. Huskisson to him as highly fitted for business and he was accordingly immediately appointed to a place with a salary (I think) of £300 a year. (Mr. A thinks of £400). From thence by his own merit and talent he rose rapidly to the highest employments. All this I correctly remember. His original residence at Paris, under the care of his maternal uncle (I believe) Dr. Gemm, arose, I believe, from the circumstance of his father, a gentleman possessing some property near Walsall or in that part of Staffs., residing there, having contracted a second marriage, which made residing at home inelligible to the children of the first, but which finally proved the means accidentally of bringing Mr. H.'s abilities and interests to a field more fitted for them than had his original situation remained more agreeable to his own wishes and those of his friends.

The Discourse to the Club of 1789 delivered 29 August 1790 was 'Sur les Assignats'. It is printed in the appendix to his Speeches, III, 643. He had often to refute the charge that he belonged to the Jacobin Club, into which he says he went but once, 'as other Englishmen did, to satisfy my own curiosity' (Speeches: Prefatory Memoir, I, 11).

---

[1] The 1st Marquis, 1721-1803.    [2] The 2nd Marquis, 1758-1833.

The introduction to Pitt came in January 1793, and Huskisson in a letter to Hayley, 18 January 1793, tells what transpired:

The Minister was not there till an hour later than his time and only stayed during dinner, at which the conversation turned entirely upon business and gave rise to the accidental circumstance which has called me to my present situation. A Lady of France having made an application to Lord Gower in the morning with respect to the means of conforming to the Aliens Bill, the question was referred to Mr Dundas and Pitt. The former said that they were in want of a person who could speak the language and direct the execution of that Bill according to the views of Government, which were to show every possible civility and respect to all foreigners whose conduct in this country had not given rise to any suspicion and especially to save the ladies the trouble of appearing at the Public Office. Mr. Dundas gave several hints that he wished me to accept of the post. I gave no answer at the time, but was so strongly advised by Lord Gower to take the opportunity of showing my desire of being useful, that I delayed it only till the morning. It was of course accepted and in such a manner that I am rather glad to have made the offer, though it is certainly not a post I would have asked for. At present it takes up the whole of my time, and even I am not able to do without the assistance of one and frequently two clerks.

In his diary for 1809 Lord Glenbervie, Huskisson's predecessor at Woods and Forests, a vain person and a scandalmonger (he claims the entire merit of the improved forestry system and insinuates that Lady Stafford was intimate with the young secretary!!), carries the career a stage further:

Huskisson was recommended by Lady Gower to Dundas, then Secretary of State for the Home Department, Colonies and War. He made him a sort of extra clerk to read and digest French documents and to see the numerous French emigrants who had swarmed to that Office, and with whom neither the Minister (Dundas) nor his two under-secretaries, Nepean and King, could hold any direct intercourse from their ignorance of their language and who, in general, even in circumstances where it would have been so useful to them, never would take the trouble to learn ours. When that office was divided and the Home part given to the Duke of Portland (11 *July* 1794) on the coalition of the alarmists with Pitt in 1794, Dundas retaining the War and Colonies, he took Huskisson with him and advanced him to be an Under-secretary of State. On the resignations at the end of 1800, he lost that situation. On Pitt's return to office in 1803, he was made Secretary to the Treasury, was removed by the Fox and Grenville Adminstration, was restored again when the King dismissed them, and has lately again resigned at the same time, and, as is understood, as having connected himself with Canning.

He has established the reputation of a very able man and one of the best secretaries of the Treasury in the Office and in Parliament, of the many I have remembered. This is the character given of him by friend and foe. His manners are dry and not obliging, and he has no eloquence. But he always seems to me very shrewd. . . . Mr. Pitt thought Huskisson one of the ablest men in the Kingdom.[1]

It is true enough that he only found himself as a speaker *circiter* 1820; but when he found himself, he was on commercial topics—I say it deliberately—as eloquent as Gladstone.

In Pitt's first ministry, i.e. to 1801, the three men with whom Huskisson came into closest contact were Evan Nepean, Henry Dundas and Pitt himself.[2] He was a glutton for work, and overdid it to the detriment of his health. Almost at once, he became the friend of his superiors and they exchanged confidences not only as to the war situation, but also as to the state of their health.

In October 1794, with Nepean away at Tunbridge Wells taking a cure for his rheumatism, Huskisson had to run the department. 'The whole of his official duties in addition to my own have fallen to me' (Huskisson to Hayley). But he desired a regular status. 'It appears', he writes to Nepean, 'that it is Mr Pitt's intention at the conclusion of the War to appoint me a kind of Under-Secretary of the India Department'—but could he not have some regular status *now*? With the death of his father and his inheritance of the Staffordshire property, his financial position was sound. He aimed at something more than a chief-clerkship, regular office of some sort, with a seat, perhaps, in Parliament. It was causing him much 'perplexity and distress of mind'. The opportunity came next year when Nepean was moved to the Admiralty and Huskisson succeeded him as

---

[1] *Diaries of Sylvester Douglas Ld. Glenbervie*, edited by F. Bickley, II, 28-9.
[2] He witnessed Pitt's will. Dundas signed the marriage register of him and Eliza Emily Milbanke, and Mrs Huskisson's niece married a Nepean.

Under-Secretary for War and the Colonies, the seals of which
department were held by Dundas. But he had made a friend of
Nepean, as he did of everyone for whom he worked, and in
1799 when Admiral Milbanke was enquiring into the character
of the young man who wanted to marry his daughter, Nepean
spoke up for him handsomely.

With Dundas as his chief, the letters between them become
frequent and intimate. Dundas in his great sprawling hand
pours out his soul—his worry about the affairs of Europe and
his own sorry health. 'For my part I would give her [the
Empress of Russia] St. Domingo or even overturn the Turkish
Empire rather than not combine Europe in the present moment'
(14 June 1796): and again 'I should consider both Trinidad
and Buenos Ayres as poor acquisitions if obtained by the sacrifice of the Mediterranean'.

There is a letter of 1798 from Dundas enclosing one from a
member of the Dundas family, at the Cape of Good Hope,
which says 'Lord McCartney, [the new governor] has arrived
safely. The troops are pretty healthy. I send two boxes of ostrich
feathers for the ladies'. Huskisson comes into the picture because in the next year 1799, at the instance of Dundas, he was
appointed Agent to the Cape. He sends out livestock from
Woburn ('2 Devonshire Heifers and a Bull £24. 0. 0.'), vege-
table seeds and agricultural requisites from 'Thos. Gibbs and
Co., Nurserymen and Seedsmen to the Board of Agriculture'.
And William Windham, the Secretary of 1806-7, reviewing
the status of the agency argued that the appointment belonged
properly to the Colonial Department and not to the Treasury.[1]

But it was Europe which caused the headache in Dundas's
time. At the end of 1796, when there was a question of a peace
mission to the Directory, Huskisson, in view of his knowledge
of French, offered his services, and though they were not
needed, the offer earned the approval of Pitt. The war with
France continued. 'The anxiety which the landing of the French
in Egypt has created in my mind will take away much of the
pleasure of my excursion and even a brilliant success of Nelson

[1] *Windham Papers*, II, 312. Windham to Grenville.

will not compensate to my feelings for the consequences of having made good their landing' (Dundas to Huskisson, 27 August 1798). But the victory of the Nile brought rejoicing when its completeness was known. Thus far Huskisson had no official concern with finance. But big sums of secret service money passed through his hands, e.g. £121,000 between 6 March 1795 and 5 April 1797; and the provision of specie to European allies involved his Department. He writes to Dundas, at the end of 1796—Pitt's loan to the Emperor of Austria is 'a question I am not competent to discuss'; but then proceeds to an expert analysis of the problem. The difficulty about the loan is the dearth of specie. Could not some part of it have been raised abroad? Already he is a critic of the Bank, for he suggests that 'our financial entanglements are not wholly unconnected with the political sentiments of a prevailing party in the Bank'. In 1799 he writes to a future Treasury colleague Henry Wellesley (later Baron Cowley), 'The negotiation for the armistice is not yet brought to any issue.' 'Clearly, if we do not [settle this matter], the boasted power of Britain as a maritime state is entirely delusive—if this will not rouse men, we are fallen low indeed.'

Some years later, namely in 1810, Huskisson was to assist in the drafting of the Bullion Committee's Report. By this date he was an ex-Treasury official, having spent the year 1809 scouring the New World for dollars;[1] and it has been argued that the rigid Treasury control over specie added to the difficulties of the Walcheren Expedition by preventing the Commander-in-Chief in Chatham from taking specie with him to pay for supplies. The Bullion Report may be right or wrong. But the one criticism that will not hold water is that its authors forgot that there was a war on. Huskisson, like Pitt and Dundas, thought of nothing else. He lived in an atmosphere of war sup-

---

[1] Cf. E. Herries, *Memoir of J. C. Herries*, Ch. III of Vol. I.

Independently of this there is in the Treasury Papers, T. 64, 329, a remarkable transaction of 1809 concerning the shipment of dollars from Mexico to London—first, three million from the Mexican Treasury, then the whole balance of the Mexican Treasury: lastly, six million from the Merchants of Mexico—all against 'Bills on the Treasury of England in favour of the Spanish Government'. The only snag was the obstinacy of British naval commanders, who threatened to seize whatever treasure they did not personally escort.

plies of every sort for all parts of the world all the way from 1793 to 1810 and not least in 1810 when Lord Wellington was writing to him from the Peninsula, 26 April 1810. 'With a strong government we could make France evacuate it. Bonaparte isn't going to have it all his own way.' It was for Huskisson a fight to the finish; and because he thought that it would conduce to the surest finish with the minimum of injurious aftermath, he took the line he did take both in the Report and in the Tract which he wrote in its support, 'The Question concerning the Depreciation of our Currency Stated and Examined', October 1810.

In 1801 Huskisson went out of office with Pitt. Lord Hobart, Dundas's successor at the Colonial Office, wrote thanking him for the services which he had rendered to the Department, and there is a second letter in the same terms from the head of the Transport Office.

On 10 May 1804 Pitt returned to power; and Charles Long of the Treasury wrote to Huskisson 'I mentioned what you desired and I have to say in consequence that Mr. Pitt desired me to propose to you the Treasury—your colleague will be Sturges. I shall probably be at the Board . . .' Huskisson and Sturges Bourne duly became joint secretaries, and this explains the entry in the Annual Register under 26 July 1804 'This day Mr. Pitt attended by Mr. Long, Mr. Huskisson and Mr. Sturges Bourne dined with the Company of Grocers'.

Huskisson had arrived. For it was a Joint Secretaryship of the Treasury and not a Commissionership of the Treasury that was the administrative and financial plum.

A Treasury Commissioner submitted to Huskisson some years later a cynical account of his duties. Twice a week the Board meets: business purely formal:

The duty of the Lords who assist is that of listening to the perusal of minutes on multifarious subjects on which they are supposed to decide. From their ignorance, however, of every matter contained in the papers, their decision upon the Principia of Sir Isaac Newton would be as necessary and as valuable as a sanction or disapproval. The only remaining branch of duty exercised by the Lords is that of affixing their signatures to a copy of the documents by which much of the business of the Empire is transacted, but the contents of which are also unknown to those who sign them . . . The great mass of its business is now in the hands of its clerks. Over these the Lords have a nominal control. (J. L. Gould to W. Huskisson, 5 May 1827)

But the Board was valued because of its prestige, and it was a passport to more solid things. The stricture on it would not apply to a man like Long who had in addition been a treasury secretary 1791-1801. He, after a short spell in Ireland, became Paymaster-General, 1810-26, and thus was close to the purse strings throughout his official life.

It is clear from Long's letter to Huskisson that Huskisson stood high in Pitt's esteem, even before he was advanced to the Treasury. There is an echo of this many years later. In August 1826, when Canning asked him about a payment of £110,000 initialled by W. H. at the Colonial Office, Huskisson replies 'I was sent for one day (it must have been in the spring of 1799) by Mr. Pitt—Mr. Dundas was with him. . . . Both Mr. Pitt and Mr. Dundas were for the bargain. The favourite policy of that day was to get possession of all West Indian Colonies, so as to bring the whole of their productions, sugar coffee etc. to this country'. Huskisson on his side worshipped Pitt, who consulted him on his private affairs and made him a witness to his will. Staying with Pitt at Walmer Castle, Huskisson writes to his wife, 3 April 1803:

Mr. Pitt and I have been walking and having a good deal of conversation upon public subjects. Everything that drops from him is so marked by superior virtue and superior sense that it is impossible not to love and admire in him something different even from all other men. Neither ambition nor interest will lead him to do anything which with the most severe judge could lessen those feelings for him, and though it is not very unlikely he may soon come into power again, the resumption of it, should it take place, will be upon terms and in a manner not less creditable to his character than his retreat.[1]

[1] The common view that Pitt sometimes addressed the House the worse for wine is not supported by the following: 'June 17, 1827. I sat next to Mr. Huskisson, who told me something of his intercourse with Mr. Pitt, under whom he had served in the Treasury. He mentioned that

When Pitt died, Huskisson felt it incumbent upon him to submit a memorandum (February 1806) on what he believed to be Pitt's financial intentions:

The sanction of his high authority and sincere wish on my part (the natural impulse of those feelings which I shall ever entertain towards his measures and his memory) that the public should have a chance of benefitting by his thoughts on the subject are the motives which induce to commit to paper the following the present statement.

The statement goes into much detail upon the continuation of the Bank's advance to the Government and the management of the Exchequer Bill issues. These 'are in high favour with the Money Market': and 'should the Treasury be pressed beyond what the market could conveniently take (an event not probable), the Bank is ready to come to an arrangement to take, from time to time, any exchequer bills which under such circumstances Government may find it necessary to dispose of'. There is no mention of the controversial Sinking Fund, but the reckless use which Vansittart was to make of it in his policy of Loan Finance is disapproved in advance by the comment on New War Taxes:

It was Mr. Pitt's positive intention to raise the property tax to 10%. This would give an addition of about £3½ million. This was known to Mr. Thornton and some other persons as well as to myself: it being his deliberate opinion that it would be better, under the present circumstances, to carry at once our annual extra-ordinary taxes as far as they can be carried without material injury to the permanent revenue, or too great a pressure on the people, and to spare our credit, keeping it as much as possible for a reserve.

The memorandum concludes:

This I may be allowed to say is no unsatisfactory statement to offer to the country: no unsatisfactory display of our remaining resources to the

Mr. Pitt was not in the habit of drinking before he spoke. He used to take a mutton chop and a glass of wine and water at three o'clock; nothing more. . . . Mr. Huskisson mentioned that Ld. Castlereagh and Ld. Liverpool both took ether, as an excitement, before speaking. He also told me that he once asked Wilberforce what made his fingers so black, and Mr. Wilberforce told him that he was in the habit of taking opium before making a long speech; and "to that" said he "I owe all my success as a public speaker".' (Lord Broughton, *Recollections of a Long Life*, II, 205.)

world: no unsatisfactory legacy from the powerful genius whose work this fabric is, to the successor on whom is now devolved the arduous task of preserving and completing it.

The last contact with Pitt relates to a theatre which Huskisson and Canning were to make the spearhead of their economic diplomacy—South America. In 1807, Sir Home Popham was court-martialled for attacking without permission Rio de la Plata, and pleaded in defence that:

When the chain of facts shall have been completely established by the concurrent depositions of Lord Melville, Mr. Sturges Bourne and Mr. Huskisson, it will not be necessary for me again to urge that on leaving England I sailed under the strongest conviction that after having succeeded in taking the Cape nothing would contribute so effectively to accomplish the views of ministers as to strike a blow in South America before the Spaniards should be prepared against it.

The Annual Register for 1807 (pp. 402-3) gives the examination in detail:

*Mr. Huskisson sworn, and examined by Sir H. Popham.*
*Q.* Had you any conversation with Mr. Pitt, in the year 1805, on the subject of South America, and particularly Buenos Ayres; and did you by his directions take any steps respecting myself?
*A.* I had many frequent conversations with Mr. Pitt, on the subject of South America, and I might say particularly with respect to Buenos Ayres.
*Q.* Have the goodness to state the nature of those conversations with Mr. Pitt in general; but I do not wish to exact from you anything that can affect the interests of the state, or of individuals, however materially such disclosures might serve my purpose.
*A.* I believe almost on every occasion Mr. Pitt conversed with me on the subject of South America, his attention was called to that part of the globe particularly by some incident or occurrence. A person brought to me a plan or chart of the Rio de la Plata, which had been recently, as he informed me, published at Paris, the original being taken from the depôt of the King of Spain, at Madrid; and he added, that he had intelligence which led him to believe that plan would shortly be of use to some part of the French navy, who would probably find their way with troops to that settlement. Knowing this person was one on whom Mr. Pitt could place

reliance, I felt it my duty to communicate to Mr. Pitt what that person told me. Mr. Pitt stated to me, generally, the views he entertained with respect to South America; and he generally conceived that it would be of the utmost consequence to this country to maintain our naval superiority, and the facilities to which that superiority would enable us in distant operations against South America, if obliged to carry on the war, as the success of the confederacy on the continent of Europe did not correspond with his wishes, and it was also desirable to prevent the French doing that which they certainly would do, if not anticipated, namely, by our taking possession of the Spanish settlements in South America; he was therefore disposed to give credit to the person who gave that information, and hoped we should be beforehand with the superiority of naval resources. This was the general subject of the conversation. I can only state very generally the purport of Mr. Pitt's desire, but I cannot say more, without being so guarded as scarcely to render myself intelligible. I did take further steps to obtain information respecting Buenos Ayres, and put a series of questions to learn whether any French force were likely to arrive there, and also took preliminary steps with a view to facilitate the capture by a British force. Those steps were taken very shortly after the explanations were given to Sir Home, and the person spoken of in these conversations as a person with whom he had communicated, and who had given him much information upon the subject.

*Q.* I think you said Mr. Pitt desired you to take some preliminary steps, as, in case of the continuance of the war, it would be of great importance to commence operations in South America, and still greater to anticipate the supposed views of France in that quarter of the world. Do you know of any circumstances which happened to occasion him to change his opinion as to the value he set on the objects of his views in South America?

*A.* I believe his views in South America were not confined to the mere object of introducing British manufactures, but I have no occasion for belief that any of his views with respect to that country were at all changed.

*Q.* Do you think his views materially increased by the extraordinary and rapid successes of the French on the continent, and from shutting up the ports of the continent against our trade?

*A.* I believe they were.

In the end Admiral Popham received only a severe reprimand.

### Rise of the Canningites
Hitherto everything had gone well with Huskisson. He had got everything he sought and won laurels in every post, and not

least in the Treasury where he played a leading part in important administrative reforms—the centralisation of Government accounts at the Bank of England, and the framing of regulations for carrying out the great Warehousing Act of 1803. The former task brought him on the Minutes of the Bank of England, Committee of Treasury, Vol. V, 13 June 1805. 'The Deputy Governor stated to the Committee that Mr. Huskisson had suggested to him the propriety that all Receivers of Public Money should keep their accounts at the Bank; and it had been intimated, that it was expected the Bank should get the bills accepted as well as paid. To which the Committee did not see any objection.' The latter task was the occasion of his briefly addressing the House of Commons for the first time after nearly ten years of membership. The bill 'for warehousing goods within the limits of certain docks etc.' passed without opposition and received the royal assent, 28 July 1804. On 30 January 1805 the docks were officially opened (see Huskisson, *Speeches*, I, 1-3).

When after the brief Ministry of the Talents he returned to the Treasury for a second term (1807-9), in the Duke of Portland's administration, his course was again set fair. On the lines of his memorandum of 1806 he helped to clear up the relations between the Treasury and the Bank of England. This raised the question of Retrenchment in the Public Services, and accordingly he was put up to reply to Mr Wardle's Plan of Public Economy in what was his first long speech, 19 June 1809. He demolished Mr. Wardle in a learned survey (the foretaste of things to come) in which occurs the characteristic sentence 'So much, Sir, for superfluous establishments in this branch of the revenue; in which, I need not remind the House, that all sinecure offices, and places executed by deputy were abolished by Mr. Pitt' (*Speeches*, I, 26).

In this year 1809 he was offered the Chief Secretaryship of Ireland, but declined it on the advice (so he told Canning in 1821) of the Ministers who made the offer, namely Lord Liverpool, the Home Secretary, and Perceval, the Chancellor of the Exchequer. The offer was repeated in 1812, 1818 and 1821.

'In 1812 I was again designated for the station united to the Chancellorship of the Exchequer in that country . . . Upon Peel's resignation his office was again tendered to me . . . I cannot take in 1821 what I declined in 1809' (Huskisson to Canning). The Marquis Wellesley, who at the close of 1809 was brought back from the Spanish Embassy to serve as Foreign Secretary under Perceval, clearly expected Huskisson to be in the Cabinet. For he wrote to Charles Arbuthnot (then at the Foreign Office) from Seville, 30 October 1809:

One loss would grieve me deeply, that is Mr. Huskisson . . . I entertain the highest regard and esteem for his talents and attainments. In any views which I have ever formed of acting in the King's Councils, I have always looked to him as the main source of assistance. From me he would ever meet with the most cordial confidence and goodwill. I hope he will not quit the King on this occasion, nor lose the opportunity of aiding us in the correction of many errors. You are at liberty to state my sentiments to him. If I could venture to use such a freedom I should have written to him.

But when Canning, after his duel with Castlereagh, refused to take office under Perceval, Huskisson retired with him and was out of office for the next five years, 1809-14. Yet even had Canning stayed in, Huskisson would not have been welcome to Perceval at the Exchequer. Rather than to Huskisson, it was offered to Palmerston, who had no experience of finance whatever, and when Palmerston refused it, Perceval carried on himself till his death in 1812. That Perceval was out of sympathy with Huskisson, the part-author of the Bullion Report of 1810, is shewn by his reception of the pamphlet in which that Report was justified:

Perceval to Croker, 11 November 1810
    I thank you for the sight of Huskisson's pamphlet. I have run through it. I cannot say *read* it, for it requires much more reading than I have had time yet to give. It is in many respects very able, in all very specious, in many, however, I presume to think fallacious, and particularly unfair in keeping out of sight so much as it does the circumstance of an interrupted commercial intercourse with the Continent, which, in my opinion, is

sufficient, together with the causes which he mentions, to account for almost all those symptoms and phenomena which he ascribes solely to the supposed excess in the paper circulation. The truth probably lies between the two extremes of opinion upon this point; but the practical danger and difficulty of the experiment so immensely, in my mind at least, weighs down the mischief which he supposes to exist from the over-issue of paper, that I should consider the measure he proposes as tantamount to a Parliamentary Declaration that we must submit to any terms of peace rather than continue the war, which I apprehend, under his project, would be found utterly impossible.

Yours very truly.

Sp. P.

I do not propose at this place to argue the issue between the Bullionists and their opponents. The sad thing was that in 1812 Canning and Huskisson were unwilling to rejoin the government, except on terms which were unreasonable.

Dr Aspinall in his edition of the Letters of George IV (I, 106) says, on the authority of MSS 38,738, fo. 258, that in 1812 Huskisson, one of the leading members of Canning's party, refused the Chancellorship of the Exchequer 'from a firm conviction that the interests of the Government cannot be adequately maintained in the House of Commons, especially at this moment, unless this office, united to that of First Lord of the Treasury is held by the person who leads the House'. But the document is no more than a draft. It was not a firm offer from a responsible quarter; and his refusal was incidental to a fantastic project in which, with Moira as titular premier in the Lords, Canning was to be Leader of the Commons, First Lord of the Treasury and Chancellor of the Exchequer! The project, of course, came to nothing. Moira went to India, and Liverpool's long reign began.

However, the side-tracking of Huskisson at this juncture surrendered the national finances for eleven sorry years to the inept hands of Vansittart, and when in 1819 Huskisson refought the battle for Cash Payments, he had to overthrow not only the paper pound, but also the lax system of loan finance in time of peace which Vansittart, through a fatuous faith in the virtues of a sinking fund, had tied up with it. Hence the closing words of Huskisson's Memorandum of 1819 to Lord Liverpool:

The mystery of our financial system no longer deceives anyone in the money market—selling Exchequer Bills daily to redeem Funded Debt daily, then funding those Exchequer Bills once a year, or once in every 2 years, in order to go over the same ground again. Whilst the very air of mystery and the anomaly of large annual or biennial loans in time of profound peace creates uneasiness out of the market; and in foreign countries an impression unfavourable with respect to the solidity of our resources. I think I have seen some symptoms which induce me to apprehend that this impression has already been made in some degree in the political circles and money markets of the Continent. In finance expediency and ingenious devices may answer to meet temporary difficulties; but for a permanent and peace system the only wise course either in policy or for impression, is a system of simplicity and truth.

This course must be coupled with our other arrangements for the Resumption of Cash Payments, or it is my conscientious belief that we shall either fail in attaining the object or, if attained, in adhering to it.

Whatever surplus of revenue we possess must be our real Sinking Fund. The growth of the revenue and the interest of the debt *really* diminished will improve the Sinking Fund year after year, whilst peace continues. Should it require further improvement, I am sure that we should find in Parliament and the country a better disposition to submit to any moderate sacrifice for that purpose, than we can possibly expect so long as the present system is persevered in. Our Sinking Fund (it is the only fund deserving of such a name) would then be whatever surplus of revenue the country can afford without too much pressure; and be its amount great or small, it will do more for the reduction of debt, for the real stability of the public credit, for the character of England abroad, and the strength and ease of the Government at home than ever can be hoped for by continuing in a system which has all the inconveniencies without any of the advantages of concealment, and is liable to all the derangements and expense incidental to complicated machinery without producing any beneficial result, even while its movements meet with no opposition. (Liverpool Papers, 38,368, fo. 222 *et seq.*)[1]

[1] This memorandum of 1819 was preceded by two earlier ones (drafts in the Huskisson Papers) one of 1816 on Country Banks and the Limitation of the Bank's Monopoly and one of 1818 on Coin and the Currency. They reveal the highest financial ability, combining theory with factual knowledge and forceful presentation. Written at a higher level than the Parliamentary Papers of the time, they are prolegomena to the Currency and Banking Policy of the 1820's.

This was the eloquence on paper which Huskisson was to translate into the eloquence of set speech before the House of Commons in the next eleven years. In that period he raised financial exposition to a height which (at least, when the speeches are seen in print) was not outmatched by Gladstone. In Parliament from 1796, he only found his voice in 1809. Then for ten years, adhering carefully to his chosen field of public finance, he earned the respectful attention of the house, and finally was able to carry it to a pitch of enthusiasm in which he would sit down amid 'lively and sustained applause' from both sides of the House.

In 1812 the Canningites received a recruit in the person of Edward John Littleton, 1791-1863, from whose MS. autobiography the most succinct account of their purpose and fortunes is to be derived. I quote later (pp. 310-311) the boyhood part, and begin here with his entry into politics:

At B.N. College I read harder than the majority and should have taken a creditable degree, if Sir E. Littleton's death in May 1812, 2 months after I came of age, had not called me to contest the County with Sir John Wrottesley—who after a long canvas declined a poll. My election at the time probably decided the circumstances and character of my life. I ranged myself under Mr. Canning's banner in the House of Commons. My early prepossession had been Toryish, but on the Catholic Question and some others of domestic policy, my feelings were with the more liberal party. These mixed sentiments naturally placed me in the same ranks with Canning, Huskisson, my colleague, Lord Granville Leveson Gower,[1] Sturges Bourne, and afterwards Lord Dudley and about 3 or 4 others. Our party didn't consist of more than 16—for Mr. Canning considered himself, with a few followers of character, as constituting a more influential party, and standing in a more commanding and freer position than if he had been a leader of 50, each of whom would probably have felt they had a claim upon him.

During the years 1812, 13 to June 1814 I lived very much in the society I have named. Having married a daughter[2] of Ld. Wellesley Oct. 1812 (an event I cannot mention without declaring it to be the most for-

[1] M.P., Staffordshire, 1799-1815.
[2] Hyacinthe Mary, Lady Hatherton. Her mother, the Marchioness, was Hyacinthe Gabrielle, 𝐡er daughter Hyacinthe Anne.

tunate event of my life) I was led into closer intimacy with all that party—
for Lord Wellesley himself belonged to it. All those whom I have named
together with Ld. Boringdon[1] and Ld. Binning and Bobus Smith used to
dine continually at Canning's house, Gloucester Lodge, Brompton, on
Sundays. Lady Granville and Mrs. Huskisson and Ld. Morley were
always of the party, and frequently some of Ld. Stafford's family, the
Gowers. With all these parties I was on terms of considerable intimacy,
and always felt my admission to their numbers as a great compliment. Mr.
Canning's unfortunate acceptance of the Embassy at Lisbon, and the
junction of others of his friends to the Government broke up our little
corps, which for 2 or 3 years had placed itself in a position in which it was
greatly courted by the Government and the Whigs.

After the peace, while the nation began to occupy itself with domestic
questions, a very independent mode of thinking began to arise in the
country. The war had united all men. Its successes bound the nation—for
a time under the spell of those who had directed it. But peace broke the
charm—and individuals, in matters of more local interest, began to think
for themselves. John Bull too had now to pay for his follies; and growled
very much about it. The Tories were no longer always triumphant. Had
Canning stayed in England, instead of going to Lisbon and had he maintained his old seat below the Gangway on the ministerial side, and there
have played a prudently popular part, which he might honourably have
done, he would have been called on in 2 years to form a Government.

From the moment that he broke up his own party, I had great doubts
what I should do. I consulted Ward[2] about it, whom I found in the same
doubt. He told me he had suspected that Canning was about to join Lord
Liverpool's Government, for he, Mr. C. had intimated to him that he
wished 'to be individualized' as much as possible. Ward said in his usual
cynicist manner 'I was travelling along the road, in the most respectable
manner, with some chosen friends, when suddenly the coachman pulls up,
and desires me and the other passengers to step out. Accordingly I had
nothing for it but to sit patiently on the bank till the Ministerial "Bang
Up" [a favourite name with coachmen] came by, and I advise you to
accept of the same conveyance'.

I accordingly in the succeeding session, keeping my old seat, generally
voted with the Govt.—opposing it however on some few questions, which
the Whig Govt. has since carried—some of these questions of Economy

---

[1] Liverpool writes to Canning, 20 July 1814, promising him a peerage for Granville and an
Earldom for Boringdon, who was made Earl of Morley 1815 (*Private Correspondence of Lord
Granville Leveson Gower*, II, 498).

[2] John William Ward, the future Earl of Dudley, Foreign Secretary of 1827-8.

but especially of questions relating to the improvement of Criminal Law. The great battles of succeeding years were the Catholic Question on which I for several years witnessed and admired Canning's unrivalled oratorical powers and in favor of which I always gave a zealous vote, and some more than a formal support, till in my County I had on that account much prejudice to encounter. The Debates, the Recorded Divisions, the Staffordshire Advertiser's Reports of General Elections, my Correspondence and my Journal tell the rest.

The letter is an interesting commentary on the nature of the Canningite party. It was held together by one man's brilliance, and when he went there was a void which could not be filled. It is enormously to the credit of Lord Liverpool that he contained this party within a party and coaxed the general will of his followers in a liberal direction.

*Sturges Bourne and Wilmot Horton*

Some of Huskisson's friends entered so continuously into his official life—Liverpool, Goderich and Canning, his premiers, and Charles Grant, his number two at the Board of Trade, that his relations with them cannot with advantage be separated from the policies on which they were jointly engaged—which will be the subject matter of a second volume. Other friends entered significantly into his life, but not continuously, and it is desirable to have a picture of them both for their own sake and for the light it throws on Huskisson as colleague and friend. Four such are selected: Sturges Bourne and Palmerston: Granville and Wilmot Horton. Of E. J. Littleton, Lord Hatherton, a full sketch is given later in 'The Staffordshire of Huskisson and Littleton' (Chapters X-XI).

William Sturges Bourne (1769-1845), Canning's 'Sturges-Burges', was the man who would not be king. Indeed, he would have been content to be remembered as the Select Vestry of an Act of Parliament—*vide* the *History of English Local Government* by Sidney and Beatrice Webb. Sometimes a man's name is better known than the man himself. This is one example: two others are Torrens and Cowper-Temple. Torrens stands for the system of land transfer based on the public registration of title

G

which was devised by Sir Robert Richard Torrens (1814-84), the first premier of South Australia, and the date of the Torrens Act was 1858 (Act 15 of 1857-8). This was after Huskisson's time, but he knew the father, Colonel Robert Torrens (1780-1864), the author of a celebrated essay on the External Corn Trade 1815; and when, on Canning's death, Huskisson left the Board of Trade, Colonel Torrens, through E. J. Littleton, offered himself for the Vice-Presidency of it, claiming that he would be found 'not an unuseful or insufficient second' in promoting those principles which Mr Huskisson 'has applied to practice with such consummate skill and discretion'.[1] But the post went to Frankland Lewis.

Cowper-Temple stands for the amendment excluding denominational teaching from rate-built schools, which became the Cowper-Temple clause in the Education Act of 1870. The Cowper-Temple of 1870 was in Huskisson's day William Francis Cowper, second son of the 5th Earl Cowper. His mother, Lady Cowper, *née* Emily Lamb, after the Earl's death married Palmerston (1839), and this son by her first husband eventually inherited Broadlands and certain of the Palmerston estates in Ireland on condition of taking Palmerston's name of Temple. Hence Cowper-Temple. The Letters of Emily, Lady Cowper, later Lady Palmerston, to Mrs Huskisson (1829-56 —39,949) refer with pride to the successful career of William Francis, who ended his life as Baron Mount-Temple (1811-88).

Sturges Bourne similarly changed his name for a fortune, adding the surname of Bourne as the heir of his uncle, Francis Bourne. From very early days he was intimate with Canning, first at their private school in Winchester, then at Christ Church, Oxford. He identified himself with Canning as fully as did Huskisson, serving as Commissioner of the Board of Control for India, of which Canning was President, 1816-21, and finally taking office under Canning as Home Secretary in 1827. Thus, in any case, he would have been intimate with Huskisson, but the bond between them was strengthened by the fact

---

[1] *Hatherton Correspondence* 1826-7.

that the two had served as Secretaries to the Treasury. Everyone from the Regent downwards respected Sturges Bourne and
trusted him—'a very efficient man of excellent understanding'
was the phrase in which Huskisson commended him to John
Gladstone (27 April 1827). But he was a poor speaker and had
no political ambitions. He refused the under-secretaryship of
the Home Department in 1801: and only accepted the Home
Office in April 1827 at the urgent request of Canning—gladly
surrendering it in the following July to Lord Lansdowne,
whose regard Huskisson quickly won. On Canning's death
Goderich offered him the Exchequer, but he declined it. He
wrote to Huskisson confirming the refusal and suggested that
Huskisson should take it along with the lead in the House of
Commons, as Pitt had done under Shelbourne, 1782-3, and
Perceval under the Duke of Portland, 1807-9. When he left
the Home Office, he consented to remain in the Cabinet with
the minor post of Commissioner of Woods and Forests, but
from this too he retired in June 1828, keeping only the Warden-
ship of the New Forest in the County of Hampshire to which he
belonged. As a Right Honourable without office he served on
the Poor Law Commission of 1832-4, being second only in
weight to Nassau Senior, who drafted its famous report. Poor
Law Reform was his hobby.

In 1816-9 there was the first general parliamentary enquiry
into the Poor Laws: and Sturges Bourne, as Chairman of the
Commons Committee, was responsible for the legislation which
bears his name—58 Geo. 3, c. 69 (1818) and 59 Geo. 3, c. 12
(1819).[1] The purpose of it was to tighten up the administration
of poor relief by creating select vestries, with salaried overseers.
In these select vestries the voting was to be proportionate to
rates paid. Sturges Bourne took as his model the close vestry of
St. George's, Hanover Square, of which he was a member. It
was by far the best governed metropolitan parish at the time.

[1] The 1818 Act is for the Regulation of Parish Vestries. Inhabitants assessed up to £50 p.a.
get one vote: others one vote per £25 of assessment up to six at most.

The 1819 Act applies the machinery of the Select Vestries to the Concerns of the Poor.
Power is given to remove chargeable persons, born in Scotland or Ireland, though not actually
vagrants.

The result was something short of 3000 vestries under his Acts, and though they were not an instalment of local democracy, they were better than what went before, and are to be ranked with those improvements in public administration which had their origin in the Treasury.

Sturges Bourne was the most restful of Huskisson's friends, and, if he had a fault, it was that he encouraged Huskisson to take the easy way for his health's sake. 'That your health would be perfectly established if you could have rest is quite clear, and if you have reason to think without it you shall fail, how will you serve the government or the country by the sacrifice of yourself?' (18 January 1828). The following letter is characteristic of his outlook on affairs—well-balanced, slightly mocking, critical rather than constructive:

Sturges Bourne to Huskisson.    Testwood 22 Nov. 1829
My Dear H,
          I am happy to say that Mrs. Bourne is at present so free from complaints, tho' not very strong, that we have just now no thoughts of migrating. But if, as the season advances, there should be need of the more invigorating air of Brighton, we should certainly avail ourselves of your hospitality.

I trust that I am not mistaken in supposing that you are in a state of robust health and that Mrs. Huskisson has benefited by her long absence from London.

With respect to Parlt. I conclude from what you say it will meet in the same state in which it separated, with respect to Parties. Patronage, I expect, is given promptly to ultra Tories who will solicit it. But yet the Govt. will have no large body of steady and zealous friends, and a yet smaller body of organised and combined opponents; and in that will consist its strength, if strength it can be called.

All who are ignorant as myself, respecting our foreign policy, will I think expect to be enlightened voluntarily by the Govt. I fear the result is too plainly as you state as concerns Turkey and Portugal. But be this as it may, our domestic questions which were adjourned in the last session and others which have arisen since, may well have an interest so much more immediate and touching that I expect they will absorb the attention of all parties. If, however, our foreign policy has the tendency you fear, nothing

ought to be subordinate to exposing and correcting it, could the whole
Cabinet acquiesce in such a system.

Believe me,

Yours ever,

W. Sturges Bourne


Robert John Wilmot Horton (1784-1841) was like Sturges
Bourne in that he had, and for the same reason, a double-
barrelled name. The only son of Sir Robert Wilmot, Bart., he
took the name of Wilmot Horton in 1823 as the result of his
marriage in 1806 with the daughter and coheiress of Eusebius
Horton of Catton, Derbyshire, on the Staffordshire border. He
was a Canningite, but a Canningite of the second generation.
Of Eton and Christ Church, and sitting continuously for Newcastle-under-Lyme 1818-30, he was, like his friend and neighbour E. J. Littleton, a keen Staffordshire man. Temperamentally he was the reverse of Sturges Bourne: restless, eager for
office, fond of a project, political or financial, an enthusiast with
a central purpose. He had emigration on the brain.

As Under-Secretary of State for War and the Colonies (1821-
7), his Chief, Lord Bathurst, being in the Lords, he took the
lead in the presentation of the Government's Colonial policy,
and he presided over the Emigration Committee of 1826-7,
which in its Evidence and Reports covers a much wider field
than the title suggests; redundancy of population: poor law:
unemployment: the Irish question: the opportunities for settlement overseas: the exact acreage of Great Britain. It was before
this committee that Malthus gave his oft-quoted evidence.
Huskisson was therefore very close to Wilmot Horton not only
because he had once held the same office, but because now, at
the Board of Trade, his fiscal reforms touched the colonies at
every turn. Furthermore, he was to succeed Bathurst at the
Colonial Office at the time when Wilmot Horton, having been
made a Privy Councillor, was surrendering the under-secretaryship in the hope of something bigger. The reliance of the day
was on voluntary methods eked out by private subscription and
niggardly parish aid. Any call on the central exchequer was

offensive to the Treasury mind, and Wilmot Horton's attempt to get such a grant roused the wrath of Robinson the Chancellor of the Exchequer who, in what was perhaps the most resolute pronouncement of his irresolute life, wrote to Peel from Downing St., 12 March 1827:

> I was as much astonished as you were at seeing appended to a printed memo submitted by Wilmot to the Emigration Committee (of which he *subsequently* sent me a copy) a suggestion that the guarantee of the Government might be made a charge upon the Sinking Fund. I lost no time in seeing Wilmot and protested in the strongest manner against any such principle: indeed, I stated that I individually had the strongest objections to the Government being a guarantee at all; but I declared unequivocally that nothing would induce me to putting it upon the Sinking Fund. In a subsequent communication to him I repeated all my objections, and I said moreover that the utmost which in my *individual* opinion the Government could undertake to do in the matter would be to consider each case upon the merits of *each* separate case, to decide first whether any assistance should whatever be given with public money, and secondly in what mode it should be given; but retaining my first impression that a positive guarantee operating through a series of years would be objectionable in every possible way. I stated also that the question of giving public money to assist in what is called a grand plan of national emigration, was a question for the Cabinet, and that I apprehended that the Cabinet never could decide such a point until the Committee appointed to collect information should have ceased its labours.

This was stalling, but at least it was resolute stalling.

In the other great colonial issue—the status of West Indian slavery—Wilmot Horton enunciated a doctrine which became as tedious a slogan as redundancy of population at home.

Wilmot Horton to Huskisson                               25 January 1824

The question is whether slave labour can under any possible series of circumstances be transmuted into free labour with the maintenance of the primary interests of the proprietors. . . . The nature of the African is to be indolent as his wants are few and those almost spontaneously satisfied in the climatic conditions under which he lives. No adage can be more trite in Political Economy than that which points out the connection of exertion with climate.

Therefore the first step must be moral and religious instruction. Possibly improved machinery might help the proprietors to overcome the labour shortage.

Political economy, in its teaching upon population and tropical labour, was qualifying as the dismal science. But this much we may say for Wilmot Horton. He fought hard to prevent his emigration policy from being nothing more than the shovelling out of paupers. His friends chaffed him about his preoccupation, and on occasion neatly enough—'I must approve' (writes Huskisson to him) 'of Littleton's plan for transporting the Lords of the soil in Ireland, thinking of them pretty much as he does. Indeed, I approve so much that I hereby undertake to subscribe one-half of whatever portion of their confiscated estates may be assigned to me, towards teaching them to behave better in Van Dieman's Land. The hand aches. The pen is worn to the stumps. W.H.' (*Hatherton Correspondence* 1826-7).

In the reformation of the Government, January 1828, Wilmot Horton, who had made way for Stanley at the Colonial Office, expected something. Ireland and Canada had been mooted— but to his chagrin he got nothing. A run of letters to Littleton describes the progress of events:

9 January 1828. The Cabinet is *dissout* and the history would take a month to tell. The Duke of Wellington has seen the King and Chancellor this day with reference to the formation of a new Government.

10 January 1828. Nothing seems sure but that the Whigs will be out. Huskisson is not over well. I am sure a continuation of the strenuous imbecility of the dying Government would have killed him.

21 January 1828. I do not in the slightest degree understand Huskisson's conduct to me. It may be everything that friendly feeling and delicacy could suggest. It may be inexplicable. But I think it might have been more satisfactory. I shall be very glad to see you. I know nothing about myself, nor do I believe that other 'minores' do.[1]

Peel got letter after letter from him. 'Where do I come in?' 'Are you aware whether Huskisson mentioned me and my

[1] *Hatherton Correspondence* 1828-9.

peculiar position and views to the D. of W.?' But all he could reply was, 29 January 1828, 'I do not know what passed between the D. of W. and H. respecting your position.' That something was in the air is suggested by a letter of 22 January from Wilmot Horton to Huskisson, which says: 'Whenever you are ready for a West India talk I am at your service.'[1] The letter concludes whimsically:

It is funny enough that in August 1821, Ellenborough [the new Privy Seal with a seat in the Cabinet] and myself were intimate acquaintances (we have not however exchanged recognition for these four years) and one day as we were sitting in the Thuilleries Gardens we argued the point whether it was the surer and easier road to high political office to oppose diligently and malignantly (in the modern sense) or to support energetically and uncompromisingly. I maintained stoutly the latter proposition, he the former. I have often mentioned the argument in disproof of the theory, but I admit he has made a gallant rally at last.[2]

Ellenborough clearly disliked Wilmot Horton. He states in his Diary[3] for 28 May 1830 that he resisted Wellington's desire to retain Wilmot Horton by giving him the Secretaryship at War, having only the day before spoken against him for Ireland. And again, 2 July 1830: 'Lord Bathurst says Mr. Horton is a gentleman. I doubted it. He rather wishes to have Wilmot in office. But the person to be got is Mr. Stanley' (*Diary*, II, 299). Consequently he was without office till the Whigs appointed him Governor of Ceylon, where he had a successful term of six years (1831-7) with a baronetcy in 1834. In the circle of literature he is remembered by the fact that he authorised the destruction of Byron's Memoirs.

---

[1] Cf. an earlier letter from Wilmot Horton to Littleton, 27 November 1827: 'Unable to get a post at home satisfactory to my sense of my own capacity for public office, as compared with other men, I decided to apply for it abroad, and Huskisson laid my name before the King for the Civil Government of Canada. That was refused graciously in consequence of the claims and application of another party—but Jamaica was proposed to me and my present position is that of an accepted or rather accepting candidate (for it was *offered* to me) for that Government. This is entirely confidential.' But Jamaica fell through, for Huskisson's position was as tottery as his, and he had to wait for something from the Whigs.

[2] This letter has found its way into the *Hatherton Correspondence* 1828-9.

[3] *A Political Diary* 1828-30, by Edward Law, Lord Ellenborough, edited by Lord Colchester.

*Granville and Palmerston*

Granville introduces us to the Spencer-Ponsonby-Cavendish world, to that rich and socially influential group of families which, though in general mildly Whig, had little liking for the faded brocade of Holland House with its imperious châtelaine whose young men came to nothing. A famous dowager, Georgiana Lady Spencer (1737-1814), Lord Althorp's grandmother, had two famous daughters. One of them, Georgiana, the beautiful Duchess of Devonshire, had a son who became the 6th Duke—the bachelor Duke to whom Paxton was head gardener —and two daughters, one of whom, Georgiana, married the Earl of Carlisle, the owner of Castle Howard, and the other, Harriet (Hary-o), married Lord Granville. Lady Bessborough, the dowager's other daughter, was the mother of Caroline Lamb, who drove William Lamb to distraction. Lady Bessborough was thus Hary-o's aunt and before her niece's marriage to Granville she was his mistress, bearing him two children. Hary-o, nevertheless, loved him enough to marry him, leaving regretfully the house of her father, even though he, after Georgiana's death, made a Duchess of the lady who had been his wife's friend and his own mistress. The Seventh Commandment did not count for much in Regency England, nor, apparently, did the breach of it wreck family life. For Lady Bessborough continued to love and be loved by her husband and children: and Granville, the lady killer and father of bastards, made an admirable husband—his son, the 2nd Earl Granville, becoming Gladstone's respected Foreign Secretary. Devonshire House: Chiswick House (where Fox and Canning died and the bachelor duke found his gardener): Roehampton in the suburbs: Holywell, near St. Albans, the dowager's home: Brocket, near Hatfield, William Lamb's place: the ducal seats of Chatsworth and Hardwick: Castle Howard in distant Yorkshire— all these we come to know from the letters and diaries of their occupants. For they were great letter writers and family ties were as close as personal morals were lax. (A Frenchman could readily understand this.) But only a dowager could write the history of a ducal house in a paragraph:

11 June 1806.

Dear Hartington's coming has given me much pleasure. . . . He arrived
heated to death with the weather and the ride, cloaked with dust, his eyes
out with flies, and made worse with crying, which he did soon after he
came in. He drank a gallon of tea, eat loads of roast lamb, pease and goose-
berry foole, drank a quantity of beer and of water, and finished all with a
plentiful saline draught. I ordered a bason extraordinary to be put in his
room, concluding he must be sick, but he waked this morning at six, drank
a mug of asses milk, and sent me word he was very well, but very sleepy,
and is sleeping still at near nine o'clock.[1]

And she disposed of Petworth and its Earl of Egremont (when
her daughter was visiting there) in a sentence—'*forty-three*
children who all live in the house with him and their respective
mothers'.[2]

Granville Leveson Gower, 1st Earl Granville (1773-1846),
was the younger—much younger—half-brother of Lord Gower
(1758-1833) and was thus the middle figure in the three generations of the family who played so large a part in Huskisson's
life. The first generation was Lord Gower, afterwards Marquis
of Stafford and Duke of Sutherland, whom Huskisson served
at the Paris Embassy: the third generation was Lord Gower's
children, and in particular his second son, Lord Francis Egerton (1800-57), whom Huskisson helped to introduce into political life and whose canal interests (for he, under the name of
Egerton, was principal heir to the Bridgewater estate) were the
subject of frequent correspondence between Huskisson and
James Loch, M.P., the financial adviser of the Marquis. Granville was of the second generation, and, being Huskisson's
coeval, was his life-long friend. He was poor by comparison
with the senior branch of the family, but if he was straitened it
was because of his fondness for the gaming table. Though Huskisson did not live in Staffordshire, he lived with it throughout
his life. Lord Gower was the County member, 1787-98: Lord
Granville followed him, 1799-1815. E. J. Littleton joined the
latter in 1812 and sat for it till 1832.

[1] Earl of Bessborough, *Lady Bessborough and her Family Circle*, 145.
[2] *Private Correspondence of Lord Granville Leveson Gower* (1781-1821), II, 474.

Before entering Parliament Granville was attaché to Lord
Malmesbury in those peace negotiations of 1796 for which
Huskisson volunteered. In the Commons he ranged himself
with Canning in unswerving support of Pitt. On Pitt's death
Lady Bessborough wrote, 'When I thought how you and the
Pope [*sc.* Canning] would feel it, the tears gush'd from my
eyes.'[1] In 1809, under Portland, when Canning was at the
Foreign Office and Huskisson at the Treasury, Granville
joined them as Secretary at War. At the end of the year, the
three went out together. In 1812 he ought to have been
asssasinated! For when ambassador in Russia (in 1804-05)
he incurred the ill-will of the madman John Bellingham,
and the assassin's bullet was intended for him. On 12
August 1815 he was gazetted Viscount Granville of Stone
(Huskisson supplying Canning with inside information of the
peerage coming through) and devoted his later years to diplomacy. As ambassador to the Hague, February-October 1824,
and to France, November 1824-July 1828, he was in constant
correspondence with Huskisson both on official and private
affairs, and being too liberal for the Duke of Wellington's
Government, he resigned with Huskisson and his friends in
1828.

In 1824 the two correspond about Falck and commercial
reciprocity with the Dutch, Huskisson concluding (19 September 1824):

F. is not the most manageable of all negotiators: and both he and his
master, I suspect, are disposed to bring rather too much of the spirit of
tradesmen into the negotiation.

'Worst year for partridges since 1816,' he adds in postscript.
He had often enjoyed the hospitality of Tixall, the historic
house which the Granvilles rented 1811-19, and knew perhaps
the story about Granville and Sir Ralph Sneyd of Keele Hall,
Staffs. 'Ask the gentlemen' (said Granville to his keeper) 'to
kill no more hens, but you need not mention it to Mr. Sneyd.'

In the pathetic months of the Goderich regime, when Hus-

---

[1] *Private Correspondence of Lord Granville Leveson Gower* (1781-1821), II, 161.

kisson was lamenting the demoralisation of the Premier, aggravated by an 'all but crazy wife', and saying of himself 'all I dare hope is to prevent my own character from being shipwrecked' (18 December 1827), Granville tries to put heart in him and assures him of his unswerving support:

It is to your indefatigable exertions, to your judgement, to your talents of concilation that the country is indebted for the blessing of the administration being combined upon ethical principles (4 September 1827). I should always be disposed from feelings of personal friendship for you, as well as from the invariable concurrence of my political opinions with yours, to follow your example in any question of resignation or acceptance of office (12 December 1827).

But the friend was a candid friend and tries to steer him wisely through the final months under Wellington:

I cannot see that your personal honour required the exclusion of Herries from the Cabinet to which you belong—the difference between you was not of a nature to justify the appearance of vindictiveness which the proscription of Herries would have assumed (28 January 1828).

However, the breaking point for Huskisson had been reached: 'I am so worn out that I must fear I shall be as much an invalid this year as I was the last' (25 January 1828). And by May 1828 he was out of office, sick in body and sick at heart. And to add to his other worries Lady Canning was bombarding him with reproaches for not securing from the nation the allowance to which, in her view, Canning's service entitled her, and her son[1] was writing him stiff letters beginning 'Sir'.

Huskisson to Granville.

I have no doubt that it was better the connections should cease now than have continued for a month or two longer with all the difficulties that were pressing upon us. The ultra-Tory adherents and the Duke's foreign policy would have required concessions which he could not have made (27 May 1828).

[1] William Pitt Canning, R.N., drowned off Madeira 1828. On the attitude of Lady Canning, cf. Howard de Walden to Bagot, 23 February 1828, 'active, bitter and personal hostility against Huskisson...' (J. Bagot, *George Canning and His Friends*, II, 435).

Nevertheless, Granville, awaiting now his own recall, could not but regret the way in which his resignation had come about:

I should have much preferred that your separation from the Cabinet had been caused by the Duke's diverting from Canning's views and system of foreign policy than by the real or pretended misunderstanding of a letter, in which, on account of a vote you had given upon a trivial question, you had placed your office at the disposal of the Prime Minister (30 May 1828).

One leaves it with this thought. Canning's principles could only be continued if a second Canning could be found. Neither Goderich nor Huskisson could fill the bill. The man who could was there in Palmerston, but his time had not yet come, and the man who would make a better premier than either Canning or Palmerston was not a Canningite.

Henry John Temple, 3rd Viscount Palmerston (1784-1865), was faithful also to the last. 'The sentiment of Palmerston,' wrote Huskisson to Granville, 3 June 1828, 'which gave mortal offence to the Duke was that the administration of the country would be deserving of support . . . exactly in proportion as it acted in all matters of foreign and domestic policy on the principles of Mr. C.' Palmerston resigned with Huskisson, and Lord Ellenborough, who had as little love for him as for Wilmot Horton, many years later, namely in 1855, told the 2nd Earl Granville how the Duke received the news:

I recollect sitting by the side of the Duke of Wellington during the unfortunate difficulty between him and Mr. Huskisson which led to the resignation of a portion of the gentlemen forming the government. The Duke of Wellington was suddenly called out of the House, and when he returned he said to me. 'That was Palmerston, who wanted to see me to tell me that if Huskisson went, he must go too.' The Duke continued: 'I said nothing; it will not do for me to fire great guns at small birds.'[1]

Thus in 1828, Palmerston, who had been quietly and competently Secretary at War outside the Cabinet from 1809 to

[1] E. Fitzmaurice, *Life of Granville George Leveson Gower* I, 110.

1828, was still a minor star. But it was bravado on the Duke's part, and in losing Palmerston to the Whigs they lost the true successor of Canning. When Huskisson was in retirement, he was fond of deriding the foreign policy of the Government, but it was no worse then than it had been in the troubled months after Canning's death, when he was Secretary for War and the Colonies under Goderich and the Duke. For Dudley at the Foreign Office was a light weight, a rich and amusing *viveur:* and as little fitted to cope with the sequel of Navarino as was his successor Aberdeen, that man of virtue with a morbid dread of war.

The letters from Palmerston to Huskisson are infrequent. A characteristic note in the light vein runs:

> Broadlands, 7 April 1828
>
> I hope you are gaining all the benefit you ought to do from a few days in the country. But you have no mercy on your colleagues, and have sent me more leaves than are to be found in the whole of the New Forest. This may be the war for manumission for the Blacks, but in the meantime it is something like slavery to the Cabinet.

But to his friend E. J. Littleton he let himself go. Littleton, like Palmerston and William Lamb, was shortly to take office under the Whigs, but he was so strong a Canningite that it had been left to him to organise the memorial to Canning. The two letters which follow were written in September 1829; and it is to be remembered that at this date Palmerston was relatively new to foreign policy. The view he takes here of the Turkish Empire he held only till towards the end of 1831, when Stratford Canning converted him to the view that it might be preserved. (Stratford Canning, Geo. Canning's cousin, had been associated with Huskisson in the commercial negotiations of the 1820's with the United States, and in July 1830 Huskisson had to deny a newspaper report that ill-health might cause him to relinquish his seat to S—— Canning (Liverpool Public Reference Library: Huskisson to Sir John Tobin, 26 July 1830).)

Hatherton MS. Correspondence 1828-9.

Palmerston to Littleton               Broadlands 16 September 1829
   My Dear L. . . .
       Well, what a pretty state of things we have in Europe, our ancient
ally at Constantinople having no other chance of existence but what he
may owe to the moderation of the Russian Conqueror, and our ambassador playing the undignified part of a mediator rejected by the Russian.
I am inclined to think from all one hears that the Russian will be very
moderate, at least as to territory and will re-establish Mahmood in all his
European Dominions and the greater part of his Asiatic, provided he
promises to be a Good Boy in future, and not take liberties with Russian
ships and subjects and provided moreover he pays a lumping sum of money
as forfeit for his failure in the War. I suspect that the Russians look upon
the Turk somewhat in the same way that somebody did upon our Gracious
Sovereign, when they said he was the best King we ever had, because he
was almost as good as no king at all; the Russians think the Turks the
next best thing to having no neighbour at all, and they will know that
Europe would not permit them to be what Sheridan said Geo. 3 was in
that house which he built at the Gate of Windsor Castle 'next-door neighbours to themselves'. I confess I should not be sorry some day or other to
see the Turk kicked out of Europe and compelled to go and sit cup-legged
smoke his pipe, chew his opium and cut off heads on the Asiatic side of the
Bosphorus. We want civilisation, activity, trade and business in Europe,
and your Mustaphas have no idea of any traffic beyond rhubarb, figs and
red slippers; what energy can be expected from a nation who have no heels
to their shoes and pass their whole lives slip shod?
       Our Govt. seems to have got their friend Charles 10th into no slight
scrape by urging him to take on Polignac,[1] which, deny it as they may,
they certainly did; although I believe they would have preferred having
him only, so as to get the foreign policy of France into their hands, and
did not wish for the Bourmants and La-Bourdonnages. The plan of not
paying taxes is too tempting not to spread and would, if adopted by the
greater part of a people, puzzle the Govt. considerably.
       It seems likely however that the Duke will be disappointed even in the
object for the attainment of which he has brought France to the brink of
a revolution, for Polignac and Charles will probably give way to public
feeling in France in their foreign policy, in order to have a chance of being

---

[1] It was hoped that Polignac, having been ambassador to England would be pro-English, but he
was not. He based his plan for the reorganisation of Europe on a Franco-Russian alliance, and
whereas the French people were Graecophil, Wellington was the reverse.

able to have their own way at home, and the French are just as strongly for the Greeks as our Cabinet is against them. There is only wanting a rise in Lisbon, upon hearing of the resistance of Terceira[1] to complete the success of our foreign system. What a different position England would now have occupied if Canning had lived.

Palmerston to Littleton.          Broadlands 22 September 1829
. . .

It is true as you say that we English are all more or less in our hearts adscripti glebae, and among the many definitions which have been given of the Human Race, as being reasoning, talking, laughing and cooking animals, I wonder nobody ever described them as being the only agricultural animals.

I find I shall not be able to leave these parts quite as soon as I expected when last I wrote to you, but shall still get to you before your musical engagement.

So the Russians have been persuaded to pull up short of Constantinople. In Dietrich's case I think I would not have done so, but it must be presumed he knows what he is about.

At all events the Russ has the Turk at his feet, and he having demonstrated to Turkey herself as well as to the rest of the world her inability to resist, the Turkish Empire becomes perhaps his best and quietest neighbour.

I hear nothing but the disappointments of Chesterfield at Doncaster; all his ladies have flown off, and have left him with three houses and all the refinements of London artists to entertain only a party of men. They say Lady Belfast refused to go on the score of propriety,[2] unless Princess Esterhazy was there too. But the Princess could not get so far north. The Duke finds it as difficult to get ladies to agree as to manage the decisions of the Govts. of Europe.

Yours very sincerely,

Palmerston

Palmerston was strong where Huskisson was weak. He was imperturbable: he could decide on his tactics; and he wrote with a classical clarity which permitted of no misunderstanding. 'On June 23' [1839], says Lord Broughton, 'I dined with Lord Palmerston. Talking of Huskisson, he said he was the most un-

---

[1] Azores, where a government was set up in opposition to the usurper Miguel.
[2] Note by Lord Hatherton, 'Mrs. L. F. . . . was then in possession of Chesterfield'.

decided man he had ever known.' During the East Retford
debate, he continued talking to Palmerston in this fashion:
'What shall I do? I wish I knew what to do; shall I vote for
or against?' . . . 'Stay where you are,' said Lord Palmerston,
and accordingly he did stay; but Palmerston told me that, if
Huskisson had had to move, instead of sitting still, he would
have voted the other way.[1]

They were talking of the East Retford vote which precipi-
tated Huskisson's resignation. Nevertheless, Palmerston had a
deep regard for Huskisson and when Littleton apprised him of
the fatality, he replied by return, 'It came upon me like a
thunderbolt,' and then at length, a week later (September 25):

The more one thinks of it, the more sensibly one feels it. All losses of this
kind are said, sometimes lightly perhaps, to be irreparable. But it is no
exaggeration to say that there is nobody now left who possesses in the same
degree the knowledge, attainments and habits by which he was distinguished, and which would have rendered him in the present times and in
discussions which must come on, and which involve most important
interests of the country, a public servant of the greatest value whether in
office or out of it. Now at last justice will be done him, and even those
who were most opposed to him while living, will reunite in acknowledging
how great a loss we have all sustained in losing him.[2]

### The Approach to High Office

Ireland, for some the stepping stone to highest office—
Wellington, Peel, Melbourne, Arthur Balfour—had, as we
have seen, no attraction for Huskisson. Yet his outlook was
always overseas, not indeed towards diplomacy, for which he
had neither the rank nor the detachment, but towards economic
action in those overseas dominions which from first to last he
called the British Empire. While Under-Secretary for War and
the Colonies he added a commercial function, the Agency for
the Cape, 1799-1800. The Cape in those days was valued as a
port of call and refreshment, and Admiral Popham was acting
in accordance with the spirit of Pitt's strategy when he used it
as a base for his South American raid, the beginning of that

---

[1] *Recollections of a Long Life*, V, 203.
[2] Hatherton MS. Correspondence 1830.

informal empire which Canning and Huskisson turned to such
rich account. But there was formal Empire waiting in the East
—in Mauritius,[1] in Ceylon and on the great subcontinent of
India. Ceylon passed from Holland to England at about the
same time as the Cape. And Huskisson became its colonial
agent. It was a salaried office, and the most continuous he ever
held. He resigned it only in 1823, on the ground that it would
conflict with his higher duties at the Board of Trade. 'The
Colonial Agency for Ceylon which I now hold, is connected
with Lord Bathurst's Department, yet I intend to resign it.
The salary £1200 is far beyond what I can conveniently spare'
(Huskisson to Lord Liverpool, 20 November 1823). It was
given him, he adds, twenty years ago as Under-Secretary of
State. This, if 'as' equals 'while', means not later than 1801.

Mrs Huskisson, in preparing the memoir, consulted Mr
Hoblyn of the Treasury on the financial position. And he replied:

It so happens that during my connection with the Ceylon Agency from
the year 1806 up to the period when my much lamented friend resigned,
every payment was made by myself in cheques upon Messrs. Herries and
Farquhar, and that he derived no other emoluments whatever from the
Agency but the sum of £800 from 1806 to 1808, and £1200 from the
latter period up to the time of his resignation in 1823. I well recollect that
it was recommended to increase the Agent's salary to £1600, and I have
no doubt that Lord L. who was the Secretary for the Colonies [sc. 1809-
12] would have acceded to it, but Mr. H. positively refused the larger
sum, and consented to that of £1200 only, which I thought at the time an
unnecessary forbearance considering the offer came unsolicited on his part.

It was customary in those days to hold West Indian appointments and discharge them by deputy, taking a rake-off from
the office. Such a procedure would have been unthinkable in
Huskisson. But more than this, Ceylon opened out a vista of
the new Empire. He writes, 4 June 1810, to an old friend—in
reference to the sale in Persia of rejected cinnamon oil, for

---

[1] Quite a health resort, if Huskisson was rightly informed. 'I have always understood that the
Mauritius, though certainly a hot climate, is a healthy and pleasant residence, frequently resorted
to by invalids from the continent of India for the recovery of their health.' (Huskisson to Sir W.
H. Clinton, 2 November 1827.)

which there was no market in Europe, and to land development generally in Ceylon by families of Dutch descent:

It is desireable to make Ceylon 'a great prop and stay of that precarious and overgrown Empire which we possess on the continent and in case of disaster here [*sc. India*]—a rallying point by the aid of which England might still retain dominion and naval ascendancy in those seas'.

To an economic historian some of the most satisfying matter in the Huskisson correspondence is to be found in the correspondence between Huskisson and Governor Brownrigg of Ceylon in 1815-6, when the two planned the melioration of Ceylon:

Huskisson to Brownrigg

I am afraid now that peace is concluded with America that the tobacco of Ceylon will not be able to compete with that of Virginia in our market, but I do not despair, with proper management and due care in the preparation of the produce, that Ceylon in a short time will be able to export indigo, coffee and other tropical productions for the growth of which the climate appears to be well adapted.

Brownrigg to Huskisson

We are well satisfied with the amount of sales of these articles and we are well convinced that a Government embarking in commerce is generally a losing concern; however the results of our experiments have done good, for they have established the value of the articles of export that find a sale in a European market, and have stimulated a few mercantile people in the country to connect themselves with houses in London and thus form a direct intercourse with the Mother Country. There is no doubt that the Colony is capable of producing almost all the exportable articles of the eastern world, Tea excepted.

*Hemileia Vastatrix* was to remove that exception! At a time when Huskisson was liberalising the Corn Law by enlarging the imperial preference, when he was pressing on a reluctant Bank of England the Resumption of Cash Payments, and acquiescing against his better judgment in the abolition of the Income Tax, he had in his Ceylon Agency a small spearhead of imperial economy. And he desired to enlarge it by official contact with the main theatre—India. He was eager to supplement the mercantile enterprise of his new friends in Liverpool and

Glasgow, path-breakers in the eastern export trade, and to carry on where old colleagues had left off—Canning at the head of the India Board of Control, with Sturges Bourne as one of his salaried colleagues in the commission. The failure to get the India Board, when Canning left it, was the sharpest disappointment of his political life—not only for friendship's sake, but because he had quietly qualified for it and saw there the prospect of a great imperial harvest. I would even suggest that at the back of his mind there was the feeling that here at least he would have the cordial co-operation of the man who was not only the victor of Waterloo, but the subduer and (along with his eldest brother the Marquis Wellesley, Huskisson's unwavering friend) the pacificator of India. It was therefore a sad disappointment to him when for tactical reasons, to satisfy the Grenvillites, the post, with a seat in the Cabinet, was given to C. W. Williams Wynn, his political junior by ten years and an admitted mediocrity. But in the *cri de coeur* which he sent up to Canning, 23 June 1821, he added in postscript:

As the Morning Chronicle has mentioned my name for the Board of Control, it may be as well for me to declare upon my honour that except for yourself, Charles Ellis [Lord Seaford] and Arbuthnot (the latter nearly three years ago and not since) I have never intimated to any human being my wishes or expectations on the subject.

When Canning took the Foreign Office, he made it his first duty to secure adequate office for the friend who had hitherto sacrificed everything for him. As we have seen, he succeeded—securing for him the Board of Trade, February 1823, with entry into the Cabinet, November 1823.[1] To the Cabinet Huskisson had a double claim. For years he had been the financial brain of the Inner Cabinet at Fife House, and knew every Cabinet secret in anything appertaining to finance; while Wynn, his junior, who had stepped over his head, was given the Cabinet at once.

---

[1] Cf. Liverpool to Peel.

Jan 17, 1823. Huskisson is not to be in the Cabinet at present.

Oct 31, 1823. Huskisson is *not yet* regularly summoned to the Cabinet.

Nov 18, 1823. I have received the King's authority to direct that Huskisson's name may be added to the List of his Confidential Servants.

And personal claims apart, a seat in the Cabinet was necessary to the efficient discharge of his duties, with a Prime Minister in the Lords. 'All measures of trade as well as all measures of finance belong exclusively to the Lower House, and you might as well make a peer Chancellor of the Exchequer as pretend to make him the parliamentary and responsible representative of the Board of Trade' (Huskisson to Arbuthnot, 26 December 1822). Yet from Canning's point of view, this reasonable insistence on Cabinet rank was his chief difficulty in meeting Huskisson's claims, and it needed all the influence of life-long friendship to prevent an impasse. By December 1822, it was straightened out. But the tangle which Canning had to unravel is admirably set out in a characteristic letter of 3 October 1822, which reads like the personal letter that accompanies a dispatch. The point of manœuvre was Vansittart at the Exchequer:

Canning to Huskisson          Gloucester Lodge Oct. 3 1822

Van is not immoveable . . . Lord L. is confident that Robinson not only would take the Chancellorship of the Exchequer if offered to him, but that he would feel himself passed by if the offer were not made. This course of management therefore would open to you Robinson's offices, the Treasuryship of the Navy and Presidency of the Board of Trade.

Having happened [Canning continues] to enquire (of Lord L) if he was as much wedded to Van and Van to his seals as ever, the answer to my infinite surprise was 'Oh no, I could get him out and would, if I saw my way to an arrangement that I was sure would satisfy all parties, but I could not get him out for Huskisson' . . .

Getting Van out of the Exchequer is so great an object for the public, the House of Commons and the Country that if it were to be ever known or suspected that that object had been frustrated by your adherence to the succession of Charles Wynn instead of to Robinson's, the best of the friends of Government and of our friends too (Littleton for example) would never forgive me.

Robinson's change [sc. from the Board of Trade to the Exchequer] would be very popular in the House of Commons . . . and further will it not be a great relief to me to have both Peel and Robinson to rely upon, in situations of equal importance instead of providing the debate with Peel alone?

Does this mean that if Robinson did not get the Exchequer he would be raised to the Lords? Had this happened, we might have missed the delicious pen picture in *Tancred*. 'I remember', said his lordship, 'seeing Ripon, when he was Robinson, and Huskisson each pulling one of Canning's coat tails at the same time' (Chap. II). They had discovered that their chief was speaking on the wrong motion!

At first it was intended that Wynn should retire in favour of Vansittart, but in the end Vansittart accepted a peerage (as Lord Bexley) and the Duchy of Lancaster, where he drifted into senility, 'opulent and without a child' in Sturges Bourne's crisp phrase.

In the negotiations the most ambiguous part was that played by Charles Arbuthnot of the Treasury. He pretended, perhaps fancied himself, to be Huskisson's friend from first to last, yet he wrote to Liverpool, October 1822: 'I cannot conceive anything in worse taste than a man endeavouring to *force* himself into the Cabinet against the wishes of the King and his own friends';[1] and when Huskisson in deference to Canning waived immediate entrance, he said 'Huskisson has assented not with a very good grace, but still he has assented, and I have written to the King to say so'.[2] The truth is that Arbuthnot was a toady, who knew Huskisson to be his superior and was jealous of him; and he used his intimacy with the Duke of Wellington to poison the latter against him. 'My strong conviction is that Huskisson is one of the most dangerous men that ever was admitted into our councils'[3] (25 April 1825).

Arbuthnot had his own standard of good taste. As patronage secretary to the Treasury he lamented that he got so little out of it himself (only a salary of £4000!). 'I owe it my Family to take most thankfully whatever is offered.' This is his language to Huskisson, 13 December 1823, when, having fished for and secured the succession to Huskisson at Woods and Forests, he was now trying to get Huskisson's Ceylon agency and give it

---

[1] *Correspondence of Charles Arbuthnot*, ed. A. Aspinall, Letter 32D. Charles Arbuthnot, 1767-1850, Joint Secretary of the Treasury, 1809-23, nickname 'Gosh' (cf. above, p. 32. below).
[2] *Ibid.*, 34.        [3] *Ibid*, 67.

to his son to be discharged by deputy. But this was too much even for Lord Liverpool, who would have agreed to it, as a sort of pension, if he had made a pretence of discharging it himself. I think that Huskisson saw through Arbuthnot and rather liked him nevertheless, for both of them had served My Lords.[1]

## Accidents and Sickness

Accidents and lengthening bouts of sickness dogged Huskisson through his life. Indeed his life was a chapter of accidents culminating in the one which caused his death. Whether it is possible out of conjugal affection to take over a proneness to accident I will not presume to say, but certain it is that Lady Palmerston's closing letters to Mrs Huskisson advert more than once to accidents to her of the type which brought to him so many letters of sympathy. Since the widow assembled the materials on which the memoir of Huskisson is based, we may rely on its accuracy hereunder:

As a child, he fractured his arm:—a few days before his marriage, his horse fell with him and he was severely hurt:—soon after, he was knocked down by the pole of a carriage, just at the entrance to the Horse Guards;— in the autumn of 1801, being then in Scotland at the Duke of Athol's, he missed his distance in attempting to leap the moat and gave himself a most violent sprained ankle, accompanied with a considerable laceration of some of the tendons and ligaments of his foot, and it was many weeks before he recovered sufficiently to leave Scotland. Indeed the effects of this accident were visible in his gait during the remainder of his life. He afterwards fractured his arm by a fall from his horse at Petworth;[2] and, again in 1817 by his carriage being overturned. On this occasion, none of his surgeons could discover the precise nature of the mischief, but Sir Astley Cooper

[1] The nature of Arbuthnot's claim on the Government is seen in this from Liverpool to Peel. 24 December 1822: 'It is quite out of my power to propose to him [Fitzgerald] Huskisson's office, as a strong additional motive for promoting Huskisson has been that I might be enabled by this means to give the office he now holds to Arbuthnot, who has been 14 years Secretary to the Treasury, is nearly worn out by the severe duties and fatigue incident to that situation, and has long looked to Huskisson's office, as a sort of retirement, but which would help him still in those confidential relations to me, which are of the utmost importance to my comfort.

I would further add that the office of Woods is become of peculiar importance from the connection which must exist between the discharge of the duties of it and the administration of the King's private affairs. For such a situation and relation Arbuthnot is particularly fitted'.

[2] This may have been in January 1807 when there is a letter from Charles Long to Mrs Huskisson condoling on Huskisson's accident.

was of opinion that the bone was split from the fracture up to the joint. The recovery was slow, and his sufferings very severe; as all kinds of experiments were employed to prevent the joint from stiffening. In spite of every exertion, he never recovered the full use of his arm, and a visible alteration in the spirit and elasticity of his carriage resulted from the injury. He was constantly encountering accidents of minor importance, and the frequency of them, joined to a frame enfeebled from the severe illnesses under which he suffered during his latter years, had given rise to a certain hesitation in his movements wherever any crowd or obstacle impeded him.[1]

Wilberforce from Stanstead, near Emsworth, Hants., condoles with him on his 'dreadful accident' (23 September 1817):

You know probably that I do not ride and a four-wheeled carriage of two and a venerable coachman, whatever merits they possess, have not that of enabling me to do much in a little time. . . . That you may entirely recover and long enjoy your health and strength is the cordial wish of, my dear Sir, Yours very truly,

W. Wilberforce

A fortnight later, he offers to drive over to Eartham for the day.

Among others were letters from the Premier, and General Sir Benjamin Blomfield. 'A bad fracture of my arm', he writes to several of them, 'compels me to use an amanuensis for urgent affairs.' 'I do not by any means' (writes Canning, 3 November 1819) 'like the accounts of the numbness in your arm.' Huskisson can never have had a very robust constitution. He complains of ill-health as early as 1794. He was at Cheltenham, recovering from a breakdown in 1798. 'I am come here to recover that health without which event that most endearing prospect of life would lose its charms' (Huskisson to Nepean, 15 July 1798)—the prospect, that is, of marriage. Huskisson hated the shifts of bachelor life, and his marriage in 1799 brought loving care and a home.

Yet it would be wrong to think of him as a semi-invalid during most of his life. To the end he was a keen sportsman. He travelled much in his own country, both visiting friends and in pursuance of his duties as Commissioner of Woods and

---

[1] Biographical Memoir in *Speeches*, Vol. I, pp. 44-5.

Forests. To a degree which we should not find today, the letters of the time are full of complaints of ill health, especially from the formidable gout, whatever that really was. (It attacked even Coke of Holkham at last, to his great indignation, when he was no more than eighty.) Huskisson outlived both Liverpool and Canning, whose end undoubtedly was hastened by worry and work: and his many hurts did not prevent him from being the most inveterate of correspondents. To the last he wrote in a clear and pointed hand with meticulous punctuation. If he had been like the Duke of Wellington—normally in good health, or at any rate saying little about his ailments—he would have been the exception. The Regent's bedside was a malodorous drug-store, at which his ministers reluctantly sat. A mutual friend of the Regent and Huskisson, Lord Hertford, lived for two things, his pleasures and his health. He was forever trying to coax Huskisson to Sudbourne to take a sea-bath treatment, and—though this was after Huskisson's death—he ran like a rabbit from the cholera. Lady Cowper writes to Mrs Huskisson, August 1832:

Lord Hertford is frantically alarmed about it, and has I know taken 2 physicians with him into the country—he always travels like a caravan—going to the sea—so that a few individuals more or less are of little consequence.

But undoubtedly the increasing ill-health of Huskisson in his last three years was a disturbing factor in the situation. The rest which was ordered for him in 1827—in the form of a trip to the Continent—was broken by Canning's death, and he hurried back, a sick man in mental distress at the loss of his adored friend and leader. Goderich's ill-fated ministry had no one who could steady it—and least of all, its ablest man, Huskisson. A longer journey in 1828, in the course of which he visited the Pope, improved his health, but a better tonic was the escape from office. Indeed, in 1829 he enjoyed a brief Indian summer. He was the indispensable man, so all his correspondents assured him; and one traces in his letters of 1829-30 (which are some of the best he ever wrote) a considerable satisfaction with the role of senior statesman. Then, unluckily,

in early 1830 came a real setback. I have not the medical knowledge to say whether he could ever have hoped to take on a
heavy burden afterwards. But here are the facts as communicated by him to Sir John Tobin from Carlton Gardens, the new
town house into which he had recently entered:

Huskisson to Sir John Tobin          Carlton Gardens, 19 July 1830
My Dear Sir,
          I have received your very kind letter of the 15th and I grieve
that I cannot answer it as I could wish, but there are occurrences in life
which one cannot control and with one of these I am now most inoppor-
tunely visited.
          The plain truth is (and it is best to make no mystery of it, at least to you)
that I was seized on Thursday evng., during the procession of the King's
funeral (at which I was), with a violent attack of strangury, and other dis-
tressing symptoms. They were sufficiently mitigated (not without most
severe discipline) by Sat. evng. to enable me to get back to Town: but the
result of a consultation, this morning, is the necessity of my submitting to
a surgical operation, as soon as possible to prevent the occurrence of
another attack which might be attended with severe danger. The operation therefore will take place tomorrow. The Surgeon (Mr. Copeland)
gives me reason to hope that I need not be confined to my bed for more
than a week and that should everything be favourable I might be allowed
to travel by about Friday seven night.
          This is all most provoking, but the case does not admit of postponement,
and there is no help for it. The writ, I apprehend, cannot arrive at Liverpool sooner than this day week or perhaps the day after Tuesday. The
Election would then be fixed probably for the Monday follg. as it would
not be desirable to begin on the Sat. Now without being sanguine I will
not despair of getting to Liverpool by Sunday evng. the 1st of August.
The possibility, however, of my not being able to travel so soon must be
contemplated. . . .

On 26 July, six days after the operation, he writes again:

I wish I could now say, with anything like positive confidence that I
shall be present at the Election, even should it stand over to this day week.
I am going on very well, but find myself weaker than I had anticipated.
And the extreme heat of the day has overcome me very much. I shall be
able to speak more positively tomorrow or Wednesday; but should I be

compelled to relinquish all hope of seeing you at the election, there will, I trust be no difficulty. I should fain hope that, with the concurrence of our friends, you would do me the honour to represent me at the hustings, unless you should think it is advisable to propose it to Mr. Bolton; but I am most unwilling to suggest this arrangement, as I fear his health would not be adequate to the fatigue of it.

Believe me to be,

My dear sir,

Yours very truly.

W. Huskisson

Excuse my dictating this letter, as I cannot sit up conveniently to write.

Handwriting, I think, is Mrs Huskisson's.

On 28 July, eight days after the operation, his doctors issued a Medical Certificate:

From the stage of debility in which Mr. Huskisson's illness has left him, we are of opinion that it would be extremely hazardous for him to undertake a long journey or to incur any unusual fatigue or exertion for some weeks.

G. Maton.

Thos. Copeland.                                    July 28, 1830

He was not well enough to go to Liverpool for the election which, however, went off successfully. But by September he was fit enough to travel, and reached Liverpool in time for the railway celebrations. He kept faith with his public.

The senior physician, William George Maton, was physician extraordinary to Queen Charlotte, the Duchess of Kent and the infant Princess Victoria. Mrs Huskisson thought very highly of him, and a common interest in botany made a bond between them.

# CHAPTER THREE

# HERRIES, PEEL AND THE DUKE

## I. HERRIES

### Clearing the Ground

We may clear the ground by dismissing a letter printed in the Lewis Melville edition of *The Huskisson Papers 1792-1830*, pp. 310 to 319: and headed by Melville 'William Huskisson to John Charles Herries, Roehampton, Dec. 20, 1829'. (Incidentally this editor writes Eartham as Eastham and Eliza Emily, W.H's wife, as Elizabeth.) This letter is not by Huskisson, nor is it a copy in Huskisson's writing: and it is not to J. C. Herries, but to Robert Herries. Later in the same volume, 38,758, f. 123, there is a letter in the same writing from Thos. H. Farquhar[1] of 4 St. James's Street to John C. Hobhouse, Esq.; and Farquhar, from the similarity of the contents, is undoubtedly the author of both. The writer was a banker (a partner in the banking firm of Herries, Farquhar & Co.), writing with a special knowledge of the foreign exchanges, and the false 'Huskisson' letter closes with an extract from the letter of a Scottish correspondent. Even were there no second letter, and even if the first had been a copy in Huskisson's hand, it could not have been by him. It is not in his style: it talks constantly of 'manufactural': and it consists of a critique, amounting to diatribe, of the whole currency and banking policy of the Government from 1797 to 1829, in the course of which it condemns 'Peel's Bill' of 1819, i.e. the Resumption of Cash Payments, which was the central aim of Huskisson's monetary programme. Finally, the transcription contains numerous inaccuracies; and the key word 'pressure' (i.e. financial pressure) is written 'purchase' and alternatively 'prepare', which make nonsense.

We may further dismiss a calumny which has no evidence to support it other than the persistence with which it was repeated. On this test Huskisson was an illegitimate alien and a Jacobin

[1] I take him to be the Sir Thomas Farquhar (Mrs Huskisson's trustee) of p. 116 below.

to boot. It was bruited when, with the approval of the King, who had a high opinion of his financial talents, as he also had of Huskisson's, Herries was offered the Chancellorship of the Exchequer, September 1827, after Sturges Bourne had declined the post. Thus Lord Howard de Walden of the Foreign Office wrote to Huskisson, 23 August 1827, 'Herries is a creature of Knighton who is disposed to risk everything rather than lose him. . . . But people don't like him as a Cabinet Minister and moreover there are some awkward stories about his connection with Rothschild. . . . The Whigs won't join if he is Chancellor of the Exchequer. . . . The general wish of course is that you would be Chancellor of the Exchequer.'

The calumny must be mentioned, if only to be dismissed, because Huskisson led others to think he took it seriously and maintained an air of mystery which made sincere collaboration between Herries and himself impossible. The detail is in the Peel Papers and relates to the conditions under which, after Goderich's retirement, Huskisson and his friends were prepared to accept office under Wellington:

Huskisson to Peel                                   14 January 1828
In consequence of my conversation with the Chancellor [*Lyndhurst*] this morning it became necessary that I should tell him that I had stated to you *confidentially* on Friday my difficulty respecting Herries. . . .

Peel to Huskisson                                   14 January 1828
I did not understand from you that the difficulty as to Herries went to the extent to which it appears from the Chancellor's communication it did go. I have been labouring most anxiously and I began to hope successfully (God knows from better motives than those of personal gratification or ambition) to facilitate a reunion.

Huskisson to Peel                                   15 January 1828
Upon a matter of such serious importance, publick and personal, as that which we discussed this morning, I wish to guard myself if possible from the influence of any undue excitement. I have therefore with much hesitation, I admit, requested Dudley, Grant and Palmerston (knowing all the facts which I trust are ever likely to be made publick) to meet and consider whether the difficulty I feel would be removed by Herries taking some other office in the Cabinet.

I should not have felt myself at liberty to take the step if Planta had not brought me, immediately after you left me, an opinion of Goderich (equally of course acquainted with the case) that I was not called upon to *resign* if Herries was removed from his present office to some other. I have since gone over the whole subject with Goderich, and although he admits that no man can make himself entirely a judge for another in a case affecting personal honour, he perseveres decidedly in his opinion.

Peel tries to make Huskisson more accommodating. 'You think the D. of W. has gone further with Herries than he has done' (15 January 1828).

Huskisson to the Duke                                     17 January 1828

My Dear Duke,      Having now received the opinions of Lord Dudley, Lord Palmerston and Mr. Grant, that, under all the circumstances with which they are acquainted, there is nothing which should preclude me from accepting office with Mr. Herries in a new Government consistently with a proper regard to my personal honour and public character, I lose not a moment in informing you that I am willing to abide by their decision. I do so on the following understanding.

That it is not your intention to continue Mr. Herries in the situation of Chancellor of the Exchequer.

That there is to be a Finance Committee.

That Ld. Althorp shall be proposed as a member of that Committee.

Upon this last point Mr. Herries and I were, from the first entirely agreed. The difficulty arose respecting the Chair.

In the end Herries gave up the Exchequer and accepted the minor office of the Mint, with a seat in the Cabinet, and Sir Henry Parnell became Chairman of the Finance Committee. It would have been possible for Huskisson to argue that the differences between him and Herries related solely to their well-known public differences regarding (a) the Chairmanship of the Finance Committee and (b) the events which had occasioned the downfall of the Goderich administration. But he was aware of the calumnies afloat against Herries, and with his sensitive regard to his own 'personal honour and public character', it was for him to say openly and outright both to Herries and Peel that he gave no credence whatever to the charges against the personal honour and public character of Herries, and that the difference between them was one of public policy on which difference was legitimate. He could not but know that on the score of administrative experience Herries's claim to the Exchequer was as great as that either of Sturges Bourne or himself, and he buttressed a difficult case of political expediency behind an altogether regrettable mystification. After the death of Herries, the sons, Edward and Sir Charles, defended their father in a lengthy Memoir,[1] but they swing over to the opposite extreme, having no sympathy with the formidable task which confronted Huskisson of securing a continuation of the Canningite policy by enlarging the administration to include such Whigs as were in sympathy with the principles of Canning. Yet, I cannot resist the opinion that if Huskisson had come to the Exchequer to find the Chairmanship of the Public Finance Committee determined for him in advance, he would have indignantly rejected so unreasonable a pre-emption of his claims. In the Tableau of the Reformed Parliament in the National Portrait Gallery, the narrow face and squeezed body of Herries suggest the pertinacity of one born under the planet Saturn.

*The Herries Family*

From William Herries, a merchant burgess of Edinburgh, who died in 1598, two branches of the family descended—the Herries of Hartwood and the Herries of Halldykes.

From William Herries of Hartwood was descended Michael Herries of Spottes (1725-99) and Alexander Young of Harburn (near Edinburgh), 1757-1842. The latter's son, as the heir of Michael Herries, took his name and estate, which has descended to its present owner, Col. William Young-Herries, whose son and heir is my recent pupil, Michael Young-Herries of Trinity College, Cambridge. Spottes is near Castle Douglas, Kirkcudbrightshire, and there I have been privileged to study the rich collection of correspondence assembled by Alexander Young of Harburn and containing letters from Burns, Scott,

[1] E. Herries, with intro. by Sir Charles Herries, *Memoirs of the Public Life of the Rt. Hon. John Charles Herries*, 2 vols., 1880.

Maria Edgeworth, J. C. Curwen and the Dalrymples (the last a connection of the Youngs by marriage).

From Robert Herries of Halldykes was descended the famous banking house of Herries and also the statesman J. C. Herries. This branch of the family has had its seat since the end of the eighteenth century at St. Julians, near Sevenoaks, Kent.

Three Robert Herries figure in the banking story. Robert Herries I went out from Annandale to Rotterdam, and acquiring there a competent fortune returned to Scotland to join eventually his nephew in a banking house in London. He died in 1791. The nephew was Robert Herries II, 1730-1815, knighted 1774. He, too, was an overseas merchant, first in Holland and then in Spain, where, with the help of the Hopes of Rotterdam, he established a business in Barcelona. He, too, found his way eventually to London, and in 1762 became a chief partner in John Coutts & Co. of Edinburgh and London. After a short while the Edinburgh and London businesses were separated, Sir William Forbes of Pitsligo taking the Edinburgh business. In 1768 Herries invented the system of circular notes of credit for foreign travel, Coutts Bank issuing them and Hopes of Amsterdam arranging for their encashment. Finally in 1772 he separated from Coutts and established in St. James's Street a banking house, which under various titles, the London Exchange Banking Company; Herries and Farquhar; Herries, Farquhar & Co.; carried on business there till it was amalgamated with Lloyd's in 1893. Huskisson banked with Herries, and the wrongly assigned letter, quoted above, is from a present partner in the banking house (Farquhar) to a former partner, Robert Herries III. It was thus as a customer and friend of the Herries house that a copy of the letter found its way into the Huskisson correspondence, and not from any connection of Huskisson with J. C. Herries.

Robert Herries III, 1767-1845, joined Robert Herries II in the bank, retiring in 1825 when the latter died. Together with J. C. Herries he bought land on which, in 1822, St. Julians was built. Here he lived, till in 1836 it was made over to J. C. Herries, from whom it passed to his son Edward, 1821-1911.

J. C. Herries was the son of Col. Charles Herries, the younger brother of Robert Herries II. He had no connection with the banking business, but the high standing of the family business in the foreign banking world meant that he had easy access to the Barings, Rothschilds and other merchant bankers˙ of his day. If Disraeli had been Prime Minister in Huskisson's day, he would probably have been accused of shady dealings with Sidonia. Perhaps he was!

*John Charles Herries*

In the field of public finance (not trade policy, but revenue policy) the accomplishment of Herries over his long life, 1778-1855—and he was in harness almost to the end—was second only to that of Gladstone. In the history of revenue administration, civil audit, income tax and public borrowing he played a central part, but in trade policy he was protectionist at heart and for this reason perhaps has not come down to us as one of the great reformers.

A secretary of Secretaries, first of Vansittart, then of Perceval, then of Wellesley-Pole at the Irish Exchequer, he rose to be a Cabinet Minister. In diligence of investigation and minuting he was a veritable Sidney Webb, and by common consent an excellent man of business, but of oratory he had nothing. A long period of war service, as Commissary-in-chief to the Army (in the course of which he converted the reproaches of Wellington into limited praise), was followed by a shorter period of peace service, as Auditor of the Civil List, a new office of 1816, which his brother, General Sir William Herries, had after him; and these offices gave him the executive experience which enabled him to shape the financial investigations of the 1820's: the Commission of 1821 into the management of the Irish Revenue,[1] which resulted in the Consolidation of the Irish with the English Exchequer: the Commission of 1818-24, which resulted in the Customs Consolidation of 1825, the Herries Consolidation as it was officially termed (Herries was now a Secretary to the Treasury): the Finance Committee of 1828,[2]

---

[1] Parliamentary Papers 1822, XII.    [2] Parliamentary Papers 1828, V.

which with Parnell as Chairman produced the Report that
terminated Pitt's Sinking Fund, and made fundamental proposals for the presentation of the Public Accounts.

The Commission of 1818-24 is the subject of a later chapter
(pp. 286-90). The line taken in the Irish Report is economy
by consolidation—consolidation of Customs and Excise, and of
the Irish and British Revenues: and fiscal unity of trade—'any
inequalities (in taxation) should be confined to branches of
revenue not the subject of commercial exchange'. The condition of Ireland is to be improved by 'educating her to the institutions and usages of Great Britain'.

The Reports of 1828 present an anatomy of public finance.
That part of the fourth Report which recommends the abolition
of the Sinking Fund apparatus and the devotion of true surplus
only to debt redemption is well-known. But not less interesting
is the way in which the Reports pursue the doctrine of Treasury
control over all expenditures, and gauge what the next generation was to call the Resilience of the Revenue. To Granville's
disgust they probed even into diplomatic pensions: 'I think
the principle adopted by the Finance Committee of requiring a
declaration of the private income of the ex-ambassador is highly
objectionable and might in some cases have a most unjust operation' (Granville to Littleton, 16 June 1828: Hatherton MS.
Correspondence 1828-9). The Duke of Wellington and Sir
Henry Hardinge gave evidence about the Ordnance Department (i.e. Artillery and Engineers): and here one learns about
the Ordance Survey—two-thirds of it completed, as well as the
whole triangulation of Great Britain (without which our holiday
tramps would not be a British holiday), and the vital importance
of military education. 'The Artillery previous to the establishment of the Woolwich Academy (which I believe was instituted
by the Duke of Cumberland), was always a corps so deficient in
service, that we were in a great degree dependent on foreigners
to fill all the high offices of rank in the Artillery service, and we
only got rid of the system of employing foreigners since the
establishment of the Academy at Woolwich' (Hardinge, Evidence, p. 234).

The problem of taxation is approached through an examination of the revenue for the period 1823-7 in the light of the important tax remissions of the time: the net result, notwithstanding the remissions, being an increase of c. £6 million through increased consumption, in the face of sharp foreign competition, unusual pressure on the agricultural interest and the commercial panic of 1825—'striking evidence (the Committee claims) of undiminished productiveness, such as can only be ascribed to a state of general wealth and industry in the country'.

From beginning to end the pen, so far as there is a single pen, is the pen of Herries. Indeed the fourth Report breaks off to advert to a long statement by him, which is printed in an appendix.

Even as Huskisson was the only Leader of the House, whose leadership was confined to a single circular,[1] so Herries was the only Chancellor of the Exchequer who did not survive long enough to present a budget. It was a national loss; for we should have had a budget statement rivalling in comprehensiveness and grasp of principles the best of Gladstone's. Whether he could have carried an Income Tax in 1828 must be a matter of speculation. But no one can digest the Reports of 1828 without seeing that this was the expedient which the time required, alike for the encouragement of consumption and the promotion of foreign trade. When Peel, after eleven years of spineless Whig finance, was nerving himself to this step, Herries wrote to him:

I have very long entertained the conviction that the burthens of this country, consisting in so large a degree of accumulated debt ought to be defrayed, in a greater proportion than they have hitherto been since the Peace, by the contribution of accumulated wealth; and that the very great preponderance assigned in our system of taxation to the duties derived

[1] Littleton preserves his copy endorsing it 'This circular was the only act of leadership of the House Mr. Huskisson ever performed, changes that occurred immediately afterwards having placed the office in Peel's hands. The circular ran:

Downing St. 26 Dec 1827. 'Sir. As Parliament will certainly meet for the despatch of business on the 22nd of January next, and as questions of the utmost importance will come under discussion at the meeting, I hope you will excuse me stating to you that a full attendance is particularly desirable at the opening of the Session—W.H.'

from manufactures and consumption, was not only impolitic, but unsustainable.

I was so deeply impressed with this belief more than fifteen years ago that when I held the office of Chancellor of the Exchequer I had come to the determination in entire concurrence with Huskisson and Lord Ripon, to propose a Property Tax by way of commutation for some of the then existing indirect taxes, which were most obstructive to the industry of the country, and consequently most detrimental to it in its then growing rivalry with the manufactures of the Continent, and also most obnoxious to the public feeling; and therefore likely to be wrenched, sooner or later, out of any Government. The change of Ministers put an end to these intentions...[1]

After his sinecure at the Mint, which was for that reason unwelcome, Herries held office for short periods only—as President of the Board of Trade, 1830-2 (when he had the satisfaction of terminating the long trade friction with America): as Secretary at War, 1834-5: and as President of the India Board of Control, 1852. He would have liked at the last to become Chancellor of the Exchequer, but other claimants had the precedence: so that Gladstone had the easy task of demolishing and succeeding Benjamin Disraeli, 28 December 1852.

*Financial Contacts*

(a) Alexander Young of Harburn was a lawyer, and in an autobiographical note[2] he tells us:

I was afterwards made acquainted with Sir William and recommended to him and Lady Forbes by their intimate friends and my relations, Sir Robert and Lady Herries; also by Col. Charles Herries, Sir Robert's younger brother, and I was well known to, and had experience of many acts of friendship from Sir Wm. even before I began business on my own account. . . . When it was suggested to me that I ought to be a Director of the Bank of Scotland I consulted Sir Wm. and I believe it was then owing to him that I was chosen one of the number.

This Alexander Young, lawyer, bank director and *littérateur*, writes to Sir Thos. Farquhar, 7 August 1828: 'When the rage

[1] E. Herries, *Memoir of J. C. Herries*, II, 208.

[2] Spottes MS., *Alexander Young and Dr Blacklock, the Blind Beggar* (and poetical mentor of Sir Walter Scott).

of speculation and adventure seized the British public not many years ago, its influence extended even to the sober society of writers to the Signet in Scotland'—including one James Stuart, who 'has set sail for America', after borrowing a large sum of money from the trustees of Mrs Huskisson in her marriage settlement with Mr Huskisson. Further letters from Scotland say that the security is unquestionable. It is a first mortgage of £30,200 at 4½% on an estate valued at £50,000. Huskisson, who was then recuperating in Italy, writes to A. Milne, Esq., of Woods and Forests (from Venice, 12 September 1828), that he is glad to hear that the security is ample and that other creditors cannot impair its validity: and regrets that 'you and Sir Thos. Farquhar as Trustees should be exposed to so much annoying trouble'.

The correspondence goes on and on and closes with an entry in Huskisson's hand, 'The Trustees, having taken the opinion of Counsel upon the articles of the proposed agreement with reference to the marriage settlement of Mrs. Huskisson, do not feel themselves warranted to consent to these articles. But they are willing to abstain from taking any legal proceeding to force a sale of the estate of Ardross and the repayment of the principal money.'

Ardross (if I have identified it aright) is on the north-east coast of Ross and Cromarty, 4½ miles north of Alness.[1] When I was a boy I climbed BenWyvis and must have seen the property, but in those days I had not heard of William and Emily Huskisson.

(b) In another note, on Walter Boyd, Alexander Young writes:

When I first knew him, he was factor or land steward to Patrick Heron, by whom he was recommended to Col. Herries, father to John Charles Herries, the later Secretary at War.

---

[1] This Ardross (the other being a ruin in Fifeshire) is not far from Dunrobin, the Duke of Sutherland's seat—'Off to Dunrobin via Dornoch' writes Lord Stafford to Huskisson, 31 July 1798. The mansion is a big place and known as Ardross Castle. Belonging for a time to the Ross-shire family of Matheson, who bought it from the Duke of Sutherland in 1842, it was acquired early in the present century by Dyson Perrins, Esq. It is a large and valuable estate. Whether the Sutherland family owned it in 1825, I know not.

He afterwards became a banker at Brussels, where he married. I had there some correspondence with him on behalf of my school fellow Mr. General Lockhart. He afterwards entered into partnership with the celebrated Paul Benfield and the great loans and cash transactions of the British Govt. during Mr. Pitt's administration were managed chiefly by them. My friend Mr. James Drummond became afterwards a partner of this house, from which at last Mr. Benfield retired. And Mr. Boyd, having settled at Paris became as eminent in the finances of that country as ever he was in this; having paid every creditor in full, both principal and interest, he bought a beautiful villa at Plaistow in the Co. of Kent, whence these letters are dated [1823] and where I believe he now resides. He was a most intelligent, agreeable and friendly person, universally beloved and esteemed in all the various situations which he has held in the course of his extraordinary and eventful career.

Boyd figures in the Huskisson Papers as a voluminous correspondent with a grievance: and there is a caustic notice of him in Sir John Clapham's *Bank of England*, II, 16-17. (Again, 'long, long I have desired to have a couple of hours conversation with you. . . . Benfield died here last spring'—Boyd writes to Huskisson from Paris, December 1810. Note the place and date. How different from World War II!. Leeves and Wright, when preparing the Huskisson Memoir, had to expose the canard that 'the assignees of Boyd and Benfield, bankrupts, found in the accounts of the said bankrupts a balance of between £20,000 and £30,000 against Mr. Huskisson which money was paid by Mr. Huskisson to the said assignees'.

It is easy to see how anyone who was connected, as J. C. Herries officially was, with the Rothschilds and other foreign bankers in collecting French funds for Wellington's forces, could later be accused of benefiting from the great loaning operations conducted by the Rothschilds in Europe after the peace. The *Morning Chronicle* uttered the slander, and Goderich, as Prime Minister, on the same day, 24 August 1827, issued a categorical denial, which was published in the *Times*.

'I owe it to you' (he wrote to Herries) 'to state explicitly that the grounds assumed in that paragraph for the delay in the appointment of Chancellor of the Exchequer are totally destitute of foundation.'[1] But mud sticks, as Huskisson himself knew only too well; and of all rumours that which imputes financial shadiness is the hardest to scotch. Herries was Leipzig-trained in Germany, Huskisson was brought up in Paris; and therefore they did not enjoy the immunity accorded to those who had an English public school, followed by Oxford or Cambridge. The old school tie was then a passport of worth. It even excused you from having a legitimate father.

## II. PEEL

*A Misunderstanding removed*

Gossip in those days floated around like floodwater seeking its level—gossip political and social, some of it good-natured (of this the Duke had more than his fair share), much of it malicious. The great diarists were gossipers in chief, and this was the way in which they earned, if not their keep, at least their round of hospitality. If a proud man condemned it, he was written down as haughty: if a sensitive man flinched from it, he confirmed suspicion. When the differences were among colleagues, they sank them in public and aired them in private. What saved them from many an open breach was either the likelihood that, before the winter was up, they would be shooting in the same coverts, or the possession of a common friend, who insisted on smoothing things between them.

The year is 1823: the day 19 December. Peel is at the Home Office: Huskisson at the Board of Trade; and both in the flesh are at Sudbourne.

Huskisson to his wife

Peel is gone out this morning to decide two bets of 150 to 100 each, that he does not bag 20 brace of pheasants. I have a bet of 15 to 10 that he does not.

And again:

Peel started in all the rain to decide a bet. .... The bets were 100 to 50, 2 or 3 times over. Baring the bettor. Peel returned at 1 drenched, having

[1] E. Herries, *Memoir of J. C. Herries*, I, 166.

won his bet, which was great doing. . . . He is an excellent shot, and has always been a lucky man.

Incidentally in this same month Peel pronounced secretarially in favour of prize fighting and pugilism.[1]

The year shifts to 1827: the month again is December. Peel for the moment is out of office: Huskisson has moved to War and the Colonies.

Hatherton Correspondence 1826-7.

Littleton to Peel.                    Teddesley 6 December 1827

My Dear Peel,

I have hesitated a great deal about the propriety of showing you the enclosed letter. But I am so disgusted with the lies invented by party spirit that I cannot refrain from availing myself of any means to destroy at least one of them.

Your brother Wm., who was here last week, referred in conversation to a Report that he had heard, that Mr. Huskisson had declared it impossible for him to continue in the Cabinet, if you were restored to it, or something exactly to that effect.

I knew it to be so impossible that he would have expressed himself in terms so much in variance with his undisguised feelings, that I ventured to assure your bro. that the report was a malignant fabrication, invented for the purpose of exciting an enmity, where none existed naturally, but when it was a party object to concrete one.

I gave to your brother some information which he must have felt constituted a complete proof of the insidious motive of the fabrication. Fearful I had committed an indiscretion, I thought it right to tell Huskisson what had passed. I enclose you his answer in the strictest confidence.

E. J. L.

Huskisson to Littleton                    Downing St. 4 December 1827

My Dear W.

Instead of thinking you indiscreet, I have to thank you sincerely for having so positively contradicted the calumnious report to which Peel appears to have given credit.

It is Mr. Peel's misfortune, I am afraid, to be rather too prone to listen to such malignant statements, and not always to be sufficiently on his guard against the motives of those by whom they are invented or propagated.

[1] Peel to Henry Hobhouse, 30 December 1823.

When I confirm in the most unqualified manner your denial of this falsehood, I have said everything that I can be expected, or that I feel myself *now* at liberty to say. The time *will* come when I shall be free to tell Mr. Peel what my real sentiments have been since his return to office, I remaining a part of the Govt., and to refer him to the present head of it, if necessary, for the truth of what I may *then* feel myself not precluded from stating. But this is not the moment for explanation. There is nothing more painful to me than to be aware of the existence of these odious attempts to disseminate hatred, and to excite personal animosities. For me at least public life has no temptations which can compensate for the growing disgust of it—a disgust, which makes me regret more and more every day that my wish to retire was over-ruled 3 months ago.

W. H.

I have received thanks from Liverpool for some of the game you were so good as to send. What a slaughter you appear to have made.

Whitehall 9 December 1827

My Dear L.

I feel very sensibly the kind motives which have induced you to write to me.

I return Huskisson's letter to you and will consider your communication as made to me in the strictest confidence.

On the day before I received your letter, i.e. on Friday last, a person connected with the present Govt. mentioned to me that very report which your letter proves to be a false one. I said at once that I did not believe it to be true, but if I were perfectly satisfied that it was true, I never would consider a declaration made at a moment when feelings were warmly excited by the death of an intimate friend and colleague as indicative of personal hostility on the part of another, or justifying it on mine. I tell you exactly what passed before I got your letter as a proof that, if the report originated in a malignant desire to excite animosity and resentment, it failed completely to produce its intended effect on me—even before it was so decisively contradicted.

R. P.

Note by Littleton

I sent the foregoing letter, dated Dec. 9 1827 to Mr. H. who answered as follows 'I return you Peel's letter and cannot express how gratified I have felt by the perusal of it. It is everything that could have been expected from the best feeling, guided by the soundest judgment'.

I sent this answer to Peel, who did not return it to me.

This correspondence was the means of smoothing the negotiations that brought the parties together again in the Cabinet in the month following.

E. J. L.

I picture the statesmen of the day as wearing cloaks from ultra-blue to radical red. No one could confuse Eldon's with Brougham's. Peel's is more blue than red: Palmerston's more red than blue: Huskisson's is neuter, with a suggestion of imperial purple. Littleton's coat was of a different sort: red or blue according to the angle from which you viewed it. He was eager to reconcile, and met everyone half way. But his impetuosity was the cause eventually of his own undoing; for as Irish Secretary he tried to solve the Irish problem by a rapid understanding with O'Connell—strange blending (Disraeli called it) of complex intrigue and almost infantile ingenuousness.[1] But to all, with the honourable exception of the imaginative Brougham, there was one unthinkable—the impossible Robert Owen: and so, when Mr. Owen asked permission to dedicate to Mr Peel the 'outline of the system of education at New Lanark', written by his eldest son Robert Dale Owen, Peel felt bound to decline the request, since he differed so materially 'from some of the opinions which you have publicly avowed with respect to the Religious Instruction of Children' (11 January 1824). Yet by October 1841 his Home Secretary Graham was to realise and confess that 'religion, the keystone of education, is in this country the bar to its progress'.

*Peel and Huskisson*

At first sight it seems that Huskisson and Peel, who was by eighteen years his junior (1788-1850), started close together and gradually drifted apart. In the long view, when we fit one career on to the other, we know that this reverses truth. The revision of the Corn Laws, which thwarted Huskisson, broke Peel. The banking legislation of 1825 was a prelude to Peel's Bank Charter Act of 1844. The tariff reductions which Huskisson inaugurated were taken by Peel in two great budgets to

---

[1] *Coningsby*, Bk. II, Ch. I.

within sight of complete free trade, and the whole of both men's work was accomplished within the pliant framework of the Tory Party.[1]

Huskisson, who had been brought into the front of the Currency arena by his share in the Bullion Report of 1810, was a member of the Commons Committee of 1819, of which Peel was Chairman and which passed 'Mr. Peel's Act' prescribing the Resumption of Cash Payments. He was behind Peel at every point, and after it had reached the statute book, he sacrificed his standing with the agricultural interest by converting his Report of 1821 on the Depressed State of Agriculture into a homily in support of Resumption. However, if we pass from the Bullion Report, which was the work of no one man, to his immediate apology for it, *The Question concerning the Depreciation of our Currency* of 1810, we realise that the approach of the two men was different. The apology is more than a monetary tract: it is imbued with the spirit of the Wealth of Nations. Our true policy is '*the interchange of reciprocal and equivalent benefit*' —reciprocal, the term which he was to make a household word in the vocabulary of fiscal reform. 'It is not in the nature of commerce to enrich one party at the expense of the other. This is a purpose, at which, if it were practicable, we ought not to aim; and which, if we arrived at it, we could not accomplish.'[2] Already he had in view a policy of trade, which could only be undertaken if the standard of value was secure and unsullied.

Peel in time drew closer to free trade, but by another route— by administrative free trade of the Herries type in the interest of good government. In 1819 he was in the interval between two long periods of office: as Chief Secretary for Ireland, 1812-18, and Home Secretary, 1822-7, 1828-30. In each office his prime duty was the maintenance of public order; and for each country he created a police force—the Royal Irish Constabu-

---

[1] Huskisson and Peel graduated in the same office—as Under Secretaries for War and the Colonies—during the same long war, Huskisson 1795-1801, Peel 1810-12. After the peace their careers bifurcated, Peel specialising in Police and the Home Department, Huskisson in Trade and Imperial affairs. But their political economy was linked by life-long service to the gold standard.

[2] *Speeches*, I, 108. *The Question* is printed there in full.

lary for Ireland, the 'Bobbies', 'Peelers', for Great Britain. By 1825 he was immersed in the condition of England question—pressure of the Irish surplus, the unemployment of hand-loom weavers, the condition of the factory children to whom his father had extended the first helping hand. In the index to the *Waverley Novels* there is an unexpected entry, 'Cotton Mills useful to the country.' Turning to the Chronicles of the Canongate (1827-8) we read:

The cotton mill was such a thing for the country! The mair bairns a cottar body had the better; they would make their awn keep frae the time they were five years auld; and a widow, wi' three or fair bairns, was a wealthier woman in the time of the Treddleses.

The son and heir of Calico Treddles could not be expected to read this without some misgiving. But he was cautious to the point of pessimism. Though it was all very sad, it could not be helped. He writes to Littleton, 31 July 1826:

We had a deputation from Birmingham on Friday last, requiring the Govt. to do something—which something they attempted to explain—but I confess I could not understand it. It seems very hard-hearted to do nothing but encourage voluntary subscriptions and local exertions—and nothing would console me for the apparent indifference but the conviction that all attempts on the part of the Govt. under such circumstances as the present to stimulate employment on any great scale are mere quackery, doing ultimately more mischief than good.[1]

And Huskisson writes to him (8 February 1827) in a vein which is dogmatically strange. It is the coldest of cold comfort —the answer of commercial Liverpool with its thriving foreign trade to industrial Manchester with its grime and suffering humanity:

Their complaint against the exportation of yarn has been a standing grievance of the weavers at all times. I am afraid that it is principally by progressive improvements in machinery that we must look toward, to maintain for our cotton and woollen manufactures the advanced stations which they occupy, and from which Germany, France and the United States are struggling hard to drive them. Abundance of capital, dear sub-

[1] *Hatherton Correspondence* 1826-7.

sistence and heavy taxation are the great stimulant to inventions for abridging labour and they are all likely to continue to operate in this country. I do not feel well enough to go down to the House today.

This, surely, is a blend of Bernard Mandeville and Samuel Smiles.

## The Growing Stature of Peel

As 1827 unfolded its troubled course, the stature of Peel grew. He is the man on whom all are coming to lean. 'I hope now', writes Sir Thomas Lethbridge from the right, 'you will take the Government of this country on your shoulders . . . I verily believe, you will be another Mr. Pitt and that the country will support you as they did him.' Wilmot Horton floods him with emigration propaganda till Peel enters a caveat, 12 March 1827, 'I really think that some effectual step ought to be taken forthwith to prevent every unemployed man in the country looking for relief from emigration.' Then, 17 July 1827, he hears that Peel and Baring have pronounced his schemes to be 'wild and visionary', and Peel sends personal comfort—'Never believe any story about my concerting with a member of the opposition in opposition to a colleague.' The clergy in shoals warn Mr Secretary Peel against concessions to Rome, and Scotland deplores the Irish invasion:

The Irish who settle in Scotland must very often do so to escape the reward of crime: they are never received but as an inferior population to that which they supplant and degrade in every respect. They undersell the native of the parish—because they go dirty and ragged during the week, and have no clothes for church on the Sabbath. (J. Maxwell to Peel.)

January 1828 closes with Littleton expressing the hope that Peel and Huskisson are now in union. 'I am one of those who consider that a union of yourself and Huskisson the most desirable of all things in the present state of the country, and I congratulate it on the realization of that event.' But in mid-February the Marquis of Camden is pressing him to stand shoulder to shoulder with the Duke, and not to let Mr Huskisson pass the Corn Bill. To bring Sturges Bourne into the uneasy ship was,

of course, impossible. Sturges Bourne refused to take charge of
the Finance Committee, this time because of his wife's health.
But Peel could ask him a question (to which, unfortunately, I
cannot find the reply):

19 April 1828. Why should not an able bodied pauper, being of military
status, after having been a burden on the poor rates for a given time, have
military service tendered to him—in lieu of parochial subsistence? Why
should not the overseer be able to say to a young and healthy labourer out
of employ 'Here are clothes for you and 13d. a day?'

Perhaps Sturges Bourne referred him to the Duke!

By the end of May the union had broken down. The letters
of resignation flow in from Lamb, Palmerston and the others;
and all of them end on a note of regret. As Palmerston put it,
'What I regret the most in all this transaction is that it separates
me from you' (1 June 1828). Beyond this we need not go. Peel
now was forty and in the prime of life, and could stand any
amount of strain and worry (with nothing more than a disturbance of the bowels); and it would have been well for the country
and the Conservative Party if he, and not the Duke of Wellington, had become the next Prime Minister. For he was, I submit,
the logical successor to Pitt; and if that be granted, there is no
more to say.

*A Famous Letter*

Even Peel now and then got a letter which raised no worry
and asked for no help. I cannot say I remember more than one,
but that one is very good. I pass over another, not to Peel,
though in the Peel Papers, which explains how Lord Cochrane
effected his escape from prison not by bribes, as he and his
friends falsely insinuated, but 'over the wall through the in-
sufficiency of it',[1] and I come to Sir Walter Scott's avowal of the
authorship of the *Waverley Novels*:

Lord  Meadowbank to Peel                          26 February 1827
    My Dear Sir,
        Aware of the interest you take in our friend Scott, I have desired

[1] W. Jones to Lushington 5 July 1822.

to be sent to you an Edinburgh Newspaper,[1] containing an account of the confession he made in public on Friday of his being the author of *Waverley* and all the other novels, and exclusively responsible for everything contained in them.

This occurred at a meeting of the Charitable Institution for the relief of decayed actors, when I happened to be present as one of the patrons and was very unexpectedly informed that the stewards wished I should propose Sir Walter's health. Sitting next him I enquired whether it was his desire that I should shape my speech in the language of mystery as to the Great Unknown, or if I might consider the humbug at an end. He told me I might use my pleasure with that personage; accordingly I said a few words in the way which appeared to me best suited for meeting the feelings of the 3 or 400 people on that subject: and after the uproar which was excited had subsided, Scott got up and made the confession you will find in the newspaper.

Altho' by us who were intimate with him no new information has been received from this acknowledgement, it would seem the public were still in doubt, and as the interest which it has created will probably be equally great in London as here, I thought you might like to see what had actually occurred.

I remain my dear Sir,

Yours most faithfully,

Alex Maconochie

### III. THE DUKE

*Elba and Waterloo*

In the MS. Correspondence of Alexander Young at Spottes I came across the following:—

(*a*) Two letters from Sir Hugh Dalrymple of the Paris Embassy to his friend Sir John Dalrymple dated Paris, 29 December 1814, and 5 January 1815.

The writer depicts in vivid language 'the magnificence of the present Court of France'. 'Everything of gold plate brilliantly lighted up.' 'There is certainly something not quite right among the troops or rather the officers, but nothing that firmness and good management may not completely overcome.'

---

[1] Cf. the Press account in Waverley Novels Introduction to *Chronicles of the Canongate*, 1st Series (1827), Appendix.

This splendour is contrasted with that of the fallen state of
Napoleon in Elba, from which Douglas, Lord Glenbervie's son,
was just returned, bringing an account of an interview of $2\frac{1}{2}$
hours with Napoleon: which Sir Hugh reports verbatim.

He said it was impossible to calculate on the burning of Moscow; that
he had staid too long upon the Elbe; that some of his Marshals had acted
like fools in shutting themselves up in the fortified towns; that he had been
overpersuaded by them at last not to enter Paris, and that he might have
created great confusion in France, if he could have made up his mind to
run the risk of sacrificing the lives of the 40,000 soldiers who remained
steady to him; that people supposed he would put an end to himself, but
that he recollected his origin and had no idea of such weakness as not being
able to survive any reverse. He took a wide range over Europe, said that
the English were wrong in supposing there was any private understanding
between him and America; that she, on the contrary, had always assumed
as high a tone with him as she had with us; but that we were right in supposing that there was a secret article in the Treaty of Tilsit, by which
Russia was bound to go to war whenever he chose. He said we could not
imagine what a scoundrel Alexander was. He said he had been accused of
turning Mussulman in Egypt; that the real truth was, he found he could
not get the military of that country to obey him. . . .

He returned again to France, and said we should have been satisfied in
forcing the French to take back the Bourbons; that we were pressing
matters too hard with respect to their boundaries on the side of Holland,
and that we might depend upon it, that sooner or later (like a vessel which
was forced to contain more air than it could hold) there would be a tremendous explosion. That France is a military country; the Bourbons had
better take care of what they were about; that there were still in France
500,000 excellent soldiers and then, making a rapid turn, he said 'but what
is all this to me? I am to all intents and purposes dead'. . . .

Amidst the most judicious remarks possible, he seemed at times to have
great pleasure in talking the most absurd nonsense. He said, for instance,
that he had no objection to abolishing the Slave Trade, but that while a
nation is composed of people of two different colours, one must always be
uppermost; that for his part, as being a white, he wished for the whites;
that he had thought a great deal on the subject; and that it had struck him
as the only way in which all this could be got the better of was by permitting polygamy; and that in this way they would soon come to be so connected together that all spirit of rivalry would cease; that he had consulted

some of his bishops upon this subject, but could not prevail upon them to agree to it. . . .

He is in perfect health; takes a great deal of exercise and is supposed to be writing the history of his life. . . .

(*b*) From the same to the same: dated Brussels, 27 June 1815. The letter begins with news of how certain friends of the family had fared at Quatre Bras and Waterloo and continues (from this point I give it in full):

We have indeed spilt torrents of precious blood; but precious as it is, it has brought its price, for it has saved Europe a second time. It is impossible for me to express myself in terms of sufficient admiration and praise of the conduct of the Duke of Wellington; since the morning of the 16th he had outdone all his former achievements. The Duke had been in the habit of getting the most correct possible information of all that went on in France; not a regiment marched that he did not instantly know of it. These sources of information I conclude had been discovered by Bounaparte [*sic*], who instead of punishing had talent enough to prevail upon the individuals to continue their correspondence, but to mislead the Duke in every particular. In this state of matters, the Duke was kept in the dark, not only as to the point of attack, but as to the arrival of Bounaparte's army, and was furnished with such proofs of the weakness of that army, that he felt secure Bounaparte would have no inducement to give up the advantage of having it to say that he called upon them only in defence of their country. Thus situated, the Duke of W had determined to await the arrival of the Russians and Austrians before he commenced operations, and was not a little surprised while sitting at dinner on the 15th to find that he had actually passed the frontiers. The Duke thus taken by surprise gave the necessary orders with the utmost composure, viz—the drawing to the part of the country where the French were entering his whole force, and then ordering on the whole force he had in this neighbourhood to stop the advance of the enemy, at all rates till such time as the rest of the army could be brought up. Can you conceive anything like Bounaparte's information? He knew that the Duchess of Richmond had selected that evening, the 15th, for a grand ball, and that all the generals of our army were to be there. The ball did take place; the generals all arrived in a state of ignorance, but their different corps were in the act of marching before they set off to join them. The Duke of Wellington staid till 2 o'clock in the morning, and appeared to have nothing on his mind, though he has since owned

K

that one of the expresses he received while at supper was to inform him that the French outposts had got as far as Genappe, within four leagues of this place. Nothing could be so tormenting for the Duke as this point of attack, as it was his extreme left, and of course forced him to fatigue his troops exceedingly, by bringing them on the right above 30 miles. With a view to general operations, however, it was fortunate, as it enabled part of both armies to operate upon his flanks. The Duke left about 8 o'clock on the morning of the 16th and just overtook the troops that had been marching from this place through the night, as the enemy made their appearance at the farm house of Quatre Bras. In this state, fatigued as all parties were—I mean the Duke and his little army; they had at once to go into action, without cavalry or artillery, and having only been joined by the generals who happened to be cantoned nearest to this place of attack. The result was most extraordinary and could only have arisen from the astonishing judgment displayed by the Duke in posting his troops and in the determined bravery of the British soldiers. The French could never drive us from the field of battle, and returned to their own position in the course of the afternoon, upon seeing immence reinforcements coming at every moment. Night came on, and the Duke had determined to attack Bounaparte's position in conjunction with Blucher next morning. I may as well here mention that when the Duke of Wellington was at the Congress, the King of Prussia offered him the command of his troops, but that he seeing this would not go down with the Prussian generals, and that it was thus likely rather to hurt, than benefit the cause, had the good sense to decline it, and to request the command to be given to Blucher, which was accordingly done, but I believe that B- has instructions on the event of a difference of opinion to follow that of W-. Thus circumstanced, the Duke was not a little surprised to find that the patroles he sent out in the night could never fall in with those of the Prussians, but on the contrary were always met by those of the French. At 7. in the morning of the 17th, and not sooner, a despatch arrived from Blucher to say that he had been forced to fall back 8 or 10 miles. Upon this the Duke had instantly to alter his plans, and to determine upon a retreat. This he executed in the most superb style, not leaving behind him anything but a few men very badly wounded, and took up a new position in front of Waterloo. Here he had a meeting with Blucher, and they determined to make a grand attack upon Bounaparte (who had in the course of the evening of Saturday the 17th taken up a position in front of that of Waterloo) on the morning of Monday the 19th, by which time it was known that Bulow's corps of 25,000 men, and another of 20,000 would be arrived. Bounaparte, however had as good information of this as they, had by incredible exertions got up all his amunition etc. and actually began the engagement about 2 hours after Blucher had left the Duke's quarters. Here again the Duke had instantly to change his plans, and to form others, which, if I had the power of detailing to you, and of making you understand, would, I am sure induce you to subscribe to anything I could say in praise of Wellington. We had 55,000 infantry, 20,000 of which only were English, 8000 cavalry, 5000 of which English, and from 2 to 3000 artillery. In all say 65,000. The French had 90,000 infantry, 28,000 cavalry, and from 6 to 7,000 artillery. The Duke resisted this enormous mass from ½ past 11 till 6 in the evening; at this time, the French had made a sort of last effort, very desperate, which the Duke had with great difficulty been able to resist. He discovered a sort of pause on the part of the enemy, and instantly ordered up the remains of the corps of Brunswickers, which after the fall of their Prince, he had ordered in to reserve. He had this corps formed in a manner to produce as much effect as possible, if the enemy, as he concluded might be the case, mistook the Brunswickers for a fresh corps. This with the cannon which at a little distance announced the approach of the Prussians, made the pause still more decided, and the Duke of Wellington, by ordering an immediate charge of his whole line, converted it into a flight. Bounaparte had felt so certain of victory, that he had ordered up his whole pack of artillery and ammunition within a short distance of the field of battle where, to the amount of 800, guns etc. fell into our hands (we never had above 120 in the action, but nothing could exceed the manner in which they were served) and the Prussians being quite fresh played the very deuce with the retreating army. From first to last the Duke did not make a single mistake, whilst Bounaparte made a very great one in allowing the English army to retire as they did on the Saturday; had he forced on an engagement on that day the consequences I am satisfied must have been fatal. If the Duke had not succeeded on the field I am satisfied he never would have left it alive. There was but one road by which a retreat could have been thought of, and it was so clogged up with all sorts of waggons that it would have been impossible for 500 men ever to have reached Brussels, and then they of course could not have escaped.

## Back in England

After Waterloo, Wellington's reputation, for as long as he might live, was invulnerable. For not only had he brought to his knees the greatest soldier of the age, but, after the tension of a long war had been relaxed, he had rescued his country from a nightmare shock. No doubt scores of such letters and thousands of personal narrations passed from the field of Waterloo to the homes and hearts of the people never to be forgotten. If he had been vainglorious, he might have become a bore, but in fact he was the most modest of men. If he had been sanctimonious he might have sat on a pedestal, but he was very human, he had his family troubles and he liked little children— and the ladies. In 1825—10 years after Waterloo—the diary of E. J. Littleton records: 'I dined today with the Duke of Wellington, and sat next to the two Chief Justices—to whom I spoke of the Memoirs of Harriette Wilson, the celebrated courtezan, who beats the D. of Wellington unmercifully. As Chief Justice Best was going away, he whispered to me "Send me that book, bring it to me in Bedford Square after Church tomorrow".'[1] When he returned to politics (for in his youth he had been in the Irish Parliament with a junior household office), he might have strained the constitution, but in fact, with unswerving loyalty, he played the constitutional game from first to last. A test case arose in October 1827, when he was commander-in-chief and out of office. The Governor-in-Chief of Canada commanded the forces there. Would the Duke claim a veto over a civil appointment carrying with it military command? Huskisson feared it would be so and indulged in his all too habitual language of contingent resignation. But the Duke accepted the Cabinet's nominee and concluded a friendly letter to Goderich, 'You may rely upon it that I am not at all disposed to render that mode of proceeding inconvenient to His Majesty's Government or injurious to his service.'

The change of office involved the appointment of Lord Dalhousie to command in India: and again the Duke was accommodating. He writes to Huskisson:

I understand that Ld. Wm. Bentinck, who is the Governor General, approves of the appointment of Ld. Dalhousie to be CiC. in India; and it

---

[1] There is a modern edition, with a preface by James Laver. Her sister Sophia managed things better, marrying a peer and becoming Lady Berwick of Attingham.

appears the wish of H.M.'s servants that he be appointed to that situation, and I have nothing to object to in the arrangement.

Ever, my dear Huskisson,

Yours most sincerely,

Wellington

In his long life he did only one mean and wicked thing; and that the perversity of the age condoned—Jeremy B. excepted. In 1829, having ordered the about turn over Catholic Emancipation, and having then been denounced by Lord Winchilsea as a Papist in disguise, he called him out. The Duke, who was a bad shot, meant to hit but missed. Winchilsea magnanimously fired into the air. If he had killed the Duke, he would have been flayed alive. If the Duke had killed him, it would have been necessary to the public peace to hush it up or distort the nature of the provocation. 'We're playing at duelling, Dukey. Shew us how a dead-er topples into a ditch.' Not pleasant to think of! But his luck held, he missed Lord Winchilsea, and as Chancellor of Oxford University gave him an Honorary Degree.

## Wellington and Huskisson

Temperamentally, need it be said, the two were poles asunder, and this turned sympathy to antipathy. For in their ideals and conception of public service, and in what in their different fields they in fact accomplished, they were complementary rather than rival. Wellington, it may be remembered (1769-1852) was Huskisson's senior only by one year.

In February 1797 Colonel Wesley reached Calcutta. In the same month by an order in Council, confirmed by an Act of 3 May 1797, the Bank of England suspended Cash Payments. In 1819, the year after Wellington, now the uncrowned king of Europe, had settled off his own bat the ticklish problem of war reparations, getting all to agree and taking nothing for England, Parliament determined upon the Resumption of Cash Payments. If Waterloo had gone against us, Cash Payments would have been as far away as they were in 1810. But the prestige of England made London now the undisputed capital of the world's finance. Wellington secured the peace of Europe, Castlereagh devised the concert of Europe; and on this twin foundation Huskisson was able to build a network of commercial reciprocity by treaties of commerce with every country, whether in Europe or the New World, that was prepared to sign them. There were those among the countries of Europe who came to think that England had caught them off their balance and committed them to unprofitable arrangements, but certain it is that Wellington desired to perpetuate peace and that Huskisson had no desire to impose unequal treaties either on Europe or Asia. When he is revising the Navigation Laws, he is always saying to his colleagues 'Our Navigation Law still forbids this and that: we must in fairness allow the same exceptions to others'. But he was not a cosmopolitan after the fashion of Cobden and Bright; his purpose was to consolidate that second British Empire which the victories of Nelson and Wellington had brought into being.

If only the Duke would keep to soldiering, Huskisson's lot would be a happy one. 'I wish to see him directing its [the country's] energies and presiding over its military character. He is the guardian of that character in the eyes of the world; a world jealous of our greatness' (Huskisson to Arbuthnot, 23 April 1827). But it was not to be.

There were two rounds in the Corn Law battle, and Wellington won them both. It was a barren victory, for whereas Huskisson was trying to reshape the Corn Laws in conformity with changing conditions of production and consumption, Wellington treated it as a military manoeuvre. There was a citadel to defend. If there was a leak, it must be stopped up. If the enemy (i.e. foreign corn) threatened to infiltrate, the defences must be strengthened: and no nonsense about it. It was not a question of misunderstanding technical detail. He had a flair for figures and knew what they meant. But whereas the purpose of Huskisson (as also of Lord Liverpool and Canning) was to restore an open trade in corn, such as the country enjoyed in pre-war days when corn flowed freely in and out, the purpose of the Duke and the landed interest was to consolidate, without regard to the course of trade, the near-monopoly which they had enjoyed in a generation of war.

Round I was in May-June 1827, when the Canning Administration was pressing forward a new general corn bill which never reached the statute book. The Duke in the Lords carried an amendment relating to the warehousing system, claiming that he had Huskisson's consent to it. Huskisson declared that the Duke had misinterpreted his letter, as no doubt was the case. But he had made the tactical blunder of communicating with the Duke without securing in advance the assent of Goderich, the Government leader in the Lords. Goderich saw the danger of the amendment. 'If it goes forward, it will be received favourably by all of whatever party who carp at the Bill and want some amendment or modification' (1 June 1827 —Goderich to Huskisson). And he was non-plussed when the Duke said he had Huskisson's assent in his pocket. Lord Melville, the First Lord of the Admiralty, reflected the general bewilderment, when he wrote to Huskisson:

What is the meaning of this strange misunderstanding and confusion as to the Duke of Wellington's Corn clauses? He shewed me your note about $\frac{1}{2}$ an hour before he moved the clause, and tho' it was obvious that it might be fatal to the Bill in point of H. of C. form, I had no doubt that if the Lords had made no other alterations (except such as Goderich consented to) another Bill might be brought in conformable to your suggestion, and I decided to vote for the clause in the express belief that such would be the case. It appears to me that our friend G. does not treat the Duke in the House very decorously in objecting to a clause which *YOU* had suggested, subject of course to the difficulty or the inconvenience on the point of form.

Poor G.! The amendment was fatal. Huskisson, pathetically anxious to have the Duke with him, had walked into a trap. It was cold comfort to be told by the Duke, 'As you say that I misunderstood the meaning of your letter of the 24th I must have done so' (4 June). For next day the Duke went on to say, 'In respect to the Bill being thrown out in consequence of this among other amendments, that is a matter that depends entirely on the Government.'

By September of this year (22 September 1827) Huskisson was telling Lord Carlisle that 'the career of politics at home is certainly the most uncertain and hazardous of all the lotteries of life'.

Round II was in the early months of 1828, when the Corn Bill, which became law as 9 Geo. 4, c. 60 after Huskisson and his friends had resigned, was on its Parliamentary way. Into the machinery of this Act and its place in the history of agricultural policy, it is not proposed to enter here, but only into the tactics of it. Huskisson, warned by 1827, feared that the Duke would interpolate extras and communicated his misgiving to Peel, who passed it on to Goulburn, who replied, 'For myself I own I cannot conceive his [the Duke] having the opinion imputed by Huskisson.' With Grant at the Board of Trade forecasting chaos to the grain trade, and Wellington as Premier urging political necessity, 'I think we could carry a measure such as that which I have above detailed. We cannot carry anything short of it', Huskisson was between two fires. Supported by Peel he secured concessions, the Duke yielding something in point of duty, Grant something in point of time at which changes in the scale should take effect. But Grant was uneasy, thought the whole thing discreditable and only under urgent personal pressure agreed to move the corn resolutions in their final form. When Grant threatened to resign, Huskisson begged him 'for God's sake' not to: 'it will bring my public life to a close in bitterness.' But tactically it would have been an excellent issue on which to withdraw, instead of on the ridiculous East Retford issue of two months later. This time it was Huskisson who offered his resignation, and he was not allowed by the Duke to draw back from it—it was resignation, and 'no mistake'. How unreal the final quarrel was is shown by a reminiscence in the *Greville Diary*.[1]

16 August 1848
I heard an anecdote at Nuneham which was new to me; Harcourt gave

[1] There is a contemptible mis-appreciation of Huskisson in the *Diary* for 18 September 1830, ending 'however, he was (unfortunately) one of the first men in the House, and was listened to with attention upon any subject'.

it on the authority of Sir Robert Peel. He said that, when the discussion took place about the East Retford question during the Duke of Wellington's Govt., *in the Cabinet* Peel was for giving the representation to one of the great towns and Huskisson was against it; that Peel was overruled by a majority of his colleagues and consequently took the part he did in Parliament; while Huskisson was induced to change his opinion and to take in Parliament the opposite line from that which he had taken in the Cabinet; he and Peel, in fact, both changing sides. His colleagues were naturally very indignant with Huskisson, and this accounts for the bitterness which the Duke of Wellington evinced, and for his celebrated 'No mistake'.

Greville indulges in sententious moralising about the discredit to both statesmen. The biographer of Huskisson reflects how easily he could have defied the Duke, if he had not committed himself to paper. For Peel (assuming the story to be true) could not have forced a quarrel with Huskisson on this issue, and without Peel, Wellington was powerless.

## 1848

By 1848 the Duke was an oracle and an institution—the man to whom everyone touched his hat in the street, the man who said this or that which every informed person was expected to know and hastened to pass on. And 1848 was the year of his last military achievement when he saved London from spoliation by the Chartists, from 'something like the siege of Jerusalem on a far larger scale'—to employ the bravura of Macaulay.

The City and the West End played up, and Lady Palmerston in one of her last letters to Mrs Huskisson tells her what a grand day Carlton Gardens had:

C. Gardens
Friday (1848)

My Dear Mrs. Huskisson,

Your letter reminded me that I ought to have given you private details of our *revolution* as the papers tho' very full could only give the public ones. Our Terrace was divided into districts all the servants made Special Constables—Ld Arundel commanded the other side of the Column and Mr. Tomline with Ld Kildare this one. The arrangements were excellent everywhere, 2,000 real Police stationed in Trafalgar Square & Regent St. & Cockspur St., where it was thought there would be a fight.

The Admiralty and all the offices were garrisoned & provisioned as if for a siege, cannon placed on the Bridges & the Duke of Wellington's arrangements so beautifully made with Corps stationed & pickets between, that they said a force of 10,000 could be collected at any given point in a few minutes—and these arrangements were his own, & everybody was in admiration of his calmness & judgment just as in the olden time when he got upon his old ground of glory. There certainly was great alarm in all quarters, the uncertainty of what number of disaffected might come in from the manufacturing districts & the very great number of foreigners in this Country, French, Poles & Germans & the daily arrival of many more, known to be revolutionists from Paris of the very worst character.

This, with all that has occur'd lately in Europe, made one of course anxious to avoid no precautions that could be taken, and I am sure it is very fortunate that the whole thing has occur'd as it has shown the good spirit of our middle classes, and almost one may say of the whole population of London as well as the activity and courage of the Aristocracy.

Meanwhile, the Chartist procession had wended its peaceful way from Kennington Common to the House of Commons. (Alfred Marshall once told me that the sight of it was his first childhood memory.) The petition weighed 5 cwt. 84 lb. and among the signatures were Victoria Rex and the Duke of Wellington.

Disraeli took its measure, and in 1867 rebuilt the Conservative Party by granting the Chartist demand-in-chief, which was not bread or circuses, but a citizen's vote.

# CHAPTER FOUR

# SILK AND SPECULATION

*If the honourable member alluded to the Company which had been formed to promote the growth of silk in Ireland, he would explain, in a few words, all the connection he had had with that Company. When the parties who had projected it came to the Board of Trade, he had specifically stated to them, that though he thought it a desirable experiment, and wished it to have a fair trial, and though, under other circumstances, he might have felt disposed to take an interest in it, yet, considering the situation he held, as President of the Board of Trade, he could not expose himself to the mis-apprehension that would be likely to arise from his so doing. When the parties applied to him, to know what number of shares would be taken, he informed them, that there must have been some misconception as to the intentions of the Government, which was desirous only of giving that degree of countenance to the experiment, which might facilitate the object of providing employment to a large portion of the population of Ireland. Such was the nature of this application, and such the answer which had been given on the part of the Government; and he defied the honourable gentleman to point out a single speculation, of any description, with which he had had the slightest connection, either directly or indirectly.*

—Huskisson in Speech on Joint Stock Companies,
5 December 1826. (*Speeches* III, 71-2)

## THE DOCUMENTS IN THE CASE

1. *Liverpool Papers, 38,276*

Memorandum from the Inspector General of Excise, Custom House, Dublin, 20 April 1819:

In some of the mountainous counties of Ireland and particularly in the County of Donegal illicit distillation has been carried on from time immemorial and has been the principal occupation of almost the whole population for several generations. The suppression of a practice so general and so ancient must be considered as little short of a complete revolution in the habits and manners of the people, and it cannot be expected that any law, however vigorous, will effect such a change either suddenly or without exciting much clamour.

But by the fining system (under the Townshend Fining Laws, originating with the Irish Parliament in 1783) the practice is much reduced, as compared with 4 or 5 years ago. Yet some smuggling will continue in the wilds of Donegal and Tyrone, while the duties remaining on spirits exist.

There are now at work in and about the County of Donegal 6 licensed distilleries, all of which have been erected subsequent to the revival of the fining system.

### 2. *Hatherton Diary*,[1] *1819-20*

Homeward bound: 3 hours at the Calais customs: news just received of the death of the Duke of Kent. 'By the event of his death [23 January 1820] the Infant Princess whom he has left stands Heiress to the throne of England—after the Dukes of York and Clarence, who at present have no children and both of whom are bad livers, thus affording the probability of a Regency during the minority of the Infant some future day.'

'Mrs. L had smuggled shamefully in her pockets, her pelisse, her work baskets, full of contraband articles—besides which she had without my knowledge taken the horse hair out of the cushions of the carriage, and filled them with silk stockings and ribbons. The carriage would have been forfeited, if the fraud had been discovered, but she rode off with them triumphantly.'

Joy at seeing England again. 'The great mixture of corn, grass and woodland and the glorious prospect of the Thames... crowded with vessels from all parts of the world. . . . Then the rapidity of travelling, the neatness and expedition in the inns, what a contrast with Germany.'

### 3. *Patent Rolls of George IV*

1823. 18 March. Doth give and grant unto Richard Badnall the younger, his excrs. especial licence for the sole use and benefit of his improvements in the throwing, winding or spinning of sewing silks within England Wales and Berwick on Tweed for 14 years.

*do* for dying (1823): *do* for winding, spinning or twisting of silk, wool etc. (1825): *do* for improvements in the manufacture of silk (1825).

---

[1] Not always a day-to-day diary: sometimes, as here, written up for a period.

4. *Customs Instructions in the Minute Book of the Customs*

16 July 1823. Officers in London and at Dover enjoined to use their utmost endeavours to prevent smuggling by Passengers having goods concealed on their persons, taking care, in all cases, to make their search, particularly in the case of Females, with the utmost delicacy and circumspection. And should the officers in a proper exercise of a sound discretion be proceeded against, the Board will protect them.

Persons of Females (Searchers). Great care is to be taken in the selection of the Women by whom the search must be made.

5. *Hatherton Diary, 1824-5*

Dec. 18. 1824. Crossed the Channel in the tiny steam vessel in 4 hours. There was on board a French Government Messenger—whom a drunken and noisy Englishman wanted to fight, because the former would not shake hands with him. At the Custom House at Dover all Mrs. Littleton's gloves, shoes and ribbons were seized as contraband. I tried in vain to procure their restoration. After dinner Mrs. Littleton, though very unwell with the crossing, went and wheedled the principal officer of the Department to relinquish them one by one; sitting down in the examining room amidst 50 passengers and hundreds of trunks, with all her own 'effets' being strewed before her. Finding that there were a few things so fairly forfeited that the officer could not give them up, she engaged him in conversation, and catching up first a Neapolitan silk hankerchief, pretended she had dropped it, and then picking it up tied it round her neck; then she threw a pair of shoes into her trunk again by admirable leger-de-main and whipped up $\frac{1}{2}$ a dozen pair of shoes. A search being made for the latter, she was obliged to relinquish them, laughing and saying 'Oh, I can't give *them* up. Well if I give them up, will you give me all my ribbons? They are only sashes for each gown,' each one yard long! Her entreaties and her anxiety about them seemed to win their hearts, and with a shake of the head, they abandoned all their prey, except a few gloves and hankerchiefs; the latter presents sent by her daughter to Lady Harrowby.

Slept at Sittingbourne.

### 6. *Hatherton Diary, September 1824-March 1825*

We arrived at Teddesley the day before X'Mas day [1824] having been absent not quite 4 months.

The interval from X'Mas to the meeting of Parliament I spent principally in hunting with my stag hounds and pheasant shooting. I had but few good runs. . . . I had very excellent sport pheasant shooting and we killed about 5 or 6 hundred, and had some pheasant parties in the house. My friend Wilmot Horton was at one of them, and was the means of embarking me in one of the new speculations now become so prevalent. While he was with me, he received a letter from Mr. Rundell, one of the great Jewellers and Goldsmiths in Ludgate Hill, asking him if he would become a Director of a Company they were forming to work mines in South America. Mr. Wilmot Horton and this firm had already united in contracting with the Columbian and Mexican Govts. for the Pearl Fishery on the Coasts of both oceans. They had published a prospectus and sent out vessels with Diving Bells, which had never been employed in the Fishery before. The Public took the thing—and my friend W. Horton has made 12,000£ by sale of Shares and may make 50,000 if he likes. But the Govt. would not permit him to put his name to another joint stock company, and I therefore beseeched him on the occasion of the formation of the General South American Mining Association to recommend me in his place. I accordingly to my surprize was appointed President—the Company it appears was formed immediately on mines being offered to Messrs. Rundell and Bridge, and as our Prospectus states, it is for procuring and working of mines. We have agents despatched to Columbia to examine those that are offered, and to Peru for a similar purpose, and we are now looking for a person to send to Mexico. On my arrival in town on 3rd of Febr. 1825 I found all the world mad about Schemes. Places and names never heard of stand in Prospectus as mines to be worked or lands to be cultivated. Nothing is too extravagant. No man thinks of the result, as no man buys shares to keep them. Therefore the only thing sought for is a fresh scheme to job in. A friend of mine, intending to do me a kindness, put my name down for 20 shares in the Columbian Agricultural schemes, I sent them to my banker desiring him to sell the shares forthwith. He did so in five minutes the next morning and for what cost me 100 £ I received 420 £.

I had three parties called on me one morning about new schemes. One was a joint stock co. to work the Ribden Copper Mines belonging to Lord Shrewsbury in Staffordshire.[1] I believe this to be a sound scheme, but I declined it. Another was, to make a company to fish choral in the Mediterranean under a grant from the Dey of Tunis. But I disliked the aspect of the concern, knowing how cheaply it is worked near the places where it is taken, and not quite liking the security.

A third party was to raise a company to cultivate silk in Ireland and in the Colonies. Though part of this scheme, the Irish part, appears the most visionary of all, I have undertaken this. It appears that in Italy many cultivators have lately taken their Silk Worms into Store Rooms; especially Count Dandolo, with the greatest success. This does away with the difficulty of managing the animal in this climate. Then we know that the mulberry will thrive very well either in England or in Ireland. The only difficulty will be to delay the hatching of the eggs till the mulberry is in leaf. I am sanguine we shall succeed by selecting sheltered spots and southern aspects for the trees, by keeping the eggs covered as long as we can with safety, and by preparing a crop of lettuce for the first fortnight of the animal's existence. I have taken the Projector Mr. Badnall and Mr. Spilsbury—both gentlemen living near Leek in Staffordshire—to Lord Lansdowne, Lord Liverpool, Mr. Huskisson and several other business personages in the Govt. and in opposition, and have prevailed on them not only to unite in patronising the scheme

---

[1] Ribden, Staffs: N. of Alton, and 7 miles W. of Ashbourne. 'There is a copper mine at Ribden, and the foundations of a smelting furnace at "Blazing Star"; but the former was discontinued in 1827, and the latter many years before' (W. White, *History, Gazeteer of Staffs* 1834, p. 725).

by lending their name, but on the Govt. to give us a Charter.
The subject has been discussed at a Cabinet meeting, for Lord
Liverpool and Huskisson doubted the propriety of lending
their names to a joint stock company in these wild times. However, the direction of Capital towards Ireland influenced them
to assent. The greatest names as Political Economists and Men
of Science have joined us, and the thing is going on well, and
appears to excite much conversation.

7. *Annual Register for 1824* (quoted in Tooke, *History of Prices,*
  II, 150-2)
    The mines of Mexico was a phrase which suggested to every
imagination unbounded wealth; and three companies—the
Real del Monte Association, the United Mexican, and the
Anglo-Mexican,—were formed for the purpose of extracting
wealth from their bowels by English capital, machinery, and
skill. Similar companies were formed, in the course of the year
for working the mines of Chili, of Brazil, of Peru, and of the
Provinces of the Rio de la Plata, and for prosecuting the pearl
fishery on the coast of Columbia. . . .

8. *B. Blackmantle*, Vol. II. *The English Spy 1826*

### BUBBLES OF 1825

    The doctor leaves his patient—the pedagogue his Lexicon,
    For mines of Real Monte, or for those of Anglo-Mexican:
    E'en *Chili* bonds don't cool the rage, nor those still more romantic, sir.
    For new canals to join the seas, Pacific and Atlantic, sir.

    Investment Banks to lend a lift to people who are undone—
    Proposals for Assurance—there's no end of that in London;
    And one among the number who in Parliament now press their bills
    For lending cash at 8 per cent on coats and inexpressibles.

    When Greenwich coaches go by steam on roads of iron railing, sir
    How pleasant it will be to see a dozen in a line;
    And ships of heavy burden over hills and valleys sailing, sir
    Shall cross from Bristol's Channel to the Tweed or Tyne.

But the most inviting scheme of all is one proposed for carrying
Large furnaces to melt the ice which hems poor CAPTAIN PARRY in[1]
They'll then have steamboats twice a week to all the newly-seen land,
And call for goods and passengers at Labrador and Greenland.

[And now in 1950 early breakfast in Iceland and lunch after Goose
Bay].

## 9. *Hatherton Correspondence 1817-25*

Huskisson to Littleton                    Eartham, 9 January 1825
    I return you Mr. R. Badnall's letter. I am delighted to hear
from all quarters of the progress making in the Silk Manufac-
tory. It is a pleasure to see that my anticipations are likely to be
realised and I may therefore hope that Baring himself will be
reconverted to liberal ideas on this subject. With these feelings
you will largely understand that I did not read with indifference
Mr. Badnall's account of the ample share which his invention
is likely to contribute to our improvement and future superiority in the manufacture. I honour the feeling which has dic-
tated the wish of Mr. B. to be allowed to present his models to
the King and to explain the nature and advantages of his improvements to H.M. Mr. B.'s object, I perceive, is to obtain a
private interview for this purpose. Now certainly I cannot say
what H.M. would decide, if applied to for such an interview;
but I have, so far as I can recollect, never heard of such an
application. The reason of my ignorance may be perhaps, that
in the ordinary course such an application would not go through
the Minister. The proper channel for it (if it is to be made at
all) would be one of the officers in attendance upon H.M. as
part of his household, probably Sir W. Knighton. What that
officer would do upon receiving such an application I cannot
venture to anticipate, tho' it is my own impression that it is not
usual for the King to go into the details and particulars of
mechanical improvements of this sort, however much justified.
He always is to know generally that they have been made, and

---

[1] In August 1948 Mr Anderson, a tailor of Orford, Suffolk (who possesses a set of livery but-
tons, as used at Sudbourne, from Ld. Hertford's time onward) shewed me in his book of press
cuttings the photo of an old sailor buried in Orford Churchyard,—John Green, 1797-1892—
'The last survivor of the Hecla in Capt. Parry's Expedition of 1820'.

L

that they are largely conducive to the wealth and prosperity and the industrious classes of his subjects.

Mr. B.'s other discovery, by which a bull's hide is to be changed into a piece of good leather, almost as rapidly as Harlequin's change of dress, is a more striking proof of the advantage which science is every day conferring upon the useful arts. I hope you will stand in this leather when you rise in your place to anathematise all railways . . .

10. *Hatherton Diary 1824-5*

12 March [1825]—In our Silk Company there are 5 of us, who call ourselves Projectors and we all meet at breakfast today at my house to discuss our concern. We shall have 10,000 shares at £100 each and call for 5 £ deposit forthwith. We propose to keep 4000 shares for ourselves, give 200 to each Director, 50 to each Vice President and leave 2000 for the Public. We have among us a Mr. Heathcote, a Devonshire man, who has 140,000 Mulberry Trees on the ground or rather had— for 40,000 of them are now on their voyage to Lord Kingston's estate in Ireland. Mr. H. was about to try the experiment on his own account. But has joined us.

16 March [1825]—Attended a Meeting of our unlimited Corporation for the introduction of the culture of the Silkworm at the King's Head Tavern—Poultry, Lord Auckland in the Chair. We revised and settled our List of Honorary Members and Corporators—and touched on the delicate question of a Division of the Shares. We agreed to divide into 20,000 of 50 £ each; and claimed 8000 for ourselves the Projectors—including Mr. Rothshild and our Solicitor and Banker, and 2000 Shares for distribution among our own friends which would leave each of the 5 Projectors 1000 each.

19 March [1825]—Mr. Rundell having called on me to tell me he had heard of a thing likely to benefit the Genl. South Amn. Mining Association, we had a long conversation about it. It turns out that 30 years ago the King, wishing to improve the Income of the Duke of York and not liking to appeal to Parlt. for an additional Annuity for him, gave him a part of the Mines,

belonging to the Crown in Nova Scotia. A misunderstanding, however, arose as to the extent of this Grant. The Treasury insisting it was limited to certain mines only. There is one Silver mine there, and another of Copper, with Coal near—on the Sea Coast—But they have none of them been proved. We accordingly agreed to see Mr. Wilmot Horton at the Colonial Office; and there we ascertained all the facts. From there we proceeded to York House, where we had a long conversation with Sir Herbert Taylor, H.R. Highness's Confidential Secretary: who recounted to us all that had passed on the subject—and hailing our offer to take the Grant off His R. Highness's hands, paying him a percentage on profits, made me write him a letter on the subject, saying it would enable the Duke to bring the matter to a termination with the Treasury. He said we could not have come at a more fortunate moment, for H.R.H. was poverty itself,—and in fact, Mr. Rundell told me, as we were leaving the house, that two solicitors were in council there at the same time, as to the best means of raising the means for the year.

11. *Huskisson Papers, 38,746*
The Countess of Egremont writes to Huskisson for some shares in the 'British, Irish and Colonial Silk Co.'
Huskisson replies briefly that he is Honorary President only (14 April 1825).

12. *Patent Rolls of George IV*
30th day of July 1825 doth give, grant, constitute declare and appoint that Joshua Walker and others shall be called, one Body Politic and Corporate by the name of the British Irish and Colonial Silk Co. to continue for ever and doth grant unto them divers privileges.

13. *The Parchment Roll*
(P.R.O. C66 14294) Twelfth Part of Patents in 6th Year of King Geo. IV.
Charter of Incorporation of the British, Irish and Colonial Silk Company.
Whereas the material from which Silks are manufactured in

Great Britain is principally if not wholly supplied from foreign parts and the manufacture and purchase thereof are attended with very great expence.

And whereas if by the breeding and rearing the Silk Worm in the United Kingdom of Great Britain and Ireland or in Our Dominions abroad sufficient of Silk for the purposes of manufacture would be obtained so as to supersede the necessity of importing into the United Kingdom Silk and Silk in the Cocoon.

And whereas it has been represented to us that the Mulberry Trees from whose leaves the food of the Silk Worm is principally produced may be planted and brought to perfection in Our United Kingdom of Great Britain and Ireland etc. . . .

And whereas Joshua Walker of London, Banker: Richard Badnall the younger and Francis Gibbon Spilsbury, manufacturers of Leek Co. Stafford: John Heathcote of Tiverton Devon, Lace manufacturer: have satisfied themselves that Silk might be obtained at prices which would be productive of the greatest advantages to the manufacturers of Silk in this Country, the climate of Ireland and Great Britain being suitable.

And whereas the processes of raising and tending worms would employ a great number of men, women and children especially in Ireland,

And whereas much time and large outlay are required for the undertaking

We do constitute Joshua Walker, Richard Badnall, Gibbon Spilsbury, John Heathcote, George Baron Auckland, Sir Robert Farquhar Bart, Alexander Baring, George Harrison, William Manning, Nathan Mayer Rothschild, John Plummer, Robert Hart Davis, Moses Montefiore. . . . 'The British Irish and Colonial Silk Company', with power to introduce, breed and rear silkworms and to spin, twist and throw the silk: the said Company to raise not exceeding £1 million, to be subscribed in Shares, and the Subscribers to shares in capital to be entitled to act as auditor and examiner, if possessed of 50 shares at least. . . .

(Long detail follows about the holdings of meetings and procedure thereat. Littleton's name does not appear as a fifth projector nor among the original shareholders.)

14. *Hatherton Correspondence, 1817-25*
Wilmot Horton to Littleton                    September 1825.

You have embarrassed my Rundell & Co. a good deal by your refusal after the consent which your silence had given (of taking some shares in a Pearl Fishery Co.[1]). On the score of prudence I think you need not hesitate as you will make from £3 to 5,000 to a moral certainty by the job—the interest of which at 5% I expect that you will specifically lay out in the preservation and increase of game and of gratitude to me. Your remarks on the salary plan are very good. We will discuss it when we meet. Francis Leveson and Fleming move the address in the Commons, Dudley in the Lords.

Ld. Bathurst told me yesterday that Lady Stanhope says that she has followed him (Dudley) on the shore at Brighton where he has been repeating his speech and that what she has heard is very good.

Did you hear what Byron said to him many years ago, in fact about one year after he ratted? Ward said to Mackintosh at Mad. de Stael's dinner, after much persiflage 'I suppose I should not find it difficult to be rewigged'. Byron answered 'But I take it you must be re-*warded* first.'

(Bathurst was Wilmot Horton's chief. John William Ward, then Viscount Dudley and Ward, was created Earl of Dudley in 1827.)

15. *Sir Robert Wilson to Littleton*
                                              6 October 1825

My Dear L,

        I see we are launched and have no doubt we shall reach the Port of Eldorado. Many many thanks to you for my proportionate share of cargo, be the share what it may.

The state of the Silk Market in England is made known opportunely and must tend to make our experiments more popular. It is certainly the most patriotic establishment that has as yet been projected....

                    Lord Hatherton's note.

(Sir Robert Wilson 1777-1849. General and Governor of Gibraltar: M.P. for Southwark 1826.)

16. *Hatherton Correspondence, 1817-25*

Ossington, 16 November 1825

J. E. Denison to Littleton

I think you draw a very true tho' no agreeable picture of Newcastle. You don't hear of any quiet snug corner into which a body might creep? If Wilmot chooses to throw his pearls before swine I daresay the produce of his diving bells will bring in [*illegible* a pile?]. I find it hard to draw 5 or 6 thousand pounds from a stiff clay soil.

(Denison, later Speaker of the House of Commons, had coal properties in Durham where Littleton had recently toured and an estate in Ossington, Notts., from which he took his title.)

17. *Hatherton Correspondence, 1817-25*

Wilmot Horton to Littleton            16 November 1825

I am richer than I need be but somehow or other I should not like to be poorer. I don't think much of the Darlington case —the level ground is the uphill question in a railroad.

(The Stockton and Darlington Railway was opened on 27 September 1825.)

18. *Hatherton Correspondence, 1817-25*

Wilmot Horton to Littleton            9 December 1825

Lord Clanricarde wrote from Huskisson's, where he was staying, to his Banker to purchase him half a lottery ticket on the day preceding the drawing, and le lendemain he received the satisfactory hint that he was to pocket 15,000 for the said half—No 10 976.

18a. *N.B.* The Marquis of Clanricarde (1802-74) married Canning's daughter in 1825. The last lottery was drawn in October 1826. Robinson, as Chancellor of the Exchequer, was responsible for the act abolishing them—4 Geo. 4 c. 60. Hence the contemporary doggerel:

O Fred'rick Robinson thou man of death!
Our scanty pittance why should you begrudge it?
Why oh! why thus in dudgeon stop our breath,
And shut us cruelly from out thy budget?'

## 19. *The Greville Diary*

20 February 1826

So great and absorbing is the interest which the present discussions excite that all men are become political economists and
financiers, and everybody is obliged to have an opinion.

21 February 1826

Old Rundell (of the house of Rundell and Bridge, the great
silversmiths and jewellers) died last week. Rundell was eighty
years old, and died worth between 1,400,000 L and 1,500,000
L, the greater part of which is vested in the funds.

## 20. *Huskisson's Speeches, II, 512*

*Exposition of the effects of the Free Trade System on the Silk
Manufacture*, 24 February 1826: extract.

. . . In a printed letter from a manufacturer of Macclesfield to
the Marquis of Lansdowne, I find the following anecdote:—
'It is the custom, in the parterres of the theatres in France to
secure the place, by tying a pocket handkerchief on the seat. I
had the curiosity, at the Theatre François, to notice the appearance of them; and, out of twenty-five, immediately around me,
there was not one Silk handkerchief.' I should have little doubt,
if a similar custom prevailed in the pit of our theatre, that this
accurate observer would find most of the seats decorated with
handkerchiefs of prohibited Silk. Nay, Sir, if strangers were, at
this moment, ordered to withdraw from the gallery; and every
member were called upon (of course in secret committee) to
produce his handkerchief, with the understanding, that those
who had not prohibited handkerchiefs in their pockets were
obliged to inform against those who had—I am inclined to
believe, that the informers would be in a small majority. Upon
every information laid under this prohibitory law, the chances
are, that the informer and the constable have Bandanas round

their necks, and that the magistrate, who hears the charge, has one in his pocket!

## 21. *Salary of the President of the Board of Trade*

### (House of Commons Debate, 6 April 1826)[1]

Mr. Robertson . . . begged to call their attention to a Charter which had last year been granted by the President of the Board of Trade, to incorporate a certain silk company, at the head of which stood the name of Alexander Baring; and he could not but consider it a very singular coincidence, that early in June last, a short time after that charter had been granted, Mr. Baring had risen in his place to propose an increase of salary to the President of the Board of Trade. He need not remind the House, that the profits of this company were to arise from the propagation of silk-worms, and it was expected to prove a most lucrative speculation. He therefore could not but feel that there must have been some secret understanding between the parties.

Mr. Baring . . ., with respect to the allusion which had been made to the company of which he had become a member, begged leave to offer some explanation. The silk company was established last year, with a view of benefiting Ireland, and with that view he had lent his name to the concern; and his expectations consequently could not have been very highly excited. . . . He had never exchanged a word with the President of the Board of Trade concerning this company.

Mr. Secretary Peel said that if the knowledge of what passed then was confined within the walls of the House, it would be ludicrous in him to notice the charge of the honourable member for Grampound; and he only did so for the purpose of repeating the declaration which had been already made by his right honourable friend (*Huskisson*), that he had lent his name to that company honourably, and without the slightest hope of participating in its advantages. If it drew to itself all the wealth of the Indies, his right honourable friend would not derive a single farthing from it; and when the honourable gentleman imputed

[1] Cf. Huskisson's *Speeches*, II, 535-7.

to the honourable member for Taunton, that on account of the miserable profits which he might realise from a venture of 200 L., he (*Baring*) was induced deliberately to propose an increase of the salary of his right honourable friend; he would only look for the answer to so unfounded an imputation, in the smile which sat upon every face the moment it was uttered.[1]

22. *Hatherton Correspondence, 1826*
Robert Percy ('Bobus') Smith to Littleton
Cheam, 23 October 1826

Here—doing nothing, pure unadulterated nothing. Not as you and your foolish neighbours do nothing—scampering after hounds, worrying poachers, getting bastards and committing clowns for that same, but sitting in the shade when it was hot and in the sun when it was cool, with my jaws half open and as happy as I can fancy a thriving turnip to be. . . .

I agree with you the distress of the country has been much exaggerated. At the same time there is something in the frequent recurrence and long continuance of these distresses which staggers one, and almost makes one doubt whether our plan of society is a safe or happy one for the most of the people. Their condition generally better, but it is surely much more precarious than in countries much worse governed, and that enters deeply into the estimate of human happiness. For I can do without a thousand things which it makes me wretched to lose, and therefore I will trouble Mr. Bumpkins to continue paying the dividends.

(R. P. ('Bobus') Smith, elder brother of Sydney Smith. Cheam was Wilmot Horton's place in Surrey.)

23. *Peel Papers, 40,390*
William Congreve to Peel                              24 November 1826

Disclaims responsibility for the affairs of the Arigna Mining Co.

---

[1] Huskisson had hitherto drawn no salary as President of the Board of Trade, but had £3000 as Treasurer of the Navy. The upshot of the debate was that the proposed sole salary of £5000 for the President was withdrawn, and instead Huskisson got £2000 as President, £3000 as Treasurer of the Navy: £5000 in all.

(Arigna, a mineral district, Co. Roscommon, in the Vale of Arigna rivulet, an affluent of the Shannon: coal and iron were formerly worked and limestone is abundant. Sir William Congreve, 1772-1828, was the inventor of the Congreve rocket.)

### 24. *Hatherton Correspondence, 1827*

Huskisson to Littleton                                    17 July 1827

... As a parting job, here is a bit of business for you: as it is to you that I owe the Honour or (as someone wished to make out) the Scrape of being President of la Grande Compagnie, as it is called in the enclosed letter.

I saw the Mr. Beardmore to whom the writer refers, last year. Since then I had heard nothing more upon the subject till I received the enclosed.

I am not sufficiently conversant with Silk to form any opinion upon the discoveries claimed by my Correspondent. But I believe there is something, perhaps deserving attention, in what he is able to suggest.

The little Pacquet of Silk which accompanied his letter, and which I now forward to you, appears to me to be very beautiful; but you will have an opportunity, if you think it worth while to move at all in the business, to decide upon its merits.

It is but fair that I should also enclose a copy of my answer to the Frenchman, in which you will see that I have been very discreet in not naming the *Membre du Parlement*, to whom I confide his correspondence. This is enough of business for a man that ought to avoid doing any.

I hope to return in autumn—if not a giant, at least refreshed.

### 25. *Hatherton Correspondence, 1827*

Letter to the Frenchman          Somerset Place, 17 Juillet 1827

Malheureusement du moment quand je l'ai reçue, l'état de ma santé ne me permettrait pas de prendre part aux affaires et mes medicins m'ont consulté d'aller passer quelque tems sur le continent pour m'en rétirer plus completement.

Dans ces circonstances, je me suis cru en liberté d'envoyer votre lettre ainsi que le petit pacquet de soie qui l'accom-

pagnoit a un des mes amis, Membre du Parlement, et qui s'est
interessé beaucoup à la formation, et au succès de la compagnie
qui s'est formée il y a deux ans, pour la culture et le perfec-
tionnement des vers à soie en Angleterre et dans les colonies
anglaises.

Je puis me fier entièrement a la discretion de mon ami, qui
ne manque pas, s'il y voit occasion, de communiquer avec vous,
avec la circonspection que vous recommandez.

J'ai l'honneur, etc.

26. *Colonial Office Letters Inwards (C.O. 323.154)*

Littleton to Hay                Grosvenor Place,
                                20 February 1828

My dear Hay,

When Mr. Rundell and I called on you the other day
on the subject of the Breton Mines, you will remember that our
object was to procure for the Genl. Mining Association a
promise of a Lease of those mines conditionally on the failure
of the D. of York's executors to establish their claim. You
seemed to think that our's might be made provided Sir James
Kempt approved and promised to look over the papers on the
affair, to try and discern if there was anything in them upon
which his view of the interests of the Colony and the Government in the question could be collected. I know not whether
you have succeeded in your research, but in case you have not
I beg to enclose you a letter from Sir J. Kempt to the Agent in
the Colony which I am sure will be quite satisfactory to Mr
Huskisson, and show him the importance of an early favourable decision on the point.

                              E. J. Littleton

                 (Draft Reply)

Coal Mines
     Cape Breton.

The Secretary of State will probably consider the private
letter from Sir James Kempt as sufficiently satisfactory as to the
Governor's opinion of the importance of putting the manage-

ment into the hands of Messrs. Rundell & Co. but it will scarcely be possible without waiting for the answer to the reference to the Governor to decide whether the proposals made by Messrs. R. are as advantageous as they ought to be to the public.

21 February 1828.

27. *Rundells to Hay*                                    5 June 1828

5 Ludgate Hill

We beg leave to inform you that Mr. Edmund Rundell will have the honour of waiting upon you at 2 o'clock this afternoon.

Rundell, Bridge and Rundell.[1]

William Hay Esq.

28. *A View of the Silk Trade* by Richard Badnall Esq. London, 1828.

To the Right Hon. Vesey Fitzgerald President of the Board of Trade, ... humbly submitted.

The author writes in support of the Government's Free Trade policy, but pleads for a reduction in the import duty on thrown silk, the semi-raw material. This and modernised machinery will enable the British manufacturer to sustain foreign competition. The tract opens and closes with a reference to Huskisson. 'Mr. Huskisson, from a sincere and most praiseworthy desire to consult and tranquillize the conflicting opinions of the throwsters and manufacturers, endeavoured to do so by acceding as far as he considered it prudent, to the earnest entreaties of both, evidently conceiving that their objects and interests were mutual; but he was probably not aware, nor do I believe that it is, even now, generally understood, that *no two* interests can be so opposite as that of the Silk Manufacturer and the Silk throwster...' (p. 19).

'From the knowledge which I possess of the industry, perseverance and enterprise of the Silk Trade, I do not hesitate ... to prognosticate that if it be once placed on such a sound and steady position, as an equality with France in our purchase of

---

[1] The eventual relation of the Rundells to the General Mining Association (of Canada), which had a monopoly of coal-mining in Nova Scotia down to 1858, is not disclosed in this correspondence. The standing of the Treasury in the grant is discussed by Bathurst in C.O., 324.75.

Italian Thrown silk would render it, we shall soon have the gratification of seeing our looms fully employed . . . our shops free from smuggled silk goods . . . and the name of Huskisson, to whom may firstly be attributed very much of the honour which such a result would confer on him, no longer held up as a subject of vilification and abuse' (p. 108).

29. *Hatherton Correspondence, 1828-9*
Vesey Fitzgerald to Littleton                    5 January 1829
   Long letter concerning the Petition of Distress from the Leek Silk Trade.
'. . . Mr. Badnall's Book. I think a very able one. He puts the facts in a very strong light, I believe in a just one.'

30. *Hatherton Correspondence*
Huskisson to Littleton              Eartham, 25 January 1829
   I return Vesey's *silky* letter. I am glad that he appears to be stout. But why not bury the question in oblivion? . . .

31. *Board of Trade Minute (B.T. 5.38)*
*Mr. Badnall*                                   23 April 1829
   Read. Letter addressed to the Right Honble W. V. Fitzgerald, from Mr. Badnall wherein he states that it is his Intention to proceed to the Continent on Commercial Business, unless it should be thought advisable to employ him in some official situation.
   Ordered that a letter be written to Mr. Badnall acknowledging the Receipt of the said letter, and at the same time expressing the perfect Satisfaction of the Lords of this Committee with the Zeal and Attention which he has manifested in conducting the confidential enquiry lately entrusted to him, and also with the several Elaborate Reports delivered in by him. Adding however that Mr. Fitzgerald cannot hold out any Hope of its being in his Power to promote his view with respect to some official Situation—And that Mr. Fitzgerald trusts therefore that he will not be induced to lay aside any Plans which he may have in Contemplation from an expectation of being enabled to procure any Official Situation thro' him.

32. *Colonial Office Letters Out* (*C.O. 324.86*)
The Rt. Hon. V. Fitzgerald       Downing St., 11 July 1829.
  My dear Fitzgerald,
        I have spoken to Sir G. Murray on the subject of Mr.
Badnall, and I find he has given so much trouble by the variety
of his schemes, as to have produced an unfavourable impression
as to the steadiness of his projects.

I am afraid, therefore, that I cannot render him any assistance, and that his case must be dealt with by the proper authorities.

                              Yrs.

                                        R. W. Hay


33. *Huskisson Papers, 38,758*
Littleton to Huskisson                    18 December 1829
  I have a letter from Badnall of Silk Company memory Proh
Pudor! to-day telling me he has established himself at Liverpool where he means to conduct periodical silk sales. It was he
who held the last, and no doubt imported the French and
Italian buyers, of whom we heard also. He is up to anything in
the way of advancing a speculation. He says the principal
parties interested at Liverpool support him handsomely, and
that from the central situation of Liverpool as regards the silk
manufacture and the extraordinary spirit of enterprise which
the merchants there always evince, when an opportunity for
any particular branch of London trade offers, he has the fullest
confidence in Liverpool becoming in a few years as great a
mart for silk as it is now for indigo, which until lately was excluded from the Liverpool market by the jealous monopolists
of London.


34. *Hatherton Correspondence* (*Leigh volume*)
Littleton to Rev. William Leigh of Bilston        August 1830
  You told me I was to be attacked about the General Mining
Co. I have long since ceased to be a member of it—or to have
any prospects in it, or interest myself about it, it was solely
occupied with mining speculation in Brazil.

## 35. *Trevethick to Giddy*

21 December 1830[1]

Yesterday I recd. a letter from Peru from Capt^n Hodge who says that the engines sent there to the pasco mines in the room of mine that was destroy'd by the spaniards are nothing more than playthings and the sheet copper pumps that was brazed have all burst and the english agents all turned oute, drunkards and robbers, and the scheam have fallen to ground with a total loss of all the property with oute even doing any thing. So much for London engineering and mining knolidge! He says that in a few months he shall return to England.

(Richard Trevethick (1771-1833) was the nearly exact coeval of Huskisson. He is writing to his friend Davies (Giddy) Gilbert, the President of the Royal Society. Whether in 1808 a certain Secretary to the Treasury had a trial run in Torrington Square on 'Catch me who can', history does not relate).

## 36. *Olde Leeke* (by Matthew Henry Miller)
### *The Badnalls of Leek*

'Richard Badnall was born at Leek on the 28th. February 1770. He was the son of Joseph Badnall, silk dyer, and Martha his wife. On 28th January 1784 he entered the Manchester Grammar School and remained there several years. In 1794 he married Harriet, daughter of the Rev. John William Hopkins, M.A., rector of Upminster, Essex, and afterward resided at Highfield House. Mr. Badnall became a lieutenant in the Leek Volunteer Corps and a magistrate for the county of Staffordshire. His first wife having died, he was married a second time (1821) to Sarah Pratt of Tean, and died at Liverpool on 28th February, 1838.'

'Richard Badnall, son of Richard and Harriet Badnall, was born at Leek in 1797. He was educated at Ashbourne Grammer School, and afterwards at Chaddesley, Worcs. In 1819 he married Sarah, daughter of Enoch Hand, solicitor, Uttoxeter, and settled down at Ashenhurst Hall, and afterwards at Cotton Hall, Oakamoor. Mr. Badnall was the author of several books,

---

[1] Quoted in H. W. Dickinson and A. Tilley, *Richard Trevethick* (1934), p. 187.

amongst which was *A Treatise on the Silk Trade*, a book now rarely met with. In 1837 Mr. Badnall contested the parliamentary seat of Newcastle-under-Lyme, his opponents being William Henry Miller (M.P. 1830-1841) and Spencer Horsey de Horsey, both Conservatives. Mr. Miller secured 669 votes to Mr. Badnall's 292. Alleging that the election had been won by bribery and corruption, Mr. Badnall petitioned for an enquiry to be held. Mr. Miller, however, retained the seat, although the Commissioners reported that much bribery and corruption did exist. Mr. Badnall died at Cotton on August 31st. 1839, aged 42 years.'

*Leek Times, 11 February, 1899*
Proprietor and editor, M. H. Miller

### 37. *Encyclopedia Britannica*
Extracts from the article on Silk (Korean, Soi).

1. 'Two Persian monks from China, versed in the mystery of silkworm rearing, secured some eggs for the Emperor Justinian. From the contents of that bamboo tube brought to Constantinople about the year 550 were produced all the races and varieties of silkworm which stocked and supplied the Western world for more than twelve hundred years.'

2. 'In 1825 a public company was formed and incorporated under the name of the British Irish and Colonial Silk Co. with a capital of £1,000,000, principally with a view of introducing sericulture in Ireland, but it was a complete failure.'

### THE QUESTION AT ISSUE
Which, then, was the better way? The way of Mrs Littleton or the way of Mr Littleton: of Hyacinthe Mary or Edward John: of French ribbons or Irish silkworms? The inhabitants of Donegal would have had no doubt: nor Adam Smith for that matter: how much, if any, have we?

# CHAPTER FIVE

# THE ART OF LETTER WRITING

*Letters as Literature*

In these degenerate telephone days the art of letter writing has nearly vanished. In Huskisson's day it was at its zenith. Letters were indeed *belles lettres*. One is struck by the promptness with which they were answered and the speed with which they reached their destination. In London they were often sent by special messenger. But to and from the country they seemed to have passed as fast as they do to-day, and faster at the weekend. The news is piping hot. Moreover, much of the handwriting, the Huskissons' in particular, is a joy to read; but it was some time before it dawned upon me that in the Huskisson Papers I was reading, not the originals, but a fair copy in his own or his wife's hand. Where in the Liverpool, Peel or Hatherton Papers I have come across the original, I found that the fair copy and the original were identical. In the case of a financial memorandum there may be three copies, the rough, heavily corrected draft, the fair copy and the 'original', i.e. the document actually sent. The difficulty, at first, was to identify the individuals referred to by the first letter in their name— Ld. L., C., B. (Lord Liverpool, Canning, Binning), etc.—and the numerous barely legible signatures. Bartholomew's *Gazetteer* places all the country seats.

I append the signatures (p. 180) of Mr and Mrs Huskisson in the marriage register.

One cannot imagine a stranger deriving from the letters of this age the notion of the strong, silent Englishman, dealing in understatements. We had not been spoilt then by a century of public schools and tropical empire. We were ebullient and playful and had no reserves. With all our friends we exchanged the condition of our bowels. Obviously having a good time ourselves, we mourned over the condition of the country, and we touted unblushingly for favours.

To define a letter, for the purpose of this chapter, is not easy.

There is no sharp line between the public and private letter. Official dispatches to embassies and colonial governors are supplemented by so-called 'private letters', which are commentaries on the dispatches. Instructions from the Customs Commissioners wear the guise of letters: starting with 'Gentlemen' and ending with 'your loving friends'. As students of banking history will recall, the cheque started life as a courtly request. And in addition to letters there are the diaries, intended perhaps for publication. These, like letters, abound in personalities. They are fruitful sources of information, but shameless in their prejudices. And the judgments they pronounce on the character and motives of a third party are of little value outside their context, and even there they frequently do no more than throw light on the personality of the diarist. It is the unique merit of Pepys's Diary that he talks primarily about himself. He takes us into his confidence, and we trust him, as we cannot trust Greville or Creevey. They injected malice in order to amuse. Croker was downright honest, but in revenge totally lacking in a sense of humour. The recently published Diary of Henry Hobhouse (of the Home Office) is a more modest work; and it commands confidence, though it perpetuates the Herries canard. But perhaps the diarist feels at liberty to say to himself what others are saying, without regard to the possibility of its eventual publication, even when the possibility is in his mind. The original is in the possession of Sir Arthur Hobhouse and the entry which has most to say about Huskisson reads:

"4 September [1827]. After all which passed in April it seemed as if the King consistently with his own professions could take no other step on Mr Canning's death than send for Mr Peel. But it seems H.M. took violent umbrage at the seceders, in which he was encouraged probably by the Premier, and doubtless by his own domestic circle. As little would any one have conjectured from experience that Ld. Goderich would have accepted the First Lordship of the Treasury, if offered to him. But little can professions be relied on. The King lost no time in naming his Lordship for that high office, and his Lord-

Letter, dated 1779, to Collector of Customs, Dunbar, signed by
Adam Smith and two other members of the Board of Commissioners

ship lost as little in accepting it. All the members of the Cabinet were on the spot, except Mr Huskisson, who had gone into Germany by medical advice for the restoration of his health. The offices of Colonial Secretary and Chancellor of Exchequer were open, to each of which Mr H. was likely to aspire. The lead of the House of Commons was also vacant. This also was likely to be an object of his ambition, tho' the state of his health ought to forbid his undertaking it, and he is not fitted for it either by eloquence or by skill in parliamentary debate or by enjoying the confidence of a large portion of the House. It soon however became understood that the seals of the Colonial Dept. and the lead of the House of Commons were designed for Mr. Huskisson, and this probably by his own consent. The difficulty was in filling the other office. For this the King named Mr. Herries, one of the Secrs. of the Treasury, originally a clerk in that Dept. and private secretary to Mr Perceval. The Whigs were earnest for one of their party to succeed, Herries being both a Tory and an anti-Catholic. On the 17th August the King held a Council at Windsor, when the D. of Portland was made Ld. President in the room of Lord Harrowby, who truer to his professions than Ld. Goderich thought that Canning's death absolved him from counteracting any longer his sincere wishes for retirement. Mr Herries was summoned to this Council to be sworn in Chan. of the Exchr. When however the Ministers arrived at Windsor, the Whigs declared that they wd. not serve with Herries, and raised a personal objection to him that he had been engaged with Rothschildt in stockjobbing. The eleven Cabinet Ministers present divided 6 to 5 agt. Herries, Ld. Goderich (as it is understood) being one of the majority. Herries was sworn in a Privy Councillor, but the ultimate decision as to his office was reserved till Huskisson's return. This took place some days after, when Huskisson had an audience of the King, who peremptorily insisted on Herries's appointment, wch. accordingly took place yesterday, when Huskisson was also sworn in Secretary of State. The Whigs notwithstanding this defeat have retained their places. It is surmised that the King's firmness in Herries's favour has in a great degree arisen from Sir Wm. Knighton's influence, and this has added to the suspicion of the truth of the imputation against Herries. Huskisson is succeeded as Treasurer of the Navy and President of the Board of Trade by Mr. Chas. Grant, who was found so incompetent to the affairs of Ireland, and he has also a seat in the Cabinet, for what reason no one can conjecture.

Mr Canning's death removed an obstacle to the D. of Wellington's return to the command of the army. Of this the Ministers promptly availed themselves, and the Duke accepted the command, but with an express reserve of his opinions on political matters."

Autobiography and the diary are first cousins. Sustained autobiography is very rare, and it is usually the glimpse of early years which the writer best reveals, e.g. John Stuart Mill and Robert Owen. The time to read Owen's autobiography is after reading the superb life by Frank Podmore; for his autobiography is like the rest of him, a monotone. I rank Owen as a greater seer than any soldier or statesman of his age, yet like Blake's, his genius was fantastic. Every one who met him said of him the same sort of thing—for example Alexander Young of Harburn, whom he visited 11 October 1812, when the New View of Society was fresh from his pen:

When Mr. O. was first seized with the insane project of ameliorating the condition of mankind by his own reveries, I had a great deal of intercourse with him and I thought the qualities of his heart much superior to those of his head. He came to my house on one occasion at 5 o'c in the morning and roused from a sound sleep Mr. Francis Jeffrey, who had not then been long in bed; but he first made me rise and conduct him to Mr. Jeffrey's room, where I heard the beginning of their conversation, but was glad to make my escape before its conclusion. Mr. J., after being compelled to awake, asked Mr. O. not in very good humour 'What has put it into your head, sir, that you are wiser than all the rest of mankind?' On which Mr. O. drawing in his chair to Mr. J.'s bedside began saying 'If you will give me leave I will explain the whole business to you in the clearest manner'. As I did not think this would be a very expeditious process I retreated immediately to bed again, and I understood that long before Mr. O.'s explanation was finished Mr. J. was fast asleep, and betwixt 9 and 10 o'c I found Mr. O. quietly awaiting breakfast in the parlour.

This letter is interesting not because the incident is unique, but because it was the sort of thing which all his friends experienced of him. A single idea, if it is really great, will last a lifetime. But the greatest of ideas, if repeated often enough, becomes a bore. In this respect the diary and autobiography are at opposite poles. For the purpose of the diarist is variety of gossip, and of the autobiographer *apologia pro sua vita*. 'What I remember' is not autobiography but a cross between it and the true diary.

Already by numerous extracts from letters I have endeavoured to elucidate the course of my narrative. At this point I will try to illustrate what the writers took for humour. Humour may be unconscious—i.e. humorous only to us who read it: or deliberate. And in its deliberate form it may be woven into the letter, as with Canning or Sydney Smith, or introduced as a joke, or an aside, as with Huskisson and most of the others.

Of unconscious humour I give this specimen from a friend (otherwise unknown) to Huskisson. He concludes a letter on matters of business with the information, 'I believe I shall be so fortunate as to form a matrimonial alliance which, although in itself the result of inclination, is equally justified by prudence.' Even more charming is a single sentence letter from the Persian Ambassador to Mrs Littleton:

London May 1819

Dear friend,
    I thank you very much for your enquiries this morning very sick and doctor say I take great deal of blood if not die until five o'clock will come to see you but I am sure not live long time when you go from here I hope you not forget where bury me
                Your old and true friend
                      Abul Hassan

He recovered, I may add, and addressed her later as 'angel of paradise'.

Huskisson was serious even in his humour, and built up his none too many jokes usually around an animal. (And his friends played up to his little weakness. Says Littleton, 18 December 1829, anent the commission for his portrait, 'The Rothwell ran at your name as a pike takes a bait.')

Remonstrating with his friend Charles Arbuthnot for trying to take on the Ceylon Agency and make a sinecure of it, he concludes:

In spite of which, whenever made, may you live to enjoy the appointment as long as the oldest lived elephant which your island ever produced, even though it should be a thousand years.

Joke two has woodcocks for Leit-motiv. He is now in retirement, and it is the censorious senior who speaks:

Huskisson to J. E. Denison.[1]                    28 December 1828

Poor creatures, they are come in sorrow to inspect your drainage uncompensated, as far as their bills are concerned, by the prospective benefits of a summer irrigation. It must be consolatory to that other biped, the Duke of Norfolk, that he is not the only one to complain of the March of Intellect in Notts; though I will not do those poor woodcocks the injustice to put their brains (quantity apart) upon a level with those of your Lord Lieutenant.

Huskisson was happier when he ended on a playful note that achieved its humour by recalling humour. The letter to Littleton about himself and the Duke of Wellington, from which I have extracted in the section on Sudbourne (p. 51), ends with a charming postscript:

P.S. There is an old story of Dudley muttering 'how do you do' to the Duchess of Beaufort; and then before he withdrew saying aloud to himself 'I think I have said enough'. I am just saying 'I owed Littleton a letter, but I have written too much—but he need not read it'.

There were good stories, which flew around the dining tables of London, that you would not dare to tell unless you got in early—such as this about Croker and Cockburn at the Admiralty, which was notorious for its departmental feuds. These

[1] Denison, later speaker of the House of Commons, eventually became Viscount Ossington of Ossington, County Notts.

two, when the Siamese Twins came on view in London, promptly visited them in order to enjoy so unusual a spectacle of navel union.[1]

Among the treasures of Teddesley Hall there is a volume of two-way correspondence between Littleton and his daughter Hyacinthe Anne from early girlhood to her death (1820-47). The Duke of Wellington, of course, comes in. It was 13 April 1842, just after the Afghanistan disaster:

I must tell you what he said 'Oh! the worst part of that business is having given up the ladies'. I enquired why? 'I'll tell you. There is no instance in all their history of a Moslem having given up his women'. And he added with great emphasis, 'There is not a Moslem *heart*—from Constantinople to Cape *Comorin*—that has not *vibrated* with *contemptuous* indignation—on hearing of that occurrence. I have marked the pauses and emphasis which are so peculiar.

The Duke was speaking in dead earnest. But as one repeats to oneself the emphasis and pauses, there comes the enjoyment that belongs to pure humour.

It is fascinating to observe how Littleton trains up his daughter from nursery jokes to political wit. By 1830, when she is old enough to attend the Cowes Regatta, she is writing to Papa:

Have you heard the new rhyme
> John and Bill went up the hill,
> To mend the Constitution,
> Bill fell down and lost his crown
> And John found revolution?

There is a breathless fun in Canning and a worldly wit in the Rev. Sydney Smith, which place them in a class by themselves, but of all the letters which I have read in the last two years— and I have read thousands—I have found none which so surely combine curiosity and humour as those of E. J. Littleton. He had an ear for everyone, and an eye for everything. This is taken from a letter to Huskisson of 11 October 1829, written from Bretby Park[2]:

---

[1] J. W. Croker, Secretary of the Admiralty: Sir Geo. Cockburn, Lord of the Admiralty. Siamese Twins, born 1811, first exhibited 1829-30.

[2] In the parish of Repton, Derbyshire, the principal seat of the Earl of Chesterfield.

Palmerston, who was to have been at Teddesley the week before last, threw us over for some fair lady in the South, and came to us just as we were stepping into our carriage to go to Shugborough, for which place we gave him a billet. He staid there 3 days and at Beau Desert till yesterday, when he proceeded to Ireland. Horace Twiss has spent a weekend with us, (highly confidential) damning the Chancellor and praising Canning. Lord Anglesey had been with Palmerston at Beau Desert—He, Twiss, is now gone to Cirencester, to sing another tune. . . . By the bye, he too went with us to Shugborough, where there was a play admirably got up— all the County there, Saints as well as Sinners—the Harrowbys, Sandons —Lady Mary Saurin—and in the evening at supper Twiss was called on for a song. He gave them a highly moral and sentimental dirge about the *Evening of Life*, which did not take with many—on which he sang them a capital song, all but indecent, about an Old Maid and a Dog's Meat Man, which, good as it was, was less entertaining than some faces at table. He also wrote and spoke an Epilogue—which had great success . . .

And Littleton's ears pricked up; and the face of Twiss was as the face of a cherub boy; and the county looked like. . . , but it needs a Macaulay to describe the scene.

*First and Last*

I give the earliest letter which I have seen from Wellington to Huskisson, and perhaps the very last letter (with its sequel) that Huskisson ever wrote, the Duke being the subject matter of it. They stand at the beginning and end of Huskisson's high career; and when he stepped across that railway track to meet the Duke, who knows but that the two jostled in his mind and added an emotional distraction to the nervousness of physical disability? Which of the two was he greeting—the co-operating soldier of 1810 or the political martinet of 1830?

Lord Wellington to Huskisson                    Vizeu,[1] 26 April 1810
    My Dear Huskisson,
        I received by the last Post yr. letter of the 19th March and I assure you that I should be very happy to be of any use to Captain Ratcliffe, and I will not forget your wishes in his favour.

[1] Portugal: 30 m. N.N.E. of Coimbra.

I am fully sensible of the critical situation in which I am placed in this country and I hope that I am not unequal to its difficulties. The Honour and Interest of the Country require that I should not come away one moment too soon; and its safety as far as that depends upon the return of this Army is involved in my not attempting to stay one moment too long. With these main considerations are involved others connected with the state of the Publick Mind particularly respecting the continuance of the Contest in the Peninsula, and with the weakness of the Govt. and upon the whole I don't know of an Instance in which an officer has been involved in more difficult circumstances.

However nothing should tempt me to endeavour to withdraw from them; and conceiving the Honour and Interest of the Country materially involved in maintaining an Army in the Peninsula, till it is necessary to evacuate it, I should be sorry to receive orders which should relieve me from all difficulties by directing a premature evacuation.

If we have a strong Govt. in England, and the *command of money and arms*, I think we might still oblige the French to evacuate the Peninsula. As it is, I don't despair. It is impossible at any time to foretell the state of the contest in the following week, but the French have made no progress since January. They lose numbers daily; and they will soon be unable without further reinforcements to hold the ground over which they have [chosen to spread][1] themselves. They will be stronger [therefore] probably when they will have been obliged to concentrate to a greater degree. But still they have much to do before they can oblige us to quit the Peninsula and the Bonapartes will more than once repent the invasion of Spain before they will make the compleat conquest of the Country.

Believe me, my dear Huskisson.

Yours most sincerely,

Wellington

Huskisson to Melbourne                              13 September 1830.

I received the enclosed from Brougham yesterday, with the request that I would put it in your hands as soon as I could. I was sorry to learn from Birch that I have no chance of doing so here, and not less sorry to find that you are prevented by indisposition. I hope that it will find you quite recovered.

The great Captain comes here tomorrow, and great are the preparations for his reception. The feelings are not confidence in, or admiration of his political character, but rather that of awe at the man that subdued

---

[1] Words conjectural, being obscured by the seal.

Bonaparte and forced the Catholic Question. It is the Indian worshipping the Devil because he is not conscious where he shall find a protecting deity.

The Duke is in his usual good luck in respect to the state of the country which he is now visiting. Nothing can be more satisfactory than the present state of manufacturing and trade, and the feeling is general that its present healthy condition is likely to be permanent. We shall see whether he takes to himself the credit of all this. But at all events he has the benefit of it.[1]

Melbourne's reply to Brougham is given in Brougham's *Life and Times*, III, 66:

Panshanger, 19 September 1830

My dear B.

I should long ago have answered your letter, which poor Huskisson sent to me here, had it not been for the stunning event of which the account succeeded so immediately. You can easily conceive the affliction it has caused me; and in a public point of view, it is unnecessary to expatiate on the loss, particularly at this moment. I have been obliged to have the operation performed for a carbuncle, which has succeeded perfectly, but which prevented me from travelling.

This saved me from being a witness of the melancholy catastrophe; and otherwise I should have regretted that it lost me the opportunity of having a full conversation with you upon the present most important and critical state of public affairs.

### The Minister and his Sovereign

No one could be more gracious when he was so disposed than King George IV. But the King's Government had to be carried on, and he looked for capable servants to serve him at home and overseas. One cannot read the Correspondence of George IV (edited by Dr Aspinall) without gaining respect for this monarch—I say nothing of his private life. He worked with his ministers, entered into their point of view, and objected only to being left in the lurch. Huskisson's tenure of the Colonial Office was brief. Two of the strongest letters which he sent out will be studied in another place. But the beginning of the story may be told here:

[1] Quoted in L. C. Sanders *Lord Melbourne's Papers*, 119.

King George to Mr. Huskisson
Secret and Confidential.

The King sends his kind regards to Mr. Huskisson. The King was desirous to have spoken to Mr. Huskisson (if he could have done so previous to leaving London) upon a matter of great interest to the King and which will contribute much to the King's comfort. The King is very desirous not to interrupt Mr. Huskisson's short relaxation from the labours of office, and which is so necessary for the re-establishment of his health, and which the King feels is so very important both for his own as well as for the service and best interests of the country, at this very critical moment. The King therefore prefers communicating his wishes to Mr. Huskisson through the medium of his pen, to the putting of Mr. Huskisson to all the trouble of a journey to the Royal Lodge, merely for the sake of a short interview of a few minutes. But now to the point—The appointment of Governor to the Island of Jamaica being now finally vacant by the Duke of Manchester's acceptance of the Post Office, the King is most anxious that Sir Francis Burton, who has been for some years Lt. Governor of Canada, and universally and justly esteemed and beloved there should be *now* appointed as the Duke of Manchester's successor; and that then Lt. Gen. Sir Hilgrove Turner[1] now Governor of the Bermudas, should follow Sir Francis Burton[2] in the situation of Lt. Governor of Canada. This will place the Govt. of the Bermudas at Mr. Huskisson's disposal and contribute very materially and essentially to the comfort and gratification of the King's feelings.

The King sincerely hopes to receive from Mr. Huskisson a good report of the speedy, if not complete, re-establishment of his health.
Sept. 20. 1827                                                    G. R.

William Huskisson to the King.          Eartham, 21 September 1827
[Huskisson, after thanking the King for his kindness, proceeds]:
Mr. Huskisson hopes it is unnecessary for him to assure your Majesty that in the discharge of these high publick duties, which your Majesty has graciously confided to him, he can have nothing more at heart than to pay the most implicit deference to every wish in which your Majesty's personal feelings and comfort are concerned. In this disposition Mr. Huskisson will communicate with Lord Goderich on the arrangements which your Majesty is desirous should take place, in consequence of the Government of Jamaica being now vacant. Until they can consider the subject, Mr.

[1] Sir Tomkyns Hilgrove Turner 1766-1843, Govr. of Bermudas 1825-31. Groom of the Bedchamber. Brought to England the Rosetta stone.
[2] Who had held the office as a sinecure, till required to proceed to Quebec.

Huskisson is confident that your Majesty will forgive him, if he asks your Majesty's leave to abstain from submitting any advice to your Majesty, upon a matter of so much importance as the appointment, under present circumstances of a successor to the Duke of Manchester.

Mr. Huskisson feels that he should be wanting in duty to your Majesty if he omitted to take the opportunity of humbly stating to your Majesty that in accepting the Colonial seals, he considered the very intricate and delicate questions which in consequence of the resolutions[1] in Parliament of 1823 have grown up, and are now pending, between this country and Jamaica, as involving the most formidable part of the labours which he has undertaken. The attention which he has since devoted to the subject has convinced him that he did not overrate either its magnitude, or the difficulties with which it is beset; and that the greatest care and circumspection will be requisite to ward off the dangers which might arise both to this country and to the most valuable foreign possession of your Majesty's Crown, from a continued misunderstanding upon points in respect to which the Legislatures of Great Britain and Jamaica are now unfortunately at issue.

Mr. Huskisson entreats your Majesty's indulgence for the liberty he has taken in presuming to trouble your Majesty with these observations. They pressed the more forcibly upon him at the moment when he received your Majesty's letter, from his having been engaged yesterday in preparing a long dispatch to the acting Lieutenant Governor of Jamaica,[2] explanatory of the reasons which will impose on your Majesty's servants the painful duty of submitting to your Majesty, at the next Council, an Order for disallowing the Slave Law Consolidation Act passed in the last session of the Jamaica Legislature; this Act being the only return which that Legislature has made to the resolutions so strongly urged upon them in your Majesty's name, and in furtherance of the unanimous votes of Parliament.

The too probable consequence of this state of things, Mr. Huskisson apprehends, may be the revival next Session in the House of Commons, with increased difficulties, and feelings exasperated on both sides, of all those topicks of irritation connected with the state of the West India population, which it has been the anxious endeavour of your Majesty's Government to set at rest. With these apprehensions of increasing perplexity (which Mr. Huskisson well knows were entertained by Mr. Canning) Mr. Huskisson feels that everything connected with the manage-

---

[1] Declaring the expediency of adopting effectual measures to ameliorate the condition of the slave population of the Colonies.

[2] Maj.-Gen. Sir John Keane.

ment of your Majesty's affairs in Jamaica will require the most serious deliberation.

Mr. Huskisson returns to town on Tuesday next, and will wait your Majesty's commands to attend your Majesty on this subject. Your Majesty will perhaps allow him to mention that Thursday is fixed for a meeting of your Majesty's confidential servants on the not less intricate affair of Greece....

## The Wine and Spirits Business

They were all in it. Such time as they could spare from the heavy burdens of official life they devoted to the slaughtering of game and the consumption of alcohol (or its antidotes). Canning claimed to be a farmer, Huskisson officially was a forester: but they never forgot their sideline.

Canning to Huskisson.                    South Hill, 28 June 1812
Dear Huskisson,
        I am amazed at your proposal to me to send a waggon to town in the course of this week. This it is to be a London fine gentleman, and to know nothing of the course of crops and seasons! I suppose you imagine that because the Hay, in the Five Fields near Chelsea and by Battersea Rise, has been cut and carried this fortnight, it must be the same with us here in Berkshire. No such thing. My hay (at least in the Gold Mead, Brook Mead and Long Moor, which you must know are my most promising crops this year) are but just fit to begin cutting: and it depends upon the rain or sunshine of the next two or three days whether this week may not be the very crisis—as that is rather a political than a rural word— the very busiest time, of my hay harvest. With such a prospect before me you cannot expect me to trust my waggons two days from home.

My hope is that you may be able, without inconvenience to yourself, to let my hock lie peacably in your cellar, till you return from summer excursions. If you cannot do this, I must devise some way for having it moved to another person's cellars (for I have neither cellar nor house of my own) in town. But in either case I should be glad to acquit my conscience by being out of your debt before you leave town....

Canning to Huskisson.                    10 February 1816 from
                                              Portugal.
Will you have the goodness to forward the enclosed letter which I am anxious that Gladstone should receive safe; as it contains a bill of lading

for a Pipe of Wine which I am sending as a present to the Mayor? Your wine is on the way from Oporto. . . . It is to be fit for drinking in three years.

No doubt, in both cases, Dobbin did as George ordered.

But Huskisson had several strings to his alcoholic bow—brother Tom in the West Indies, and friend Hammond in Paris, who writes (13 November 1817) of 'some difficulty in executing your commission respecting champagne, owing to harvest failure. 3 frs. 10 sous a bottle formerly: now up to 7 frs'. *Mon Dieu!* And as Agent for Ceylon he kept an eye on its produce—'Arrack, casks of, 227—for Sale by Candle at No. 38, Mincing Lane—September 1814.'

*Jane Austen rediviva*

Miss Austen lived on, after 1817, in Bath in male attire. For the Prime Minister betook himself thither, that Prime Minister who had all too often to cope with a resigning Huskisson. In 1821 the latter was at the end of his patience. He was sore at missing the Board of Control, and thoroughly disgusted with Woods and Forests. 'I am most unfairly and awkwardly used', he writes to Chatterbox Binning 6 December 1821. And then suddenly the sky cleared for no apparent reason. For he had still to wait nearly two years for the Cabinet.

But 'fidgetalis' (as Huskisson dubbed the Premier—the pot calling the kettle black?) knew his Huskisson: and a single, suave letter, pure Jane Austen from start to finish, did the trick:

Liverpool to Huskisson                    Bath, 6 December 1821
. . . I have found this place not very full for the season, but evidently improved since I saw it last in 1817. Buildings which then were stopped are now in progress—and shops of every description appear to be increased in numbers and are certainly greatly improved as to luxury and taste. Milsom Street contains, I think, more splendid shops than Bond Street or any other street of its length in London or the provinces, and things are very cheap particularly when you consider that you get the best of everything. The choicest pieces of meat at 5d the lb.—you may contract for a family, taking choice and other cuts at 4½d. Fine fowls at 2/3 apiece and other articles in proportion. I have no doubt that a family might live cheaper here, enjoy-

ing the luxuries as well as the necessaries of life, than in almost any town in Europe.

> Believe me to be,
> My Dear Huskisson,
> Very faithfully yours,
> Liverpool

It acted. 'I have given up all idea of Immediate Retirement,' he replies 11 January 1822. Once again, by quiet tact, Liverpool had held his unruly team together. The gods, I think, acted unfairly by him when they denied him a spell of painless retirement in which to watch how the steeds would break apart as soon as his hand was withdrawn from the guiding reins.

## Oxford v. Cambridge

As the world knows, the difference between them is profound. Oxford excels in philosophy and culture: Cambridge in science and sums. While Oxford claimed co-partnership with the Deity, building to Him churches and refashioning His creed, Cambridge swore by lab. and lexicon, deriving man from the monkey and polishing heathen verse. It is not surprising, therefore, that when there were rewards from on high Oxford should get the premier plums and Cambridge the residue, which, however, on occasion was worth having:

Christchurch to Cambridge      Foreign Office, 2 June 1825.
via Mr. Huskisson
My Dear Huskisson,

Lord Camden called upon me yesterday to talk to me of something which (as he said to me in his note, asking an interview) concerned 'the character and memory of Mr. Pitt'.

This something was as follows. A subscription was raised for a Statue to Mr. Pitt. The committee, at the head of which was Lord Camden, thought proper to add to the Statue (which is to cost £7,000 and to be erected in Hanover Square) a Project for founding a Pitt Press at Cambridge. They calculated (or assumed without calculation) that they should have money enough for both.

They have not. And Lord Camden's object was to propose to me to follow the example of the Bishop of Lincoln, the Duke of Grafton, Lord

Lonsdale (and I suppose himself) in giving £100 towards completing a
Pitt Press at Cambridge.

The application seems to me quite preposterous. The Statue is a national undertaking, the Press is clearly a University object—with much
more of Cambridge than of Pitt in it.

All those whom he mentioned were Cambridge men.

£100's are not so plentiful with anyone (except the Puisne Judges) as
to make it a matter of indifference whether one throws them away upon
the Caput at Cambridge or not. And I am much inclined to send to Lord
Camden a letter such as the enclosed.

But before I do so I wish to know if you happen to have heard anything of this project, and of the canvass for subscriptions upon it.

Ever yours,

G. C.[1]

Cambridge to Christ Church, *cri de coeur* direct

Castle Prison, Cambridge.

14 June 1816

My Lord,

You will, I trust, be disposed to consider this appeal to your Lordship's benevolence as extorted from me by a cruel pressure of most dis-
tressing circumstances which at this instant threaten to immure me within
the walls of a Prison for life and wholly deprive a wife and seven young
children of my care and protection. Struggling, My Lord, year after year
against a train of calamities which originated in the baleful effects of a fire
in London while I was connected with Merchant Taylors School, the
hour of trial is at length arrived in which, if unaided by the great and good,
I must drink the bitter cup of affliction to the dregs, to be hastened perhaps
to a premature grave leaving completely destitute the tenderest objects of
my regard. My creditors are about to seize upon my small collection of
Books and House-hold furniture, which are my all and without which the
literary labours of my past days will become as waste paper and my future
life blank. I have lately published an 8vo volume of Miscellaneous Criti-
cisms of the late Professor Porson by which I have not earned a fraction.
The singular humanity of the Syndics of the Cambridge Press has enabled
me to reprint Dacres *Miscellanea Critica*, of which the Preface, the first
Sections and Appendix are out of the Press.

---

[1] Cf. Lord Colchester's Diary 25 April 1825. 'I went with Sir Charles Long to Chantrey's. The
price of Mr. Pitt's statue . . . is to be 7000 £. The rest of the stock about 14,000 £ to be paid
afterwards to the University of Cambridge in aid of the intended printing press there' (III, 379).

My Lord, after this short and simple account of my unfortunate situation I hope I shall not intrude too far upon your Lordship's indulgence:- That I may not be considered altogether unworthy your Lordship's attention by stating that I have lived not only an irreproachable life, but as far as my talents and learning as a scholar and a Divine have enabled me, I may presume to add an useful life. I have entirely devoted the whole of my time to the duties of my profession, to the instruction of youth and to the pursuit of studies most honourable and liberal.

Seven years My Lord I was second Master to Merchant Taylor's School nor did I quit the situation till compelled by ill-health, ten years I have been an instructor of Private Pupils and nineteen years have I been engaged in the service of the Church of England. I am now My Lord arrived at the Age of Forty-six years and after all the time I have bestowed upon the improvement of others I am not only not possessed of property still less of any certain means of livelihood, but I am within the walls of a prison, leaving my wife and children upon that world in which I have so long laboured industriously indeed for others, but most unprofitably for myself.

Thus situated, my Lord, thus pleading not for honours and for distinction, but for mere subsistence for myself and family, I hope I may be excused in supplicating the consideration and benevolence of your Lordship.

Permit me, My Lord, to subscribe myself with sentiments of profound respect.

Your Lordship's

Most obedient

and grateful

humble servant

Thomas Kidd

The bowels of compassion were moved. For as the British Museum catalogue indicates, Thomas Kidd, Minister of St. Swithin's, Norwich, has six works to his credit, including the Miscellanea Critica of 1815. He had called his son Richard Bentley Porson in loyalty to the classics; and if there was still a Kidd to come, he presumably was named, in Christ, Robert Banks Jenkinson—or, if feminine Roberta, like Brighton's Old Macaw.

Round I goes to Oxford. In Round II the protagonists are Palmerston of John's and Mr. Home Secretary Peel of the

House. It is a story at the one place of proctors and 'cruising'
ladies and a spinning house where no one span; and at the other
of Peel and Lord Douro and his tutor the Rev. Bull, who sent
him down after detecting him in revelry by a timely visit to 'the
Yews'—a mean trick, the Duke averred and seemed like
making a Cabinet issue of it. This round goes to Cambridge.
For Oxford is monastic and spies privily on its cloistered youth,
while proctorial Cambridge fights cruiser actions on the Cury
Main with *Saucy Sall* and *Maria Jane*. But I leave it to the
Winstanleys of to-morrow (whether or not they come from
Merchant Taylors' School) to tell the two stories from the Peel
Papers, 40,374 and 40,376, in an octavo volume by the Pitt
Press.

*Revenons à nos moutons.* For we have strayed a long way from
Huskisson and his fiscal policy; and the English tongue has no
monopoly of the courtly phrase. So, remembering that his first
economic address was in French, let us close our study of letter
writing with the following from a French admirer to his widow,
dated from Paris 8 Aôut 1831:

Madame,
    Je ne puis vous exprimer combien je me trouve honoré et flatté
par l'envoi que vous avez bien voulu me faire de la collection des discours
de l'homme d'Etat illustre dont vous étiez la digne compagne.
    Ces discours sont des monuments de génie et de sagesse faite pour servir
de leçons aux hommes d'état et de guides aux legislateurs des peuples
civilisés.
    Ah! Madame Huskisson, ces mêmes discours ont un prix de plus a mes
yeux par l'indulgente estime dont leur auteur a bien voulu de m'honorer.
    Son biographie aurait dû parler de la liberalité des communications qui
caracterisait M. Huskisson. J'aurais pu fournir l'exemple le plus notable
à cet égard.
    En 1824, lors de mon dernier voyage en Angleterre, je souhaitais vive-
ment connaître à fond les nouvelles maximes commerciales suivies par le
Gouvernement Brittanique, dans ses rapports avec les nations étrangères:
je fis pars de ce désir à M. Huskisson. Alors cet homme d'état, plein de
bonté, fit recueiller toutes les pièces officielles et inedites relatives à ces
innovations commerciales, les mes en dépot dans un Cabinet à côté du sien
propre, au Ministère du Commerce (Board of Trade) et me permit d'y

travailler quinze jours, pour en extraire les faits qu'il m'importait de connaître.

Je citerai soigneusement cette noble liberalité, quand je publierai la partie de mes voyages dans la Grande Bretagne relatives au commerce extérieur.

En vous renouvelant l'expression de ma gratitude

    J'ai l'honneur d'être

    avec un profond respect

    Madame

    votre très humble et très obeisant serviteur

        Mon. Charles Dupin

          Conseiller d'état

# CHAPTER SIX

# HUSKISSON TO HIS WIFE

IT should be explained that Admiral Mark Milbanke (*c.* 1725-1805) by his wife Mary Webber had two daughters:

1. Harriet, who married Mr Tilghman of Philadelphia, and whose grandson, William Huskisson Tilghman, inherited Eartham on Mrs Huskisson's death in 1856.
2. Eliza Emily, who married William Huskisson and had no issue.

Two of the Admiral's brothers were: Ralph Milbanke, the 5th baronet, and John Milbanke, the writer of the first letter in this series.

Mrs Huskisson was the grand-aunt of William Huskisson Tilghman and the first cousin

1. of Ralph Milbanke, the 6th baronet (who had no son and was the father of Anne Isabella—Lady Byron):
2. of his brother, John Milbanke (who, dying before the 6th baronet, was the father of Sir John Peniston Milbanke, the 7th baronet):
3. of their sister, Elizabeth, wife of Peniston 1st Viscount Melbourne and mother of William Lamb, the future premier.

Mrs Huskisson died 1856, and Eartham then passed to William Huskisson Tilghman Huskisson (taking the additional surname of Huskisson) and on his death in 1866 to the son of the 7th baronet, namely to Sir John Ralph Milbanke Huskisson (taking the additional surname of Huskisson), the 8th baronet, who died at Eartham in 1868. Since then the Baronetcy has descended thus:

9th—Sir Peniston Milbanke (his son) of Eartham House and of the banking firm of Milbanke and Co., Chichester, died 1899.
10th—Sir John Peniston Milbanke, V.C. (his son), killed in Dardanelles 1915.

11th—Sir John Charles Peniston Milbanke (his son), died
    June 1947.
12th—Sir Ralph Mark Milbanke (brother of the last), died 1949.

The Will and Codicils of Mrs Huskisson, ELIZA EMILY
HUSKISSON, were proved on 25 June 1856 by Humphrey
William Freeland and William Huskisson Tilghman.

The principal beneficiaries under the trust are William Hus-
kisson Tilghman, 'the eldest son of my late nephew Richard
Milbanke Tilghman deceased and Godson of my deceased
Husband': and his issue failing, 'Sir John Ralph Milbanke
Baronet, eldest son of my Cousin, Sir John Peniston Milbanke
Baronet deceased': and his issue failing, Richard Milbanke
Tilghman, 'youngest son of my said late nephew Richard Mil-
banke Tilghman deceased.'

The properties disposed of are
1. 'Hereditaments in the County of Norfolk.'
(In 38,760 there are particulars of Norfolk properties under
consideration by Huskisson: £7000 estate, near Lynn, recommended as a purchase for Mrs Arbuthnot or Mrs Huskisson
(date 1811): estate in Gedney, Lincs.: a Lincs. Fen estate: a
Clench-Warton Norfolk property, with name of Thos. Hoseason
on back of memo.)
2. Leasehold in Tilney St., Park Lane.
3. Eartham estate with freehold mansion.
4. Other property in County of Sussex (Yapton rent charge:
    hereditaments at New Fishbourne).
5. Mortgage, under will of Admiral Milbanke, of £10,000:
    then held on Lord Methuen's Estate.
6. Shares in Sun Fire and Life offices.

Bequests of sentimental interest include
1. 'The Vase presented to my late husband by the Inhabitants
    of Chichester and the Liverpool Candelabrum'—to go
    with Eartham Mansion as heirlooms.
2. 'Silver inkstand now at Eartham which was valued by my
    late husband as having belonged to and been constantly

used by his uncle Dr. Gem'— to go with Eartham Mansion as heirlooms.

3. The Trustees to pay the 'expenses attendant on my grand nephew William Huskisson Tilghman taking his degree of Master of Arts at Cambridge'.

4. To Edward Leeves £500 for 'superintending the edition of the Speeches of my late husband'.

5. Picture by Henry Williams of Rome to the Director of the National Gallery. (Now in Tate Collection, on loan to Newcastle, March 1949.)

6. To West Sussex, East Hampshire and Chichester General Infirmary Dispensary £500.

7. To each poor widow in Eartham £5.

The substantial legacies are all to her side of the family. On Huskisson's side Mary Ann Kinnaird and Elizabeth Huskisson get £100 each, free of duty.

APPROXIMATE VALUE OF MRS HUSKISSON'S ESTATE

When the Trustees sold the Eartham Estate to Sir William Bird in 1905 (the house then being in urgent need of modernisation), the price was £37,000. The house was reconstructed by Sir Edwin Lutyens in Queen Anne style; and Sir William Bird resided there still (1949). Now the estate of Coke of Holkham, which produced in 1841 a net rental of £30,000, produced in 1911 a net rental of £15,000. I conjecture, therefore, that in 1856 the value of the Eartham property was around £50,000, and that of her whole estate close on £100,000. On the margin of Huskisson's will there is a note that *his* estate did not exceed £60,000.

(Death Duties in 1856 were as follows:
(I) *Probate*. On Estates valued at £50-60,000, testate, £750.
(II) *Legacy and Succession*. 1% for children and direct descendants,
3% for brother and sister, and direct descendants,
up to 10% for strangers—
which after 1853 were payable by real, as well as personal, estate.)

Particulars of Mrs Huskisson's Estate are in 38,770, as of 7 April 1856:

| | | *Duties paid* | |
|---|---|---|---|
| | | Probation Duty & | |
| Cash at Bankers | £1200 | Proctor's Account | £590 |
| Tilney St. Furniture | £1000 | Funeral Expenses | £200 |
| Plate & Pictures | £4265 | Duties on Legacies, | |
| Wine at Eartham & | 400 | Ranging from 3 to 10% | 167 |
| Tilney St. | | Succession Duty | ?(*sic*) |
| Farm Stock | 700 | | |
| Mortages | | | |
| 'Mr Barrill's' | £10,000 | Dividends p/a | |
| Lord Methuen's | £10,000 | [1]Sun Fire Shares | 390 |
| | | Sun Life Shares | 75 |
| | | Life Annuity etc. (including divi. of £2 10 0 from Wey & Arun Canal) | 180 |
| | | | £645 |

NB.—No 7 Tilney St. rented from Lady Guernsey.

For Mrs Huskisson's pedigree, as given in a legal document subsequent to her death: *see p. 184.*

The Letters (other than the first from Uncle John) are from Huskisson to his wife at Eartham, their Sussex home. The main series is from London in January 1819; and the last few

---

[1] The Sun Fire Office was founded 1710: the Sun Life Assurance Society was constituted by Deed of Settlement 15 June 1810 (the latter with a capital of £480,000 in 4800 £100 shares, £10 per share paid up).

S.L.A.S. had a separate entity, but the same 'managers' (i.e. directors) as S.F.O.

William Huskisson was a director of both—from 8 July 1814 (in S.F.O.) to his death 15 September 1830. On 29 July 1812 and at various dates to 1 August 1823 he purchased in all 60 shares in S.F.O. which on 24 August 1832 were transferred to his widow, and sold 1 December 1857.

He does not appear as an original subscriber to the S.L.A.S., but must have become a shareholder in it between 1810 and 1813. Sometime between 24 December 1813 and 1 November 1836 Mrs Huskisson became the assignee of the 50 shares of W. Huskisson in S.L.A.S. Sometime between 30 March 1853 and 8 December 1858 the 50 shares held by Mrs Huskisson were assigned by her executors, Humphrey William Freeland and William Huskisson Tilghman Huskisson, to E. J. S. Lefevre and J. W. Watson. (Details by courtesy of Sun Fire and Sun Life.)

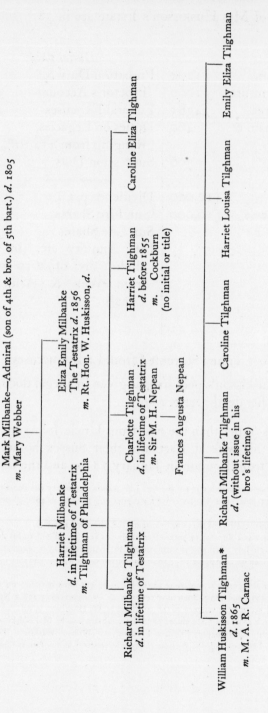

Mark Milbanke—Admiral (son of 4th & bro. of 5th bart.) *d.* 1805
*m.* Mary Webber

Harriet Milbanke
*d.* in lifetime of Testatrix
*m.* Tilghman of Philadelphia

Eliza Emily Milbanke
The Testatrix *d.* 1856
*m.* Rt. Hon. W. Huskisson, *d.*

Richard Milbanke Tilghman
*d.* in lifetime of Testatrix

Charlotte Tilghman
*d.* in lifetime of Testatrix
*m.* Sir M. H. Nepean

Frances Augusta Nepean

Harriet Tilghman
*d.* before 1855
*m.*    Cockburn
(no initial or title)

Caroline Eliza Tilghman

William Huskisson Tilghman*
*d.* 1865
*m.* M. A. R. Carnac

Richard Milbanke Tilghman
*d.* (without issue in his
bro's lifetime)

Caroline Tilghman

Harriet Louisa Tilghman

Emily Eliza Tilghman

* Foster, *Men at the Bar* : Inns of Court Records :—
Tilghman William Huskisson: afterwards William Huskisson Tilghman Huskisson. Eld. s. Richard Milbanke Tilghman,
Adm. pens. at Trinity, 27 Jan. 1847. Matric Michs, 1847; B.A. 1851; M.A. 1856. Adm. a student at Lincoln's Inn,
30 May 1851.

are from London, Sudbourne and the New Forest in the late summer of the same year.

(Letter from my Uncle John in answer to my father's announcement of my marriage.—E. H.):

To Admiral Milbanke, Upper Wimpole St. London.
*Pelham* [*i.e. franked by*]                              January Sixth 1799
   I very sincerely partake in your anxious moments and know what parents feel when they are to decide for the future welfare of a beloved child. I have had a private conversation with Mr. P. He says the gentleman in question bears a very good character, he was an eleve of Ld. Gower's and was brought forward by him during his Embassy at Paris, he stands very high for his official and political abilities; and he is Mr. Dundas's confidential secretary.

Such a man will always be employed and may have a good income for his life—but a father must look for substantials. You will naturally secure her fortune and what Mr. H. can bring forward in case she should be left a widow and with children. I could not help saying so much, but you have good and wise friends at hand that will be with you in these trying moments. I feel a comfort that you have so competent a friend in Mr. Nepean, he certainly can give you the best advice and he has always been friendly to you. God protect and direct you, Mrs. Milbanke and your dear child.

     Very sincerely and affectionately yours
Stanmore.                                                    J. Milbanke[1]

(Uncle John himself was well married to Lady Wentworth, and his anxieties should have been reserved for the 6th baronet, Annabella's father.)
The 'Huskisson to his wife' series starts with

              4 January 1819.
. . . we performed our journey with more than ordinary animosity. I suppose the Post Boys thought that the bastard sprig of Royalty, who was my companion, was entitled in this respect to the same compliment as Royalty itself. The consequence was that we passed C. Wyndham who had 4 horses and the start of us by a quarter of an hour at Chidingfold, and got off from Moon's before him. However, the racing was continued on his

---

[1] Huskisson Papers, 39,949.

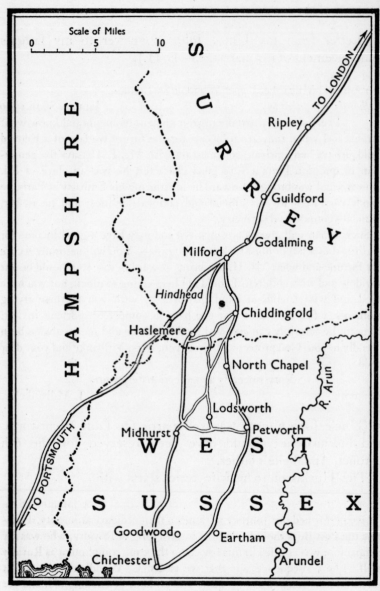

Sketch-map of the route from Chichester to Ripjey

part and he passed us at the entrance of Guildford. Here I put a stop to it; and we went on more soberly, but got to town in 4 hours and ten minutes, safe and sound; but with the boot a little injured by the springs, in consequence of the weight before, and of the leather giving, as it will in new carriages. We were but two or three minutes above the two hours from Petworth to Ripley!

Richard is just come in, having brought back one of the hares, in consequence of poor Mother Chapeau having breathed her last yesterday morning. I have been at Fife House all morning, when the weather was very fine. Now it rains torrents and blows hard. I have sent the £10 to Cad. for Mrs. Webber[1] and received the £40 which is placed to your account. Tomorrow I will go to Herries's.

*Explanatory Note.*

Eartham to Petworth 8-9 miles v. hilly.

| Petworth | 0 | 25½ miles in 2 hrs and |
| Chiddingfold | 9½ | 2 or 3 minutes |
| Godalming | 16 | 12½ m.p.h.! |
| Guildford | 20½ | (tell it to Ripley!) |
| Ripley | 25½ | |

| Cobham | 30½ | 25 miles in 2 hrs and 8 minutes. |
| Kingston | 38½ | 11 m.p.h. |
| London | 50½ | 50½ miles in 4 hrs and 10 minutes. |
| | | 12 m.p.h. |

Distances London to Chiddingfold taken from 'Brittannia Depicta', or Ogilby Improved, 1724.

The road described is as it was before motor by-passes. South of Chiddingfold Ogilby marks 'turning to Petworth'. This is now a straight good road with few and easy gradients. Apart from Guildford High Street there is no steep hill and no long gradient between Petworth and London (except, perhaps, east of Kingston). From London to Godalming the road is the main Portsmouth road, much used by Nelson. From Godalming onward it is the Chichester Road—with, according to Ogilby, a turning through Northchapel to Petworth. But the Chiddingfold route to Midhurst is no longer used. The road from Godalming to Midhurst and Goodwood now runs through

---

[1] Mrs Huskisson's mother was a Webber.

Haslemere. The main road from Chiddingfold now goes straight to Petworth.

Monday 5 January, 1819
40 m. past 5.

I cannot, my dearest, perform my promise of writing today; for I went to see Castlereagh (who is upon his couch in his bedroom at 4 o'c.) and he has detained me to this minute. The last Bell[1] was gone when I came in, so Boswell had put up the paper, which I hope you will receive safe. I enclose the Farmer's Journal for Martin. I took Herries's in my way to Castlereagh, and put £400 to your account at Ridge's.[2]

This has been a fine day; but I could not get further than St. James's Street and Square. I have not called yet at Melbourne House, as the Papers announce that Lord M. is at Pansanger.[3] Everybody asks me if he is going to be married.[4]

I have no time, my dearest, today for an epistle, having been most unmercifully detained at the House of Commons, where we were sworn in according to the order of our Counties in the alphabet. . . .

I am going to dine with Charles Grant.[5]

9th. January 1819

Yesterday, my dearest, I had not time to write to you, and today I cannot recollect anything to say. We had a pretty pleasant dinner yesterday at Chas. Grant's with Peel, Croker, etc. But I was obliged to leave it early, Castlereagh having appointed me a little after nine. He (Castlereagh) is far from about, and has not been off his couch since he had the first attack of the gout. However, he is going today to the country, to try to recruit a little till the opening. I saw Lord H.[6] yesterday; indeed he and I (being both Sussex) were next to one another in being sworn. He told me he had *five or six* shots and Harry *eight or nine* without being able to kill anything.

---

[1] I.e. the bell-ringer who collected letters—Charles Povry's idea (*d.* 1743) and continued for London till 1846. The bellman carried a locked bag, with a slit for inserting the letter, and the persons dropping letters in paid the bellman one penny for each (cf. Howard Robinson, *The British Post Office*, Princeton, 1948).

[2] In *Kent's Directory* 1825 there is 'Ridge S. Stockbroker and Ridge John, Army Agent'; and in the *Post Office Annual Directory* 1814 among the Bankers, 'Biddulph, Cocks and Ridge & Co. of 43, Charing Cross.'

[3] Panshanger, Earl Cooper's seat in Herts.

[4] Elizabeth, Lady Melbourne, had died in 1818.

[5] Charles Grant 1778-1866 (Lord Glenelg), later his Vice at the Board of Trade—the son of 'St. Grant', so-called because of his enthusiasm for Indian missions.

[6] Lord Henry Howard, member for Arundel.

We had a most tremendous gale last night; it broke the skylight, and has, I see, blown off tiles in many places. Today, it is very fine; and a brisk air. I shall try to inhale a little of it presently. I have heard nothing of what the world say about Lady W.[1] Indeed I have seen no world to talk of it. Binning is in town, and he is my Gossip on such points; but I have not yet fallen in with him. Today we go together to dine at Canning's. I have sent Rd. to enquire what Mr. Briant will charge for a pair of horses for the half day (that is to take to dinner and back), for Binning has no carriage and it is a great bore to go to Hogmore Lane and back in a damp nasty hackney(?).[2]

I do not believe one word about Lord Melbourne's marriage. He appears to me very reasonable and resigned.

You will be glad to hear I have some prospect of getting the perfect gentleman off my hands by sending him to a situation at £250 a year at Liverpool. I have desired him to call here to make him the offer. In the meantime, I have a bothering letter from his father-in-law.

Lord Colville[3] is come to attend his Parliamentary duty! He has called here.

After my letter of Thursday was written, Liverpool sent a message to know if I dined with him. I answered that I had no invitation. He replied that one had been sent a week ago, but I cannot find—to dinner. An afterthought; or there was some mistake here, but I cannot trace anything of it.

Richard begged the hare that old Mrs. Chapeau could not eat; and as Boswell begged nothing, I gave him a pheasant. The rest I have contrived to eat. Tell the Vicar[4] he must send me a little game by Eileen. Partridges I shall prefer.

13 January 1819

Send me by the return of post the report of Pitt's trial.[5] It is wanted in the Office.

Your account, my dearest, of the foolish proceedings respecting this poacher is a vexatious instance of the meddling of fools with matters they do not understand. You will find the history of this man's being taken up in the enclosed letter, which I received from Squire Dixon (and for which I have thanked him) on Monday morning. As it was quite clear that there

[1] Kitty Pakenham, Duchess of Wellington.

[2] The word written is 'agony', which does not make sense, unless it is a pun on hackney. Hogmore Lane is the old name of Gloucester Road, renamed thus from Gloucester Lodge.

[3] Lord Colville of Culross 1768-1849, a Tory Representative Peer of Scotland 1818-49.

[4] Difficult to identify. There was an interregnum at Eartham at this time. Can it be Cockburn Vicar of Boxley?

[5] Pitt the Poacher, not Mr Pitt!

was not the shadow of *legal proof* against Goble to justify his detention for
five months, Dixon ought to have told his people to let him go; but as he
has sent him over to Woodson, I concluded that he would take him at
once to Mr. Johnstone's Office, where the business would have ended by
the man's discharge, and therefore I troubled myself no further about it.
This is what ought to have been done, and what I told them to do in all
cases of any poacher being taken whilst I was away.

It is a most serious business, to have detained this man in the manner he
appears to have been detained; and if he should be aware of the hold it
gives him over all concerned in it, he will make them feel that it is so; for I
am satisfied that if he can get any Attorney to bring an action, that a Jury
would be instructed by the Judge, to give very considerable damages. I
hope that before you receive this, the man will have been taken to Chichester, and discharged; but still I wish you would send for both Gold-
smith and Woodson, and tell them that it is my special direction in the
event of their taking any poacher or of any poacher being given over to
them, that they should, without loss of time, take him to Mr. Johnstone's
Office at Chichester, to be dealt with, as Mr. Johnstone or Price or Freeland[1] may direct. When I say without any loss of time, I mean, if taken
in the daytime, immediately, if at night, as soon as Mr. Johnstone's Office
is open in the morning. To frighten the keepers, you may tell them what
would be the consequences of Goble bringing an action for false imprison-
ment, but caution them not to speak of the subject or it might put it in his
head. I have no doubt Goble is guilty, but as it is clear that nothing could
be proved, they were not justified in detaining him at all.

I enclose to you these letters for Harriet and Cockburn[2] which came
this morning. One of them is from Dick and probably later than his former
epistles. FitzClarence says he knew him very well—that he had been
extravagant, but he thought he would do in time.

You should have given me a hint before I left Petworth that Sir
Gorgeous[3] was separated from his Wife. As it was, it came too late. When
I got out at Stable Yard, I went up St. James's St. to see if there was any
dinner party at Arthur's, but before I got to the Club door, I met Sir G.
walking with the Attorney General,[4] when he offered me some dinner,

---

[1] His solicitor, and a witness to his will. (Mrs Huskisson's will (1856) was proven by Humphrey
William Freeland and William Huskisson Tilghman.)

[2] In Mrs Huskisson's will there is a legacy of £1000 to 'my Niece Harriet Cockburn'. 'Dick'
in the next sentence may be Harriet's brother, Richard Milbanke Tilghman. Harriet had only
one brother; and this fits the clause in Mrs Huskisson's will 'I give to my Niece Harriet Cockburn widow the Tortoise-shell fan sent to me from India by her dear brother'.

[3] Duke of Wellington, also written Sir Gor., Sir Geo., Sir G.          [4] Sir Samuel Shepherd.

which I accepted. When I went at 7. the first thing was to ask after Lady W. He made a face, and said she had thought proper to separate from him. I could not find that there was any other ground than *incompatibilité d'humeur*. He said he had agreed to give her a handsome allowance, and that she was at her Brother's in St. James's Square. I should like to hear her story.

Monday the Arbuthnots had the Regent's Box; and I went there to see Jane Shore and the Pantomime. The Tragedy was nearly half over before I arrived; but Mistress O'Neil was very good in what I saw, and looked very well. Mistress Somerville in Alicia quite horrid. I wonder that she is at all tolerated.

In point of tricks the Pantomime is not very good, and the only thing very clever is the appearance of Lord Humpy Dandy(?) before he becomes clown.[1] If you were amused or shocked with the taking off the old Queen[2] last year, you would be more amused or shocked, according to the temper of your loyalty, with the manner in which the said Lord takes off the Regent. His coat, his projecting bottom, his way of sliding about the room are quite perfect; and supremely ridiculous.

Melbourne is returned from Pansanger. He has called here and I am going to dine with him today.

Tomorrow we choose the Speaker.[3] Peel is to move and Lord Clive to second his nomination.

Whitehall Place, 14 January 1819

. . I went yesterday to dinner at Melbourne House.[4] Before dinner Lord M. took an opportunity of complaining of Lady C.'s violence. I understood or rather inferred from what he said that she had been breaking some more heads with candlesticks and other missile weapons.[5] This was a preliminary to his stating his intention of parting with Whitehall. He wishes he said, to remove to some other house near Lady C. partly because it would be more comfortable in itself, and partly as the means of getting rid

[1] In Regency England morality was satisfied by performing, before the pantomime, 'George Barnwell' or 'Jane Shore'. Mrs Siddons, as Jane, drifting half-starved through the streets of London, made her audience think she really was dying from want. The prince of clowns was Joseph Grimaldi 1779-1837 (cf. M. Wilson Disher, *Clowns and Pantomimes*).

[2] Charlotte, consort of George III, died 1818.

[3] Manners-Sutton, Speaker from 1817 to 1835.

[4] The second Melbourne House and now known as Dover House, Whitehall. The first Melbourne House (eighteenth century) became the Albany, Piccadilly. It was exchanged by Lord Melbourne for the mansion of the Duke of (Albany and) York in Whitehall.

[5] Cf. Faringdon Diary, VIII, 75, 28 June 1815, 'One of Her fancies is to keep *a Page*; and she lately fractured the skull of this attendant with a poker'.

of this nuisance. He would, he added, increase their allowance and they must learn to keep house and shift for themselves. Upon the whole I think it is the best thing for Lord M. The moving will be something to do, and tho' Lady C. may be a resource occasionally, she is at other times a plague and makes a disturbance which William will not and he cannot controul or put down.

At dinner we had her Ladyship (tolerably well behaved). Mrs Lambe with a bad cold—Wm. and little George and Frederick. Frederick is gone to Middleton with the Cowpers. We despatched the dinner and went, all but the Ladies, to the Pantomime at Drury Lane. We were there in time to witness the last scene of Brutus, and consequently the whole of the Pantomime; which I can only describe by saying that I understood nothing of the story; and that it is by many degrees the worst thing of the sort I ever saw.

Lord M. asked me to dine again today; but Lady C. threatened to carry us all at $\frac{1}{2}$ past 8 to see the wild beasts fed. For that I have no fancy immediately after my own dinner, and I therefore declined, and shall get a mutton chop at home.

I am glad Goble is discharged, as there were clearly no means of convicting him. I am not much surprised that young Greystock missed 22 shots; but how came his noble sire to be such a bungler? He used to do better. Tell Cockburn that Lord Bathurst said he had dreadful complaints of the hares. I hope, therefore, that he will be able to kill a few, but I do not want the Keepers to kill them.

It appears not impossible that the Winter may pass without any more frost, sufficient to fill the ice house. Do not you think therefore that it should be secured as well as possible, to preserve what we have. If another frost should come, it will not be much trouble to open it again, and if it should not, remember that half a loaf is better than no bread.

I see a list in the Papers of the deaf and dumb children that have been elected. But from not recollecting the names, I do not know whether either of the Chichester candidates have been selected.

My rooms are warm enough, but the weather is very nasty; and the streets are abominable. I conclude by enclosing Bryan's bill for your amusement.

P.S. Manners-Sutton has been unanimously re-elected.

The attendance was very considerable.[1]

---

[1] Cf. Journal of the House of Commons 14 January 1819:

'The House then again unanimously calling Mr. Manners-Sutton to the Chair, he was turned out of his place by the said Mr. Peel and Lord Viscount Clive, and conducted by them to the Chair; where standing on the upper step he returned his grateful acknowledgements to the House,

14th. January, 1819

. . . . .

The Regent has made Lord Fife[1] his (Poulett's) successor in the Bed Chamber. He seems determined to have all the greatest *Roués* in the country in his service.

Did I tell you that I had met Sir W. Houston[2] on Saturday? He said he had been at Stowe, where there had been famous doings—'Well,' I said, 'and you are now going to Woburn', where there are to be famous doings this week—the bets are that 1,000 pheasants will be killed. The Duke of York is to be there. What do you think was his reply. 'We are very much pressed to meet H.R.H. but Lady Jane wishes to get home; and so home we are going on Monday in our way to Brighton.'

This only proves to me that their intended and long vaunted trip to Woburn was only in prospective, when they set off for Stowe, that from Stowe they offered themselves and were refused. I suppose at Woburn Abbey they have heard from their new neighbour Lady Holland, that she is too bad even for Lauderdale.[3] So the General must end the season by killing stray pheasants (if any) that may still be left at Burton.

I will make the enquiries at Murray's the first day I can get there.

I will send the Farmer's Journal for scribble tomorrow. I have not had time to read it today. I wish you would send me the provincial Papers of this week as I want to see what is done at Quarter Sessions in our County and Hants.

There are several bills come in. Shall I send them to you or let them wait till you come? P.S. Castlereagh is come back to town from the country much mended.

18th. January 1819

. . . . .

Lady Binning[4] is come to town with her spouse; but I have not seen her Ladyship. He is more fidgety than ever. In proof of this take what

---

for the great honour they had been pleased to confer upon him by unanimously choosing him to be their Speaker.

And thereupon he sat down in the Chair; and then the Mace (which before lay under the Table) was laid upon the Table.'

[1] James Duff, fourth Earl of Fife 1776-1857, Peninsula soldier, Lord of the Bedchamber.

[2] Lt.-Gen. Sir William Houston, K.C.B. 1815, married in 1805 Lady Jane Maitland, daughter of James, seventh Earl of Lauderdale.

[3] James Maitland, eighth Earl of Lauderdale 1759-1839—the author of *Inquiry into the Nature and Origin of Public Wealth*, 2nd edn., greatly enlarged 1819.

[4] Thomas, Earl of Haddington 1780-1858—styled Lord Binning—Baron Melros of Tyning-name 1827, Earl of Haddington 1828, married Maria, d. of George, fourth Earl of Macclesfield.

o

follows: On Saturday I called to take him to Gloucester Lodge[1]. The door of the carriage was opened to let him in, but by the time he had reached the street door of his house, he returned to the dining room to communicate with Lady B, who was gnawing her bone by herself. He then came back to the door—returned again to her Ladyship and repeated the manoeuvre a third time, till I nearly lost all patience, as it was blowing and raining furiously all the time. We travelled on to Canning's, his Lordship in horrible bad humour, but when I brought him back, he had a little recovered his serenity. This could not be the effect of a good dinner, for a worse neither I nor Major F. Clarence (who had been a fortnight at Petworth) ever saw. There was, however, one new dish, a brace of pheasants dressed boiled-turkey fashion with sellery in the first course. I did not taste it.

Turner has been here this morning. He has lost a brother, a veterinary surgeon at Reigate, and is going to the funeral. Talking of the matted grass in Windsor Forest, he said it was choaking the young trees just as your matted grass (fiorin) is doing on Crouch Ham. Have you had any of it cut away?

I called yesterday in Foley Place.[1] I do not think your Sister[2] looks unwell, but her arm is no better; and I hear is not likely to be so. Pritchart was there and is giving her medicines, which she seems disinclined to take, and I rather encouraged the disinclination, if they are merely intended to operate on the arm; for I am very sure that internal remedies will not reach the seat of the disorder if external ones cannot.

By their account Mrs. C. appears to have died of the consequences of a fit—and her maid seems to have kept the knowledge of her decease to herself for many hours after it took place. I should think there could not be many valuables in the house. If she has considered your promised legacy as such, and packed it up, I shall not break my heart; for the old trumpery tea cups will give as much plague with the Legacy Duty Office as if they were of any value.

What can Lady Henry mean by sending me a common single letter to frank. Is not her Lord at hand? or is she going to cut him as too tiresome, a V. . .[3] de Lady W[r].?

Sir Gor. says they are to live upon the best of terms together when they casually meet, as persons who have a great esteem for one another. All this seems very ridiculous but I think she will suffer from it more than he will.

[1] Gloucester Lodge, Brompton, in Kensington Parish. Foley Place is now Langham St. and runs into Foley St.

[2] i.e. Harriet Tilghman, who married Cockburn.

[3] The word is illegible. 'Victim' would make sense.

Lord Melbourne continues to plague me for Griottier, who I suppose is a great plague to him, but I do not see how it can be done. He is a foreigner, and what is worse a drunken foreigner—two bad recommendations.

I think if George did not reach the opposite coast before the late gales, he must have had a bad time of it. Hoffman complains of the tempestuous weather at sea. He has had a ship 19 days on her passage from Portsmouth to the River.

20 January 1819

I am glad to find by Mary's letter which I return that George and her boys got safe over with only a moderate share of fright and lots of sickness. The misery is being a succession of days in these nasty packets.

You took for granted that the perfect gentleman would jump at the Liverpool offer, but this is not the case: as becomes such a gentleman, he has begged for a week to [*think it over*]. . . .

I think you had better have nothing to say to the Stansted[1] Chapel. I do not wish to give more countenance to these methodists than I can help; and I think it would look odd to go such a distance at such a time of the year, upon such an errand. Besides Way has behaved ill to our Bishop,[2] is at war with all the Clergy, and I therefore consider it better, even with reference to them, that you should not put yourself to the inconvenience of getting up at a very early hour in order to reach Stansted in time. Besides the invitation I see is only to the Clergy, and only few of them will go; and you seem to have a tolerable share of racketting about for the week without this attraction.

I am going to Castlereagh's dress dinner today. He has asked twice as many as he can conveniently accommodate, and is not himself well enough to dine; so it will be a bear garden. This morning I went to the City to receive my little Sun Fire[3] allowance and am more than tired. I should have been walking all day in the country.

I am pestered with applications for old Leaven's place, all stating that he is dying. I therefore presume that he will soon make a vacancy. If he admires either of the Gage[4] girls, I do not see why one of them should not become Mrs. S. Dickins.[5] He will have enough to be perfectly comfortable without looking for a fortune with his Wife; and I agree with you it is high time that one of them should be married.

[1] 7 miles N.W. of Chichester. Wilberforce lived here.      [2] John Buckner.
[3] Mrs Huskisson's will mentions shares 'in the Sun Fire and Life offices'.
[4] The daughter of Uncle John Milbanke, had married John Gage, brother of the third Viscount Gage.
[5] Mrs Huskisson leaves £50 to Charles Scrase Dickins. Scrase is a Sussex name.

I met Sir Geo. in the street yesterday, and I rather infer that something has occurred to ruffle a little the perfect esteem with which the separation was going on. If I were to guess, I should say some pretty heavy debts which he is unexpectedly called upon to pay for her Ladyship.

22 January 1819

There is a letter from Tom,[1] announcing his safe arrival at Barbadoes after a good passage, but reporting that he had not been able to get any wine for me. (*Feeble Government start: Opposition left unanswered.*) They all agreed that it could not be Canning, because he was the Corps De Reserve, and the other four are all useless logs that could not be moved: so that the day ended with the Opposition having what is called the best of it.

We got away by seven, and Canning and I walked home with Binning who fed us. . . .

Mr. Peel did very well in seconding the address except that he *oped* too often and talked of the *ouse* as we Staffordshire men are apt to do. (*The sitting brought on headache.*) The first day always does, and made me feel upon the whole very uncomfortable and deucedly languid.

23 January 1819

(*Worried over Emily's health*). . . .

I suppose Lord Henry will be forced up to town on the 2nd. of Feb. as it appears to be settled there is to be a very great battle that day, and one in which, in some shape, I fear., I shall be forced to take an active part, as the contest is the Bank and Cash Payments. This will make me busy next week in looking over the former speeches and documents on the subject. Between ourselves the Govt. are very much embarrassed what to do, and will not, I apprehend, have the best of it. However, for this as for many other scrapes, they may thank the genius of old Mouldy (*sc. Van*). L is in one of his grand fidgetts. Yesterday he said if Tierney were to beat us, it would be fatal, if not to the whole Govt., at least to the Treasury—At least L. added, I do not see how I could remain at the head of that Department. Upon which Vansittart said—I think it would bring down the whole Govt, *for I am sure I do not see how I could either*. It is impossible to avoid laughing at such simplicity, and fortunately I am so circumstanced as to have very little feeling of a different nature; caring not a straw, provided it takes place without disgrace.

[1] Tom Huskisson, his half-brother. Capt. R.N. 1784-1844.

*At Murray's bookshop, executing Mrs. H's commission. Met Lady Carol-ine. Lady Westmoreland, 'another madwoman', is in the Press—a novel with Longman's called Monduro). . . .*

I could not go there without buying something, so I ordered Hallam's *Middle Ages*, of which I have had a very good account as a book fit to be in a Library. Being in the humour to spend money, I also ordered a com-plete set of the Parliamentary Debates as reported by Cobbett. This will cost a good deal, but it is a Book of Reference, which I am always wanting in town. . . .

25 January 1819

......

*(The perfect gentleman accepted the Liverpool job.)*
Liverpool beats Binning as figitalis. He ought to be Grand Cross of the Order, but all his talk will end in vapour. I dined yesterday with Peel, his brother William is laid up with the gout.

26 January 1819
*(Interested in the state of his pheasant coverts, and killing off the old hens and cocks.)*

I called upon poor Melbourne[1] on Sunday. He seems to sit moping at home very much; but however he has made his arrangements for breaking up his Whitehall establishment.

*(Books arrived from Murray—Miller's 4 Vol. Dictionary by T. Martyn,[2] Prof. of Botany, University of Cambridge.)*

I am sent for to the House (I know not why, for Castlereagh is unable to attend and the business put off for another week).

27 Jan 1819
*(Detail about the separation of William and Caroline.)*

I saw her this morning upon her horse at Whitehall, with a mob around her. . . . She clearly manoeuvred not to see us—Arbuthnot, Van, and myself, who were walking together.

*(Weather miserable: Government 'hobbling along'.)*

[1] The premier's father.

[2] T. Martyn (1735-1825 Sidney) appointed 1761 and succeeded 1825 by J. S. Henslow (Joh.). The two held the Chair between them 100 years (1761-1861). There is a stencil on the wall of Corpus 'Henslow Common Informer'—he discovered the fertiliser value of coprolites, and was accused of acting as spy at a post-Reform Act election.

Whitehall Place, 30 January 1819

......

I am so worried with the grand figitalis at Fife House, with other figi-
tales who force their way in here, that I have not yet had time to look up
Mr. Barton[1] or any other things I must read before Tuesday. Tomorrow
I mean seriously to begin. Ricardo is too hard and stiff to send by the Post;
but you might send me by that conveyance the Edinburgh in which he is
reviewed (either the last or last but one) and that would answer my purpose till you come, when you may bring me the author himself. After all
I begin to hope that I shall not be obliged to say anything on Tuesday.

......

Lord Colville called here again yesterday when I was at Fife House.
Do you suppose he wishes to be Lord High Commissioner in the room of
Lord Errol[2] who has left 13 children with nothing but their high blood
to support them? It is miserable.

Warrender[3] has lopped £300 a year off his Lady's allowance in consequence of her sending in Debts to the amount of £3,000, which he has
been obliged to pay by granting an annuity to that amount. He is quite
right.

2 February, 1819

(*Lovely day—went to*) Gloucester Lodge where I was forced to go to
talk some matters over with Canning, who has something the matter with
his knee. Whether gout or not remains to be seen. We are a hobbling set,
and likely so to continue. On my return I found the Vice Chancellor (*of
Court of Chancery?*) and others here on Windsor Forest business. . . .

3 February 1819

......

I had no occasion to speak; indeed I had some reasons for not doing it,
as I might have got into some arguments, which were better kept in the
background, until we have more fully ascertained whether we are likely

---

[1] Presumably John Barton of Stoughton (6 miles N.W. of Chichester). John Barton of Stoughton wrote in 1833 'An Enquiry into the Expediency of the existing Restrictions on the Importation of foreign Corn'. He writes as a Sussex man, and refers in it to Huskisson. 'Mr. Jacob was
employed by the Government at the suggestion, I believe, of Mr. Huskisson.' . . . 'The present
system of graduated duties was devised by Mr. Huskisson, confessedly the ablest Advocate of
Free Trade.' He says that he began his studies '17 years ago', i.e. 1816, and quotes from the
Lords Committee of 1819 on the Bank of England. In 'Geography of Plants' 1827 he quotes
under *Beeches* Cowper's lines on the woods at Eartham, and at the end are notices of two earlier
economic tracts, with a review by Sismondi.

[2] Lord Errol, Lord High Commissioner to the General Assembly of the Church of Scotland
1817-18, died on 26 January 1819.

[3] Sir Geo. Warrender, Lord of the Admiralty.

to agree. I mean by *we* the men in office, for they cannot expect Canning and myself to recede from our principles upon the subject of Restriction....

Van was therefore *commanded* not to touch upon the principles of the question (*and did as he was told*)....

Enclosed is the list of the Committee,[1] which will be ballotted for to-day. You will see that it includes a large sprinkling of the Opposition, and a good deal of the talent of the House, with a less than usual proportion of Country Gentlemen as make weights....

I have a letter from Sir C-C today asking for Madras. This is too bad. Scotchmen ever will be Scotch men.[2]

H of C ½ past 5, 4 February 1819

......

Is it possible there should be such a fool in the world as to give £18,000 for Salt Hill.[3] It must have been some Jew, who made his money, as such fellows often do, without one grain of common sense. The old Newland must have been born under some lucky planet; for if he does not get his French claim, this would almost make him amends for it.

I believe the Canal is in bad hands, and will soon be in a bad way. I wish Lord E for his own credit, would look a little into their proceedings, for the world gives them credit for countenancing all the rascality of this Portsmouth and their contractors.

......

The House of Commons Postman waits—so God bless you.

[1] There is no enclosure, but assuming that the Committee is the Commons Committee on the Expediency of the Bank Resuming Cash payments, which took evidence from 11 February to 1 May, the Rt. Hon. Robert Peel in the Chair, the List of those giving evidence is:

| | | |
|---|---|---|
| George Dorrain | Swinton Colthurst Holland | Isaac Lyon Goldsmith |
| Charles Pole | Thomas Tooke | Ebenezer Gilchrist |
| Jeremiah Harman | David Ricardo | John Smith |
| William Haldinand | Hieronimus Burmester | Robert Muskett |
| William Ward | Nathan Meyer Rothschild | John Ward |
| Samuel Thornton | Lewis Lloyd | Vincent Stuckey |
| John Irving | Samuel Gurney | Hudson Gurney |
| John Gladstone | Alexander Baring | Thomas Smith |

And the List of the Committee is:

| | | |
|---|---|---|
| Viscount Castlereagh | Mr Grenfell | Mr Littleton |
| Mr Chancellor of the Exchequer | Mr Huskisson | Mr Wilan |
| Mr Tierney | Mr James Abercromby | Mr Stuart Wortley |
| Mr Canning | Mr Bankes | Mr Maury |
| Mr Wellesly Pole | Sir James Mackintosh | Mr Frankland Lewis |
| Mr Lamb | Mr Peel | Mr Ashhurst |
| Mr Fredk. Robinson | Sir John Nicholl | Sir John Newport |

[2] General Sir Colin Campbell 1776-1847 (K.C.B. 1814)?

[3] Probably Salt Hill, W. of Chichester. (Warren Hastings wrote his memorandum of 1800 from 'Salt Hill', and it may be the same seat. See p. 282.)

5 February 1819

......

We are obliged to have an evening meeting at nine at Castlereagh's—
for he (C) lies in bed so late in the morning that there is no time for it
before the Committees meet. Liverpool has therefore desired that I would
dine with him, that we might proceed to Castlereagh's at nine—and this
I am going to do. . . . A legal joke of Jekyl's in the Chronicle of to-day. . . .
He said the business of the Court of Chancery was divided into two parts
—the one under the Chancellor was oyer sans terminer, and the other
under the Vice Chancellor was terminer sans oyer. . . . It is worthy of a
place, I think, in your collection.

6 February 1819

P.S. If Lord E[1] is so anxious for a respectable Bishop, he should set the
example of not giving us such raffish parsons.

Whitehall Place, 26 July 1819

I am returned, my dearest, from a broiling Inspection of Richmond
Park. . . .

26 July 1819

I saw Long's new house at Bromley Hill, which was put up last summer,
by far the most dressed and furnished villa I ever saw.[2] L[iverpool] has this
morning pressed me to stay over Monday and to dine and sleep at Combe
(nr. Kingston in Surrey). Canning has got a touch of the gout.

29 July 1819

. . . The Regent kept me waiting till ½ past three and has been boring me
from that time to the present moment (½ past five) and the worst is, that
before I left him Liverpool was gone, but Liverpool I must see and then
Blomfield after L before I can stir. . . . I must also see Canning, whom I
only saw yesterday in the crowd, and who is unfortunately for himself, as
well as me, detained by his gout at Gloucester Lodge.

. . . If I can manage matters, so as to be in my carriage by three o'c. tomorrow, I will set off. That will bring me home by ten or a little after,
but if I am not by eleven, you must give me up, and Liverpool will have
had his own way.

We had a very bad dinner yesterday; but otherwise it went off very
well. The Frenchman and his wife are the two most ridiculous creatures

_____

[1] Egremont.　　　　　[2] For was he not the decorator of the royal palaces?

in the world; more heavy than lead; and having nothing about them which could be deemed fashionable or even gentlemanlike. . . .

Lord W. Bentinck[1] has finally declined Madras after giving Canning every reason to believe he would accept it. His wife has prevailed.

The Regent was gracious to me yesterday and reasonable, and tolerably good humoured today, when I had to discuss with him some knotty points.

Sudbourne, Sunday night (1819)

Grant's new carriage (brand new) met with an accident as we were going into Colchester, which obliged us to abandon it and all our baggage there, leaving the servants in charge and getting in ourselves in a hack chaise as well as we could.

(*Caused by* 'furious driving'. *A lucky escape.*)

Sudbourne (1819)

(*Few servants about: did not want to trouble* 'Yarmouth's gentleman'. *A box of powder had burst over his clothes*).

3 *Parties in the shoot yesterday* 1. The Speaker and Yarmouth, 2. Grant and I, 3. Lord Beauchamp and Horace Seymour.[2] . . . Birds were very wild.

I shot as I always do in company, badly. But by Yarmouth's account far better than the Speaker.

They (*the Hunters*) have the neighbouring place 'Rendlesham'.

Sir G. Warrender and Croker were to have been of the party but could not come. . . .

We rise at 7 and breakfast at ½ past 8.

8 September 1819

Yarmouth gave me 4 brace of red legs.

(*So he has sent off* 1 *brace for Fife House and* 1 *for Mrs. H*). . . .

This domaine upon the whole is fine and huge, and for shooting admirable. It amounts to about 26,000[3] acres., in a ring fence, having the

---

[1] 1st Governor-General of India 1833.          [2] H. S., a member of the Hertford family.
[3] The parishes which formed the Sudbourne Estate were:

| | |
|---|---|
| Orford | 2,703 acres |
| Havergate Island | 268 „ |
| Gedgrave | 1,810 „ |
| Iken | 2,668 „ |
| Sudbourne | 4,878 „ |
| Chillesford | 1,855 „ |
| | 14,182 acres |

The 'two Ravins' would be the Butley Creek and the Alde River; which fits in with the probable boundary. If the western boundary did not follow the parish boundaries closely, the total of

sea in front, which is about a mile from the house, and two ravins for boundary on two sides. The woods are magnificent and well scattered and the shooting ground is pleasant; as it looks upon the Bay, where there are generally some ships at anchor and others passing. The house is a bad one and very ill-placed, as it has no view of the sea.

Rendlesham, 12 September 1819

We are come over here today and are to shoot our way to Woodbridge tomorrow morning: from thence we shall proceed a part of our way to town; so as to get in at a reasonable hour on Tuesday.

Whitehall, 14 September 1819

(*With the jolting road from Sudbourne to Rendlesham*) Mrs. Seymour was taken unwell, and was before morning delivered of a fine boy; as we were informed when we came down to breakfast. This did not interfere with our plans. We took the field a little before 10 and left off at ½ past 2, having brought to bag 51 brace of Partridges. We then proceeded to Colchester where we slept, and this morning came on to town arriving about four.... Today we feed with the Speaker.

(*Dining with the Melbournes tomorrow.*)

16 September 1819

......

There are Cabinets today and tomorrow of the few Ministers that are in or near town. After this Lord Liverpool moves away to Walmer next week and Castelreagh to Ireland....

I think of proposing to Milne[1] to come down with me, and he will probably accept and stay till I go with him to the New Forest.

(*Reference to a visit to Wilmot and the Granvilles.*)

New Park, 29 September 1819

... Our road from Southwick to Creech Lodge,[2] about 2½ miles, was for the last mile about the very worst a carriage ever went over. It frequently came to a dead standstill and by the advice of the boys we got out and walked. At the Lodge we found our nags, which we mounted, and proceeded on our inspection till ½ past five, so as to finish our out-door busi-

the Sudbourne Estate might have reached 16,000 acres. Huskisson's figure is therefore too high by 10,000 acres, unless he meant to include the Rendlesham Estate. This in 1819 was owned by Lord Rendlesham, a Thellusson.

[1] Of Woods and Forests.        [2] Near Fareham, S. Hants.

ness at Bere.[1] . . . Between 3 and ½ past 5 inspected some of the Plantations here, being a very fine afternoon for the purpose. . . .

God bless you[2]

W H

All the time one is reading letters one is building up a picture of the writer; but from time to time one wonders also what sort of person was he or she to whom the letter is written? for undoubtedly just as there are good listeners, so there are good letter readers. Mrs Huskisson, absorbed in her husband, nevertheless had a personality of her own. She was fond of news and society, but at the same time a pure and pious soul. The one little pen picture we have is in the Letters of Hary O—'Mrs Huskisson said the other day (c 1803), twisting her little body into every sort of shape "I should like to go to Paris, merely to pique Buonaparte, by not being presented to him" ' (edn. G. Leveson Gower, p. 50). We all of us at Cambridge remember a gracious lady who, surviving her famous husband for twenty years, enjoyed an Indian Summer of widowed happiness, devoted to the perpetuation of his fame. So it was with Mrs Huskisson. Both these ladies loved children, though they had no children of their own; and there was no suggestion of inferiority status in their marital relation, for their husbands were so entirely dependent on them. And when towards the end one reads letters from Lady Palmerston condoling with her more than once on a nasty accident, one wonders if she did not say in reply 'I am going on well, thank you, but it is nothing compared with what poor William had to bear'. What a find it would be if there were at Panshanger or Broadlands the replies of Mrs Huskisson to the run of letters (1829—c. 1856) in Add. 39,949(b) from Emily Lady Cowper, afterwards Lady Palmerston, to Mrs Huskisson.

[1] S.E. border of Hants          [2] A variant on his usual 'Yours aff[ec].'

# PART II
## THE GEOGRAPHICAL APPROACH

# CHAPTER SEVEN

# WOODS, FORESTS AND CROWN LANDS

## 'Estates Bursar' to the Crown

MORE than once in compiling this narrative I have been struck by the considerable analogy between the subject of it and a friend no longer with us: both of them Treasury (and Insurance) experts with a primacy among their fellows: both of them with town houses and places on the Sussex Downs: Eartham and Carlton Gardens, Tilton and Gordon Square: the Southdowns of the one, the Dairy Shorthorns of the other: the cicerone of Lady Hamilton, the patron of theatrical art: speaking unpalatable truth in the Report of the Bullion Committee or the Economic Consequences of the Peace: reluctantly admired when their policy was adopted and eagerly denounced when it seemed to receive a check: above all, uniquely able by formal treatise or set speech to cast their economic thought in the mould of enduring literature. But let me halt the omnibus and present briefly the Rt. Hon. William Huskisson, 'Estates Bursar' to the Crown, whose revenues he so greatly enlarged. Though, to be sure, he was never a fellow of Eton, yet he enjoyed in fee venison one buck and one doe from Windsor Great Park yearly. And what is the dignity of a barony beside the thrill of waking up one fine morning in February 1815 to hear that His Majesty has appointed you to be Keeper of the Gawle in the Forest of Dean, and also Riding Forester and Ale-Conner within the said Forest?

If you are 'Estates Bursar' to the Crown or, speaking more correctly, First Commissioner of His Majesty's Woods, Forests and Land Revenues, clearly the first thing is to make yourself agreeable to the wearer of it. This Huskisson did. For pinned to the Crown Lands copy of the 'Survey of Pall Mall included in the Plans of Houses and Ground within the Cities of London and Westminster and the Borough of Southwark held under lease from the Crown: finished 1804' (the giant tome on which the Office works today), I found an inked slip, which on being unfolded read 'His Majesty intimated to Mr. Huskisson his pleasure that the leases of houses on the South side of Pall Mall Westward of No. 105, occupied by Louisa Manners, might be renewed'. The Manners property was west of Carlton House, the royal residence, and occupied approximately the site on which the Royal Automobile Club stands today.

The next thing is to oblige the First Lord of the Treasury, whose town residence was Fife House, where the inner cabinet met. In 1822 its amenities were threatened by alterations in the vicinity, and particularly in Little Scotland Yard adjoining Fife House. Lord Liverpool desired a lease of certain plots of ground, including the site of the old Stationery Office, for his protection. His architect, Jno. Soane Esq., recommended that the property should be fenced: which (say the Commissioners) 'is desirable and essential for the comfortable habitation of Fife House'. Furthermore, it would fit in with improvements at the South East end of Whitehall Place, 'as thereby they will be properly enclosed and kept in order as garden ground.' Mention is made also of the 'Terrace of Fife House Garden near the River', and the Commissioners recommend that His Lordship should have liberty to embank the land, after securing 'the concurrence of the Corporation of London and the deputed Conservators of the River'. Of Course My Lords of the Treasury agreed, and the First Lord of the Treasury was obliged.[1]

The next thing after this (some would have said the next thing before this) is to oblige the victor of Waterloo. But here Mr Huskisson failed owing to an unfortunate misunderstanding—on the part of the Duke. The matter did not reach the official records, but the nature of it is disclosed in a lugubrious letter from Huskisson to Lord Liverpool in 1816. The Duke desired from the Crown a slice of the New Forest for his new

---

[1] The old Fife House site is now covered partly by the War Office building, by the Whitehall Court roadway, and by the Whitehall Court buildings (south-west of the National Liberal Club).

Fife House was erected in the eighteenth century as the London residence of the Earl of Fife. It was occupied for some years by the Earl of Liverpool during his premiership and he died there in December 1828. It was used later as a receptacle for the East India Museum and pulled down about 1862 to make room for improvements. *See map on p. 38.*

estate. The difficulty was that the commoners had rights of
pasturage over the Forest. The Crown had only 300 acres out
of 90,000 acres of forest in severalty.

Like any other waste this is a mixed property—the timber, venison and
the game belonging to the Lord of the Soil, but the pasturage of their
cattle to all who have rights of common. By an act of the 9 and 10 Wm.3
the Crown is empowered to enclose 6,000 acres for the growth of Naval
Timber, but these enclosures are to be thrown open as soon as the timber
shall be grown beyond the reach of cattle: when other enclosures to a like
amount may be made: so that even this partial right of enclosure is confined to a given object and to a limited time. . . . It is desirable to enclose
the whole of this Waste (*sc. the New Forest*) by Act, but interests are too
complicated to permit of the requisite consents to get an Act through, and
if so gotten there would be years of claims and compensations . . . tho' I
have no doubt that the Duke's popularity and their wish to see him settled
among them would go with many of the parties. Up Park (4 *miles S.E.
of Petersfield*) would be a better purchase for the Duke if he can afford
it. . . .[1]

In the end the Duke built at Strathfieldsaye on the Berkshire
border.

Huskisson still had a few lines to spare and it was the custom
in those days to fill your double sheet. Canning did it with
P.S.'s, and P.SS.'s relating entirely to himself. Huskisson's custom was to append remarks on the prospects of the harvest or
the condition of the people; and so this letter ends: 'Part of the
healthy and able population on the poor rates—such is the
present state of almost every parish in the district. The farmers
are destitute and without credit, but if corn should preserve its
present price, things will be better after the harvest.'

But although he failed with the Duke of Wellington he did
better for the Duke of Richmond who, until his elevation, had
sat with him for Chichester. In the records of the Commissioners there is a disquisition of portentous length upon property at Oldbury and Seabeach 'long in possession of the Rich-

---

[1] Huskisson to Lord Liverpool 1816. Incidentally, Emma Hart began her career at Up Park
as the mistress of Sir Harry Fetherstonhaugh, from whom the Hon. Charles Greville took her
and educated her before passing her on to his uncle, Sir William Hamilton, at Naples.

P

mond family and intermixed with their hereditary estate'. It was decided (1819) to sell the timber to the Duke of Richmond as tenant of the Crown, and certain land to Lord Henry Howard (i.e. to the Norfolk family at Arundel). Four years later (1823)—and it was the last piece of business transacted by Huskisson before he left the office—the same property was under discussion. The Duke of Richmond was now buying further property here, which included the hamlet of Halnaker,[1] and the price was reduced by £2,500 to £4,557 14s. 0d., the Crown solicitor having reported that Halnaker itself had belonged to the Duke all along. In the language of another, the studio had discovered that it did not own it!

'Makes you feel like Cromwell. Doesn't it?' said Mr Huskisson.

'Ah!' said My Lords of the Treasury.

They smiled indulgently. They were kindly men at heart, and they liked their Dukes and Earls to be happy.

## The Wood Book of the Treasury

The source from which these items are taken is the Wood Book of the Treasury in the Public Record Office: and the volumes covering the period of Huskisson's tenure are numbered T.25, 6 to 11. Vol. 6 starts at 1 January 1813: and half way through he comes into the picture, signing with his colleague Henry Dawkins a report for buying out the holders of fuel rights in the New Forest for 20/- a load at twenty years purchase. The Treasury agree over the signatures of N. Vansittart, B. Paget and C. Grant Jr.: Vol. 11 starts at 28 February 1823, the month in which he handed over, but as the Treasury only weeks or months later took action on the Reports of the Commissioners, the greater part of this volume too contains Huskisson matter. Throughout he signs the important Reports, but frequently for routine business there is only the signature of his assistants. There are always two signatories.

From 1810 to 1828 the First Commissioners of Woods and Forests (as they are commonly styled) were:

---

[1] Halnaker, popularly Half-Acre, is near to Eartham.

| 31 July 1810 | Sylvester Lord Glenbervie. |
| 21 August 1814 | Rt. Hon. William Huskisson. |
| 8 February 1823 | Rt. Hon. Charles Arbuthnot. |
| 31 May 1827 | Geo. Earl of Carlisle. |
| 23 July 1827 | Rt. Hon. William Sturges Bourne. |
| 11 February 1828 | Rt. Hon. Charles Arbuthnot. |
| 14 June 1828 | William Viscount Lowther. |

The assistant commissioners throughout were William Dacres Adams and Henry Dawkins.

It will be noted that three of the above First Commissioners were former Secretaries of the Treasury—Huskisson, Arbuthnot and Sturges Bourne, while Lord Glenbervie, as Sylvester Douglas, was a Lord of the Treasury 1797-1800. Therefore, all that it meant for them administratively was that they stood on the other side of the counter, answering queries, where formerly they had propounded them: writing reports, where formerly they had endorsed them under the signature of My Lords.

I did not encounter any case where a Report was rejected by the Treasury, though sometimes small amendments were suggested.

The overall impression is the miscellaneity of the business: lands and houses: town land and agricultural land: royal parks and old forest: occasionally, mooring chains, market tolls and ferries: purchases as well as sales: exchanges of property: transactions in all parts of the country: and in the London area much business, not only in the West End. In particular one gets used to the words 'allotment' and 'peppercorn'. Allotment means the allotment of a specific area as the result of enclosure, in this period mainly the enclosure of moor and common waste, in which the Crown had an especial interest. (Later an allotment will mean the allotment of a few strips to the parish poor and thus pass into the allotment of the rural allotment movement out of which grew the urban allotments that so many of us enjoy today.) The peppercorn was the consideration short of nothing which the tenant paid in the first year of his ninety-

nine-year building lease. Thus on 12 February 1822 the lessees
of the Argyle Rooms east of Regent Street, having asked to be
compensated for the 'ruinous expenses they have incurred' in
entering upon the property, are informed that 'the peppercorn
will be extended to two years'.

It is clear that the Commissioners are very much masters in
their own house vis-à-vis those without; and it had not always
been so. Thus on 18 August 1815 at the outset of the Huskisson regime, Charles Arbuthnot (from the Treasury) approves
the surrender, for a consideration, by the Bishop of Rochester
of his Receivership of Crown Rents in Essex, Hertford, Norfolk and Hunts. My Lords of the Treasury consider that 'much
benefit for the Crown Estates may reasonably be expected from
the adoption of the plan now submitted by you', i.e. the appointment of surveyors to collect direct. Therefore the Commissioners should draft a bill specifying the amount of compensation, but the accounts must be kept as before under the Audi-
tors of the Land Revenue—Treasury sovereignty is to be
maintained. From first to last the Commissioners of Woods
and Forests, like the Commissioners of Customs and Excise,
are financially a limb of the Treasury.

In selling property or granting leases the Commissioners had
to follow the course of the market. In October 1816 after asking for authority to dispose by auction of enclosure allotments
in Denbigh and Flint, valued at £6,000 odd, they found that
there was no buyer and therefore let the principal lot on a
twenty-one year lease. In the same year, when trying to sell a
Lincolnshire estate, 'our Surveyor' reported that 'the shock
which had been experienced in landed property was felt in a
greater degree in the City of Lincoln, from the failure of so
many of the banks, than in most other counties'. But after a
delay of two years it was found possible to 'dispose of it now by
private contract' (1818). As a rule, the method of sale was by
public auction, but when the property was withdrawn, the local
surveyor might report later that a suitable purchaser had been
found at the required price.

Building land, actual and prospective, had its own problems, and here the Commissioners were strong sellers because able to afford the long view.

Thus in 1817 the Crown offered forty-five acres of grassland in Islington to a certain Mr Felton for £7,000. He submitted that 'as the property was so contiguous to his estate and might in some degree contribute to his comfort, he was willing to give for it £6,750. More he could not upon any principle of justice to himself afford to pay'. In his next letter, however, he did.

In November 1820 the projected new Haymarket Theatre asked for easier terms in respect of ornamental outlay on their frontage 'because of the present depressed state of Theatrical Properties and of that Theatre in particular from the extended period to which the Winter Theatres now continue their performances'. The Commissioners turned down the request, adding that the ground could be easily let to others for the rent now demanded.

The country business varied from tiny transactions, such as the disposal of two acres of escheated land at Grantchester, near Cambridge, to large transactions inwards and outwards with well-known names. There is a payment in 1818 to Charles Rose Ellis (later Lord Seaford) for the purchase by the Crown of the Claremont Estate for the late Princess Charlotte—£65,400. Alex. Baring, the member for Taunton (later Lord Ashburton), buys tenements at Taunton—£4,000, 'to be paid into the Bank of England.' There is the lease of a large property to Lord Calthorpe, comprising the Manor and Demesne Lands of Hampton in Arden, Co. Warwick. The allotments from enclosure in Wales lead to sales large and small: in the north to the families of Mostyn, Grosvenor and Kenyon: in the south a big allotment from Brecknock Forest to Mr John Christie of Mark Lane— £15,000, 'this being the Board's[1] reserve price.'

There is a big, and to a layman, complicated transaction with Lord Holland, who holds the estates of Ampthill and Millbrook (Co. Bedford) on the life of the Duke of Bedford. The Crown's interest, 'after the life of the Duke of Bedford' is

---

[1] The Commissioners often refer to themselves as 'the Board'.

valued at £14,500; and the Commissioners recommend the Treasury to part with it for this sum.

Sometimes, when the Board differs from its valuer, it states its reason. Thus Lord Westmoreland comes up to the Board's figure of £4,600 for property in Sharleston (near Wakefield). It was valued at £4,420; 'but as it appeared to us that the value would be greatly increased in the case of an Inclosure in the Common Fields, and it would enable the purchaser to lay together the lands which are now very much dispersed,' the higher figure had been asked. Again and again the counties of Denbigh and Flint are mentioned. The Crown seems to have had many small and scattered properties in Wales, which it sold off, or in the case of quarries, leased: e.g. 'Jan. 1823, a slate quarry in Wales for 31 years to a gentleman of Liverpool and another.' In 1816 there were negotiations with Lady Penrhyn for the lease of slate quarries for a money rent plus one-ninth of the slate produced.

There was one class of property on which the Crown rightly took a special stand. It was raised by the Marquis of Anglesey's offer in 1815 to buy Carnarvon Castle, of which he was the Keeper. The Board's policy was—no freehold alienation, but a ninety-nine-year lease. 'As to the sale of this or any similar castle our opinion is decidedly adverse to the alienation, from the Crown, of these Monuments of its Antient Grandeur.' Conformably with this, the Gaol Site and Castle Ruins of Flint were leased in 1820 to Sir Thomas Mostyn. Tintern Abbey today is a Crown property. Worcester Castle crops up in connection with the Worcester Castle Estate. In 1818 the Dean and Chapter, after a dispute over the Crown's title, agreed to buy a certain part of it. In 1820, when the parcels were offered, the Dean and Chapter turned the offer down. In 1822 they were still at it, but the negotiations were now triangular, the Corporation of Worcester having entered. There is mention of the Castle Hill and its 'Pestilential Gaol'. The detail extends over pages, and at the end the Commissioners say: 'having collected all these particulars for the information of your Lordships, we leave the decision to you.' Turning *faute de mieux* to Dugdale we learn that King Edgar's Tower in Worcester is 'supposed to have been formerly attached to a castle, and is the only remaining part of it'. But of pestilence not a hint!—'indeed, for beauty, cleanliness and respectability . . . no visitor will be disappointed on his arrival at the City of Worcester and but few will leave it without regret.'

Quite unlike the Minutes of the Customs, which are analysed rulings for the guidance of the Customs Service, the Wood Book of the Treasury contains scarcely anything about office routine. There is, however, one instruction from the Treasury, dated 25 June 1822, relative to deductions to be made from the Salaries of Officers and Clerks and other persons in Public Employ towards the formation of a Superannuation Fund, to commence from 5 April last. This presumably was sent to all departments.

More than once in the correspondence contained in the Huskisson Papers, Huskisson, when announcing the time-table of his progress from one stately home to another, speaks of going round by a particular way in order to look at some Crown properties. I confess I should like to have visited a few of them, e.g.:

(i) *Newmarket*

On 4 July 1816 the Office of Woods reports that their valuer has recommended the sale of the Racecourse to the Jockey Club at £7 10s. 0d. an acre, or £1282 10s. 0d. in all, and informed them that 'the lowness of his valuation proceeds from the circumstance of the ground being much injured, not merely by the racing, but also by the continual exercising of horses upon it: which has considerably lessened its value as a sheepwalk'! The Board agrees, but with the proviso that 'if not continued as a race course, the Crown may repurchase at the same rate'.

Signed W. Huskisson<br>H. Dawkins

Next year, the 'Royal Palace at Newmarket was disposed of in lots'.

## (ii) *Threapwood Common*

Between Malpas in Cheshire and Hanmer in Flint. Extra parochial: 200 acres, 'enclosed by encroachments which are still going on': and 'occupied by a lawless disorderly set of people, who have principally subsisted by receiving as inmates persons who find it convenient to withdraw themselves out of the limits of Parish Jurisdiction in order to avoid legal authority and control'. Prayer: a grant of land for a chapel site by renouncing the Crown's interest in certain acres.

'Recommended,' say Woods. 'Agreed,' say my Lords— '*most* laudable.'

## (iii) *The Bullo Pill Railroad*

Stockton and Darlington we know, Liverpool and Manchester we know, but who are you? 'Bullo Pill, a coaling port, in a fine reach of the Severn, $1\frac{1}{2}$ m. S. of Newnham W. Glos' (Bartholomew). Hence the following under date of 20 March 1822:

We beg to acquaint your Lordships that an application has been made to us, on behalf of the Bullo Pill Railway Company, for permission to make a collateral branch of railway from some collieries in Dean Forest called the 'Folly and Whimsey Coal Works' to join their Road at a place called the Dun Head in that Forest.

Mr. Masham our Deputy Surveyor of this Forest having inspected the proposed lines of Road has reported to us that the land over which the same is intended to pass is very wet and quite inapplicable to the production of timber and that the substitution of a Railway for the present numerous Tracts of Road will be an advantage to the Soil of the Forest, that the length of road applied for is 1100 yards, for which the sum of £10 a year would be a proper rent to be required for the same in proportion to what is paid for the other railways in the Forest, and that the Severn and Wye Railway Company have signified that there will be no objection to the construction thereof.

Under these circumstances we submit that this appears to us to be a proper case for the exercise of the powers given to your Lordships by the Act of the 52 Geo 3 cap 161 sec 7, whereby it is made lawful to grant leases for terms not exceeding 31 years of such parts of the Royal Forests as may be necessary for making Railways, Tram Roads or Inclined Planes for the purpose of facilitating the removing and carrying away any free-stone limestone and other stone slate, coal etc. which may be dug and got therein.

The Treasury agrees—22 April 1822.

The railway age had arrived—ahead of the steam train. But it was not the Board's first contact with transportation or cinders. In 1815, when the Board was strongly 'timber-conscious', it was agreed that David Mushet might work the ore in Dean Forest provided that he should be absolutely restrained from following the veins into the Enclosures. The smoke and effluvia of his works must not be suffered to damage the plantations.

In 1818 it sold some 'slips of land' to the Thames Isis Navigation for a Navigable Cut: and in the same year a Denbigh coal property to a worthy clergyman and his wife, not for the mining of coal, but 'as a protection against the defacing of their residence'. The figure was fixed at £1500, the property as such being valued at £790 and the balance being added because of the added amenity value! Not that the Commissioners were anti-clerical; for they gave Newmarket a free burying ground, and built churches on their Great London Estate, to which we now turn. Everyone has heard of Lord Liverpool's grant in 1818 towards church buildings as the Government's constructive remedy for the cure of social malaise. Most properly Huskisson was proposed as one of the Commissioners, for it was on the Crown Estate that four of the additional churches were to be built; and in modest language he accepted the honour.

## Regent's Park and Whitehall

Marylebone Park.

As the interest which the Duke of Portland held jointly with the Crown expired in 1811, the Commissioners had directed plans to be prepared, not only for the formation of the Regent's Park, but also for the further object of making a more direct and commodious line of communication between Marylebone and Westminster, as suggested by Mr. Fordyce in his 4th Report of 1809. The Plan suggested by Mr. Nash, as one of the architects to the Department of Woods, which included the making of the Regent's

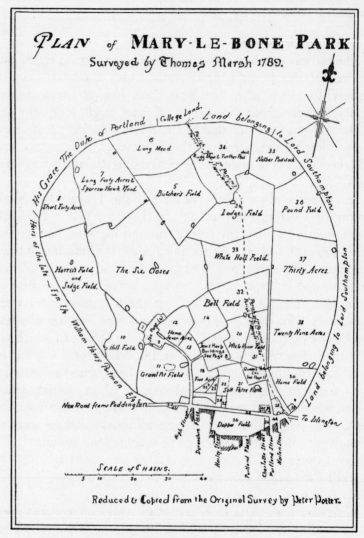

Marylebone Park in 1789

(*Reproduced by permission of the Office of the Commissioners of Crown Lands*)

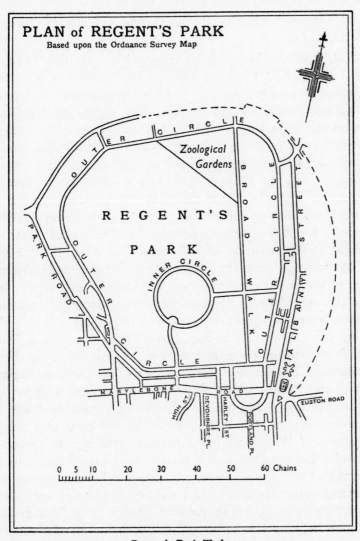

**Regent's Park Today**

*(Based upon the Ordnance Survey Map, with the sanction of the Controller of H.M. Stationery Office)*

Canal, was recommended by the Commissioners and was, after some alterations approved by the Government, adopted.[1]

P.P. 1868-9, (XXXV), Public Income and Expenditure, I, Pt. II, p. 440.

Vol. 6 of the Wood Book runs from 1 January 1813 to 31 August 1815. Half way through, the address to the Commissioners changes from 'My Lord and Gentlemen', 27 August 1814, to 'Gentlemen', 29 August 1814, signifying that Huskisson had taken over from Lord Glenbervie. Already in Glenbervie's term of office the metropolitan development was in hand, as the Parliamentary Paper of 1868-9 indicates: and on January 1814 the Treasury gave formal sanction to a 'loan of £300,000 from the Royal Exchange Assurance Corporation for making a more convenient communication from Marylebone Park and the Northern parts of the Metropolis to Charing Cross'. In the remainder of Vol. 6 and right through to the end of Huskisson's time, the development occupies an increasing part of the Board's business, and the values which it involved greatly exceed the aggregate of other business, including minerals and woodland. It became so important that an additional office known as the New Street Office was opened, from which the special business connected with it was done. New Street and Marylebone Park are what we know as Regent Street and Regent's Park. But the business dealt with by the Whitehall Office and the New Street office must be taken in conjunction; for they were complementary parts of a single program of West End Metropolitan Development reaching from St. James's Park and Whitehall to the northern limits of Regent's Park. It would need a historian of London to map out the development in detail, and I must content myself with some observations on its technique and finance. The fundamental relation between the owner and the occupant was the ninety-nine-year building lease; and that is why in 1918 and thereabouts the majority of the leases in Regent St. became due for renewal at the greatly enhanced figures which the land values of 1918 justified.

[1] As the maps show, the shape of Regent's Park today is that of the original farm.

I had the pleasure of a conversation in the summer of 1949 with Sir George (Granville) Leveson Gower,[1] who was Commissioner of Woods and Forests from 1908 to 1924. 'The Treasury fixed the price: and we had the job of explaining to the occupants why they had to pay so much more.' The statesmen who held fast to Regent's Park and Regent St. did as well for the English public as Disraeli when he bought the shares in the Suez Canal—in the very long run perhaps better.

John Nash 1752-1832 was one of the Board's architects, and the 'New Street' Development, as it was commonly called, was based on his plans. From Victoria Bus Station as far as Camden Street (I am supposing that you are saving shillings by proceeding in this way to Cambridge) you are with John Nash most of the way—Buckingham Palace, Hyde Park, Marble Arch, Regent St., Regent's Park. It might be better architecture but it is magnificent beside the dreariness of Camden Road and the horrors of Holloway and Hornsey. Nash repaired and enlarged Buckingham House, his large gateway for which, the Marble Arch, was removed in 1851 to its present site. His style (says the D.N.B.) 'lacks grandeur, and great monotony is produced by his persistent use of stucco'.

The wealthy Dudley, the Foreign Secretary of next year, writes to Littleton in 1826:

They have offered me a plot of ground on the New Terrace. I am more than half inclined to accept it. If I do not like to live there after the house is built, it will always be a very marketable article in such a situation. I see you take four windows. If it is a fair question,—and if it is not you will consider it as unasked—what do you expect it to cost you? This would be a sort of guide to me. Have you anything to do with Nash? I have some thoughts of letting him give me a plan, and having it executed by the best builder I can hear of. I suppose £20,000 would do something really handsome and substantial. This (sc. *Park Lane*) is in many respects a delightful situation—but Parliament, the clubs, the southern aspect and

---

[1] Sir George told me that when he came down from Balliol to act as Private Secretary to Mr Gladstone (1880-5) he handed over his rooms to G. N. Curzon: and also that in his day he had played games with four Prime Ministers—whist with Mr Gladstone and (I think) Lord Rosebery: indoor tennis with Lord Salisbury: outdoor tennis with Mr Balfour.

the increasing airiness and magnificence of that part of the town give it a great advantage.[1]

This New Terrace was *not* in Regent's Park, but was the future Carlton Terrace, facing St. James's Park. Huskisson later built in Carlton Gardens and thus ended his town life as a tenant of the office which he had formerly administered. There would be small likelihood of a statesman, especially if like Dudley he was a wealthy coal owner, living in Regent's Park stucco. (Not that there were no smart houses there—cf. Dudley writing from Park Lane, 8 August 1829, 'Town almost empty, but not quite. Great dinner today at Lord Hertford's in the Regent's Park,'[2] : and Richard Wellesley from the Stamp Office, 30 September 1829, 'Lord and Lady W. are now in the Regent's Park').

Nash was Littleton's architect also, and there is a letter of 1826 from Nash (No. 14 Regent Street) to him concerning the plans for a town house. To this letter Lord Hatherton (i.e. Littleton) has appended the following note: 'The Architect of Regent St., Regent's Park, Carlton House Gardens, the Marble Arch opposite Buckingham House and various other parts of London, also of Aqualate, the Restorer of Ingestre'[3] (Hatherton MS. Correspondence, 1826-7).

As with all architects and plans, there were changes and extensions as the work proceeded. One great change on the original was imposed by the Board. Nash revelled in squares and circuses and crescents: the Board, with St. James's Park and Hyde Park in mind, insisted on a much larger Regent's Park, devoted to public recreation, than Nash proposed. His fee, according to a minute of 6 June 1818, took the form of half-a-year's ground rent (the full rent, not the peppercorn!).

As I understand it, the Crown leased sites for others to build on, under covenant, according to the general plan. There are scores of references to the letting of plots, sometimes to the

---

[1] Hatherton MS. Correspondence, Letter 38—1826.

[2] This would be the lodge of St. Dunstan's, where his lavish entertainments earned him the *sobriquet* 'The Caliph of Regent's Park'.

[3] Littleton, being a Staffordshire man, mentions Nash's work in his county.

prospective occupier of a single house, sometimes to the builder
of a block of houses. The names of Pascoe Grenfell, Sir Thomas
Clarges and Mr Baxter occur frequently: e.g. proposed lease in
New Street to Mr Baxter (1818) at £1639, 'Mr. Nash to approve the covenants and clauses.' It is common to read that
they must be 'houses of the first class'. In Portland Place there
is to be 'a circus of houses of the first rate'. The 'United Services Club' (1819) must be 'of stone or near stone and uniform
in colour', and the property must be insured. It is stipulated,
e.g., that 'the lessee should enter into covenant for keeping the
premises insured against fire in the Royal Exchange or such
other Assurance Office as this Board may appoint' (1822). In
January 1823, on the eve of Huskisson's departure, there is a
list of certain Marylebone Leases, carrying fire insurance of
£36,000, with apportioned ground rents of £1,300 (odd). The
Board might keep amenities in its own hands. Thus in a Marylebone Park lease 'the ornamental garden of 18 plots is to be
reserved in the hands of the Crown with a view to avoiding
difficulties and disagreements among them as to its management'.

I was not able to form a clear picture of the comparative importance of the New St. development and the rest of the
Crown's London Estate. There is naturally more about it, because it is new, but the big figure for *single* plots seemed to be
in the Whitehall area. In July 1820 the Duke of Richmond
offers to sell 'Richmond House near Parliament St.' for £4,300.
Huskisson, before building in Carlton Gardens, lived in Richmond Terrace, and you may still see Richmond Terrace and its
Mews—approximately opposite the Cenotaph at the point
where Whitehall becomes Parliament St. In 1823, when Peniston Viscount Melbourne gets a renewal of his lease in Whitehall, 'it is no longer necessary' (says the Board) 'to repeat the
clause for resuming the premises by the Crown, in the event of
the rebuilding of Whitehall Palace.' After New Street, Whitehall gets the most mentions, but there are considerable property
deals in Spring Gardens, Great Tower Hill, Wardour St. and
Soho.

To finance their developments it was necessary for the Board to borrow under authority of Parliament, as given by:

53 George 3 c 121 Appendix III (Crown Lands, Regent St.)
　　　　　　　Appendix VI (London Buildings, Regent St.)
54 George 3 c 70 Crown Lands.

Under this authority the Board borrowed £300,000 from the Royal Exchange Assurance Company, and by 1817 needed a further £300,000. When the Royal Exchange decided not to take up the second loan, application was made to the Bank of England, which found that it could not legally make such a loan. Enabling legislation, however, was promptly passed through Parliament and received the Royal assent 23 May 1817 (57 Geo. 3 c 97, 98): whereupon the loan was made.

In 1820 there was a further loan of £200,000. In 1825 £600,000 was repaid partly by a loan from the Consolidated Fund and partly out of Land Revenue.

*Forest and Woodland*

Some of the Crown forest land had no timber on it and perhaps never had: most of its farm land carried timber. But, as an office, Woods and Forests were specially and primarily concerned with Crown forest which carried wood and was available for replantation or new plantation: where possible with Navy Timber. In December 1815 the Treasury instruct the Commissioners to continue the experiment suggested by the Admiralty of stripping the timber in the royal forests before it is felled. Presumably the Commissioners reported adversely, for several months later they are instructed to follow the old method of felling. (This, incidentally, is the only *technical* suggestion from outside which I detected).

The old Crown forests with which the Wood book chiefly deals are:

　　　　The New Forest　　　　Hants.
　　　　The Forest of Dean　　Gloster.
　　　　Salcy and Whittlewood　Northants (respectively 7
　　　　　　　　　　　　　　　miles S.E. and 6 miles
　　　　　　　　　　　　　　　S. of Northampton).

| Wychwood | Oxfordshire (4 miles N.W. of Witney). |
| Alice Holt | Surrey (near Farnham). |
| Delamere | Cheshire (10 miles N.E. of Chester). |

New plantations required enclosure for the protection of the seedlings. In December 1814 there was an enclosure of this sort for Navy Timber in the Forest of Dean. In December 1815 land was purchased in Parkhurst Forest, Isle of Wight, and a Treasury Warrant was issued authorising £6050 to be carried to the 'Navy Timber Nursery Fund'. Two months later authority was given for felling Beech Timber in Alice Holt for the use of the Navy. The lease of a farm in 1815 within the 'disafforested Forest of Braydon, Co. Wilts' (the hamlet of Braydon is near Cricklade) reminds us that throughout we are dealing with something which in former times was much greater. The Board, however, was not prepared to mix afforestation with charity and in 1817 declined to rent land for 'the employment of the labouring poor on planting oak'.

The timber transactions decline after 1815. There is less reference to Forests and more reference to Parks and especially to Windsor Great Park, which occupies a prominent place throughout.[1] Windsor Great Park (with Virginia Water), Hampton Court, Bushey Park, Richmond Park: Hyde Park, St. James's Park and Marylebone Park—these figure frequently because of the outlay on their upkeep. The former group, furthermore, were royal residences or under the special control of royalty. The Duke of Kent was keeper of the Home Park at Hampton Court: the Duke of Clarence at Bushey: the Princess Elizabeth at Richmond. Windsor Great Park with its

---

[1] Windsor Great Park was under Special Commissioners, and Huskisson writes to Lord Liverpool 1 March 1822 that he cannot take cognizance of the Report of these Commissioners and of the King's wishes thereon, unless the Board of Woods receives the King's command under the sign Manual or instructions from the Lords of Treasury. 'I have so often stated to you that the powers exercised by this Commission are in my judgment contrary to law and incompatible with the existing powers conferred on the Board of Woods according to law.'

A letter of C. Tennyson to Huskisson 6 July 1830 opens, 'I saw the Duke of Sussex this morning. We had much conversation on Public Matters'. The King (William IV) had given him the Rangership of Windsor Park—which is about 4000 £ a year, and Cumberland Lodge.'

Q

fine timber was in a class by itself, since here at the Royal
Lodge the Regent himself lived. In 1823 the question arose of
defraying the cost of additions to His Majesty's Lodge by felling timber. The King's ruling was: yes, as regards the timber
in Cranbourne and Swinley Wood: no, as regards that in
Windsor Forest. This is about as far as the examination of day
to day transactions takes us. What we need is an overall view of
the whole: which fortunately is available in P.P. 1868-9,
XXXV, Pt. II.

### From Edward the Confessor to 1950

When Huskisson accepted the Commissionership of Woods
and Forests it looked as though he might combine in an empi-
rical fashion three different functions which would one day
branch out into as many different ministries: a ministry of
essential supplies, a ministry of agriculture and a ministry of
town planning.

It was the first function which led to the appointment of a
man of Huskisson's calibre. It was still the age of the wooden
ship; and England in respect of Navy Timber was a deficiency
country. The Napoleonic blockade had cut off Baltic supplies
and it was not clear in 1814 that the need could be met from the
Colonies. As it turned out, it could be so met, and later the
arrival of the iron ship permanently removed the national
danger. By 1823 the issue was between Baltic and Canadian
timber, and this shifted it, as a question of policy, to the
domain of the Board of Trade.

The second function was never more than implicit. But if
any one in high office might be expected to possess an official
knowledge of agriculture it was the Commissioner of Woods
and Forests; and Huskisson did become the official spokesman
for agriculture in an informal way. The old Board of Agriculture was in principle not a ministry: it was a sort of Agricultural Organisation Society, with a grant from the State, and its
main function was publicity. By 1822 it was considered to have
done its work and was dissolved as a measure of economy. The
Royal Agricultural Society, established in 1838, did what the

old Board had done from a different angle and by voluntary means. But it was not because the Crown had agricultural properties that Huskisson became the spokesman of government. This contact was incidental. It was the part he played in the Corn Law of 1815 that brought him into the centre of the agricultural picture, and when he changed his attitude to the Corn Laws, the agricultural interest refused to follow him and considered him, henceforth, their leading opponent.

The third function was very important to London, but it was local and was outside the current of national policy. While, perhaps, it was for this reason that a man like Joseph Chamberlain would have liked to hold an office concerned with metropolitan development, Huskisson was not by inclination a local government man. He thought first and last in terms of Empire; and if he managed the New Street office well, it was merely that he could manage most kinds of knotty business—the disposition of the Privy Purse under the Regency Acts, the financial adjustment of the Queen's divorce, and so forth.

He was in fact a square peg in a round hole; and he came to dislike it thoroughly. He writes to Canning 23 June 1821, 'In this disagreeable office originally entered upon against my own judgment I have now lingered for seven years;' and he was to linger in it two years longer. The truth is, he lacked the equanimity which enabled Palmerston to make himself at home in a subordinate office till he could step cheerfully into the highest rank. Huskisson agonised about his future; for example, when offered the Governorship of Madras he compiled anxious columns of the pro's and con's before refusing it, where Palmerston would have dismissed it with a guffaw in the Premier's face. Nevertheless we must not leave it at this, because, disagreeable as the office became to him, it introduces us to a strand in our national history which runs from the earliest time to the present day.

We may divide the story into three periods:

Period I     Medieval.
Period II    The Administrative Revolution (1786-1814).
Period III   Modern.

## PERIOD I: MEDIEVAL

In the Domesday Survey, the Crown retained the 'ancient demesnes' of Edward the Confessor, and later acquired other land by prerogative, viz.: escheat, forfeiture and feudal delinquency. It was held that such later acquisitions might be disposed of by the King at his pleasure, though Parliament claimed the right to void the gifts if they were exorbitant. William II squandered the great estate of the Conqueror, and it was only gradually that the Crown estate was rebuilt by resumptions in succeeding centuries. Henry VIII increased it greatly by the Dissolution of the Monasteries, but quickly alienated the greater part. James I also granted lavishly, but under strong conciliar control the administration of the Crown Estate was both efficient and economical. Charles I sold Crown land or borrowed on its security in his struggle with Parliament, and the victorious Commonwealth sold off the balance; but these last were voided at the Restoration. The public purse, however, did not benefit greatly thereby, owing to easements and concealment of revenue; and when William of Orange in his turn used the Crown Lands to finance his succession, the revenues sank, till in 1702 they were at the paltry figure of £6000 a year. The Crown was restrained from further alienation by an Act of 1702, and in 1760 the medieval period drew to a close when the Crown's Land Revenues were surrendered to Parliament by the King, together with the rest of his hereditary revenues. During the administrative changes of the 1780's they were brought to the credit of the Consolidated Fund (1787). But, though the Crown Land revenues were thus surrendered, the surrender is technically for the lifetime of the sovereign only, so that the public, as it were, is a life tenant for the King's life.

## PERIOD II: THE ADMINISTRATIVE REVOLUTION
### 1786-1814

Burke in his speech on the Plan of Economical Reform 11 Feb. 1780[1] advocated the sale of the Crown lands; and he had behind him the high authority of the Wealth of Nations:

[1] *Works*, ed. 1852 III 365.

The revenue which, in any civilized monarchy, the crown derives from the crown lands, though it appears to cost nothing to individuals, in reality costs more to the society than perhaps any other equal revenue which the crown enjoys. It would, in all cases, be for the interest of the society to replace this revenue to the crown by some other equal revenue and to divide the lands among the people, which could not be done better, perhaps, than by exposing them to public sale.[1]

Fortunately for the public this short-sighted economy was refused; and the crown estate was retained for the reforming zeal of Pitt. The management of the Crown Lands was given to two Surveyors General: (1) of Land Revenue (2) of Woods and Forests. Revenue collection was placed under central control, and fixed salaries replaced fees. John Robinson[2] was (1727-1802) the first Surveyor General of Woods and Forests, and was followed in 1803 by Lord Glenbervie. The Government was now working to a plan, as prescribed by a special commission of enquiry, a device of unique importance in the history of economic reform, which later was applied to the reform of the Customs and the Excise. Later still, with greater power and publicity, often under pressure from without, it embraced those famous investigations into Poor Laws, Factories, Mines, Health, Housing and Truck, which formulated the social legislation of the nineteenth century, and from which (Report and Evidence) we write so much of our economic history.

In 1786 special Commissioners were appointed 'to enquire into the state and condition of Woods, Forests and Land Revenues belonging to the Crown'. They reported to the Treasury, and the Treasury laid the Reports before Parliament. In seventeen successive Reports, 1786-93 (and let me confess

---

[1] *Wealth of Nations*, Bk. V, Ch. II, Pt. I, Funds of the Sovereign: ed. Cannan, II, 309.

[2] Secretary to Treasury 1770-82. Surveyor General 1787-1802. Cf. John Robinson to Lord Hawkesbury (1st Earl of Liverpool) from Syon Hill 20 September 1788:

'I have been so much engaged in Windsor Forest, that I did not come to Addiscombe [*nr. Croydon*] last Saturday . . ., and am this morning going again to Virginia Water. The Soldiers' Working Camp in the Forest does not break up from thence until the 27th.'

An oily gentleman and briber-in-chief to the Government—'Name! Name!'. 'Yes. I could name him', cried Sheridan, 'as soon as I could say Jack Robinson.' But a great favourite with George III, for he knew all about sheep and planted at Windsor millions of acorns, and 20,000 oak trees.

I have only skimmed them), they covered the complex field; and they are of high value not only from the full and detailed information relating to the Crown Lands contained in them but also from the important and valuable improvements recommended by the Commissioners and subsequently carried into effect. In their 17th Report 1793 they noted that the three branches of fee farm rents, demised estates and woods and forests still yielded only about £6,000 p.a. on the average of 1760-86; and they recommended a single Board of Management. But as with Customs Consolidation, the major change was delayed by the proclamation of war.

The next move came from Dundas as First Lord of the Admiralty in December 1804. The correspondence is in the Huskisson Papers, and I abstract the substance of it:

*Dundas to Glenbervie Dec. 5 1804*
Navy Timber, especially oak, is very deficient. Were it a case of famine or pestilence, everyone would be alive to the danger. But as the danger is gradual no one heeds. Individual proprietors cannot grow it on the scale required. The only resource is Crown Lands and Forests.

*Glenbervie to Dundas.* From 'Office of Woods' Dec. 6, 1804
The Commissioners (*sc.* of 1786-93) denounced the constitution, powers and practice of the Forests Department. The Surveyor General of Woods and Forests (*i.e. Glenbervie himself*) acts under the Treasury but has inadequate power. The Officer of Lord Warden is antiquated. Crown Lands and Forests do not co-operate. Wanted a Board or Commission with executive power—analogous to the standing Commission of the Privy Council for the Board of Trade, the members of it to be composed of leading political figures, together with experts and a president who attends regularly. This machinery can be financed by Forests. But large scale enclosure and plantation will require either a grant from Parliament or a proportionate contribution from the Navy.

Glenbervie appends a copy of the order in Council of August 1786, dissolving the Committee of the Privy Council on Trade and Foreign Plantations and substituting a new one with Lord Hawkesbury (*1st Earl of Liverpool, father of the future premier*) as President.

In 1810 the Board was constituted, and perhaps because it was sensed that the timber side, with its patriotic appeal, would play a subordinate role, the large council of notables was dropped. The Surveyor General of Land Revenues and the Surveyor General of Woods, Forests, Parks and Chases were united; and His Majesty was authorised to appoint not more than three Commissioners of H.M. Woods, Forests and Land Revenues, to whom the duties of the Surveyors General were transferred and under whom the arrangement of Crown property was placed.

| | |
|---|---|
| Salary of 1st Commissioner | £2,000 |
| Salaries of 2nd and 3rd Commissioners | £1,200 |

Reports were required. They were triennial to 1827, and thereafter annual.

With the passing of 53 Geo. 3, 121 (1813) for the improvement of the north part of the metropolis (the New Street Act) we reach the point at which Glenbervie, now aged seventy, retired and Huskisson entered.

It was Huskisson's method, before making a big speech or taking important action (e.g. on silk or American reprisals), to call for memoranda; and in 38,760 there is an undated (but c. 1814) 'Memorandum for Mr. Huskisson on Woods, Forests and Crown Lands'. This repeats the matter covered by Glenberbie's letter to Dundas and sketches the progress made during Glenbervie's tenure. Again I abstract:

Under the new system the annual income of crown lands has risen by £100,000 per annum. As to forest, in 1803, when Lord Glenbervie became Surveyor General of Woods, the only timber enclosures in the Royal Forests were (1) 676 acres in the Forest of Dean and (2) 1207 in the New Forest, with fences and improvements in a state of neglect. Lord G. fenced, drained and planted with such energy that there are now 40,000 acres of enclosed timber, which at first were under the Surveyor General and now are under the Board. All the work, except the putting in of the plants, has been done under contract, by open competition. In regard to Forests and Crown Lands as a whole, the present commissioners have sold off the parts more expensive to manage (these fetching from 1810 to date

£300,000).[1] This sum has been laid out in timber land and the improvement of the Crown Estate in London. Were all non-forest land sold, it would still be necessary for the safety of the timber supply to have Crown Forests, and it is to the public advantage that the Crown should be represented in every part of the country. Adam Smith's criticism [the writer leaves it to us to locate the passage!] does not apply to the present system of management, and overlooks the innumerable difficulties to their sale, namely (1) the long leases of town houses which tenants have improved in the expectation of a renewal, (2) the difficulty of finding good purchasers for large country properties, (3) the 'qualified interest' which the Crown has in much of the remaining forest.

Experience speaks, and I conjecture that the memorandum was written at the Office by the Second or Third Commissioner.

### PERIOD III: MODERN

For the remainder of the nineteenth century the Board pursued a chameleon career, shedding here and adding there, with changes in the balance of functions within the office and in its relation to the rest of the Government: arriving eventually at its present title 'Commissioners of Crown Lands' (1924). In 1826 it took over the Crown Revenues of the Isle of Man from the Stanley family: in 1828 the Irish Crown Revenues from the Excise: in 1831-5 the Scottish Crown Revenues from the Barons of the Exchequer in Scotland. Conversely, it parted with its foreshore rights to the Board of Trade 1866, and with its Land Revenue Record Office to the Public Record Office in 1903-4.

In 1851 by the Crown Lands Act of that year, Public Works and Buildings and Royal Parks (bar Windsor) were transferred to the Commissioner of Works, salary £2,000: while Royal Forests and other possessions of the Crown stayed with Woods —with two Commissioners at £1,000, both ineligible for Parliament. In 1906 the President of the Board of Agriculture became *ex officio* Commissioner of Woods unpaid. In 1924 Forests were transferred to the new Forestry Commission, the title of Commissioner of H.M.'s Woods, Forests and Land Revenues being changed to Commissioners of Crown Lands;

[1] This figure is suspiciously high.

and, on the retirement of Sir Geo. Leveson Gower (see p. 221),
the Minister of Agriculture and Fisheries *ex officio* (a politician)
and the new permanent Commissioner of Crown Lands (a civil
servant) became jointly responsible for the management of the
Land Revenue. By 6 and 7 Geo. 6, c. 7 (1943) the Secretary of
State for Scotland is also a Commissioner *ex officio*.

In the modern period there have been other important transfers. In 1837 its Lighthouse Rights passed to Trinity House at
a valuation of £300,000: in 1942 its coal mines to the Coal
Commission at a valuation of £2 million. In 1902 Osborne,
Queen Victoria's private home, became a Crown estate.

But the figures of most interest are those relating to the
growth of values which the enterprise of the Commissioners
brought into being. The 1776 acres of enclosed forest in 1808
had risen to 33;000 planted acres in 1849, valued at £1 million;
and in 1924 the whole 120,000 acres of Forest Land passed to
the Forestry Commission at £1,680,000. Thus the Forestry
enterprise was a public success; and much more so the urban
development, represented by the London Estate in chief. Between 1813 and 1839 large quantities of capital, met from
loans and steadily mounting revenue, were called for; and it
was only in 1839 that net revenue from this source emerged.
Since then it has grown cumulatively. In the ten years 1938-48
the net revenue from all Crown properties (urban and agricultural) paid into the exchequer averaged one million a year: the
London Estate being by far the largest contributor. There was
a moment not so long ago when the Canadian buffalo had
dwindled to a single herd in Mexico. It was salvaged and con-
served, and now Canada has as much buffalo as her National
Parks can carry. Canada is justly proud of this, and I suggest
that we, too, have good reason to be grateful to those Commissioners of Woods, Forests and Land Revenues who built up
the all but vanished asset of Burke's day to the present estate in
the hands of Crown Lands or the other public departments to
which parts have been transferred. Suppose Burke had had his
way and suppose that now in 1950 the West End had decided
to become the owner of itself, what huge sums would have been

demanded in compensation, what paeans would have been sung
to the record of private enterprise, what dirges uttered on the
perils of nationalisation! My friends of the Conservative College
like to hear me on Empire, but sniff politely when they think
they scent Labour.

### No. 2 Carlton Gardens

No. 2 joins on to No. 1, the official residence of the Foreign
Secretary. In World War I it was occupied for a time by Lord
Kitchener and it is now, as the result of damage in World War
II, in a state of disrepair.

When in 1827 Carlton House was pulled down, the Treasury
approved the erection of houses on the site and grounds in
accordance with a lay-out prepared by John Nash. Building
leases were offered to various influential people, including Huskisson, who, writing from Somerset Place on 31 May 1827,
accepted terms for building a house in Carlton Gardens. It was
built just in time to be occupied by Huskisson, whose last
London letters are headed 'Carlton Gardens'. The house had
its own garden, which Mrs Huskisson speaks of as 'our Garden
at the end of Carlton Terrace'.

On 15 March 1830 Huskisson received from the Office of
Woods a statement of the terms finally arranged, namely:
£1,752 5s. 6d., being the purchase price of 'three-quarters of
the yearly rent agreed to be paid by you to the Crown, for the
site of the house lately built by you in Carlton Gardens', plus
an annual rental of £28 4s. 0d.: together with two further payments, one in lieu of land tax, and the other for the piece of
garden ground next to St. James's Park and attached to the
premises. After his death a lease was granted (3 May 1831) to
his widow for a term of ninety-nine years as from 5 July 1831
—the property being described as 'a plot of ground (part of the
site of Carlton Palace) with a messuage thereon'.

Huskisson had secured Treasury assent to a gate opening
into the Ordnance Passage which ran between his house and
Marlborough House, with a view to having a private way into
the Park. The original intention was to make the Ordnance

Passage a thoroughfare. When this was dropped, the Treasury agreed that, 'provided the privacy of the Ordnance Passage was preserved, there would be no difficulty in allowing me a private access to it' (Huskisson to J. Pennethorne: Eartham, 13 October 1829, 38,758, f. 20); and on the strength of this, he built a gateway and steps. It was hoped thus to placate the Duke, who, as Master General of the Ordnance, resisted what he considered to be an encroachment. But even so he was not satisfied: and after Huskisson had incurred the expense of gateway and steps, the Duke ordered the door to be removed. The correspondence goes on and on, and the matter, so far as I can find, was not adjusted in Huskisson's time. Yet another misunderstanding! Under escort I descended these steps (28 January 1949) to the still barred doorway flush with the alley, still known as Ordnance Passage, which separates Carlton Gardens from Marlborough House, the residence of Queen Mary. What a lot London has to tell us, if only we know where to look!

# CHAPTER EIGHT

# THE SUSSEX OF HUSKISSON AND HAYLEY

## *William and Emily Huskisson*

To the memory of the Rt. Hon. William Huskisson, for ten years one of the Representatives of this City in Parliament. This station he relinquished in 1823 when, yielding to a sense of publick duty he accepted the offer of being returned for Liverpool, for which he was selected on account of the zeal and intelligence displayed by him in advancing the Commercial Prosperity of the Empire. His death was occasioned by an accident near that Town on the XV of September MDCCCXXX and changed a scene of triumphal rejoicing into one of general mourning.

At the urgent solicitation of his constituents he was interred at the Cemetery there amid the unaffected sorrow of all classes of people. . . .

This last was literally true. Town and Country: Tory, Whig and Radical: alike mourned him, from Ebenezer Elliott the Corn Law rhymer:

'Oh Huskisson, in vain our friend'

to the stolid yeomanry of West Sussex—the one class of his countrymen with whom John Wesley failed. In general 'their life is supremely dull; and it is usually unhappy too. For, of all people in the kingdom they are most discontented; seldom satisfied either with God or man'[1]—but to Huskisson the salt of the earth. In the malaise of 1819 he writes to Arbuthnot, 'the yeomanry are still within your reach and to them in my opinion we must look' (24 March 1820). Huskisson was then a member of the Government, but ten years later he almost regrets their emotional immunity. 'The men of Sussex seem to be a subdued race. It is an old custom in the Weald to leave their wagons in the first slough till the return of fine weather. With the same resignation they look to the present slough and seem to trust to the D. of W. to get them out of it' (to J. E. Denison

[1] Wesley's Journal, V, 192.

10 January 1830). In November 1830, when he had been two months dead, the Agricultural Labourers' Revolt reached Sussex, and it was the county in which the farmers kept their heads, calmly meeting the deputations of the men and accepting their reasonable demands, even though 'each farmer had an incendiary letter addressed to him in his pocket'.[1] By comparison with other southern counties the subsequent deportations were few.

The statue, a fine piece,[2] with the above inscription on the pedestal, is in Chichester Cathedral; and in an adjoining bay is a beautiful memorial to Mrs Huskisson: the widow kneeling before an angel: her elbows resting on an open book and the hands raised in supplication:

Sacred to the memory of Eliza Emily, wife of the Rt. Hon. William Huskisson, M.P. for this city. She died at Eartham where she is buried in the churchyard of that Parish April 13, 1856. This monument, designed and executed by John Gibson, R.A., is erected by him to record her Christian virtue and his grateful sense of her many acts of kindness during their long and uninterrupted friendship.

'Unto thee O Lord do I lift up my soul'

The tablet to her in Eartham Parish church is equally satisfying: white marble on a black background with the name of Ellis at the bottom:

Sacred to the memory of Eliza Emily Huskisson.
Youngest[3] daughter of Admiral Milbanke and wife of
the Rt. Hon. William Huskisson.
Born May 28, 1777.
Died April 7, 1856.
Beloved and respected by her family and friends and
by this village where she had lived so long.

[1] Cf. J. L. and B. Hammond, *The Village Labourer*, 247-8, 308.
[2] By Carew: yet not, I feel, by one who understood him as Gibson did. John Gibson (1790-1866), a Liverpool Welsh boy, did early work for Sir John Gladstone and a bas relief of Mr Blundell in Sefton Church. He attracted the notice of William Roscoe, who introduced him to Italian masters and so to Rome, where he met Canova and lived many years. Mrs Huskisson visited him there. For an appreciation of his work see the notice by Lady Eastlake in *Encyclopaedia Britannica*.
[3] Her elder sister was Harriet. I know of no other.

Huskisson, as M.P. for Chichester, was not the big townsman representing little townsmen, but the statesman prominent
in the counsels of the nation, who had honoured Chichester in
making his home close by and identifying himself with its
interests. At Eartham he knew nearly all the happiness of his
life. During years of uncongenial office in London he found
compensation not only in the seclusion and hospitalities of
Eartham (friends looked forward to his coverts), but in the
activities and politics of the lively little town where Eartham
shopped and made social contact with the county and the diocese. I have halted by the wicket which leads from Eartham
House to Eartham Church and understood entirely why she
wished William to lie there, where she also would one day lie,
and not in far-off Liverpool. Yet were I a conjuror I would call
up, not the worshippers within its walls or the long row of Mil-
bankes on its walls—but the contents of the Eartham post box
during the eighty years from 1776 to 1856.

There had, of course, to be a London life. That was in the
day's work and the social season; but three lives—Sussex,
London, Liverpool—were more than Mrs Huskisson could
face, and Huskisson himself only went to Liverpool with un-
feigned reluctance. I quote from the late George Veitch, who
knew every line of the story:

Liverpool was more eager to give than Huskisson to receive. He was as
reluctant to desert Chichester as Chichester to surrender him. 'If, *multa
gemens*, I am to be transferred to Liverpool,' he wrote, 'I cannot cast off
Chichester as I would an old shoe' . . . But in the upshot he yielded to
importunity rather than imperil the seat at Liverpool which Canning had
come to regard as the corner-stone of his political authority. And incidentally Chichester went over to the Whigs.

And again:

When Huskisson arrived in Liverpool late on 10th February (1823), he
found that a contest, vexatious, but not formidable, nevertheless awaited
him. 'The Rabble of this place', he wrote to his wife, 'will *never*, I see
clearly, allow an election without a contest . . . I am now wishing heartily
I had been at Chichester—so quiet and so complacent—instead of having

the battle to fight here.'[1] You could hardly call Huskisson a democrat—
not even of the Cam Hobhouse, Francis Burdett type.

## The County Town of West Sussex

> I will gather and carefully make my friends
> Of the men of the Sussex Weald.
> They watch the stars from silent folds,
> They stiffly plough the field.
> By them and the God of the South Country
> My poor soul shall be healed.
>
> I will hold my house in the high wood
> Within a walk of the sea,
> And the men who were boys when I was a boy
> Shall sit and drink with me.
>
> (Hilaire Belloc)

The Sussex of Huskisson and Hayley was West Sussex: and
more particularly that quadrangle of it which is bounded on the
north by Midhurst (sacred to the memory of Cobden), and
Petworth (Huskisson's post-town), and on the south by Chichester and Felpham, which last we visit to gaze at Hayley's
turret and fall in love with Blake's cottage.

> Away to sweet Felpham, for heaven is there
> The ladder of angels descends through the air;
> On the turret its spiral does softly descend,
> Through the village then winds, at my cot it does end.
>
> The bread of sweet thought and the wine of delight
> Feed the village of Felpham by day and by night
> And at his own door the bless'd Hermit does stand
> Dispensing unceasing to all the wide land.
>
> (To Mrs. Anna Flaxman, Sept 14 1800.)

Eartham and Slindon, where Belloc spent his youth, lie next
to one another, and the Rector of Slindon does duty at both
churches. In Slindon church a newly erected tablet notifies that

[1] George S. Veitch, *Huskisson and Liverpool*, 23, 26.

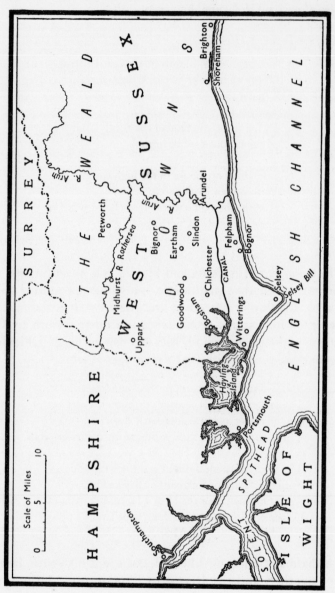

West Sussex

Stephen Langton, Archbishop of Canterbury, came from the parish.

The Eartham and Slindon properties are flanked by the ducal houses of Richmond at Goodwood on the west and Norfolk at Arundel on the east. To the north over Bignor Hill in true Weald lies Petworth, where in Huskisson's day lived Geo. O'Brien Wyndham, third Earl of Egremont (1751-1837), a Westminster boy and the patron of fine art.

'Hold my house in the high wood, within a walk of the sea.' This fits for the South Downs of West Sussex which, unlike those of East Sussex, are liberally wooded. But it is a long walk by reason of the peculiar relation in which Chichester stands to the sea. For though it has a harbour, this is but one of several winding creeks (Bosham, the artists' paradise, is the chief of them) which flow by a roundabout course into the roadstead of Spithead between the mainland and Hayling Island. Felpham, six miles S.S.E. of Eartham, is Eartham's seaside: East and West Wittering are Chichester's, about six miles away to the S.W., with Selsey Bill between them and Felpham. Therefore, from Eartham you look down towards Selsey Bill over a deep stretch of corn and dairyland, with the rim of the sea just visible on either side of the Bill.[1] Chichester, named from Cissa, son of Aelli, is one of the most ancient towns in England, and one may read on the wall of the Council House, close to where it was found, a stone bearing the inscription:

To Neptune and Minerva this temple is dedicated for the welfare of the divine house by the authority of Tiberius Claudius Cogidubnus, king and legate of Augustus in Britain, by the Guild of Wrights and its associates, the site being granted by (Pud)ens, son of Pudentinus.

This puts the gilds of our medieval history into their proper modern place.

With its Cathedral and famous Market Cross (from which North, South, East and West Streets lead out to their respective gates), and its still more famous St. Mary's Hospital (where

---

[1] Cf. Journal of House of Commons 1819—'Selsey Enclosure Bill: that Mr. Huskisson, Sir Godfrey Webster and Mr. Walter Burrell do prepare and bring it in': Huskisson in his 'woodcocks' mood would have punned it.

R

old ladies live as they have lived since the thirteenth century, in a sort of great barn with a chapel at the end, in quarters as pleasant as an undergraduate's rooms at Cambridge), Chichester symbolises cohesion and continuity. And its rich variety of Georgian houses, with no trace of slums anywhere, gives an inkling of a prosperous past, dignified and well-proportioned, up to which its modern buildings, public and private, successfully live. Yet there is no sense of sleepiness about it. Indeed, it is only too lively today with its ceaseless stream of Southdown buses, and what the congestion of the South Coast will be now that the petrol shortage has eased baffles the imagination.

In 1700 Chichester (for Sussex was then an iron county) had an important industry. It was the chief needle maker of England, but this was soon lost to the West Midlands, to the Black Country that was coming to be; and eighteenth-century Chichester had to look elsewhere for its future, which it found in the growing productivity of its agriculture, or, as Huskisson would have said, in the industry of its yeomanry.

The boom to which Chichester owed its resurgence was brought about by a new development in the corn trade. Whereas formerly Sussex farmers had sent their surplus corn overland to Farnham, the great grain market of southern England, a few moneyed men of Chichester and the neighbourhood had taken to buying up the corn and lodging it in granaries, which they had built near the Crook, and after milling it themselves exported it by sea to London. Farnham's loss was Chichester's gain. Improved methods of farming contributed to the boom, and the Chichester corn market became one of the most flourishing in England. Hay, the Chichester historian, estimates that by 1800 three times as much grain was being produced in the surrounding country as a hundred years earlier. But today the Corn Exchange is a cinema theatre.

On this agricultural base local trade throve, and Chichester became the home of many traders, wholesale and retail, whose custom was enlarged by the increasing attraction of the Downs as a site for stately homes, which, with the improvement of roads, were increasingly accessible to London. It was also great

hunting country. The Charlton Pack: the Goodwood Pack: the
Cowdray Pack: followed in succession. More distinctive as an
assembler of population was the growth of Goodwood as a
racing centre at the instance of its owners, the ducal House of
Richmond. '1801—the new race course on the Harrowby near
Goodwood is now completely formed.'

The 1st Duke was the natural son of Charles II by Louise
de Kérouaille, Duchess of Portsmouth. The 2nd Duke built,
to the design of Sir William Chambers (the architect of Somerset House), the immense stable block, which is still the finest
architectural feature on the estate. The 3rd Duke, tree planter,
cabinet minister and mighty hunter, equipped 'Glorious Goodwood' with its first grand-stand. The 4th Duke, Huskisson's
coeval, 1764-1819, became Governor General of Canada,
dying of fox-bite in Quebec, and the repercussions of the fatality
enter the political story. This Duke was Wellington's soldier
friend whose Duchess gave the famous ball at Brussels. The
5th Duke, Charles Gordon Lennox, Earl of March, was Huskisson's colleague in the representation of Chichester and, as
Duke, continued the family tradition of soldiering and sport,
becoming President of the Royal Agricultural Society (1845-
60). Is there some relation between soldiering and sport? Does
the open field of baronial and civil war give place to the enclosure of the pheasant covert, the race course and the mena-
gerie of wild beasts?[1] Did the hunt welcome enclosure for its
hedges? Be that as it may, there never was a chase so famous or
so thrilling as that which Goodwood's royal ancestor staged
along these downs with himself as fox and Cromwell's soldiery
hot on his trail. Now cantering, now hiding, the monarch and
his trusty guide sped cunningly till at last by a miracle of fortune well-deserved they found ship at Shoreham.

But there is a sport on green grass more English even than
horse-racing. Richard Newland came from the parish of Slindon. A left-hander and the finest bat of his day, he made 88 for

---

[1] Cf. T. G. Wills, *Records of Chichester*, p. 73: '1725. Now about was brought to Goodwood
the great novelty of many wild beasts, birds and other animals, and there kept in dens, with iron
gates made for them to be seen through, which draw a great number of people thither to see them,
a lion, tiger, man tiger, bears, egles, ostrich.'

England against Kent in 1745. It was he who taught the art to Richard Nyren of Hambledon, Co. Hants., and when Nyren had trained his Hambledon eleven serious cricket was born. The early contiguity of racing and cricket is marked by the fact that in 1825 the Earl of Egremont won the Goodwood Stakes with 'Stumps', and the Goodwood Cup with 'Cricket'. Does Slindon blood run in Australian veins? I trow not. But Thomas Henty, John Trigg, Tommy Hills, George Page and David Grey—of whom more anon—might enlighten us, if only they were here to tell the tale.

### Chichester's M.P. (1812-23)

Chichester sent two members to Westminster: the earliest of all being a certain 'William of Eartham' 1295,[1] our William of Eartham coming 517 years later. Some continuity! The election indentures of the period, signed and sealed by the Mayor, are in the town archives: for 1812 Huskisson and the Earl of March: for 1818 *ditto*: for 1820 Huskisson and the Rt. Hon. John George Lennox, brother of the new Duke. In 1823 'in the place of the Rt. Hon. William Huskisson, who since his said election hath vacated his seat by the acceptance of the office of Treasurer of His Majesty's Navy' was chosen William Stephen Poyntz of Cowdray Park in the County of Sussex.

The phraseology of the indentures may be illustrated by the special election of 1814:

8th day of August in the 54th year of our Sovereign Lord King George the third. This indenture witnesses that the Rt. Hon. William Huskisson, who was lately chosen one of the citizens of the said City of Chichester for the present Parliament of our Lord the King and who since the said election hath vacated the seat in the said Parliament by the acceptance of the Office of one of the Commissioners of his said Majesty's Woods, Forests and Land Revenue, the said Mayor Aldermen and Citizens have again made choice and election of the said William Huskisson to be a Citizen for the said City of Chichester to attend at the said present Parliament according to the tenor of the said warrant.

[1] P.P. 1878, LXII, Pt. I, Willielmus de Ertham, Chichester City.

Chichester, as to one half, was a pocket borough. Throughout the eighteenth century one of the members was usually a Lennox; and from 1784 onwards there was an arrangement by which the Duke of Richmond nominated one member and the electors the other. The electors were all those paying scot and lot—i.e. the ratepayers, together with the corporates (aldermen and councillors) and the freemen (honorary freemen of the merchant gild, and *ex-officio* freemen, like the bailiffs). It came to be the custom for the Mayor to nominate each year two honorary freemen, one a Tory and one a Whig, and in the Corporation Minutes for September 1818 a well-known Cambridge name appears:

Mr. Mayor proposed and nominated Stephen Gaselee Esquire, Barrister at Law, to be admitted to the Freedom of the Merchant Guild within the city.

In 1819 the Common Council contained one Earl, two Lords, one Honourable and two Baronets. In this way town and county were blended both for local and political purposes.

Was there bribery? Were votes bought and sold? The oath which the electors took was definite enough.

I do swear I have not received . . . directly or indirectly any Sum or Sums of Money, Office, Place, or Employment, Gift or Reward . . . in order to give my vote, and that I have not been before Polled at this election.

In his election address of 1820—the Regent having ascended the Throne—'to the free and independent electors of Chichester', Huskisson had need to say very little—in substance only this: 'I throw myself on your personal kindness. From no other influence do I look for countenance or support.' Was this a sly dig at the other half of the picture? for it was reported to the Municipal Corporation's Commissioner of 1835 that Lord Arthur Lennox (the Lennox representative of the day) 'is returned chiefly through the influence of the Corporation (of which his brother, the Duke of Richmond is Lord High Steward), which body appoints the Magistrates of the City, they regulating the Licences of Public Houses, and elects Corporates and Freemen, whereby an undue influence is exercised over many who have votes for Parliament'.

But large expenditure might be legitimately incurred in bringing voters to the poll; and there was other expenditure of a more doubtful order, at which the Report of 1835 hints. Beer flowed freely when there was a serious contest. An unsuccessful candidate, John Fuller by name, spent £1100 on ribbons. And in addition to beer and favours there was a liberal supply of organised noise—though mainly before Huskisson's time. Rival parties of 'White-boys' constituted themselves the candidates' constables and paraded the town during the election, beating the other side up. But by 1820 it was the elections for the county and other boroughs that provided most of the fun. Huskisson loved having a finger in the election pie—of his neighbours. Witness this to Lord Liverpool of 6 February 1820:

The enclosed answer from Lord E. respecting our county representation I received yesterday just as my carriage was driving off to come down here. I called upon Lord E. in my way thro' Petworth, and in conversation he strongly urged your Brother's losing no time in ascertaining from 2 or 3 of the leading interests in the East of the County, Lords Ashburnham, Chichester, Abergavenny, Gage and 'blast' Fuller (the latter not to be omitted), whether they will support him. Lord E. has no doubt of his receiving an affirmative answer from all of them. Then we, of the West, may declare ourselves. I can see the Duke of Richmond, Lord Selsey, the Bishop etc., and Mr. J. [*Jenkinson*] may rely upon my personal assistance, if wanted, in securing the Freeholders in and around Chichester. From the part which I took upon the Corn Bill[1] and little services which I have done them, I know that I can influence a great many of the yeomanry in this neighbourhood, who at the last election [1818] signified to me by whole parishes their readiness to vote according to my wishes. But I agree with Lord E. that there will be no occasion for such an exertion. At Brighton and Lewes there are some Whigs, and the Duke of Norfolk may influence a few Freeholders round Arundel; but I have every reason to believe that he will not bestir himself for so discredited a character as Sir Godfrey W.

I have long been convinced of what Lord E. hints respecting the in-

---

[1] I.e. in support of the Corn Law of 1815. He had not yet written his 1821 Report!

decision and speculation which enabled Sir G.[1] to step in at the last election. But with Lord Chichester's age and state of health it would be too much refinement to be calculating a second time upon the County remaining misrepresented for the chance of his son being returned 6 or 7 years hence.

I shall repair to Chichester tomorrow. All is quiet there; tho' Arundel sets a bad example. They have now 4 Candidates with open houses; and many of our lower orders look with envious eye, and craving thirst to the scenes of jollity and drunkenness which are going on there.

Yours very truly,

W. Huskisson

So away, boys, to Arun's Dell. There's naught doing in our sleepy burg these days!

When duly elected, the two citizens were the mouthpiece of their fellow-citizens to Westminster.

Huskisson soon won the confidence of the county. The wool growers of Eastbourne thank him for his service in securing the repeal of the vicious Act of William III restraining the carriage of wool in Kent and Sussex. To a constituent anent the proposed Corn Law of 1814, he explains his opposition to Parnell's violently prohibitive duty, and at the same time (for the country was still at war) stresses the need for home supply. 'Let the bread we eat be the produce of corn grown among ourselves. I for one do not care how cheap it is; the cheaper the better.'[2]

The only mentions I have found of Huskisson in the Town Minutes concern addresses which he and the Earl of March are requested to present in their own person: one in 1816 congratulating the Regent on the Marriage of his Daughter, another sympathising with him after the flagrant attack on his Royal Person. Arundel might wobble, now with a Protestant and now with a Catholic Duke of Norfolk, but Chichester was

---

[1] Sir Godfrey Webster, see above, p. 241 *n*.

[2] The letter was later printed. Cf. the Acts of the Apostles, XII, 20 'and having made Blastus the king's chamberlain their friend, desired peace; because their country was nourished by the king's country'. When Sir John Sinclair quoted this at him, Huskisson by return replied (unhappily there is no date) 'that not the authority of Blastus, nor of all the Chamberlains who had held the golden key from his time downwards, would shake his confidence in the principles of free trade, or induce him to prevent the importation of foreign grain' (*Memorials of Sir John Sinclair*, II, 325).

Protestant throughout, pronouncing in 1812 against the repeal of Catholic disabilities, since it would be 'an encroachment on that venerable monument of British wisdom and patriotism, our unrivalled constitution'. There existed in Chichester, and still exists, along with its Mace of 1689, a dining-club named 'the Mayor and Corporation of St. Pancras', which on 4 December celebrates by a dinner the landing of William of Orange at Torbay. Huskisson was a member of it (and Mr Stephen Gaselee, surely).

In the Huskisson correspondence for 1818 there are adjoining letters, one from Lord Egremont concerning the Chichester election, another from an exuberant excise officer, Rotton by name, returning thanks for an appointment—'Oh, my dear sir, how different are my prospects now to what they were but one month ago!'

In 1819 Lord Liverpool was subjected to a polite bombardment of the same nature at the instance of Huskisson himself.

*Huskisson to Ld Liverpool* April 25. 1819

At the request of several of Mr. Powell's friends I forward to you the enclosed paper, and I have much satisfaction in doing so because I am confident your best exertion will be employed to accomplish the object it is intended to promote.

Mr P., collector of customs at the Port of Chichester, had a large family and a small income (just like Mr Rotton); and most of Chichester signed the petition.

Lord Liverpool replies in the standard language of regretful refusal, and, as the same petition was presented by the Earl of March, he asures both that he will do his best, if an opportunity offers. But 'I will add that in the Port of London nearly all the higher class of officers are selected, when vacancies occur, from the next subordinate class at the same port', as Huskisson knew full well.

One gets quite used to the 'refusal' letter of this Premier— now to an official of the Customs or Excise, now to a bishop or army officer, now to a brother politician. No wonder in the end he had a stroke. For he had to write scores of them, and they are usually in his own hand. Peel in a similar situation (before he was Prime Minister) generally concluded 'but why not ask the Duke?'. Canning, less patient, would let off a little steam:

I know that very generally a notion prevails that short cuts by individuals are better than the practised roads of office for obtaining individual objects; but I do assure you—that opinion is erroneous.[1]

Palmerston, needless to say, took it in his stride:

My Dear Sandon,
     Mr. Sealey's case is only that of every man who takes a post by storm. After having moved Heaven and Earth to get the office, he next sets to work to make it better than he finds it! or to change it for one he fancies would suit him better. I fear, however, that Mr. Sealey must divide with the 'Contents'.

Yours sincerely,

Palmerston[2]

## The Arun Navigation and Public Works

The point at which local history touches regional or national history raises delicate problems for the economic historian. The Victoria County History was faced with the regional problem. If all or nearly all of a great industry is located within a single county, such as the Lancashire cotton industry or the Stafford-shire pottery industry, the story can be coherently told under one county. If it is definitely tripartite, like the woollen indus-try—West Country, East Anglia, Yorkshire (West Riding), it can, by prior arrangement, be co-ordinated. But I do not see how any county history can come to terms with Birmingham and the Black Country, which involves three contiguous coun-ties, Worcestershire, Warwickshire and Staffordshire, without scrapping the county unit.

The national problem is of a different nature. A local trouble may stimulate the formulation of a national problem, and ap-proximately the same problem may be voiced from many differ-ent quarters, e.g. the protests against the new corn law or the

---

[1] Canning Box: Liverpool Public Reference Library.
[2] Sandon Box: Liverpool Public Reference Library. Viscount Sandon (1798-1882) sat for Liverpool 1831-47.

distress petitions of hand-loom weavers. If in our local history such
an example occurs, we may present the example, while taking
care not to exaggerate its importance. Where, however, a local
problem is raised by a statesman who is also close to the heart
of things, it comes significantly into the national picture, and
where a parallel problem is raised by a correspondent in another
part of the country, who has intimate relations with the statesman aforesaid, the dual statement takes on more than local
importance.

In 1785 a body called the River Arun Navigation was incorporated to improve the navigation of that modest stream. Its
minute book (which is among the county archives in Chichester)
opens with the act of incorporation, empowering it to purchase
land, make surveys, levy appointed tolls, etc. etc. It was a small
but in the end remunerative undertaking, which was able to
declare a 7% dividend on its stock in 1830: receipts £1500,
expenses (wages, taxes, bond repayments, reserve) £800, dividend £700.

In 1816 a bill was promoted for a larger venture, namely to
connect Portsmouth with the Arun by a canal passing to the
south of Chichester and roughly parallel with the Portsmouth-
Chichester-Brighton railroad of the future. Discussion between
the Corporation of Chichester (which had its own little coal
dock at Dell Quay), the River Arun Navigation and the new
Canal resulted in adjustments, Chichester connecting by a
branch and leasing tenements needed by the Canal. Eventually
it was built, but it had a disappointing life, and is now derelict,
part of the course being dry. This was the canal for which Huskisson, as we shall see, sought aid in 1816 as a measure of
national policy. In 1817 he was able to secure that £750,000 of
the Exchequer Bills for the year should be devoted to public
buildings and fisheries, but whether any portion reached the
Portsmouth-Arundel Canal Company, not having seen the
canal records, I am unable to say.

In the financial furore of the mid-1820's a more grandiose
project was mooted: namely, a 'grand Imperial Ship Canal
through the Counties of Surrey, Sussex and Southampton with

a branch from the same to the River Thames at Cherry Garden
Stairs, also a branch from Arundel to the sea near Littlehamp-
ton made under the direction of Nicholas Wilcox Cundy Esq.
Architect and Civil Engineer, Nov. 1827'. The plan, when the
sheets are pieced together, is over ten yards long, but there it
ended, for Arundel was not the Manchester of the South.

The case that Huskisson argues is central aid for local effort
in a season of post-war distress, and his emphasis on the de-
mobilised war arsenal of Portsmouth raises the broader problem of national adjustment to the condition of peace. This is the
point at which, in the sequence of ideas, Canning's Quaker
friend, James Cropper of Liverpool, enters. Unless my judgment is altogether at fault, this second letter is a masterpiece. I
dislike slogans, but surely he is on the track of what we call
'full employment'; and he states the problem of supply in excess
of wants in terms which Lord Keynes has taught us to associate
with the later Malthus. Note in particular the role of consumption in the programme of recovery and its pertinence to the idea
of the multiplier.

I cannot prove that Canning turned over the letter to Huskisson, but as Huskisson was his economic repository it is
highly probable.

Some people are intrigued by anticipations (or survivals),
and almost write their economic history in terms of it. I am not
one of them, for single ideas or episodes, in isolation and un-
developed, lead nowhere. It is when ideas are combined and
built into a sequence that they engender policy. And I think
that Canning and Huskisson might in their day of full power
have said to Cropper: 'Agreed, but we have found by now that
the way to entice men accustomed-to-accumulate to spend for
employment is to provide them with the facilities for warehousing, shipping and an extended foreign trade, which is the
object of our commercial policy; and this involves as a bye product the importation of foreign grain for the ill fed poor.' By
this route the Huskisson of the 1815 Corn Law could pass
consistently into the Huskisson of Ebenezer Elliott. The two
letters are:

*Huskisson to Lord Liverpool* from Eartham: proposing that Government should take shares in the Arun and Portsmouth Canal:[1]

It would be the means of securing the execution of such a work in the interval of peace, when labour and materials are cheap; and of giving employment to many artisans, bricklayers, carpenters etc. (in the construction of the docks and bridges), who by the cessation of the war are thrown out of work at Portsmouth and its neighbourhood, as well as to country labourers, of whom there is now a great excess.

The case is simply this—that the advance of a comparatively *small* sum by Govt. for a work in which it is admitted the State has a material interest, is necessary at this moment to enable individuals to lay out a much *larger* sum of their own in the same work, and without any other inducement than the probable benefit they expect to derive from the speculation; a benefit which, whatever it may be, will be equally shared by the Govt. in proportion to its subscription. Such a subscription could never have been asked for at all if, from the present state of the country, all the ordinary means of raising money upon securities had not been suspended, so as to preclude the present list of subscribers from adding, as many of them would be desirous to do, to the amount of their subscriptions, and entirely to shut out many other persons from subscribing at all. This unfortunate state of affairs by the stagnation which it creates in most branches of labour and industry, seems of itself to point out to Govt. the propriety of this advance. If between this time and the meeting of Parliament the subscription should be filled by individuals, no advance will be asked, but it is essential to obtain the assurance that this aid will not be refused, in case it shall be wanting to complete the amount of private subscriptions.

Liverpool 4th Mo.10 1817.[2]

Geo. Canning
    Respected Friend,
        Since my return from London it has afforded me great pleasure to learn that Govt. had decided on lending money on Public Works, and as this is a subject which has occupied much of my attention for several months, I shall request their attention to a few additional remarks on this subject.

What I have before stated went in substance to prove that we had plenty of everything in the country (in good seasons) and that we only

---

[1] *Liverpool Papers*, 38,292, f. 100: undated (1815-16).
[2] Canning Box: Liverpool Public Reference Library.

wanted something to give circulation and this would be better done by domestic improvements than it had been by war.

What I have now to state is that I consider the great improvements in machinery for saving manual labour as one of the chief causes for the unparalleled exertions of the last war as by affording the necessaries and comforts of life with less manual labour a greater portion of our Population were set at liberty for military employment etc. and that which was so great a benefit in war may, if it is not our own fault, be equally beneficial in peace, for surely it is a consolation to consider that our present distress arises not from a wasted or exhausted country nor anything which if rightly considered should cause despondency, but quite the contrary. It is the mighty surplus power of the country now lying dormant and waiting to be directed to some useful object. It is a power which, if turned to domestic improvement will astonish the world, as much as it did in Military exertions.

If it is true, as I believe it to be, that we may enjoy as much foreign trade as ever (tho' not precisely of the same kind), if we enable our population to become large consumers of foreign articles, then all our Public Works are a clear gain to the country from a state of peace, and if, as I have before stated, we cannot suffer a diminution of our population either from emigration or from any other cause without great and general suffering, it forms an additional inducement for giving employment.

There is another point of view in which I wish to place this apparently surplus population. Nothing can be more natural than to suppose that if we have too many people we shall cure the evil if we allow them to be reduced, but I trust I can show that nothing can be more fallacious. All our present wants can be supplied with a less portion of manual labour than they were before the war. We must therefore invent some new *wants* or we cannot employ them. If our present population are one-tenth part more than we want and that one-tenth part were to emigrate or be in another way reduced those who were left would still be in the same relative situation. There would still seem to be one-tenth too many and so on until a ruinous depopulation followed.

What then are these new wants to be? If the surplus wealth of the country was generally in the hands of the landowners, it is probable an increased consumption of domestic or foreign luxuries would give additional employment to the Poor, but this surplus wealth being more in the hands of men accustomed to accumulate, our *new wants* must be something in their way, something likely to bring in an income—as Roads, Bridges, etc.

Thus if we are willing to enjoy the luxury of fine roads comparatively short and level, to see the country improved and ornamented, we shall with it see *immediately* the sufferings of the poor relieved and the weight removed from the parishes which have supported them; we shall see a *gradual* improvement in agriculture and manufactures from an increasing demand, a *gradual* increase in our foreign trade from an increasing consumption of foreign articles, and a *gradual* increase in our revenues from all these causes united, and we may trust to see at no very distant period the present depression and distress turned into a state of prosperity and happiness of which we have known no parallel.

One of the principal objects of my writing now is to state that views directly the opposite of these are very prevalent amongst men of all political parties, but I have also found that these feelings in a great proportion at least may be removed if proper means are used, and I have been glad that in this respect thy views accord with mine, because if in introducing the proposed measure, its prospective advantages were stated fully to the House of Commons, it would be incomparably the best means of recommending the measure and of removing the present groundless despondency.

A very grand plan for a chain bridge at Runcorn was produced, and if we had been fully satisfied of its practicability, it is probable the Committee would have endeavoured to obtain leave to bring in a bill this session. The expectation that Govt. might probably grant a loan towards the completion of the undertaking was received with general satisfaction —the Bridge alone is estimated at about £100,000.

I am very respectfully,

thy friend    James Cropper

## William Hayley of Eartham and Felpham

Eartham was the ancestral home of William Hayley (1745-1820), 'the poet of Eartham', as he called himself, and as fantastic a soul as ever had the refusal of the laurel-wreath. Huskisson's relation with him was not simply that of one owner following another, but of an old friend relieving his *cher père*[1] of the precious haven which in the buffetings of life had become an encumbrance. The friend and disciple of Cowper, whose life he wrote in the form of a commentary on his letters: the intimate of Romney, whose life he wrote also, and of Flaxman

---

[1] The pet-name arose from the fact that Hayley's name was William also, and that Huskisson was born several years after Hayley's marriage.

who befriended his invalid son Thomas: the irritating patron, in his Felpham days, of Blake, he poured out criticism and verse in indiscriminant profusion. Anything and everything set his muse going: the day's work, his wife's nerves, his son's illness, the literary arrangements with Cowper in the matter of editing Milton:

> Ne'er shall my name in pride's contentious line
> With hostile emulation cope with thine.

He has been called 'stupid and stubborn poetaster'.[1] Stupid he was and stubborn, but stubborn in his friendships also, and there was no malice in him. Of course, he exasperated a genius like Blake, but when Blake was hauled up on a charge of sedition, Hayley was there to swear him off.

As soon as Hayley made a friend, it was his purpose to get him or her to Eartham, where they could talk poetry at one another; and Miss Anna Seward, the Swan of Lichfield (1747-1809), promptly delivered the goods—to William Hayley Esq. on leaving Eartham, his seat in Sussex, September 1782:

(The House *is* on the edge of a reverse slope and when you get to the right spot on top, you *can* see Chichester spire and the sea, and the Isle of Wight in bold outline beyond.)

> The full luxuriance of yon sloping wood,
> Circling the golden field with pomp of shade,
> And, where mild Comfort's downy pinions spread,
> The village, bosom'd in the leafy glade.
>
> The path-way fence, with shrubs and florets strewn,
> Soft as it winds the bright mount's steepy side;
> While, on th' opposing hill, dark forests frown
> On the noon's glory, in their sombrous pride.
>
> Green as the livelier eminence ascends,
> The champaign splendours bursting on the sight,
> Where far and wide the dazzling vale extends,
> Clos'd by the distant main, that rolls in light!

[1] Mark Schorer *William Blake*, 17

But to some the prose of William Cowper (1731-1800) wil be more satisfying than Miss Seward's verse:

Aug. 6 179:
Here we are in the most elegant mansion that I have ever inhabited and surrounded by the most delightful pleasure grounds that was eve seen. . . . They occupy three sides of a hill which, in Bucks., might wel pass for a mountain, and from the summit of which is beheld a most magni-ficent landscape, bounded by the sea, and in one part of it by the Isle o Wight, which may also be seen plainly from the windows of the library i which I am writing.

Yet before the visit was up he was home-sick for Weston:

Aug. 26 179:
The genius of Weston suits me better, it has an air of snug concealmen for which a disposition like mine feels itself peculiarly qualified; wherea. here I see from every window woods like forests, and hills like mountains a wildness in short that rather increases my natural melancholy.

George Romney (1734-1802) was the real friend. As early as 1776 Hayley persuaded him to exchange for a while 'the noxious air of London for the cheerful tranquillity of our Sussex coast', and he returned every autumn for the next twenty years. The last visit was in 1799. Romney brought Flaxman (and there is a noted mantlepiece by Flaxman in the big bedroom of Eartham today), and when young Hayley died in 1800 Flax-man in friendship carved the monument to him in Eartham Church.

The two artists decorated Hayley's library, and Romney had a paint room outside known as Romney's Nook. Romney from Eartham made frequent pilgrimages to Petworth to the great advantage of his health. There was the long walk to and fro and, when he got there, that warm bath of sea water, for which he was so grateful that he adorned the walls of Petworth Villa with his brush.[1]

Some time before 1800 Hayley built himself a little villa at Felpham, his 'Marine Hermitage' as he called it, and leaving

[1] In Creevey's account of Petworth (John Gore, *Creevey's Life and Times*, 273-8) there is no mention of Romney.

the large house at Eartham to his sculptor son (the young artist
was to live in one part, and the rest to be let to lodgers 'at a
liberal monthly rent'), he made Felpham his future home. And
when Thomas Hayley died in 1800, he sold Eartham to a
friend of some years standing—William Huskisson.

The friendship arose in this way. William Hayley, on his
father's early death, was taken by his mother to London and
educated from there at Eton and Trinity Hall, Cambridge. The
London circle included George Selwyn, Edward Gibbon,
William Cowper, George Romney—and in particular the Rev.
Dr. Warner who accompanied Lord Gower to the Paris Embassy as domestic chaplain in 1790. The Rev. Dr. Warner was
an old friend of Huskisson's great uncle Dr. Gem, with whom
Lord Gower was already acquainted, and in this way Huskisson
became Lord Gower's private secretary. In the August of 1790
Warner persuaded Hayley and Romney to visit him in Paris,
where Huskisson thus would meet both poet and painter. After
the tourists got back to England the correspondence between
Hayley and Huskisson, which fills a large part of Volume I of
the Huskisson Papers (38,734), starts. Huskisson's father died
in 1790 and his favourite brother Richard, who had been
brought up with him in Paris, in 1794; and from 1790 to 1800
he poured out his soul to *mon cher père*, more ardently at the
outset, perhaps, as was the way with Hayley's friendships. And
Hayley responded with his own enthusiasms, being the more
juvenile of the two. If Hayley had several small commissions
for Huskisson, such as pushing a play or advancing a protégé,
Huskisson had one important commission for him, the laureate
of mortuary verse, in memory of a dearly loved brother. Huskisson, just because he had no actual home, reacted gratefully
to Hayley's offer of a spiritual home at Eartham, which finally
he made his own. And Emily Milbanke became his spiritual
daughter-in-law from the moment of her engagement to Huskisson, whom she married on 6 April 1799. Hayley writes to
her on his son's approaching death, interpolating the inevitable
verse and signing himself 'your affectionate afflicted Hermit';
and there is a second letter to 'Dear William and Mary' con-

s

cerning his own re-marriage. Later there seems to have been some estrangement, in which finance may have played a part. For Hayley's finance was as fantastic as himself. The bare facts are that Dr. Gem[1] had a mortgage on Eartham, which Huskisson converted into ownership, after Hayley had left Eartham for Felpham to patronise Blake and become the sight of that aspiring sea-side resort. Royalty visited him from Bognor. When he was ill, a daily bulletin of his health was posted; and when he was well the curious brought telescopes to watch for him on his horse with military spurs and umbrella blowing inside out and, if luck was with them, in the act of tumbling off. (According to Miss Seward, Hayley, like her editor Sir Walter, was lame.)

The last contact I know is in the List of Subscribers to Hayley's 3 Volume Life of William Cowper, under date of 4 January 1806. They include, in addition to Earl Cowper and other friends of the family:

|  | £ | s. | d. |
|---|---|---|---|
| Rt. Hon. William Pitt | 10 | 10 | 0 |
| Rt. Hon. Henry Addington | 10 | 10 | 0 |
| The Lord Bishop of Llandaff | 6 | 6 | 0 |
| William Huskisson Esq. | 6 | 6 | 0 |

two Prime Ministers: the Lakeland Bishop, whom Romney painted (and no Fellow of Trinity will persuade me that the background of their Romney is Welsh mountains): and Pitt's promising young man, joint secretary to His Majesty's Treasury.

*Extracts from the Hayley-Huskisson letters*
*(i)  Lady Hamilton*

Paris, Oct. 13 1791

With respect to the other fair object of admiration she was received by Lady Sutherland as Lady Hamilton—both in singing and performing her attitudes are the most astonishing spectacle I ever saw. She was gone long before I received your letter, but I am much obliged to you and Mr. Romney for your thought.

[1] I could not find Dr. Gem's will at Somerset House, possibly because he died (1800) in Paris, when the country was at war.

Huskisson had discharged in advance the pleasantest commission in his life—to attend on the fair Emma, whose county
by adoption was West Sussex also.[1] And what Huskisson saw
of her in Paris, Hayley had already seen in Naples. 'She performed both in serious and comic to admiration, both in singing
and acting; and her Nina surpasses everything I ever saw, and
I believe, as a piece of acting, nothing ever surpassed it.'[2]

But Lady Hamilton combined with charm the courage that
was to win the love of England's greatest son: as foreshadowed
in this from Huskisson to Hayley 1798, 'The escape of the
Royal Family from Naples in a terrible storm was due to the
resourcefulness of Lady Hamilton.' For 'the boldest measures
are the safest', as Nelson, quoting Chatham, said to her.[3]

## (ii)  The French Revolution

At first both were ardent for the Revolution (Huskisson
having been present at the taking of the Bastille), but Hayley's
ardour outlasted Huskisson's.

*Huskisson to Hayley.* 'In the first horror of great events' (the
flight to Varennes) he feels that he is relating a dream. 'The
assembly has behaved vastly well' (22 July 1791). He has heard
of Burke's new book (The Reflections on the French Revolution), and asks for a copy to be sent to the Embassy at Paris. 'I
have not read a word of Burke's publication, but I am shocked
at his strange romantic doctrines.' Then, with the September
massacres, violent recoil. He is back in England now, but looking back on France.

## (iii)  *Huskisson to Hayley, London, 12 September 1792*

Report must have made you acquainted with the scenes of horror and
cruelty which have disgraced humanity in France and rendered its capital

---

[1] At Up Park. Cf. p. 209n.

[2] Wm. Hayley, *Life of Geo. Romney,* 171.

[3] A letter from Earl of Carlisle to Huskisson 10 November 1805 adverting to Nelson's death
says that Nelson once told him that the victory of Aboukir would have been impossible if Lady
H. had not procured provisions from the Government of Naples. Nelson's letter of 3 October
1798 ran—'And may the words of the great Mr. Pitt be instilled into the ministry of this
country,—"*The Boldest measures are the safest*".'

uninhabitable. The change in the government which took place on the 10th August obliged Lord Gower to return to England; the obstacles opposed to Englishmen who wished to leave Paris so great that it was almost impossible, joined to the daily expectation of the terrible events which have since taken place in the beginning of last week, determined me to embrace the offer of returning with him to this land of true liberty.—I have left my Uncle and many friends in Paris.

As the terror deepens, Frenchmen become 'rascals and madmen'. 'If fate had placed me in any station in the French Empire, I would as a citizen go to some unfrequented part of the world, there to hide from the opprobrium of a title at present dishonoured'.

### (iv) The Theatre

To Hayley all this was very sad, not only in itself, because it destroyed the chance of having a play which he had written in French performed on the Paris stage. Huskisson had supplied him with tips of the convenances. 'The despotism of the theatre still remains here in all its force, so that it will be impossible to change the scene more than once, and never but at the end of an act.' And fatal objection, there was a courtezan in it, which the propriety of France would not tolerate!

### (v) The Death of Richard

'Politician sold Oxley Estates for Money to Continue Career'—is the caption of a three-column article in a Wolverhampton paper, of as recently as 10 January 1949. But domestic sorrow soon supervened on the winning of financial ease.

### (vi) Huskisson to Hayley, 21 August 1794

'My brother is no more. So soon after our first separation in life, I am thus deprived of the companion of my infancy, of my education, and of almost every hour of my existence.' He goes on to say that he has 'directed a monument to our father's memory to be erected in the Chancel of Bushbury Parish Church', and asks Hayley for assistance in the inscription. The monument, in white marble on dark stone against the decorated chancel wall, reads:

In memory of William Huskisson Esq. of Oxley in the Parish of Bush-bury, who Died the 12th of February 1790, Aged 47 years, and of Eliza-beth his wife, who died the 19th of September 1774 Aged 31 years.

Also of Richard Huskisson their second Son, who served as a Naval and Military Surgeon first in the Thetis Frigate 1795: afterwards at the reduction of Martinique and St. Lucia, and finally of Guadeloupe, where he expired in the 24th year of his age, 1794.

The verse is in small capitals:

> Brave, sensible, humane, thy mind and heart
> Completely fashioned for the healing art,
> Led thee, young Huskisson, with guardian care
> To rescue valour from perdition's snare:
> Teaching the mariner, in noxious seas,
> To foil the hovering harpy of disease:
> Thy bolder piety laboured to sustain
> The soldier drooping with contagious pain,
> Where death that nature to her rage might bend,
> Robb'd her of thee, her salutary friend.
> Humanity and honour joined in grief
> When they dejected lost thy dear relief,
> Paying to virtue their acknowledg'd debt,
> Gave thee a foreign grave with fond regret.
> A brother who in thee could once rejoice
> (His bosom friend by nature and by choice),
> Feels and records on this thy vacant tomb
> Pride in thy work, and anguish in thy doom.

It is good as mortuary verse goes; and it breathes sincere affection.    Farewell, William Hayley!

★    ★    ★    ★    ★

*Launceston to Chichester (1832-3)*

Our Launceston is on the Tamar in Cornwall County, Tas-mania, or, as they called it then, Van Diemen's Land. The letters are from a recent emigrant to a friend at home: and they found their way to Eartham, presumably because the recipient hoped that Mrs Huskisson would forward them to the Colonial Office. The places mentioned on the Australian Mainland can be easily identified from an atlas. Hundreds of such letters no doubt crossed the ocean from every quarter of the globe to some town or village of the British Isles; and if we had but one per cent before us, we could attempt a real history of emigration. Social history, says the Master of Trinity, is the history of a people with the politics left out. A more serious lack (for what is high society with the politics left out?) is that it so seldom gets down to the thoughts and experiences of the rank and file who make it. How many were there who combined, as the writer of these three letters did, business enterprise with a fondness for agriculture and the curiosity of the collector? When I emigrated myself to Canada nearly thirty years ago, having read of Peter Robinson in history and seen the name in the Catalogue of the Treasury Papers, I went at once to Peterboro', Ont., to find out how his emigrants had fared. Disbanded soldiers, I found, had blazed the trail, looking for 'some farming with shooting and fishing'. Peter Robinson, ably assisted by a naval officer, who had seen service with Nelson, moved the settlers in. Lumbering provided the community's cash, the settlers the population: family A aged 19, 18, 17, 13, 11, 9, 2 and so on—for they were poor Irish. With Launceston and Peterboro' both in mind I answer provisionally that natural leaders are few and the New World brings them quickly to the top; and further that what turns the trickle of emigration into a flood is the letter (possibly with passage money in it) sent home by the pioneer.

The letters are in the Huskisson Papers 39,948. They are from Thomas Henty of Cormiston, near Launceston, Van Dieman's Land.

They are long letters, and I would dearly like to reproduce them in full. For I have read enough of the official Correspondence of the Colonial Office for 1827-30, to and from Australia, to realise that such settlers' letters again and again touch the heart of the matter. Here I can only allow myself a few extracts of local interest to Chichester folk:

(i) To shew you that a little judicious application of interest is highly useful here Tommy Hills of Chichester came out here without any property but brought with him a letter from the Duke of Richmond to the

Governor and the consequence was a Maximum Grant of Land (2,600 acres) was immediately given him.

(ii) A high rate of interest here 10 or 15½% can be obtained on the very best security, and I am laying myself out as a Negotiator for Capitalists in England. In the hope of hearing from you occasionally with the kindest remembrances to your respected brothers and to Mr. and Mrs. Freeland.

Believe me my dear Sir<br>Yours very faithfully<br>Thos. Henty

P.S. On applying the other day to Gov$^t$ for the loan of a Bricklayer to assist in building me a House I had assigned to me a Chichester man by the name of John Trigg transported for Rioting. His friends may like to know that he is quite well but heartily tired of being transported. He is expecting a commutation of sentence from home.

(iii) I have seen beautiful Samples of Barley and Hops, grown only to a small extent, but I am assured are more productive and better than the English Hop and the Crop more certain. Although Agriculture is in its infancy, we grow more than we consume. We have no profitable Market for our Wheat or we could by a proper system treble it. The growth of fine Wool is the staple Article of this Colony, and I shall stick to that as the main produce for Investment. The papers say we last year sent home upwards 1,200,000 lbs. more than was sent from the older country New South Wales.

(iv) If an opportunity offers give my respectful Compliments to Mrs. General Dorrien. Tell Boniface I am quite sure he was pleased at my making the Rogues at Arundel disgorge the Money they had robbed the Bank of Savings of, and I hope proceedings have been successful respecting the Commission of Sewers.

(v) I have a right to consider my wool, and sheep, about the very best to be found anywhere, and no sheep I have ever heard of have been so much distributed. They are a breed peculiarly my own, and I have beat everything I have shewn against, both in Carcass, Wool, and Cloth made from their wool. And to be frustrated in not getting Land proper to keep them upon, will go hard to break my heart.

## Chichester to Launceston (1950)

Is that Launceston? Chichester speaking. Yes, the Henty's still flourish. They're the principal brewers of the district. We have William Humphry's house in West Gate on our Electoral Roll for 1835, and there are Humphrys galore in the 'phone book of today. You may like to have

General Dorrien's address in 1842—Lavant House. Can you tell us any-thing about John Trigg and Tommy Hills? By the way, did George Page and David Grey ever get out to you? We have their bed in our Guildhall. It's a wooden bed. They carved beautifully:

|  |  |
|---|---|
| George Page | David Grey Transported |
| Sept. 4 1830 | 7 years. June 27, 1843 |

No trace of them? Well, Cheerio! Sussex for ever! We mean to have those Ashes back next time.

# CHAPTER NINE

## THE THAMES-SIDE OF HUSKISSON AND DEACON HUME

*The Thames*

> The time shall come when free as sea or wind
> Unbounded Thames shall flow for all mankind,
> Whole nations enter with each swelling tide,
> And seas but join the regions they divide,
> Earth's distant ends our glory shall behold,
> And the new world launch forth to seek the old.
>
> —Pope, *Windsor Forest*

How others come at a place I do not know. I find it un-profitable to read descriptions of places which I have not seen. With fiction it is different. Jane Austen's Bath: Sir Walter Scott's Borderland: the London of Dickens and Conan Doyle —these never let you down. The interest of the tale makes them live. My normal mode of locomotion is the push bike, but you cannot cycle for any length beside the Thames, still less on it, and therefore you must go by steamboat, which until lately was not easy. But happily one day in the early summer of 1948 I was invited by Sir Ralph Milbanke, Mrs Huskisson's collateral descendant, to a river trip on the good ship *Jamaica Rum* from Westminster Bridge to Greenwich and back. It was a chilly evening and I sat on deck at first, shyly explaining to a few fellow-passengers where we were—Billingsgate, Custom House, London Bridge, The Tower, East and West India Docks, Surrey Docks; and when they left me, which was soon, I was alone with my thoughts, the first of which was—the probable whereabouts of Quilp's Wharf.

Are you fond of the river? One of the most amusing places is the steam wharf of the London Bridge or St. Katherine's Dock Company on a Saturday morning in summer—in the company of Mr Percy Noakes, on the *Endeavour*, sailing from the 'Cus-tom-Us'.... And then the bell at London Bridge Wharf rang, and a Margate boat was just starting, and a Gravesend boat just starting, and people shouted, and porters ran down the steps with luggage that would crush any men but porters. . . . But soon the wind freshened considerably. 'Will you have some brandy?' 'No,' replied Hardy, . . . 'what should I want brandy for?' (Cruikshank has drawn the agonies of the Dining Saloon.) But all things come to an end, and at about two o'clock on the Thursday morning the party arrived off the Custom House— dispirited and worn out (*The Steam Excursion—Sketches by Boz*).

But sometimes there was more sombre business afloat. After a darkening hour or so, suddenly the rudder-lines tightened in his hold and he steered towards the Surrey shore. 'In luck again, Gaffer? I know'd you was in luck again, by your wake as you come down' (*Our Mutual Friend*).

And next I saw an ugly little devil with a blowpipe in his mouth. 'Pile it on, men, pile it on,' cried Holmes. 'By Heaven, I shall never forgive myself if she proves to have the heels of us.' We had shot through the Pool, past the West India Docks, down the long Deptford Reach, and up again after rounding the Isle of Dogs . . . (*The Sign of Four*).

But here *Jamaica Rum* turned about, and thoroughly cold I went below, where all was merry and tight (a round hundred in a small saloon). Dark faces beamed; society women saluted their males by pet names; the independent member for Oxford University released some quips; we drank our host's health again and again. My supper that evening consisted of two skewered half-sausages and seven of Rum Punch. That was good, but there was better to come. For I found myself wedged next to Hay's Wharf, and after we had exchanged cards, I had leave to see at a later date some of the firm's records, which go back to the eighteenth century.

Around the Thames-side of 1800, when the congestion was at its height which led to the building of its docks—West India 1802, London 1805, East India 1808, Surrey Commercial 1810—a great historical romance could be written. The commercial facts are in J. G. Broodbank's *History of the Port of*

*London* (1921); the social detail in Sir Patrick Colquhoun's *Police of the Metropolis* (1795), with its classified criminology of night plunderers, light horsemen, heavy horsemen, game watermen, game lightermen, and the rest. On the river was congestion and chaos: by its side piracy and pillage. Moreover, the country was at war; and in 1797 there was a mutiny at the Nore, which the enterprise of Trinity House, if the evidence of its spokesman many years later be correct, prevented from causing calamity.[1]

A deputation of the Brethren was dispatched to the extreme points of the channels of the river; and they succeeded in destroying, almost in view of the mutinous fleet, every buoy and beacon that could serve as a guide for its passage out to sea. This was as decisive a blow, as it was unexpected, to the criminal projects of the mutineers, who however still adhered to their purpose of carrying the fleet over to the enemy; and to enable them to do so, they had collected above 20 masters of merchant vessels, whom they had taken out of their ships for the purpose of piloting the men of war. The mutineers were so enraged against the Trinity-house, for destroying their means of escape, that they declared they would hang the first Elder Brother they could catch; and one of them, Captain Calvert, coming up in his yacht from Broadstairs, was brought on board the Sandwich, and taken down to the ward-room, where the delegates were assembled, to be tried for that act. But the openness and manliness of his manner and conversation disarmed them of their resentment; and they contented themselves with exacting from him all the information they required, as to the state of the public mind in England on their mutinous proceedings. He, at the risk of his life, unhesitatingly told them, that the whole country was against them, and that they would assuredly be brought to condign punishment. Upon this unwelcome intelligence, he was immediately ordered to depart out of the ship; but on reaching the Sandwich's quarter-deck, those masters of vessels, whom I have mentioned, came to him in a body to ask him what they should do; that they were threatened with being hanged, if they did not carry the ships out to sea, and there were no buoys to guide them. He answered, that all he could say to them was this 'That if they

---

[1] The Nore anchorage is in the estuary of the Thames, 3 miles N.E. of Sheerness and 47 miles E. of London Bridge. With his pocket glass the Uncommercial Traveller could see the Nore Light from Chatham Dockyard.

The evidence is by W. T. Money before the Foreign Trade Committee of 1825 (Lights, Harbour Dues and Pilotage) with Wallace in the Chair, p. 292 *et seq.*

did carry them out to sea, they would certainly be hanged', upon which he
was immediately ordered by the mutineers out of the ship.[1]

## Adam Smith at Edinburgh

Having written a book *Great Britain from Adam Smith to the
Present Day*, I like to start everything from Adam Smith, and
here for once it is legitimate. For Adam Smith, after publishing
*The Wealth of Nations*, wisely wrote no more (who can improve
on perfection?) but devoted the sunset of his life to administer-
ing the custom laws and restraining those gentlemen who,
though no doubt highly blameable for violating the laws of
their country, were frequently incapable of violating those of
natural justice, and would have been, in every respect, excellent
citizens, had not the laws of their country made that a crime
which nature never meant to be so—to pluralise the master's
words.

Adam Smith sat at Edinburgh, but the Scottish Customs
Records are in London in the Custom House Library, and
housed alongside the copy of Johnson's Dictionary which
Hitler picked off with a bomb just opposite the definition of
Excise (the page has the splinter of shell wedged into it). The
Library also has Adam Smith's copy of Crouch's *Complete View
of the Customs*, with his book plate in it.

Adam Smith was a Commissioner from 24 January 1778 to
his death in 1790—his place being filled on 7 January 1791.[2]
He was most regular in his attendance and often took the chair,
signing the Minutes with his clear A.S. Twice towards the end
he signs in full in his sloping schoolboy hand, *Adam Smith*.

His superiors were My Lords of the Treasury, who kept a
tight hand alike on Edinburgh and London, which at that time

[1] Ibid p 297.

[2] The year, incidentally, for which the entry survives—
'Excise Gauger, Dumfries, 1st Footwalk 1791.
Robert Burns, the poet, does pretty well, aged 32, 3 years employed, 7 in family.'
Pretty well at gauging, and at epitaph superb:
        'Here lyes wi' death auld Grizzel Grim,
        Lincluden's ugly witch,
        Oh death! thou surely are not nice,
        To lye wi' sic a bitch.'
Lincluden is on the Nith, just above Dumfries.

were co-equal[1] in authority. Almost the first question aimed at him was on 26 March 1778 by Mr Robinson, one of the Secretaries of the Treasury (this would be Thomas Robinson, second Baron Grantham, father of F.J.). 'What is the difference between culm and coal?' They referred the question to Dr. Black and other learned men and returned the answer in due course. But what the answer was the Minutes do not say.

On 3 March 1770, when he was in the chair, the first business was to reprimand a gentleman who had certified to a discharge of coals at Kirkholm, near Stranraer, without actually seeing them—'for the very next offence he will be dismissed.'

A month later (28 April 1778) they commented on 'the unfitness of the said vessel for the suppression of smuggling, as it is now carried on upon the West Coast by sailing vessels of great force, extending from the Firth of Clyde to the Mull of Galloway'. The country was then at war, and in June 1778 permits were issued to the Carron Co. to send by sea: swivels, 2 to 12 pounders, and ½ to 12 lb. balls.

The Treasury letters are numerous. Several ask for information about Scottish Ship Registry since the Union and the Scottish African Trade 'as far back as possible'. Mr Rose (George Rose) is advised 3 December 1788 that 'the total abolition of fees and a suitable compensation to the officers of the Customs in Great Britain for the losses they may sustain thereby, would tend very much to the improvement of the Revenue'. Mr Arbuthnot,[2] 5 June 1784, asks 'how many Busses were employed last year in the Bounty White Herring Industry?' Adam Smith was in the chair and must have itched to remind their Lordships that the said busses commonly set out for the sole purpose of catching, not the fish, but the bounty.

At Inverness (22 July 1784) one feeble Customs Officer let in some French wine at the Portuguese rate, but the Commis-

[1] Although occasionally the Treasury might refer the Scottish Board to the English Board for advice and assistance in some particular matter, and although the Scottish Board would often refer to the more comprehensive knowledge and wider experience of the English Board, yet the Scottish Board was jealous of its constitutional equality.

[2] Senior to our Charles Arbuthnot. Between 1770 and 1830 there is always an Arbuthnot and a Cushington (usually several) in one or other of the public services. Charles Arbuthnot was of Irish stock.

sioners felt sure that his action 'proceeded from ignorance or timidity rather than from any bad intention to prejudice the Customs'. Adam Smith from the Chair, 31 December 1788, has nice things to say of a Salt Inspector (this is in one of the Minutes to which he appends his full name). A little later he has to tell a drunk that, if it occurs again, he must go. There is, of course, much about drawbacks, bounties and debentures, and on 13 November 1788 big money: 'authorised, the remittance in bills at par to London: £40,000 for Customs, £5000 for Salt Duty.' Only once did I encounter a piece of business allowing of economic acumen in the presentation. On 26 August 1788 the Treasury, having decided to buy out the exemption of the Pitferrane Collieries (Dumfries) from Export Duty and having asked what they should give, the Commissioners, Adam Smith in the Chair, recommended £4000 and appended a note which reads like a snippet from the *Wealth of Nations:*

Tho' the Revenue will be considerably increased after the purchase of the exemption, yet such increase will be more in England than in Scotland; for the English coals being of a stronger quality than those in Scotland, it is natural to suppose that, when there shall be no exemption, the exporter will go to the places where the best coals are to be had.

And at that let us leave him and his fellow-commissioners of different years—Mr George Clerk Maxwell, Mr J. H. Cochrane, Mr Basil Cochrane, Mr James Edgar, Mr David Reid and others. But I think it mean of them not to have told us what *was* the difference between culm and coal. It is like reading *Mansfield Park* in any but the *de luxe* edition to which Lovers' Vows is appended.

*The London Custom House,* (*1814-28*)
The scene shifts to 1814. Napoleon was down and out and My Lords of the Treasury were in a benign mood.
1815. '4 Aums of Wine (*164 gallons*) to be admitted duty free for Mr. Goulburn and other commissioners plenipotentiary who had been employed in negotiating a Treaty with the United States at Ghent.'

1814—11 June. 'The luggage of Viscount Castlereagh, who had been on a special mission to the continent ordered to be forwarded to His Lordship's residence at St. James's Square ... and Sundry Packages containing wine etc. etc. delivered free of duty at various periods between the 11th of June 1814 and the 5th August 1815.'

1814. 30 Japanese silk dressing gowns to be admitted duty free as curiosities 'being presents from the Emperor of Japan to the Court of Directors of the East India Company'. (Victory brings prestige, prestige presents.)

1816—14 Nov. 'The suite of Mr. Canning to be treated with the same respect as that shewn to H.M. ambassadors on their return home.' (Canning thought that this was the very least due to him.)

1818—August. '35 Cases of Works of Art collected by the Duke of Wellington sent to Apsley House in charge of an officer and delivered duty free.'

And when the tumult of victory had died down, there was still a kindly welcome for curios and antiques. It was an acquisitive age, and there was the spoil of Europe and the East to be acquired. When one recalls that Charles Long (an Emmanuel man like John Harvard) of the Treasury and the Customs Commission assisted his royal masters in the decoration of their palaces, one sees how it all fits in.

1822. 'Golden Image of the Idol Vishnu to be admitted as a curiosity.' An ungodly proceeding, but excusable perhaps as an offset to

1820. 'Lord Rollo allowed the drawback on the materials used in a Church built by his Lordship.' (This and other exemptions in the same category intrigued Deacon Hume, who found in it an argument for the exemption of Baltic timber, used in the construction of British ships!)

And England in her turn could be chivalrous on the outward voyage—

1819-20. 'Horses allowed to be shipped duty free: 50 for the Emperor of Austria, 36 for the King of France'—to be followed five years later by a tropical counterflow.

1825. 'Sundry articles delivered free to Sir Stamford Raffles, late Governor of Sumatra.' Hence the London Zoo,[1] and private Zoos or rather Whipsnades in the seclusions of rural England. 'Yea, in his bowler hat he kneeled before kangaroos—gigantic, erect, silhouetted against the light—four buck-kangaroos in the heart of Sussex.'

But 1814, the year of victory, was the year when the old Custom House was burnt down and many records lost.

1814—12 Feb. 'In consequence of the calamitous event of the Custom House being burnt down this morning the Board assembled at the official house of their secretary in Trinity Square.'

*Pro tem* the Customs business was transacted at the Commercial Sale Rooms in Mincing Lane. (For a similar reason to-day the Customs are at City Gate House, Finsbury Square.) The East India and Customs House Corps volunteers prevented much plunder and confusion, it was reported.

Already two years before the fire it had been determined to build a new house. For the old house was antiquated and far too small, so that many branches of its business had to be conducted in a variety of City offices. The old house was thus no more than a head office, with its Long Room 127 feet long and 29 feet wide, which originally was honoured by the personal superintendence of the Commissioners themselves. One can imagine them parading its stately length. 'They're coming,' signals the look-out boy, and all is diligent silence.

During 1816-17 the building was going up, and 'the Treasury gave their assent to a new Quay being constructed in front of the Custom House then building by open tender under the direction of Mr. Rennie'. In 1817 it was decided that it should be lighted externally by gas and that insurance of the premises against fire should be effected to the extent of £100,000 with

---

[1] Cf. R. W. Hay, Under Secretary for Colonies, to Governor of Ceylon, 23 August 1828:

'A Zoological Society has lately been established in London and a few acres of ground in the Regent's Park have been laid out as a Garden for the reception of curious beasts and birds from all quarters of the world in imitation of the Jardin des Plantes at Paris . . . I have ascertained that you could not confer a greater favour on the Society than by sending home a young elephant'. . . (C.O., 324, 85).

the Globe, the Imperial, the Four-in-hand and the Union. But this was only a beginning. The original estimate of £450,000 had risen by 1829 to £650,000, owing, in part, to the new central foundation having given way. And the New Custom House had barely been completed when its counterpart in Dublin was burnt down (1833). Conflagration in those days was almost a fashion—the London Custom House: the Dublin: the Royal Exchange: the Houses of Parliament (14 October 1834).

I have taken the above extracts from the Minutes of the Customs, analysed alphabetically, for the period 12 February 1814 to 31 December 1822 (Vol. 7) and 1823-29 (Vol. 8). They make fascinating reading, as one drives in tandem through the alphabet: from Ambassadors and Articles free of duty to Sufferance Wharfs and Superannuation. In Vol. 7 Quarantine and Preventive Coast Guards head the list in number of entries. In Vol. 8 the growth of dock companies and the warehousing system is reflected in the numerous regulations pertaining to them. Here and there throughout are homely items, such as— November 1821: 'It having been intimated to the Board that some of the junior clerks are frequently in the habit of assembling in some of the offices and by their conversation and improper conduct disturbing the attention of the well-disposed' ... ordered: a periodical return of good conduct—discontinued January 1823.

It was said of Rudyard Kipling that he knew Navy talk as well as any member of the Senior Service. So, too, the Customs have their language and idioms, on which the amateur can easily go astray, even when fortified by a useful compilation like Charles McCoy's *Dictionary of Customs and Excise* (1938). They do not speak of uniform, but of uniform clothing. To them a debenture is not a gilt-edged security, but a first charge on duties, payable at sight. To 'stamp a survey' has come to mean to 'fabricate a return'—the offence for which Thomas Paine[1] was dismissed. It is an example of an ancient figurative

---

[1] This gallant fighter in the cause of liberty, author of the mighty trinity—*Common Sense, Rights of Man, Age of Reason*—knew no rest even in his grave. When Lord Norbury (John Toler, Ireland's facetious 'ultra' Chief Justice) was asked what Cobbett meant by bringing home Tom Paine's bones, his answer was—to make a broil (Peel to Liverpool, 30 December 1824).

T

usage which, once common throughout the language, has survived only in the Custom's Service. The *O.E.D.* gives a quota-
tion of 1581 from Bell's translation of 'Walter Haddon against
Osorius'—'Out of these two monstrous falsely forged pro-
positions, he stampeth a conclusion . . . no less false than
malicious', i.e. to fabricate (faber=smith) a false inference out
of something. Hence to 'stamp an entry', is to make an entry
(in a book), which is intended to deceive. Tom Paine was discharged for 'stamping a whole survey', i.e. he made entries in a
survey book inferring that he made a particular survey, when
in fact he did not go near the place.

This use of 'stamping' is thus different from its more direct
and obvious sense of certifying as correct after inspection: in
which latter sense it recalls to us the emotion of Serjeant Buz-
fuz. 'Sometime before his death, he had stamped his likeness
upon a little boy. With this little boy, the only pledge of her
departed exciseman, Mrs. Bardell shrunk from the world, and
courted the retirement and tranquillity of Goswell Street.'

A Tide-waiter is the officer who boards vessels on the in-
coming tide to prevent the evasion of customs regulations. A
Land-waiter is the officer, stationed on land, who sees that duti-
able goods are brought to duty. A Coast-waiter discharges these
functions for the coast-wise trade. A Piazza-man is a Tidesman
stationed on the Custom House Quay. A Jerquer is a searcher
and defined thus in the *O.E.D.*, 'A clerical officer who examines
and checks a ship's papers, to see that all the cargo has been
duly entered and described.'

All this is a matter of language, but there are institutions
which may need for their understanding a historical note.
For example:

### SUFFERANCE WHARFS AND LEGAL QUAYS

The 13th Report on Public accounts, 1786, says The Legal
Quays are those which have been set out and appointed by
Commissions issued from the Court of Exchequer: and the
business transacted off these quays or at 'illegal places' is done
under the authority of a special sufferance made out by the

proper officer in the Long Room and signed by a Commissioner in the Port of London, and granted and signed by a Collector and Controller at an Outport. (Extract from Minutes.)

This refers to business done '*off* these quays' not in the sense of *from* or *alongside*, but in the sense of *away from* or *otherwise than at*.

### LONG ROOM

The Public Room in the Custom House of each port, where the indoor business, concerning the arrival and departure of ships, is transacted.

*Historical Note.* On the destruction of Churchman's Elizabethan Custom House in the Fire of 1666, Christopher Wren was commissioned to rebuild it, and sensing the propriety of a familiar term spoke frequently of that 'Great Long Room'. When the building was taken into public use, the term stuck, and spread to other Custom Houses, including those in the Plantations. The Long Room of today, though now tenantless, has not been seriously damaged. It is the offices on either side which were wrecked: and it is possible that when these have been rebuilt the Long Room will come into service again.

### COAST GUARD

The term 'Coast Guard' having been only first adopted under the minutes of the 19th Feb 1822, when the forces for the prevention of smuggling consisting of 'Prevention Water Guards,' 'Cruizers,' 'Riding Officers' were consolidated and placed under the authority of the Board of Customs, all entries relating to the Coast Guard in this Volume (1814-1822) will be found under those heads. (Extract from Minutes.)

*Historical Note.* In 1815 the long generation of privateering, blockade running and reprisals under letters of marque came to an end; and the Admiralty with a wealth of experience and command personnel at its disposal asked for the Customs Cruizers to be put under them. This was done, and for six years the Revenue Service afloat was in the hands of the Navy. But the change proved costly to the revenue, and accordingly in 1822 the Service was returned to the Customs and denominated Coast Guards. The subsequent shedding of services not connected with the collection of revenue left as a separate institution the coast guard in its modern form.

### James Deacon Hume, (1774-1842)

James Deacon Hume was the perfect civil servant. At the Custom House he was Huskisson's trusted ally, compiling in its service, at the instance of the Treasury, the indispensable complement of Huskisson's fiscal returns, a codification of the Custom Laws, with clearly defined tariff schedules on which policy could operate. It was not his business to raise or lower the tariff, but its simplication at his hands was an important aid to its reduction. He was a man of immense industry, and yet very far from being a mere assembler of facts. He could give his chief far-seeing advice at the highest level, as will be seen in the last section of this chapter; and his complete familiarity with the actual course of trade first under war conditions and then under peace conditions enabled him to speak with authority on monetary policy also. Thomas Tooke published the first two volumes of his *History of Prices*, covering the period from 1792 to 1837, in 1838. He (1774-1858) and Deacon Hume were coevals and close friends; and the effective criticism which Tooke makes of the central argument of the Bullion Committee's Report of 1810 is set out, and with even greater clarity in Letter V, one of a series on the Rights of the Working Classes, addressed by Deacon Hume to the Editor of the *Morning Chronicle* in January 1834. Anyone familiar with Tooke's reasoning will wonder if he is not reading Tooke himself in such a passage as this:

There was not a space on the globe at which we could gain access with some goods as a valuable consideration, from whence the gold and silver did not spontaneously flow to us; and there was not a country in the world in which so large a quantity of desirable goods could be obtained, in return for an ounce of gold, as in England. But the error which those good people have fallen into, is this—they are thinking of the facility of smuggling gold, and forget the difficulty of smuggling goods.

And again:

The only goods which can affect a question of currency in any country are those which it naturally and habitually exports . . . in England calico, hardware, sugar and coffee. The price of agricultural produce, here, had no more to do with the subject than the price of admission to a theatre at Paris. And yet one of the modes of accounting for the strange misconceptions into which the bullionists fell, notwithstanding the light of their excellent principles which they had for their guide, is, that they assumed a general rise of prices, from the dearness of agricultural produce; a fresh proof, by the by, of the mischievous predominance of a land bias on every question.[1]

In 1829, when Huskisson was out of office, Deacon Hume was moved to the Board of Trade, as joint secretary, and held that post till his retirement in 1840. After Huskisson's death in the fiscally barren years of the 1830's he carried aloft the torch lighted by Huskisson till it could be placed in the right trusty hand of Peel. It was only in 1840 in the Import Duties Committee of that year that the Whig and Radical politicians shewed anything like fiscal courage, recommending radical simplification and reduction, but still fighting shy of an income tax to fill the revenue gap.

Deacon Hume gave evidence before this Committee, whose chairman was another and unrelated Hume, Joseph Hume or 'Economy Hume', as he was nicknamed from his obsession. Strangely enough the worthy Haydn in his *Book of Dignities* confuses the two, announcing '1829 Secretary to the Board of Trade Joseph Deacon Hume'. Of Joseph Hume (1777-1855) it will here suffice to say that he, too, was a stout admirer of Huskisson. In 1824 Huskisson had been of service to him in removing certain hardships caused to settlers in Trinidad by the method of levying transport duties, and later in the same year he wrote approvingly of the reduction of the duties on horses, which Huskisson had effected. And on 30 May 1828, Huskisson being no longer Secretary for the Colonies, he said in the House, 'The Rt. Hon. Gentleman who lately filled that

[1] The H.B.T. Letters (i.e. Hume Board of Trade Letters) are given in full in Charles Badham, *Life of James Deacon Hume*, pp. 63-127.

office was commencing a system of kindness and conciliation, which was calculated to produce union and peace in our colonies: and if a different system be now adopted, both will be banished and discord and disunion will prevail in their stead.'

As between Deacon Hume and Huskisson the admiration was mutual and lifelong. The civil servant was fond of recalling how the statesman handled his opposition. In evidence before the House of Commons Committee on the Laws affecting the Export of Machinery (1841) he said:

I can very well remember, upon one occasion of a deputation to the Board of Trade, when Mr. Huskisson held up one of those small articles of machinery to the gentlemen who attended that meeting; and he said 'So, gentlemen, then the prosperity of the trade of this country depends upon our preventing this thing from being carried out of it.'

And two years before in less known evidence (before a Committee to enquire into the Fresh Fruit Trade, 1839), he stated, 'Mr. Huskisson did not investigate the expenses of the silk manufacturers, but he said a certain sum is as much protection as you ought to have and if you cannot do it at that, you must let it alone.'

*Q.* Do you suppose that Mr. Huskisson took that course without reference to any gentleman engaged in the silk trade?

*A.* I know that he did and I know that it came out as a matter of great astonishment to the trade: it never was mentioned in a single instance to the manufacturers spoken to on the subject till it was determined.

*Q.* Did that give satisfaction, his acting without any communication with the persons engaged in the manufacture?

*A.* I never heard that the want of communication was a ground of dissatisfaction, but the silk trade showed dissatisfaction enough, certainly; altho' they soon doubled their trade afterwards.

The forthright servant of a forthright chief! And the chief in a well-known passage of his most famous speech more than returned the compliment:

I am free to admit, that we never could have succeeded in our undertaking, without the assistance of an official gentleman, in the service of the Customs, a gentleman (footnote, J. D. Hume Esq., Comptroller of His Majesty's Customs in the Port of London) of the most unwearied diligence, and who is entitled, for his persevering exertions, and the benefit he has conferred on the commercial world, to the lasting gratitude of his country. Of the difficulties of the undertaking, the House will be enabled to judge, when I state, that there were no fewer than five hundred statutes, relative to the Customs alone, to wade through; independently of the numerous enactments, concerning Smuggling, Warehousing, the Plantations etc. In the performance of this duty, we had innumerable difficulties to encounter, and battles without end to fight. And now, Sir, in one little volume (Laws of the Customs by J. D. Hume Esq.) which I hold in my hand, are comprized all the Laws at present in existence, on the subject of the management and the revenue of the Customs, of Navigation, of Smuggling, of Warehousing, and of our Colonial Trade, compressed in so clear and yet so comprehensive a manner, that no man can possibly mistake the meaning or the application of them.[1]

'No man can possibly mistake the meaning.' That was the quality on which Sir James Stephen,[2] his opposite number

[1] Speeches, II, 486-7, Effects of the Free Trade System on the Silk Manufacture, 24 February 1826.

The laudatory Minute of the Board of Trade forms a fitting footnote to the Presidential commendation in Parliament. It is in the form of a Letter to J. C. Herries at the Treasury of 28 July 1827: the Letter to say:

'That during the last two years and more particularly during the sitting of Parliament the Lords of this Committee have on many occasions found it necessary to avail themselves of the assistance of Mr. Hume, Controller of His Majesty's Customs in the Port of London, who, from his great practical knowledge and experience in Custom-House Affairs, has been enabled to afford their Lordships most valuable information and advice on various points connected with the business of this Department.

'That the Lords of this Committee feel themselves bound in justice to express the high sense they entertain of the zeal and ability which have at all times marked that Gentleman's conduct in his communications with this Board.

'That their Lordships are of opinion that it will be necessary for the public service that they should continue to avail themselves of Mr. Hume's services.

'That they think it, however, incumbent on them to state that they must consider the services so rendered by him as extra-official, in as much as the business on which he has been or may hereafter be employed by this Committee must of necessity occupy a very considerable portion of the leisure he might otherwise enjoy, and cannot be regarded as forming part of his official duty as Controller of Customs.

'That under these circumstances the Lords of this Committee consider Mr. Hume as fairly entitled to remuneration for such extra services and that should their opinion meet with the approval of the Lords of the Treasury the Lords of this Committee would submit that Mr. Hume should receive an allowance of £500 per annum; so long as he continues to be employed by their Lordships—the same to take effect from the Midsummer of 1825.'

[2] 1789-1859: permanent counsel to Colonial Office and Board of Trade 1825; Under Secretary for Colonies 1836-47; unpopular in the colonies; a strong abolitionist.

The 1820's saw the emergence of the great civil servant, Deacon Hume, and Stephen blazing the trail.

on the legal side, laid emphasis, when paying the last tribute.

Paradoxical as it may sound his unacquaintance with the phraseology and the technicalities of the law was of the greatest possible use to him in accomplishing his work. Writing on a subject with which he was profoundly conversant, he succeeded in the invention of a legal style so concise, so clear, and so popular, that everyone readily seized his meaning; nor can I remember a single appeal to the courts at Westminster to ascertain it so long as he continued in office.[1]

And if nevertheless a man did mistake the meaning, it was merely his laziness.

Board of Trade, 11 Nov 1833

My dear Sir,

I do not know anything your friend can do except to petition either the Customs or the Treasury. He has transgressed as plain a law as ever was written, which is much more easily to be accounted for by his never having looked at the law at all, than by its complicated character of which he complains.

Yours very truly,

J. D. Hume[2]

William Wainewright, Esq.,

Who, then, was this Admirable Crichton of the Customs and how did he reach this pivotal position? He was the son of a Commissioner of Customs and Excise and entered the family profession in 1791 at the age of sixteen. He had his schooling at Westminster, that seminary of so many distinguished and distinctive figures in this generation—Edward Gibbon, Warren Hastings, Jeremy Bentham, William Cowper, John Russell; and Deacon Hume's nephew, the Rev. Charles Dodgson, who was also of Westminster, perpetuated in his offspring the distinctive vein. He married in 1798 Frances Elizabeth, daughter of Edward Whitehouse, Esq., who had an appointment at the Custom House and was gentleman usher at the Court of St. James, thus linking Thames Side with Whitehall.

---

[1] C. Badham, *Life of James Deacon Hume*, 331–334.
[2] Liverpool Public Reference Library, Wainewright Box, V.2.

James Deacon himself bridged the interval by packing off his family to St. Omer and taking a lodging in Westminster, so as to be near his parliamentary sources when compiling his *magnum opus*. But he is not an immigrant Scot looking for a better job. He is an old Westminster boy in familiar surroundings wielding a disciplined pen. His official career at the Custom House was marked by the following steps:

1799—Deputy Comptroller Outwards, acting for the Earl of Guildford.

1813—Assistant Comptroller Outwards: salary £700.

1821—Comptroller Inwards and Outwards: salary £1000.

In 1801 he blossomed into anonymous authorship with 'Thoughts on the Best Modes of Carrying into effect the system of Economy recommended in His Majesty's Proclamation'. The copy in the Library of the National Liberal Club is inscribed (in, I think, his own hand) thus:

(by J. D. Hume)
   The profit which may arise from the Sale of this Publication will be applied to the Subscription for Soup Shops now open at Lloyd's Coffee House.

He divides his argument into a preface and two parts. 'I eat no bread and have reduced meat by nearly one-half.' But personal economy must not be frustrated by lavish public entertainment or the wastefulness of servants: nor should these be discharged, for that only shifts the national problem. Following the recommendation of the Proclamation, he advocates the substitution of rice and fish for bread and butcher's meat—of rice, taken as course I for dinner and of fish with but little melted butter. In Part II he reveals an unexpected superstition. 'Two successive unproductive harvests are certainly the act of God, not of man' (p. 31). Then, after reiterating that the poor, because there are so many of them, must all do their little bit, he concludes:

If the scarcity of corn is artificial, the price will necessarily be lowered by the consequent lessening of the consumption, without the interference of a maximum: if it is real, a commensurate price will be the surest means of husbanding the stock, and making it last to the end of the year, but which might, by the interference of a maximum, be destroyed.

Once again we might be reading Tooke on Prices or listening to Tooke's voluminous evidence on the grain trade before a Committee of the House. Now there happens to have survived in the Liverpool Papers (38,191, f. 87 *et seq.*) a manuscript on this same problem, the scarcity of 1800, by no less a figure than Warren Hastings writing from Salt Hill. In imaginative power and constructive technique it surpasses anything that Deacon Hume or Tooke was capable of. With the experience of a lifetime behind him in a country where famine was famine, he submitted to the England of 1800 a plan of crop inspection conducted at three levels, parochial, regional and national, which would enable the authorities to distinguish between real and contrived scarcity. They had done it (he contends) in India with entire success and a minimum of legal prosecution; and a reference to supporting documents in the India Office (East India 158 Home Series Misc. (1782), pp. 350 and 493) shows that the great proconsul was not romancing, and that this was how they defeated the middleman in the scarcities of 1769 and of 1780 and 1782-3 in Bombay and Bengal.[1] But while England has often been willing to enforce on the East her own notions of trade policy and land legislation, she has rarely been able to conceive that the lessons of the East could have any application to her.

With Deacon Hume's outlook on thrift and his ability as a draftsman, it is natural to find him presiding over the Customs' Benevolent Fund established by Act of Parliament in 1816. It originated with the proposal of a certain Charles Ogilvy, a Long Room clerk in 1816. But as the Directors many years later recorded, 'it was worked out and brought to maturity entirely by the ability and influence of Mr. J. Deacon Hume, for many years from the commencement of the institution, Presi-

[1] In 1795 there was a forerunner to the memorandum of 1800, which clearly followed the same line. 'In the year 1795, when a scarcity was apprehended, Mr. Hastings wrote a letter to my father, suggesting a plan "not," he says, "as the means of remedying that evil, which I hope has no existence, but as the means of remedying the effects which proceed from the belief in it" ' (John Sinclair, *Memoirs of Sir John Sinclair*, I, 199).

dent of the Fund'. As a Fund, it was in three ways distinctive:
(1) To ensure that the claimants—the children and widows of
Customs officers—should have a certain and permanent provision, the power of subscribers to dispose of their assurances
was strictly curtailed. (2) To increase its financial attractions,
power was obtained to levy a poundage charge of one penny on
all salaries. (3) Still further, to increase its attractions another
source of income was provided in a curious way—the profit
from the Bill of Entry Office. The Bill of Entry was a journal
which supplied a daily account of ships and merchandise at the
Custom House. For this information, merchants were prepared
to pay a fee. The patent for it was formerly in private hands, but
Mr Ogilvy was instrumental in securing that it should be acquired for the benefit of the Custom-house Fund and he managed it on behalf of the Fund from 1817 to 1832. The Customs
Service had thus a direct interest in seeing that the Returns
were accurate and serviceable, and in the 1830's, when the
institution came under parliamentary review, it was yielding a
profit of some thousands a year.

These revenues were additional to the subscriptions paid by
members of the fund in the ordinary way of annual premiums.
Needless to say, the Fund has continued to the present. One of
its activities in former days was the protection of responsible
officers holding posts secured by bonds. These local collectors
were responsible for the conveyance of specie, sent with armed
outriders from the outports to London, and they were able,
through the Fund, to insure against loss in transit. With the
growth of the Banking system this form of remittance (and the
risk attaching to it) ceased. A Customs entry for 30 April 1825
reads, 'Contracts to be made with bankers at ports of England
for remittance of crown's money in case of every port in which
the amount suffices to induce bankers of wealth and responsibility to enter into security for the remittance': and in course of
time, when remittance became internal to the banking system,
it was a matter of book-keeping only.

In 1823, Deacon Hume being now Comptroller Inwards
and Outwards, his great quinquennium, like that of Huskisson,

began; and its progress may be traced in the Minutes of the Customs:

1823—21 June. 'The Treasury directed the Board to select officers to prepare a general law and set of laws for the Consolidation of the Customs of the United Kingdom.'

1823—4 Aug. 'Mr. Hume, one of the Bench Officers selected to prepare the consolidation of the Customs Laws, to be assisted by Mr. Thackeray of the Solicitor's Office and by Sir Thomas Tomlins (for Ireland).'

1823—25 Sept. 'The Board of Customs in England, Scotland and Ireland to be consolidated and to consist of 13 Commissioners at £1,400: 4 Assistant Commissioners at £1,000; with an extra daily allowance for the President.'

1823—28 Nov. 'The Board determine that the Warehousing Act of last session (4 Geo. 4, c. 24) decidedly repealed all former Warehousing Laws.'

1825—19 July. 'An octavo edition of the Consolidated Laws of Customs to be prepared and published by Mr. Hume, who may be allowed the profit which may be devised from the sale thereof.'[1]

1826—20 Jan. 'Certain officers to be remunerated for services in the Revision of the Customs Laws viz:-

| | |
|---|---|
| Mr. Hume | £6,000 |
| Mr. Thackeray | £2,000 |

1827—28 July. 'Hume's Supplement to the Laws for 1827 to be supplied as usual.'

1829—July. Ditto.

1829—22 July. 'Mr. Hume, the Comptroller having resigned in consequence of his appointment as Joint Assistant Secretary to the Board of Trade, the Board expressed the high sense of his services and their regret at losing his valuable service.'

Thus was written the Custom House Bible. But just as before Watt there was Newcomen, so before Deacon Hume there was Nicholas Jickling.

1814. 'A Digest of the Law of the Customs having been completed by Mr. Jickling, the Collector at Wells, the Treasury sanctioned the expense of printing 1000 copies—and desired that the copies not required for

[1] The Consolidated Laws had received the Royal Assent 5 July 1825.

public use should be sold to individuals. The remuneration to be granted to Mr. J. to be regulated by the value and accuracy of the work.'

'Mr. Frewin, late Chairman to the Board, selected by the Treasury to prepare an abstract of the Laws relating to the Import and Export of Merchandise, and allowed the assistance of Mr. Jickling.'

For this, Mr Frewin was paid £3,000 in 1815, and more later. In 1818 Mr Jickling was put on to the Colonies, and Sir Thomas Tomlins brought in for Ireland.

The Customs Bible, when consulted by the student, reveals itself as a thing of numerous editions with modifications and additions to keep it up-to-date. The title remains the same throughout: 'The Law of the Customs: compiled by direction of the Lords Commissioners of His Majesty's Treasury by J. D. Hume, Esq.'

In the 'New Consolidation' of 1833 by Poulett Thomson, Vice-President, the 'Standard Acts of Mr. Herries's Consolidation'[1] are reproduced, with a note to the effect that the changes between 1826 and 1833 'consist almost wholly of Reductions of Duties and Easements of Restrictions'. Its purpose, as a guide to practice, is indicated by the wide margins and the instruction, 'The binders should be particularly cautioned not to reduce the margins unnecessarily.'

The ten Standard Acts were:

1. For the Management of the Customs.

2. For the General Registration of the Customs ('The distinction between Management and Regulation is that the first relates to the Establishment and Officers of the Customs, the second to the business of the Merchants').

3. For the Prevention of Smuggling.

4. For the Encouragement of British Shipping and Navigation ('The 'Acts of Navigation', as commonly termed).

5. For the registering of British vessels. (Under this Act provision is made for the division of property in ships into 64 parts or shares: and in the 1833 edition for 'Joint-stock companies owning any ship or vessel or any number of ships or vessels, as the joint property of such company').

6. For granting Duties of Customs. (This contains the Tariff schedules.)

---

[1] J. C. Herries was Secretary to the Treasury 1823-7.

7. For the Warehousing of Goods.

8. To grant certain Bounties and Allowances of Customs. (A dwindling list.)

9. To regulate the Trade of the British Possessions abroad. (This lists the free ports of the colonies: to which the Transportation and Exportation of Goods was confined.)

10. For regulating the Trade of the Isle of Man.

(In the Statute Book these Acts are 6 Geo IV, c. 106 to 115: all dated 5 July 1825: and preceded by two long repealing acts, c. 104 and 105.)

Appendices supply matter closely related to the Customs Service. Those in the 1833 edition deal with the Corn Law of 1828: the quarantine regulations: certain commercial treaties: the Reciprocity Acts of 1823 and 1824: the Passenger Acts of 1823 and 1828.

Thus the Custom House Bible was a compendium of law simplified and arranged for office use. It is, perhaps, needless to add that it was only valid because in it the law was correctly set out.

*The Commissions of Enquiry into Customs and Excise, (1818-24)*

Professor Postan sometimes reminds us at Cambridge that we economic historians deal in the same few sets of facts, to the neglect of many others which are available. It struck me how true this was in my own case when I was wading through the Patent Rolls of George III in search of Mr Bramah's beer pull. I came across it at last:

1796-7. J. Bramah 31st day of October. Doth give and grant unto Joseph Bramah and his Excrs Especial Licence for the sole use and benefit of new methods of retaining, clarifying, preserving and drawing of all kinds of liquors within England, Wales and Berwick upon Tweed for 14 years thereof.

I had no notion that there was all this to a beer pull: still less was I prepared to be confronted with dozens of inventions year by year of a kind and by men unknown to me. I recognised a big name here and there—Watt, Cartwright, Wilkinson, Cort, though even here the particular invention was sometimes un-

familiar. Many, no doubt, were repetitions, and many duds;
yet I felt that I was on the surface of a great stream which I
identified only by its eddies.

So, too, with the Resumption of Cash Payments in 1819.
Why drag in England: why not keep to the country where cash
belonged? Lord Liverpool was duly notified in a despatch from
Pekin of 4 February 1819. The Sublime Emperor (he was informed) was so satisfied with the annual statement of the Bank
of Pekin, which revealed a balance of twenty millions of sacred
metals sealed up from the profane and vile peoples surrounding
the Wall, that he graciously authorised the managers of the
Bank (without any waiting period such as disfigured the resumption of the barbarians) to button their trousers with gold,
and to collar with silver the pet dogs of their harams: gold for
man and silver for beast, a nicely calculated bimetallism safe-
guarded by bronze cannon guaranteed not to go off.

So too, finally, with the story of fiscal reform. I (and others
perhaps with me) start off with the London Merchants' Petiti-
tion of 1820 and then settle down to Wallace and Huskisson,
Navigation Laws, Reciprocity and Silk. Had I been set the
question: Tell the story to 1824 without mentioning any of the
above, my mark would have been 0 or nearly so. Yet, seen
through the spectacles of Customs and Excise, there is plenty
to say once we open the sixteen Reports of the Commissioners
appointed by H.R.H. the Prince Regent to enquire into Customs and Excise—the Regency Reports, as the service styles
them:

1820—1st  Feb. 1818 (which refers back to the House of Commons
           Select Committee on Finance of 1797).
       2nd  Oct. 1818  Warehousing system.
       3rd  Nov. 1818  Reweighing Goods for Exportation.
       4th  Aug. 1819  The Long Room.
       5th  Aug. 1819  East India Department.

The above are issued as a single publication of 1820 by the
Treasury under the signature of S. R. Lushington; and the
Commissioners signing the individual reports are Charles

Long, Charles Grant Jnr., R. Frewin, J. C. Herries, W. J. Lushington.[1]

1821— 7th  Warehousing.
       8th  Solicitor's Department—signed by W. J. Lushington only.
       9th  Trade of Liverpool.
      10th  Customs in Ireland.
       Also Special Reports.
1822—11th  Scotland.
       Also Special Reports.

Reports 1 to 10 were referred to the Excise Department; and the latter, adverting to a pending Excise Enquiry, observe that 'it is of the very essence of the excise system, that all officers should be instructed in the whole of the duties'.

1823—12th  Outports.
      13th  Outports—General System—Coastguards.
      14th  Conclusion of Customs Reports—notice being given that the problem raised by a joint duty of Customs and Excise will come within the purview of the Excise Enquiry.
1824—15th  Excise.
      16th  Excise.

At which point the Commissioners say farewell:

Since the Commission under which the act was issued, other Commissioners have been appointed by the legislature, who have the power of examination under oath, and who, having had the question before them, so far as regards Ireland and Scotland, are, we understand, about to enter into a similar enquiry into the Excise Department in England.

Treasury minutes are interspersed with the Reports. It is not a question of exposing abuses or framing a report on which action may or may not be taken. Britain's sovereign executive is quietly at work, and when the information is to hand, action will result. We possess, now, the middle ground which carries us through the half century from Pitt to Parnell. In 1787 Pitt consolidated the duties of customs and excise, the old system having involved a separate calculation at the Custom House for each of the different subsidies, and the complications being

---

[1] William John, brother of Stephen Rumbold Lushington.

such, that scarcely any one merchant could be acquainted by any calculations of his own with the exact amount he had to pay. In 1836 Parnell's Excise Commission in its 20th Report reached the broad conclusion that 'whatever business relates to the Export, Import or Coasting Trade obviously belongs more properly to the Customs than to the Excise, and therefore should be transferred'.

This was done shortly. Why Pitt could not do it, the Select Committee of Finance had explained:

> It has been deemed expedient to divide the Collection of some of the largest duties on Imports between the Customs and the Excise, in order to secure the Revenues, by checking the Ireland Transit of Goods, which have been clandestinely brought ashore.

But with both services maintaining coastal staffs, friction between them was inevitable. It is on record that the Excise, on being informed of a 'run', intercepted it, only to find that the runners were Customs Officers. Seizure brought rewards; each service was supposed to report them within twenty-four hours: it is easy to see what a temptation there would be to conceal the location of a haul. An improved coastguard service and lower duties, diminishing the profits of smuggling, were required before all import duties could be restored to the service to which they logically belonged. As late as 1819-20 we have the entry in the Customs Minutes: 'Officers transferred from the Customs to the Excise in consequence of the collection of the duties on tobacco, tea etc., having been placed under that Department'—by 59 Geo. 3, c. 53, s. 4. That gave unity—under the Excise. The final reform was unity—under the Customs.

And there was a further pressing need which the Committee of 1797 had outlined under the heading:

### WAREHOUSING OF GOODS IMPORTED

> The policy of such a measure, carried each to a wider extent has been certainly long since sanctioned by the ablest writings (Wealth of Nations, 3rd Vol. Bk. V, ch. 3)[1]; and your Committee are now warranted by the official opinion of the present Inspector of the Commerce of the Empire

---

[1] In the Cannan Edition, II, 368.

u

(Thomas Irving) in recommending its limited execution as safe for the Revenue, and as likely to be productive of very great national advantage.

Wealth of Nations: Empire: National Advantage. We are approaching high policy here. In due course, and in step with London's first docks, followed the Warehousing Act of 43 Geo. III, c. 132, which was amplified before long into a code embracing the United Kingdom and British Possessions overseas. It would be no exaggeration to say that to Canning and Huskisson, the members in turn of the growing port of Liverpool, the Warehousing Code meant as much as did the Acts of Navigation to the statesmen of 1650-1750. It was now up to commercial enterprise to finance and build the docks, with warehouses attached or adjacent, where bonded goods could be housed under lock and key. This was done in London and, in time, elsewhere. In this great improvement the Customs Service claims a high place for one of its staff—Samuel Pellew, Collector of Customs at Falmouth, a brother of the famous admiral. He is to be credited (they say) with introducing the tonnage duty on convoys: suppressing wholesale smuggling: suggesting, as a surgeon, quarantine reform: and 'devising the system of bonding in the Customs, which has been used ever since its introduction in 1803'. Bonded goods paid no duty until taken into home consumption. Goods for re-export no longer had to pay duty and then recover it on an export debenture. The entrepot was a true entrepot. Walpole had triumphed at long last.

We may think of docks and warehousing as an aspect of the great enclosure movement: enclosure of the open fields: the gathering of spinning jennies and weaving looms into factories: the park walls of great houses: the consolidation of customs and excise in the new fiscal unit of the United Kingdom: the replacement of fees and perquisites by the all-in salary: efficient government: big business: the anatomy of modern capitalism.

## High Policy from Thames-side

Is there such a thing as imperial economy? Deacon Hume would have denied it. To him the timber preference was one of

the many heads of the Protectionist serpent, to be chopped off
as soon as might be. To him the Canada of 1897 and Sir
Wilfrid Laurier would have been suspect: the Canada of 1911
and Sir Robert Borden crazy. And yet both of these great
Canadians, not less than their successor Mackenzie King,
would have acclaimed the memoranda by him which I am about
to quote. For as the history of the First Empire shows, taxation
and the control of trade are next door neighbours, and a novice
entering the wrong door might cause an imperial broil. The
legislation of 6 Geo. IV, enshrined in the Customs Bible, was a
Customs Consolidation relating to Colonies and Plantations, as
well as to the United Kingdom. Deacon Hume at Thames-side
and Huskisson in Whitehall set the course of imperial policy
because, when the world was at peace, the main contacts of the
colonies with the Mother Country were economic. It was in his
four years at the Board of Trade 1823-7 and not in his nine
months at the Colonial Office 1827-8 that Huskisson did his
imperial work. Whether with four years at the Colonial Office
he could have so reconstructed its business, grouping trade
policy with communications and land settlement, as to make it
an office of the rank to which Joseph Chamberlain lifted it
later, must remain a matter of speculation. At any rate he did
not; and when he left the scene, Deacon Hume constituted
himself the keeper of the Huskissonian conscience, and soft-
pedalling all that side that was dearest to Huskisson, advertised
him as the Great Free Trader. Successive Secretaries (civil
servants) of the Board of Trade, Deacon Hume, John Mac-
Gregor (incidentally an ex-Canadian emigrant), G. R. Porter,
T. N. Farrer (1st Baron Farrer), ruled the dogmatic roost,
prophesying with departmental intensity, and in the teeth of all
the signs, the approaching conversion of the world to Free
Trade. And yet, when he had Huskisson beside him to keep
him to the work for which he was fitted, Deacon Hume could,
and did, render great imperial service.

The issue on which Huskisson called for information in 1826
concerned the bearing of the recent legislation on the statute of
18 Geo. III, c. 12 (Taxes, Colonies)—commonly called the

'Declaratory Act', which reserved to the Imperial Government the power to impose duties 'for the regulation of commerce, but allocated the net proceeds of these to the colony in which they were levied'.

Deacon Hume was in the strong position of being able to say, 'I drafted the legislation of 6 Geo. IV (1825) and I know what I meant by it—whatever the Colonial Office, in the persons of Lord Bathurst and Wilmot Horton, may contend.' His answer took the form of two memoranda, the originals of which are in the Huskisson Papers, 38,766, f.'s. 127-34.

The first (10 March) is a preliminary statement under the heading 'Duties in Canada—whether applicable to payment of Salaries of Officers of Customs'. His answer is—'No'. Listing the relevant legislation: 18 Geo. III, c. 12; 3 Geo. IV, c. 44, s. 7 and 8; 3 Geo. IV, c. 45, s. 9 and 10; 6 Geo. IV, c. 114, s. 10; 6 Geo. IV, c. 106, s. 9 and 10; he concludes: 'I well remember that it was not intended to give any such power in the act of last session. The reliance was expressly upon the concurrence of the Colonial Legislatures.'

The Legislation thus listed was: 18 Geo. III, c. 12 (The Declaratory Act):

Whereas taxation by the Parliament of Great Britain for the purpose of raising a Revenue in His Majesty's Colonies, Provinces and Plantations in North America has been found by experience to occasion great uneasiness and disorders among His Majesty's faithful subjects, who may nevertheless be disposed to acknowledge the justice of contributing to the common defence of the Empire, provided such contribution should be raised under the authority of the General Court or General Assembly of each respective Colony, Province or Plantation—

No tax to be hereafter imposed by the King and Parliament of Great Britain on any of the Colonies in N. America and the W. Indies 'except only such Duties as it may be expedient to impose for the Regulation of Commerce; the net produce of such Duties to be always paid and applied to and for the use of the Colony etc. in which the same shall be respectively levied, in such manner as other duties collected by the authority of the respective General Courts or General Assemblies of such Colonies, etc., are ordinarily paid and applied'.

So much of 7 Geo. III as imposes a Duty on Tea imported from Great Britain into America repealed.

## 3 Geo. IV, c. 44 (24 June 1822):

Act to regulate trade between His Majesty's Possessions in America and the West Indies and other places in America and the West Indies.

S. 7   On Importation of Articles into the Ports mentioned in Schedule A, certain duties specified in Schedule C to be paid for the use of the Colonies.

S. 8   How duties are to be applied in Colonies having no General Courts or Assemblies.

## 3 Geo. IV, c. 45 (24 June 1822):

Act to regulate Trade between His Majesty's Possessions in America and the West Indies and other parts of the world.

S. 9   Scheduled articles to pay certain duties, which shall be paid by the Collector of the Customs to the Treasurer of the Colony in which they are levied and applied as directed by the General Courts or General Assemblies of such Colonies.

S. 10  When there are no General Assemblies the Net Proceeds of such Duties to be applied in like manner as any other duties levied in Colonies where there are no General Courts or Assemblies.

## 6 Geo. IV, c. 114 (5 July 1825):

Act to Regulate the Trade of the British Possessions abroad.

S. 10  Nothing in this Act or any other Act passed in the present Session of Parliament shall extend to repeal or abrogate or in any way to alter or affect an Act passed in the 18th year of the Reign of His late Majesty King George III, intituled an Act for removing all Doubt and Apprehensions concerning Taxation by the Parliament of Great Britain in any of the Colonies Provinces and Plantations in North America and the West Indies.

## 6 Geo. IV, c. 106 (5 July 1825):

Act for the Management of the Customs.

S. 9   Officers taking any Fee not allowed, to be dismissed. Penalty £100.

S. 10  Oath of Office, not to take Fees etc.

The second and longer memorandum (16 March) reiterates his interpretation of the term 'net produce' and continues:

I hope I have made it appear that the Powers of the Crown, as they existed at the time of the General Consolidation of the Laws of the Customs, have been effectively preserved in the New Law—and I have, therefore, now only to submit my opinion, as to what those powers are with reference to the purpose for which it is proposed to use them. As the humble individual on whom the mechanical duty of framing the Act now in force devolved, I hope I have not betrayed Parliament into a breach of its Solemn Engagement pledged to the Colonies by the Act of Declaration. If such an encroachment has been made, it must be treated as an error and deemed inoperative. I shall therefore consider the Act of Declaration as the Existing Law and examine its intention and force.

Adverting again to the two features of this Law, already defined, I beg leave to say that the 'Regulation of Commerce' contemplated was for general national objects for which the Colonies were called upon to submit to restraints, rather than to receive benefits:—and that the duties, which it was stipulated might be imposed for the purposes of those objects, were considered merely as the most convenient instruments for affecting them. Various measures have, from time to time, been adopted for the purpose of enforcing our Colonial system: Certificates—Bonds—Oaths—Penalties—Forfeitures—Punishments—and even Rewards have all—and many more such modes—been resorted to and used to the same end, and if to the efficacy of such modes of enforcement the Colonial System had been entrusted without the aid of a single protecting or regulating Duty of Customs, Establishments of Custom Houses would have been equally necessary. When, therefore, a stipulation was made that duties *might* be imposed in the Colonies for the 'Regulation of Commerce' (as an exception from the engagement not to levy any duties for the benefit of the Crown)—but with the condition that the 'net produce of such duties be always paid, and applied to and for the use of the Colony, Province or Plantation in which the same shall be respectively levied etc.,' it does appear to me that a very limited construction must be put upon the words 'net produce'—and above all that no deduction can be made from the gross produce for the direct benefit of the Crown, or the easement of the Revenue of the Mother Country. The support of the Establishment of H.M.'s Customs can, on no account, I think, be made a charge upon this fund.

But to show the inutility of any attempt to absorb their duties in such charges, against the will of the colonial legislatures, it is only necessary to examine the existing law a little further, when it will be seen, that power is expressly given to those Bodies to put an end to any such struggle by levying colonial duties of equal amount to the Parliamentary. This Provision is taken from Mr. Robinson's Acts[1] and is conclusive proof, to my mind, of the General Intention of Parliament—to do no more than to make the payment of a certain sum of money, by a particular party, the instrument for effecting a determinate effect.

The case is this—Parliament declares that a duty of 5/- shall be paid in the Colony upon the importation of a Barrel of Flour from a foreign country;—the object is protection and favour to the British producer of flour, and, to show that this is the *only* object, it goes on to say that if the Colonial Legislature shall think proper to impose such a duty to the same amount, the Colonial duty shall take precedence of the Parliamentary, or of so much of it as the Colonial duty shall be sufficient to displace.

I am quite at a loss to comprehend upon what ground Mr. Wilmot Horton can lament the loss of Mr. Robinson's Acts; they appear to me, in their direct enactments for the appropriation of the monies collected under them, to have been framed with scrupulous attention to the Compact of the Act of Declaration, and as if fearful at any time a different construction should be put upon them—they have, by the peculiar provision I have just been describing, put weapons into the hands of the Colonies with which to defend themselves, by rendering the Law *inoperative* as soon as it became effective.

Having ventured, therefore, according to the view I have taken of my duty, to offer my opinion upon the actual state and genuine intention of the law—I must beg leave to advert briefly to the manner of proceeding in the general consolidation of all the Laws relating to Customs, Navigation and Colonies.

I was directed in an early stage, to enact the abolition of Fees in the Colonial Custom Houses. This was readily effected in the Act of Management Cap. 106. Some discussion took place, and many occasional observations were made, in which, as far as they came to my knowledge, reliance was always placed on the ready concurrence of the Colonies in the measure, for the sake of the benefits of which they might be expected to pay the price of it. These benefits were not confined to the abolition of fees. Relaxation, almost to abandonment, of the old Colonial System, was the valuable consideration for which they were expected to give their concurrence: but their concurrence was always deemed to be necessary; and in

[1] i.e. of 3 George 4, when F. J. Robinson was President of the Board of Trade. The section in question is s. 12 of 3 Geo. 4, 44 (24 June 1822), starting 'If upon the importation of an article charged with Duty by this Act, the article is also liable to duty under any Colonial Law equal, etc.

the event of a refusal, the only alternative ever contemplated was the with-drawal of the benefits of the new and liberal system.

Very shortly after the end of the last session Mr. Wilmot Horton sent for me for the purpose of considering what steps should be taken, and I certainly thought that I left him fully impressed with the view of the sub-ject I have been endeavouring to describe.

No inference of opposition on the part of the Colonies is to be drawn from the present state of the question—because it does not appear that any measures have been taken for ascertaining their disposition—but I would submit that it is highly expedient that no further delay be suffered to inter-vene between the consideration of the question and the final decision of it.

Surely a great State document! But as the author had an aversion to sitting for his likeness, no portrait of him exists. His biographer (a relative) says that 'in person he was of about the middle stature, his features strongly marked; his forehead high and intellectual; his eye singularly expressive'.[1] One pic-tures him at his desk at midnight writing hard, with his auth-orities in front of him: or in the Freemasons' Tavern at a meet-ing of the Political Economy Club (which he helped Thomas Tooke to found in 1821), dining with moderation and talking with gusto, never weary of his faith nor deep enough to be misunderstood. The keeper of Huskisson's conscience, he kept one half of it only.

[1] C. Badham, op. cit. 349.

CHAPTER TEN

# THE STAFFORDSHIRE OF HUSKISSON
# AND LITTLETON

*The Huskisson Family*
### *The Name and Crest*

ARTHUR YOUNG said that Frenchmen deliberately mis-
spelt English names to show their indifference to the language.
Year by year some of my pupils write George Stevenson, and
others Coke of Hokam. I have never dared to pronounce Coke,
as the family does, Cook, from a fear of the examinational aftermath; and when I take Huskisson to his first school at Brewood, near Stafford[1] (Brewde in Domesday), I am reduced to a
scholastic limerick:

> There was a young lady of Brewood,
> Who wouldn't eat pears in the newood,
>    For she was such a prude,
>    That she thought it was rude,
> To be peeled by a lady of Brewood.

But at least they call him Huskisson, and not Huskinson, as so
many of my friends and colleagues for some reason do.[2] May I
remind these of an acrostic current in the Huskisson family?

> My first was burnt at Prague for faith in God's word,
> In my second both children and lovers excel,
> Both parents rejoice at the birth of my third,
> And my whole is the name of a charming young belle.

The crest (with which Huskisson sometimes seals a letter) is
the head of an elephant inside a collar, which carries the motto

---

[1] In fact it is near Wolverhampton, but 'near Stafford' saves a post, owing to the way mail is
routed.

[2] They do it, I think, partly for the pleasure of making an ugly sound, partly by confusion with
Jenkinson, Robinson, etc. The Parish Clerk of Birtsmorton suffered from the same complaint,
writing Huskisson's father as Huskinson twice over in the Register of Christenings.

297

*At secura quies,*

this being the first half of the line from the Georgics of Virgil
(Book II, 467) which reads *At secura quies, et nescia fallere vita,*
'But . . . quiet slumbers and a life innocent of deceit.' And of a
truth, our Huskisson was a man without deceit.

### THE FAMILY

The Huskisson family belonged to the Midlands and was
widespread there, as I first realised when searching for Huskisson's will at Somerset House. Huskisson had no children, but
I had the good fortune at this point to make the acquaintance
of Mr William Marshall Huskisson, born 1865, a retired civil
engineer in London, and he introduced me to his distant cousin,
Miss Florence Mary Huskisson, born at Greenwich in 1863
and resident at Warlingham, Surrey. Miss Huskisson is the
grand-daughter of Huskisson's half-brother, Thomas. These
two seniors have in their homes, besides numerous family portraits, documents relating to the family and its property, on
which they have allowed me to draw. In Huskisson's family
tree the names William and Samuel occur again and again, as
they also do in the genealogy of my friend Mr W. M. Huskisson, which runs thus:

William Huskisson of Loughborough 1726-70.
Samuel Huskisson 1757-1819, who bought the (London) Swinton Estate.
William Huskisson of Mecklenburgh Square, London 1793-1872.
William Huskisson of the Swinton Street Chemical Works 1827-73.
William Marshall Huskisson 1865—

Miss Florence Huskisson's pedigree is:

William Huskisson 1743-90 (Huskisson's father).
Thomas Huskisson, Capt. R.N., 1784-1844 (Huskisson's half brother).
Francis Huskisson 1827-1902 of Greenwich Hospital and R.N. College.
Florence Mary Huskisson 1863—

I have one other link with the present in a letter of 5 October
1948 from Miss G. K. Everett, the daughter of Mrs Everett,
who lived formerly at the Old Vicarage, Weston, Staffs., and
died there in 1923. Mrs Everett, the grand-daughter of Capt.
Thos. Huskisson, was Huskisson's great-niece. Needless to

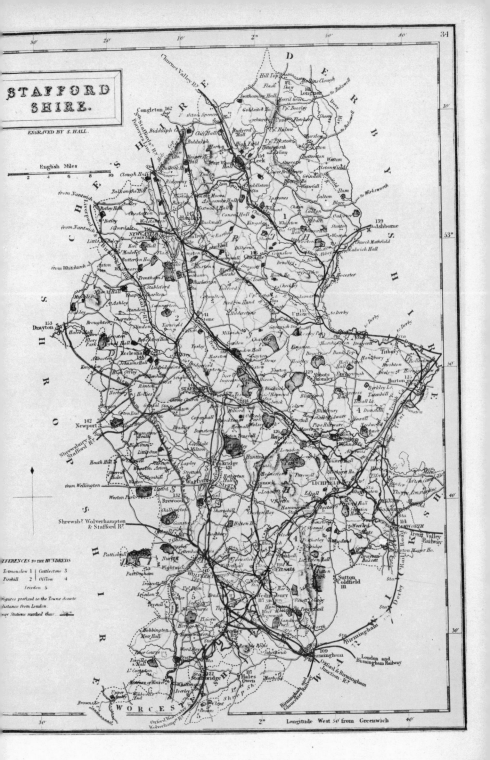

Map of Staffordshire in 1849

say, this letter also says that they have in the family papers 'a printed account of his being killed by that engine'.

In the pedigree[1] of our Huskisson one notes:

(a) *In the generations above him*: the names of Huskisson, Rotton, Grundy, Gem and Swinfen.

William Huskisson, his father, was a second son, the elder being Samuel. William Huskisson, his paternal grandfather, was an eldest son and married twice, but the children were by the first wife, *née* Grundy.

Elizabeth Rotton, his mother, was the daughter of John Rotton and of Jane, his wife, *née* Gem. His maternal grandmother married twice: (1) John Rotton (2) William Huskisson, our Huskisson's grandfather (i.e. widow married widower).

Jane was the daughter of Richard Gem, whom I assume to be the father also of Dr. Richard Gem, Huskisson's great-uncle and benefactor. If this is so, Huskisson was connected with the Gems on both sides—directly through his mother, the daughter of Jane Gem, and indirectly through his grandfather, Jane's second husband. In making Huskisson his heir, Dr. Gem was keeping well within the family. When Mrs Huskisson was preparing the memoir of her husband (1830-31), Huskisson's brother, Charles, wrote to his other brother, Samuel:

I have been informed by the late Mrs. Baswick she was descended from a very respectable family of the name of Statham in Worcestershire; and that the Rottons resided at Oxley so long back as the Revolution in 1688. At that time there were two brothers, John and Richard both of which had been in the army.

This fits in both with the pedigree (for the Gems were Worcestershire people)[2]; and with the following entries in the Bushbury Parish Register of Marriages:

[1] The pedigree runs from *c.* 1700 to the present day, but is to elaborate for reproduction.

[2] *Cf.* Huskisson's will, p. 12 above, 'I give ... my freehold ... Fockbury and all other ... estate in ... Bromsgrove in the County of Worcester ... to ... my Brother Major General Edward Samuel Huskisson ...' Jane Gem's father is described in the pedigree as 'of Fockbury Co. Worcester'. Fockbury adjoins Bromsgrove. Bromsgrove was a nail town. How could Huskisson not know all about nailers and truck?

1768 July 3 by Licence Robert Baswick of the P. of Chipping Wycombe Co. Bucks, and Jane Rotton of this P. Witn. William Huskisson, Eliz. Rotton. [I take 'the late Mrs. Baswick' of the letter to be Mrs. Robert Baswick.]

1769 March 12, William Huskisson and Elizabeth Rotton both of this Parish by Licence. Witn. Samuel Huskisson, Sarah Huskisson. (Samuel and Sarah were the bridgroom's brother and sister.)

1771 June 26, John Corsar of the P. of Sheriff Hales (Staffs.) and Sarah Huskisson of this P. by Licence. Witn. William Huskisson, Mary Bowker. [This tallies with the pedigree.]

It was to the Swinfens of the day that Huskisson paid his respects when returning from Paris in 1792, as mentioned by Lady Stafford (cf. p. 65). Thus for generations back, Huskisson on both sides was pure Midland. His friends twitted him with retaining to the end the broad Midland accent. Quite possibly he did, and was proud of it. I remember that when I came to King's College I enjoyed accentuating my northern origin to the cultured produce of Eton and the South.

(b) *In his own generation:* his full brothers (he being the eldest):
Richard, Samuel and Charles; and his half-brothers:
John, Thomas, George.

Richard, as we have seen (p. 261), died in the West Indies, 1794: Samuel became a Major-General[1]: Charles remained a country gentleman with a seat at Hazlewell Hall in Worcestershire.[2] Since their mother died, aged 31, September 1774, about three weeks after Charles was born, the boys had no normal home life, and the father's widowhood and remarriage in 1780 (solemnised in St. Peter's, Wolverhampton, 11 December 1780) to a young wife, who bore him five children between 1781 and 1788, accounts for the two elder boys going out to Dr. Gem in Paris in 1783. There is evidence of the friendliest relations between Huskisson and his half-brothers.

---

[1] Monument in Kensall Green Cemetery: 'Samuel Huskisson Esq., General in Her Majesty's Army: third son of William Huskisson of Oxley Co. Stafford, Died 30 December 1854. Aged 81 years.'

[2] In King's Norton Churchyard, Co. Worcester: 'To the memory of Charles Huskisson Esq., of Hazlewell Hall in this Parish, who died December 12th, 1857, aged 83 years. He was brother to the late Right Hon. William Huskisson and to the late General Huskisson.' Hazlewell is on the Worcester-Warwick boundary. Boundary adjustments around Birmingham complicate county references for Shrops., Staffs., Worcester and Warwick.

They executed commissions for him abroad: he helped them at home. Thus John Huskisson, who was in the army, became Deputy Surveyor of Bere Forest[1]; and Capt. Thomas Huskisson, R.N., entered the Navy Pay Office. There is a correspondence between the two about a 'financial abstraction', November 1828, which evoked Vesey Fitzgerald's dismay—'The whole Department seems to feel it deeply,' and Captain Huskisson had to find out how far back into Huskisson's Treasurership the 'defalcation' extended. And Sir James Graham, writing to Mrs Huskisson from the Admiralty 16 July 1831, wishes that he could have done more for 'the brother of his late friend', to wit Captain Thomas Huskisson, recently appointed to Greenwich Hospital. The third half-brother George was for many years a Collector of Customs in the West Indies (St. Vincent).

(c) *In the generations below him:* the names of William Milbanke Huskisson and William Swinfen Huskisson.

William Milbanke Huskisson, Tom's son, was named after the family of Huskisson's wife, Emily Milbanke; and it is believed, on the Huskisson side, that had he not predeceased her, Eartham might have passed to him. Tom's grandson, William Swinfen Huskisson, marks the repetition of an old family name.

Miss Huskisson has at Warlingham full-length portraits of her great-grandparents, William and Jane Huskisson (1788): portraits of Thomas, George and a sister as children (1788): also of Francis Huskisson, Tom's eldest son, her own father. These are her ancestors. In addition she has a bust and prints of the Statesman and a portrait of his brother, Samuel Huskisson, the Major-General, at the age of 18, which reached her through Sir Francis Rotton, who left it to her brother, now dead.

Huskisson, though he regarded himself as a Staffordshire

[1] In his will he leaves to John Huskisson a life annuity of £100; and the same John Huskisson wrote to him from Ceylon 7 December 1818 enclosing a £500 bill for investment in the funds. Similarly, in her will Mrs Huskisson leaves £100 to 'Elizabeth Huskisson, the daughter of the late Captain Huskisson RN', and presumably named after her.

man, was, along with his three full-brothers, born in Worcestershire at Birtsmorton Court, as stated in the Introduction. The
postal address of the Rector is Birtsmorton Rectory, Malvern,
Worcs.: and the entries in the Parish Register read:

William, son of Wm. & Eliz. Huskisson baptised March 18, 1770.[1]
Richard,                 —do—                    May 26, 1771.
Samuel,                  —do—                    March 14, 1773.
Charles,                 —do—                    August 21, 1774.

(Huskisson was born 11 March 1770.)

In 1776 Huskisson's father, who only had a lease of Birtsmorton Court, returned to Oxley: in 1790 he died. Huskisson
and his brother Richard left for France in 1783; and in 1793,
soon after his return thence, he sold the Oxley property. Moreover, from 1776 to 1782 he was at boarding school. Therefore
it was only in the holidays that he can have lived at Oxley. But
as he grew up he would get to know Staffordshire well from the
visits 'which the Doctor annually made with his young charges
to England'.[2]

## The Oxley and Bushbury Properties

Huskisson's grandfather is styled in the pedigree as 'of
Appleby and after 1753 of Oxley, Co. Stafford': Huskisson's
father as 'of Birchmorton Court, Co. Worcester, and after 1776,
of Oxley': Huskisson as 'of Eartham', all three being named
William. I will call them William I, William II, William III.
Oxley and Bushbury were adjoining properties on what is now
the southern fringe of Wolverhampton. Both were manors, but
Oxley was a hamlet, and Bushbury a parish with a fine parish
church.

The manor of Oxley belonged in the time of Charles I to Sir
Richard Leveson, who made his residence at Trentham and
gave Oxley to his servant, one John Langley. Samuel Swinfen
of Swinfen (*near Lichfield*), Co. Stafford, purchased it from the
Langley family in 1753 and entailed it upon his nephews

---

[1] The Register is badly stained. It may be March 14.
[2] Memoir (prefacing the Speeches), 5.

Samuel and William Huskisson (William II), the sons of his sister Dorothy (the first wife of William I). Samuel Huskisson, the elder brother, died unmarried in 1776 and was succeeded by his brother William II, whose son William (afterwards the Right Honble. William Huskisson—(III)) cut off the entail and sold the manor in 1793 to James Hordern, Esq. Samuel Swinfen himself never lived at Oxley: its occupants in turn were William I: Samuel (Swinfen's elder nephew): and William II (Swinfen's younger nephew).

The manor of Bushbury was in the Grosvenor family till 1721, when it was sold to the son of Bishop Chandler of Lichfield. The son's widow sold it to William I in 1774, who, dying in 1781, left it to his eldest surviving son, William II. The latter died in 1790, whereupon the manor, with the mansion-house, demesne lands, etc., were, under the will of the said William II, sold in the same year, 1790—the purchaser being Peter Tichborne Hinckes of Tettenhall Wood. It must be remembered that William I, though he lived at Oxley 1753-1774, did not own it—it belonged to his brother-in-law, Samuel Swinfen. The owners of Bushbury and Oxley after Huskisson's time were as follows:

*Bushbury* passed from P. T. Hinckes to his only daughter, who was the lady of the manor till her death *c.* 1875. She was a generous benefactor to the parish, helped to restore the church and gave the site for and built the parish schools; but, being the owner both of Bushbury and Tettenhall, she built her next mansion in the latter. In 1879, said the Vicar, the old manor house was 'in the present excellent tenancy of Mr. Lovatt, who most liberally gives me the free possession of the mansion house as a residence for my curate'.[1]

*Oxley* passed from James Hordern to Alexander Hordern and then to the latter's brother-in-law, Henry Hill 'of Dunstall and Oxley Manor J.P. Deputy Lieut.', who was succeeded by Alexander Stavely Hill, Q.C., M.P., of Oxley Manor. At a presentation to him and his wife, 1893, Mr. Stavely Hill said that:

[1] Rev. Moorhouse, *Wolverhampton Chronicle*, 24 September 1879.

Just a century ago, his great uncle purchased the estate from the family which formerly held it. . . . The Secretary to the English embassy in France was Mr. Huskisson, the owner of Oxley. Pitt having failed to raise sufficient money to carry on the war, a 'loyalty loan' was set afoot, and among those who contributed was Mr. Huskisson, who sold his estate for the purpose of helping the government to defeat the foe (cheers).[1]

Be the tradition right or wrong, it is refreshing to find a memory which does not introduce the railway engine.

Huskisson thus as a landowner was only connected with Staffs. as seller, for whatever reason, of the family property. Incidents from both sales have survived.

### BUSHBURY *1790*

I have heard some of the details of that sale (by auction in London) from one who heard it from eye-witnesses who described what would seem a curious state of things to us in this day—the lack of all sort of advertisement given, the scanty information to intending purchasers, the hurried rush of would-be buyers to London, when one of them found himself too late for the bargain. (Rev. Moorhouse, *ibid.*)

### OXLEY

W'hampton Dec. 28. 1793

Sir. Yrs. I have just recd. and have since waited upon my Atty. who informs me that I have a just right to the Estate from my agreement and I think myself very ill used if you convey it to any other person. If you do you will oblige me to take such steps as will be very disagreeable to you.

I am yours. etc.

Geo. Pountney

Wm. Huskisson Esq., Oxley.

Oxley, Saturday 28 Dec. 1793

From the conversation I had with you and Mr. Phillipps last night you have, must have, perceived that I considered myself as irrevocably engaged to Mr. Hordern for the Purchase of my Estate. The price he had engaged to give was equal to the sum I had demanded and he gives it under the present Lease which, without a consent which my brother is by no means disposed to grant, cannot be cancelled. The engagement Mr.

[1] *Midland Evening News*, 22 August 1893.

Horden had entered into previous to the 23rd inst. was certainly binding on his part:—on mine perhaps it might have been considered as not valid in Law; but I do not conceive that I could (even if disposed to do so) have departed from it, without forfeiting the character of a Gentleman and of a Man of Honour, and this I shall always value more than a pecuniary Consideration. As I shall therefore sign an agreement this morning before I leave Oxley I have only to express my regret at the trouble you have had on this occasion, and at the impossibility I feel of meeting you at the Talbot.

I am, Sir etc.

William Huskisson

Huskisson is 23. How true it is that the style is the man from youth to old age!

The result of these sales (in which other members of the family shared) was to free Huskisson from any pecuniary straits, and since in 1800 he inherited Dr. Gem's estate, after having married on 6 April 1799 Emily Milbanke, the co-heiress of Admiral Mark Milbanke, the Huskissons were comfortably off, even apart from the emoluments of office. When these are included, I figure them as having throughout their life an income of well over £5,000 a year. On 15 December 1794 he writes to Evan Nepean that his financial position is now sound—the Staffordshire sale brought him £13,500, increased by the death of his brother Richard to £16,000. 'When an old relative now of 87 dies, there will be a further £8-10,000.' (This is perhaps his grandmother, Jane Huskisson.)

Of other legal documents possessed by Miss Huskisson, one relates to the sale of the Advowson of Bushbury inrolled in the High Court of Chancery 9 June 1795, in which 'William Huskisson of Pall Mall, in the Parish of St. James, Westminster, Esquire' is of the second part. Another is an Indenture between William Huskisson of Clarges Street, Piccadilly, and others of 20 March 1799, relating to a mortgage which Huskisson had taken over from Dr. Richard Gem in 1796 and which the executors were now paying off. It concerned some Rotton property, and Huskisson's grandmother, described as Jane Huskisson of Birmingham (she died at Edgbaston in 1799), comes into it. Another is an extract from a Tithe Commutation Deed of Bushbury Parish (confirmed 31 July 1847), which prescribes a Rent charge of £8 16s. 1d. to Alexander Hordern, 'the Devisee in Trust under the will of William Huskisson of Oxley, deceased.'

When Huskisson returned from Paris he left his uncle behind, and in England he looked after Dr. Gem's property. In 1798 the Bushbury lawyer writes to him:

I shall be happy to hear from you when convenient respecting the Doctor's Land Tax—what is best to be done, and it will be a guide to me respecting my own Land Tax [i.e. whether to redeem under the Act of that year].

And a little later Huskisson writes to Hayley:

My uncle's name is Richard Gem. I received this morning, the remittance of the money from Staffs. But the rogues have sent a bill payable 31 days after sight. However, if you want the money sooner it may be discounted.

This, I take it, refers to the purchase of Eartham.

Today, neither Bushbury nor Oxley exists as a seat: though some of the panelling from Oxley Manor (demolished 1928-9), together with several windows having the letters W H worked into their pattern, survives in the home of a Wolverhampton builder at Springhill Park, Penn. Bushbury has its church, Oxley is a building estate. On the 'bus from Wolverhampton to Stafford one notices an Oxley Avenue, a Bushbury Fruit Stores. The great house of the region is the Goodyear Tyre and Rubber Company, with its works, its playing fields and its hive of population. The Industrial Revolution has reached it, but thanks to modern technique, it is no longer necessary that it should drape the countryside in black. Witness the Wedgewood of 1950, a rural annexe of Trentham, electrically driven, with not a wisp of smoke in the sky.

### The Education of Youth

The youths in question are William Huskisson and Edward John Walhouse, who later took the name of Littleton.

The memoir compiled for Mrs Huskisson states that Huskisson, on his mother's death, was 'placed at an infant school at Brewood in Staffs': that he was afterwards removed to Albrighton, and lastly to Appleby Magna in Leicestershire, where even then he evinced a 'peculiar aptitude for figures and calculation.' And at the Liverpool Election of 14 February 1823, Huskisson himself said, 'I was born and educated in England, in England I received the rudiments of my education, of which a reverence for the free constitution of my country formed a part; and I never left my native shores until that education was nearly completed' (Speeches, III, 649). There is an ample local history of Brewood and Albrighton, including its schools, but there is no evidence that he was enrolled as a scholar at any school in these two places. The one and only piece of solid evidence comes from Appleby Magna.

Appleby Grammar School,[1] founded and endowed in 1697 by Sir John Moore, Lord Mayor of London and East India Merchant, was closed as such in 1904, but the Headmaster of the Primary School, which replaced it, lives in the old headmaster's house in the school building; and during World War II, when turning out the old stable, he found under a heap of rubble the original Admission Registers. These have been searched and disclose:

| When entered | | | |
|---|---|---|---|
| | 1712 | Mar. 27th | Huskisson John. |
| | 1712 | May 8th | Huskisson Sam. |
| | 1719 | Jan. 18th | Huskisson James. |
| | 1723 | Jan. 7th | Huskisson Thomas. |
| | 1753 | Sep. 3rd | Huskisson William. |
| | 1782 | June 25th | Huskisson William. |
| | 1782 | June 25th | Huskisson Richard. |

The two last are our William and his surgeon brother. By a glance at the pedigree it will be seen that William Huskisson of 1753 is Huskisson's father. The first four, all in the pedigree, are of the generation above, to wit:

| | | | |
|---|---|---|---|
| 1712 | John Huskisson | Bapt. at Appleby | 1698. |
| 1712 | Samuel Huskisson | —do— | 1700. |
| 1719 | James Huskisson | —do— | 1708. |
| 1723 | Thomas Huskisson | Bapt. | 1711. |

[1] Sir William Wilson, the architect of this school, was associated with the decoration of Weston-under-Lizard.

The school[1] was built originally for boys of Appleby Magna and the five adjacent parishes, but in 1770, by which time it had grown into a select school of some distinction, it was made free (i.e. open) to all England, and so in 1782 William and Richard could come from Oxley to the school of their father and their father's people, who belonged to Appleby and round-about. The panels of black oak in the Main Hall of the old school are covered with the carved autographs of the boys. Among them is N. J. Chavasse, a surname celebrated in the epis-copal history of Liverpool,[2] but if our surmise is correct that William and Richard were there only for a short while, their names are not likely to be found.

Brewood Grammar School is an ancient grammar school, which flourishes still.[3] Founded in the time of Queen Mary, it was enriched and enlarged by two former scholars, Richard Hurd 1720-1808, bishop of Lichfield and Worcester, and Sir Edward Littleton, the (great) uncle of E. J. Walhouse, who on becoming his heir took his name—hence Edward John Little-ton, later first Lord Hatherton. There is in the Hatherton MSS. a fascinating volume of correspondence between Bishop Hurd and Sir Edward, relating to the management and extension of the school. At five or six Huskisson would be too young to attend such a place. There is no trace of him in the School records, which, however, are imperfect for the period, and it is possible that he attended a Dame's School in the vicinity, of which, in 1830, there are known to have been several from advertisements in the Wolverhampton papers. Before leaving for Albrighton he may have attended classes at Brewood Grammar School, but this is pure surmise.

At Albrighton, a little one-street town in Shropshire (but only a few miles from Brewood) to which he went next, the evi-

---

[1] The school grounds are in two counties, Leicestershire and Derbyshire. An old boy recalls that the Headmaster's pigs strayed from their sty through the doorway into the next county, and a permit was needed to bring them back. The county boundary runs through the middle of the school hall. When I lectured there March 1949, I was in Leicestershire, my audience in Derbyshire!

[2] Francis James Chavasse, Bishop of Liverpool

[3] Cf. *History of Brewood Grammar School* by Ch. Dunkley, Vicar of Brewood, Chairman of the Governors 1901-27. Prebendary of Lichfield.

dence is equally negative. There was a school near the old Toll Shop, no longer standing, of which a local history compiled between 1800 and 1825 relates:

Mr. John Brownhall had the Tolls of the fairs allotted him by the Lord of the Manor for the education of 6 poor boys belonging to the boro'. He built a good house near the Toll Shop, and kept a considerable boarding school and has seldom less than 40 boys. . . . A new school has been erected in the room of the Toll Shop in a more convenient place. . . .

But it is very possible that he boarded at the Vicarage of Albrighton, St. Mary's. We know, of course, the incumbents of the living, which was in the gift of Christ's Hospital:

|      |                 |
|------|-----------------|
| 1748 | John Hale       |
| 1782 | Henry Binfield  |
| 1795 | Thomas Lloyd    |

We know, further, that Henry Binfield of Pembroke Hall, Cambridge, M.A. 1761, 'laid out a good deal of money in improving the vicarage house. He had kept a school near London, and took a few young gentlemen here' [*Albrighton*]. This, however, is just too late for Huskisson; and whether John Hale had similarly taken a few young gentlemen, we cannot say.

When we pass to our second Staffordshire youth, E. J. Walhouse, the evidence is sure and rich. His uncle was Chairman of the Trustees of Brewood Grammar School and sent his nephew there: and the nephew tells us about his school life in a short autobiography inserted in the Reverse of his Diary, Volume V. Edward John (twenty-one years the junior of Huskisson) was born in 1791. Hatherton and Teddesley are adjoining estates east of Penkridge, Staffs. Grandfather Walhouse owned Hatherton. Sir Edward Littleton owned Teddesley. The grandfather left Hatherton to his wife, who was the sister and only surviving relative of Sir Edward Littleton; and eventually the grandson became the owner both of Hatherton and Teddesley. Teddesley is the larger property, and there is a story that, when raised to the peerage in 1835, Littleton took the title of Lord Hatherton to avoid the nickname of Lord Teddy-Sly. The school reminiscence runs:

On our arrival in Staffordshire [he was then in his ninth year] I was sent to Brewood School—at about 6 miles distance from home—because my father and my uncles had been educated there. I continued there for 6 years, during which time even with better capacities I could have learned but little—for Mr. Harrison the Headmaster had a very defective system of education. His love of more gainful pursuits, the little attention he paid to the school, and his violent temper completely disqualified him for the situation—from which indeed he was afterwards dismissed by the Trustees. At the age of 15 I went to Rugby School, where, if I made but little progress at my studies, I had at least the advantage of a more numerous society, there being nearly 300 boys there at the time I left it. I was put into the 5th form on my arrival, and soon afterwards, in consequence of a private examination at Latin Composition which I underwent with some of the boys above me, Dr. Inglis made me stand before them in his class— a thing seldom done after boys had once gained the 5th form. I contended once in vain for the Annual English Prize Poem. I was more successful in my competition for the prizes for Declamation, which I won every half year. During the last year I was there Macready, who was intended for the Bar, but who has since gone on the stage, Mr. Ricketts and myself got up some plays. Dr. Wooll gave us the Great School for our theatre and Rickets and myself painted a complete set of scenes from the Revenge. Macready acted Zonga and Don Alonzo. We were allowed to invite the Gentry resident about Rugby and we played with brilliant success to an overflowing House.

I had been at Rugby about a year and a half when I was one day visited by Mr. George Parker, a solicitor and very distant relative of Sir Edward Littleton's, whose private affairs he had been consulted upon—he had come from Birbury[1] the place of T. Biddulph Bart., who was also a relation of Sir E. Littleton and who was appointed executor and trustee in his will. His object was to put me on my guard respecting my conduct with Sir E. Littleton. He told me of offences my father had given Sir E. Little-

[1] Birbury, alias Birdingbury, 6 miles S.W. of Rugby. To keep the records straight, Littleton got from his trustee a statement of the liquor drunk at his coming-of-age. The letter reads: 'Birbury. Dec. 19 1829.

I send you the account of the liquor drunk at Teddesley when you came of age
14 hogs of strong beer.
8 dozen and 2 bottles of port wine.
5 dozen of sherry.
1 dozen and 9 bottles of rum.
6 bottles of brandy.

Signed (Sir) Theophilus Biddulph Bart;'
and in return for this information the Bart. asks for the loan of Littleton's rabbit man.

ton and of other things which would aggravate his displeasure if known. He reminded me that he had other nephews and that there was the West-cote family (the Lyttleton's[1] of Haxey). I carefully transmitted our conversation to my Father and ventured to advise him to be more quiet and cautious. This advice I constantly repeated to him to the period of my father's death.

When I left Rugby, Dr. Wooll, the Head Master, selected me out of the ordinary course to deliver the Latin Harrangue to the Trustees at their annual meeting for the examination of the boys for exhibitions. He wrote the address and made me recite it.

Being then 18 years old, I went immediately afterwards to Brazen Nose College (I never could learn any satisfactory reason why that College was preferred except that Sir E. Littleton objected to Christ Church on account of the Dissipation that reigned there). At B.N. College I read harder than the majority and should have taken a creditable degree, if Sir E. Littleton's death in May 1812, 2 months after I came of age, had not called me to contest the County with Sir John Wrottesley—who after a long canvas declined a poll.[2] .... (The rest of this short autobiography is given on pp. 79-81 above.)

The headmasters of Brewood School in Huskisson's and Littleton's time were Rev. George Croft, D.D., 1780-91, and Rev. Hamlet Harrison, B.D., 1792-1809. The Rev. Croft—fellow of University College, Oxford, and Bampton lecturer 1786—gave Brewood a headmaster who is in the Dictionary of National Biography. In his time most of the local gentry had a spell at the school—the Moncktons and the Chetwynds among others—which, on the whole, flourished during the Napoleonic

[1] As to the spelling, in reply to a query from Littleton, Lord Lyttelton replies from Althorp 25 January 1831, 'My Friend, Pitcher, Namesake and Cousin! As to the name of the descendants of "the Old Buck of the Tenures"—eight spellings of it—and in the first two editions of the Tenures no author's name. Lord L. concludes by offering help to L "in your most laudable anti-truckations".' William Henry, third Lord Lyttelton, succeeded to the title in 1828. If I have transcribed 'pitcher' correctly, what does it mean—fellow-sportsman?

[2] Cf. *Rugby School* by G. H. Bettinson, O.R. (1929):

P. 31—'Entrance (1806) E. J. Walhouse, afterwards Lord Hatherton and Secretary of State for Ireland.'

P. 32—'On Oct. 15 this year, the boys' company acted the 'Castle Spectre' in our school, the following being the cast': out of which I select:

Reginald ⎫
Motley ⎬ Doubled by W. C. Macready
Hassan (Lord Hatherton)

wars, though there were outbreaks of 'school fever' at this period that caused serious mortality at Brewood and presumably in other schools also. But Littleton's years at the school co-incided with a bad patch in the shape of a headmaster who was so unsatisfactory that the Trustees dismissed him in 1809. The evidence given at the meeting of the Trustees (held in the Littleton Arms Inn, Penkridge, August 1809) has survived.

'Mr. Harrison left it to his assistants to read the prayers and take the classes, never sitting in the Upper school except to hear a few boys of the Upper class, and as often as not in his private parlour.' A witness, resident at Brewood, stated that 'he has seen him at all times of the day, both in school hours and out, and in all directions attending to his farming business: that Mr. Harrison is a considerable farmer and has a large quantity of cattle of all sorts—holding about 90 acres of land with a proportionate farming establishment'. But what finished the Rev. Harrison was the evidence of Benjamin Wootton, breeches maker, his next door neighbour but one:

Has seen Mr. Harrison at all times of the day engaged in farming business —has worked in the field for him with other labourers, when Mr. Harrison has come to them and if the least thing was wrong has thrown himself into the most violent passions possible cursing and swearing, and calling them by the worst of names—he particularly recollects Mr. Harrison calling Joseph Till 'a damnation lousy son of a bitch. . . .'

Other evidence showed that he had flogged mercilessly and dragged one sick lad into school, saying, 'See I can work miracles—I can make the lame to walk.'

How many Harrisons in this generation were there over England as a whole: how many Squeerses in the next?

The history of a particular school is of interest principally to its old boys. But with a number of such histories before us, we might unravel a chapter of social life which to me, at least, is very obscure. These grammar schools, small and great, reflect the changes and stresses of the age. The masters, like the vicars or rectors, were usually Oxford or Cambridge men and thus were links of culture or at least of latinity between their neighbourhood and the world without. In Bishop Hurd's time, we are told, the Trustees bought the two houses opposite to the school and turned them into residences and school rooms for the second master, thereby converting what had been a village road into the present School Lane within its grounds. It was a sort of scholastic enclosure out of the open village and no doubt improved the quality of the scholastic product. Similarly, when Appleby became 'free' to all, what this meant was that it was open on payment to all England, instead of serving gratis the children round about. A few of these schools grew to famous institutions: as it happens, not in Staffordshire, but on either side of Staffordshire, at Shrewsbury in Shropshire and at Rugby in Warwickshire. Dr. Butler at the one, Dr. Arnold at the other, put them on the map for all time; and then the smaller schools became, in part, feeders to the larger institutions, until the special preparatory school emerged to oust them.

Just as improved transport reacted favourably on agriculture, so also it must have been with schools. On macadamised roads the boys could travel easily to and fro in vacations. But there was the further problem of numbers. Population in the eighteenth and nineteenth centuries increased too rapidly for the local grammar schools to become the basis of a national education. They were, so to speak, squeezed up into a middle-class status, and the whole vast problem of educating the masses had to be started afresh. It was tackled as a problem of industry, and its industrial origin is marked by the connection between the growth of factories and the certificate of attendance at school, as a condition of entry into factory employment.

### General View of the County[1]

A county of stately homes and green fields on a rolling landscape scarred by the random outcrops of industrialism—that is the county as I saw it from a cycle—first west to east from Albrighton to Burton-on-Trent, over against Appleby Magna: and

---

[1] The Dyott Diary of General William Dyott, of 1781-1845, makes an excellent background to this and the next section. He was a frequent visitor at Teddesley, with its beautiful hostess, and admired Littleton as a county member and agricultural reformer, who in twenty years, 1812-32, had transformed the Teddesley estate from 'a waste' into a 'highly improved cultivation'.

then south to north from Wolverhampton to New Chapel, which looks down on the Cheshire plain. Some of the stately homes have vanished. Beaudesert is dismantled: Trentham Abbey an amusement Park: Tixall a ruin: Drayton Manor is no more—some part of it, they say, has been removed to the U.S.A. Dudley's place at Himley Hall, which he built for himself at the mouth of a coal pit, is the headquarters now of the regional Coal Board. But many survive, and, unusually many are tenanted by their owners—Weston-under-Lizard, Chillington, Wolseley Hall, Ingestre, Sandon—to mention some of those I have been privileged to view. The county, moreover, is almost co-extensive with the historic diocese of Lichfield (the present Bishop being the ninety-first in succession), and one comes on numerous small places—Brewood, Bushbury, Croxall, for example, possessing churches rich in historic associations and architectural beauty. The early bishops of Lichfield, hunting in Brewood and holding ordinations there, made of the parish church a young cathedral, where *mirabile dictu* catholics and protestants, under the influence of the Giffards and Boscobel Oak, lived happily together, and where catholic bishops were interred in the parish church. At Bushbury, another refuge of Charles II, you may still see the beech trees and chancel door where George Borrow and his gypsy friends attended service in 1825.

Croxall church, on the Derbyshire border, has in it the chantry monument to Eusebius Horton of Catton Hall and the wall monument to Sir Robert Wilmot Horton (the R.W.H. of our narrative) and his wife Ann. She it is who for Byron 'walks in beauty like the night of cloudless climes and starry skies'. Staffordshire, indeed, is chockful of literary associations, though I confess I cannot recognise Ilam in the pages of Rasselas. But perhaps the Johnson scholars only leave Lichfield for London.

It has become a convention, almost as binding as a reference to Domesday, to begin an account of Stafford with an extract from Robert Plot's *Natural History of Staffordshire*, 1685. He deals, as his admirers know, in earthquakes and strange noises—in the earthquake which at Bushbury Hall 'caused the great pot they boyled their meat in to leap up from the ground': in the 'tremulous echo there is at Elmhurst Hall on the tarrass walk . . . which was shown me by the Worshipful Michael Biddulph'. But Plot was writing in the full loyalty of 1682; and pride of place goes to Boscobel Oak, which 'though in the County of Salop yet even there he rested in the Lap of a Staffordshire Gent, Collonel William Carlis of this neighbourhood, who having constantly followed his Majestie's fortunes, with much difficulty had also made his escape from Worcester'.

Cycling one Easter afternoon from Albrighton to Lichfield I traversed the base line of Huskisson's Staffordshire, halting first at Weston-under-Lizard, whose house is in Stafford and park wall in Shropshire. The Earl of Bradford (the owner of Boscobel Oak, which he contends is the original) showed me, at Weston, the library which houses the Letters to Selina, the huge silk carpet which Disraeli gave her, woven by French Huguenots at St. Petersburg, the white cock parrot which laid a dozen eggs (they are preserved in a silver box) and then died, the Gobelin tapestries, the Vandyke heads of Charles I, the sporting prints of George Morland, the silver-mounted tail of the Derby winner of 1892. On the wall was the family's founder, Sir Orlando Bridgeman (1606-74), the great conveyancing lawyer, whose skill created the family settlements by which estates like this were held together.[1]

My road was the Watling St. running south-east towards Atherstone. It passes, after several miles, under the aqueduct built by Thomas Telford in 1832 for the canal which winds through the grounds of Chillington Park and Brewood School. At Galey, a little to the south of Penkridge, whose church is full of Littletons from Elizabethan days to the present ('Here lie 2 Knights, Ye Father and Ye Sonne, Sir Edward and Sir Edward Littleton'), I crossed the Wolverhampton-Stafford road. To my right were Oxley and Bushbury on the outskirts of Wolverhampton: to my left Hatherton and Teddesley with

[1] See *Country Life* 9, 16, 23 Nov. of 1945 for three richly illustrated articles by Christopher Hussey on 'Weston Park Staffordshire, the Earl of Bradford's Home'.

the coal pyramids of Cannock Chase almost on top of them. Then I edged up towards Cannock to strike the road that runs down into Lichfield, noticing the warnings on the road 'Beware of Subsidence'.

From Lichfield, having rested at the George Hotel, where Farquhar, while recruiting for the Guards, wrote the Beaux' Strategem, I rode north to the Potteries: past Rugeley, Wolseley Hall, Shugborough (the Earl of Lichfield), Tixall, Ingestre (the Earl of Shrewsbury), Sandon (the Earl of Harrowby), Stone and Trentham. Next day I toiled through the Pottery towns, along single streets of undulating ugliness, till I reached 'Brindley-land'—New Chapel, Kidsgrove and Harecastle Tunnel. The picture that was left with me was of two industrial Staffordshires, Black Country and Potteries, separated by a broad expanse of tillage, pasture and elevated woodland. And it was in this intermediate land that as a historian I brooded over the great families that were there a century and a quarter ago. I envisaged it thus. Supposing that one were required to construct for England in 1827 an all-Staffordshire cabinet, could it be done? Here was my answer:

| | |
|---|---|
| First Lord of the Treasury | Earl of Harrowby (Sandon) —in fact he thrice refused the Premiership |
| Chancellor of the Exchequer | William Huskisson (Oxley) |
| Home Secretary | Robert Peel (Tamworth) |
| Foreign Secretary | Earl of Dudley (Himley) |
| Board of Trade | E. J. Littleton (Teddesley) |
| Secretary for War and the Colonies | Wilmot Horton (Catton, by Croxall) |
| First Lord of the Admiralty | Viscount Anson (Shugborough) |
| Chancellor of the Duchy of Lancaster | Earl of Shrewsbury (Ingestre) |
| Lord President of the Council | Marquis of Stafford (Trentham) |
| Lord Privy Seal | Lord Granville (Tixall) |

| Board of Control (India) | Marquis of Wellesley (his wife died at Teddesley) |
| Governor-General of Ireland | The Marquis of Anglesey (Beaudesert) |

And presumably it would not be beyond the wit of an Orlando Bridgeman to provide a suitable Lord Chancellor.

Now, let anyone take any other county (excluding Middlesex, to which everyone with a town house in a sense belonged) and try to construct for himself a full Cabinet, with names of Cabinet standing; and I should be surprised if anything like so strong a list could be drawn up. Politically, Staffordshire was the hub of Regency England; and Huskisson, with a second home at Teddesley, had an ear at the centre of things. It strikes one how small at this time was the showing made by Lancashire and Norfolk, the banner counties of industry and agriculture, in the political field.

Staffordshire is pear-shaped and some fifty miles in length from stem to crown. But the main lines of communication cross it from south-east to north-west: the valley of the Trent, which rises at Biddulph on the Cheshire border and leaves the county north of Lichfield, being the determining feature. This was the direction followed in turn by the London-Holyhead road[1] via Chester, by Brindley's Grand Junction Canal, and by the London and North Western Railway. I have before me that delight of scholars, panels from the road maps of John Ogilby, the King's cartographer of Restoration England. Coming from London we enter the county by Sutton Coldfield and then pass Swinfen Hall to Lichfield. The next two panels take us from Lichfield to Stone—past Beaudesert, Cannock 'vulgo Cank Wood' Rugeley, Wolseley Park, Tixall, Ingestre, Sandon—parallel with the Trent from Rugeley to Sandon. At Sandon there is a choice of ways: north-west to Madeley, thus avoiding the Potteries, or alternatively by Darlaston, Trentham and Newcastle to Talk—north of which, in either case, is Cheshire. The former, roughly, was the route of the Liverpool to Birming-

---

[1] Huskisson in 1819 served on a Committee of Enquiry into the London-Holyhead Road and Irish Mail Services (J.H.C., Vol. 74, p. 35).

ham (Grand Junction) Railway: the latter, roughly, the route of
the (later) Manchester to Birmingham line via Macclesfield
and Stoke. Celia Fiennes, her aunt being Lady Wolseley, made
Wolseley Hall her headquarters in 1702 for tours in every
direction.

In the canal age the great engineering feat was the piercing
by James Brindley (1716-72) at Harecastle of the high border
land between north Staffordshire and the Cheshire plain. (The
Manchester to Birmingham railway tunnel later ran beside it.)
This brought the Potteries into the orbit of modern industrialism, the china clay coming around from Cornwall up the canal,
and the finished pottery leaving by canal. In Huskisson's day
the Bridgewater Trust controlled the canal system of the Bridgewater and Grand Trunk Canals, engineered by Brindley. But
this is not the end of Staffordshire's canal story. There was
scope for a more direct and more level route from Birmingham
to the Mersey, leading off from the Staffs. and Worcestershire
Canal north of Wolverhampton and joining the Ellesmere-
Chester Canal near Nantwich. It was authorised May 1826,
and it is the canal which Telford carried by aqueduct over the
Watling Street.

By this date the canal interests were fearing the threatened
competition of the railways, and the prospectus with a sketch
map gives a view of the strategy of the undertaking. It reads:

This, which may be called the main line of the Canal, provides an
additional road from Birmingham and Staffordshire by the town of Wolverhampton to Liverpool, saving 21 miles in distance and 60 locks: it affords
also another and better road between the Midland district and Manchester,
as the Ellesmere and Chester Canal not only falls into the Mersey, but
unites the Grand Trunk Canal, by a new branch at Middlewich; by this
new line, also, North Wales and Chester, are placed in direct communication with the interior of the kingdom, and through Wolverhampton and
Birmingham with the Metropolis, the intercourse with which has been
hitherto clogged by heavy expense in land carriage.

The canal was built, but the railways, doing the same thing
better, reaped the harvest. The county town of Stafford, like the
railway towns of Crewe and Wolverton, pivoted thenceforth on

*Contemporary Map of Canals in Lancashire and Cheshire, 1830*

the railway. Dickens has drawn the picture. 'It seems as if its whole population might be imprisoned in its Railway station. The Refreshment Room at that station, is a vortex of dissipation, compared with the extinct town-inn, the Dodo, in the dull High Street.'[1] The railways, while they brought increase to some places, isolated others by destroying their coach route. Brewood was one of these, but it got level with Puffing Billies in the end; for it produced at its school T. A. Walker, who engineered the Manchester Ship Canal.

## The County Member

E. J. Littleton (1791-1863) was the ideal county member: and he met every requirement befitting the county that the Staffordshire of his day was coming to be. Bred and educated in the county or its vicinity, he knew every feature of it, its people, its occupations and its communications, from A to Z. In 1812, when his uncle died, he succeeded him both as his heir and as member for the county, which he represented continuously from 1812 to 1832.

Teddesley was a centre of hospitality not only for the county but for statesmen of all parties. To be at Teddesley was to be at the centre of things: a sort of Westminster in recess. Its coverts were famous; the stories told in its dining room and library more famous still. Here county petitions and demonstrations were organised. Here political opponents were brought together and reconciled—not as Lord Hertford did it by arranging that there should be no politics, but by smoothing things out and by acting as peacemaker. The anteroom which leads into the great library was Littleton's place of work. It was here that day after day I read the Hatherton MSS. with the Rothwell Huskisson looking down on me; and here that I re-enacted a scene from the Diary, involuntarily overhearing what the Duke said:

Nov. 20, 1821. We were a little alarmed today by the arrival of Mr. Arbuthnot, Secretary of the Treasury, from town for the purpose of an interview with the Duke and Mr. Huskisson. I found out that the object of the interview was to induce Mr. Huskisson to remain in office. Whether

[1] Reprinted Pieces, *A Plated Article.*

the negotiation to bring in Mr. Canning had failed is not as certain, but I found out that Mr. Huskisson insisted on retiring if he had not a seat in the Cabinet. I heard the Duke say to him 'Come, Huskisson, this is more a matter of passion than of feeling with you'. Huskisson afterwards owned to me that I had been right in my conjecture; but begged me not to mention it. He said he had been long enough engaged in rowing the boat, while the Cabinet Ministers sat idle in it, and instanced Lord Maryborough and Frederick Robinson—who sit there like dead weights, though the latter is a clever man (Hatherton Diary 1820-1).

There was in those days no county (least of all Northumberland and Durham, the home of the improved Shorthorn) which could be adequately represented unless the representative had an enthusiasm for agriculture.[1] Lord Althorp and Littleton talked politics at Westminster (they were colleagues in Grey's Whig administration), but at Teddesley and Althorp they admired each other's stock. Both owned allegiance to the great Coke of Holkham; and it surprises me that I do not read of Huskisson attending a Sheep Shearing—too much Whiggery there perhaps. The 1st Earl of Bradford was an active disciple of Coke, and the home farm buildings at Weston were accounted 'one of the noblest architectural products of the Agricultural Revolution'. Our staple source of agricultural knowledge is, of course, the County Surveys prepared under the auspices of the old Board of Agriculture, with Arthur Young's Norfolk at the head of the list, but we get an even closer view from the letters of the time, when one landlord writes to another—e.g. G. Tollet to Littleton from Betley Hall, 2 July 1826:

The calamity threatening this part of the country from the drought is truly great. The spring corn upon the light lands is absolutely vanishing and I have 5 fields of barley that promised 40 bushels per acre of good quality that will not turn out 50 of bad quality, and some late sown oats upon land of light quality will be a total loss. Upon the stronger lands of my farm I have wheat and oats looking well. The hay crop not more than a third, and for the present not a prospect of a single acre of turnips. I

---

[1] Huskisson's father was a keen cattle man, and Miss Huskisson has a painting of a huge cow with Oxley Manor in the background, and Tilt, the dairyman, by the animal's head.

began to sow swedes, they came up and I have not a single plant left. I must abandon all thoughts of sowing any more of that sort as I consider it too late—nor any more till rain comes. Judging from my own farm, I ask what must be the fate of Shropshire and of Norfolk. The accounts I had from my friend Mr. Tayleur from his district of Shropshire are truly deplorable. The wheat is beginning to be affected and upon one field of light land I shall not have half the crop I expected. If you have not had more rain than we have you must be suffering greatly upon your Cannock lands. We have not had a soaking rain since X'Mas and of late absolutely none. I never remember at any season of the year anything at all like it, but in this *early* part of the year it is the more ruinous. Our cheese farms are if possible worse off. They have neither grass nor fodder. What will become of their cattle, no one can tell.

Cunliffe wrote to me this day three weeks saying that we were within a week of great rain. What would he say now? What is remarkable is, the drought seems mostly to affect those districts that have been usually the most showery: viz. Lancs., Cheshire, Derbyshire, North Staffs. and Shrops. A servant of Lord Anson's was here yesterday who said that it rained at Shugborough[1] from 11 o'c on Fri. night till 7 o'c yesterday mng. We had not a drop. You perhaps have yr. share. You will think me truly μαντις κακων when I add that we are in considerable alarm for the potato crop—which to the poor of these districts would be the worst of all evils. The early sorts are undoubtedly much injured and if the drought continues the like will happen to the later ones. When once the tuber is formed and checked in its growth—it grows again when rain comes and the quality is worthless. I hope a good deal of this is news to you and to the greatest part of the Kingdom. To the North I take it they are worse off than to the South.

This is the pen of an educated man, with a thorough grasp of his subject and an eye to differences of districts and crops. It is the sort of thing that Sir James Caird worked up into his *Times* letters of 1850-1. From another angle the Liverpool grain merchants and William Jacob, Comptroller of Corn Returns, supplied Huskisson with information about grain imports and crop conditions overseas. He, too, also exchanged crop news with his friends, so that he had a balanced view of the food problem as a whole: and he never subordinated to statistics the

---

[1] Six miles N.W. of Newcastle-under Lyme, on the Cheshire border.

qualitative judgments of those directly engaged in food production.

As Professor W. H. B. Court has shown in his *Rise of the Midland Industries 1600-1838*, industrial capitalism grew there in the interstices of the older society. South Staffordshire was rich in coal and iron; and local landowners, not surfeited with the profits of overseas adventure, welcomed the development of mineral enterprise on their land. But by 1830 the rift between landowner and manual worker was deep. The county M.P. might work for the latter, but could not speak with his voice. The industrialism of the great towns, and the insurgency of thought which it bred were distasteful to the county. To Littleton this dangerous new voice was represented by Thomas Attwood the banker (1783-1856) and the Political Unions of Birmingham. Attwood writes to Lord Liverpool from Lombard St. (16 March 1820) of the bad conditions in Staffordshire:

... extreme poverty of the working classes, very hard labour for 16 to 18 hours a day for very low wages of 9/- to 10/- a week and the stock of iron and of nails again accumulating beyond demand, and tho' produced cheaply worth less at market than this low cost—Life sustained by labourers and their families on very small consumption—with very little meat, reduced to potatoes, and almost to grass and leaves for their children, and neither farmers nor manufacturers able to employ those who want work and bread, and obliged *all* to employ and to *feed* numbers for whom they have no useful occupation, still less profitable, but fear to make them desperate thro' hunger and absolute destitution. ... The poor's rates 40/- in the pound, the rents (never raised) only 30/- an acre. ... The young men of the forge at 30, debilitated by extenuation and labour to the appearance of 80.

But Attwood was a radical and a currency crank, and his remedies, political and economic, were subversive. The county would have none of him. We can see that though the unreformed House may have adequately represented the county, the towns needed a reformed channel for the expression of their true voice, for which, meanwhile, the crank was better than nothing.

Teddesley was in South Staffs.; the Potteries in North Staffs.

under the shadow of Staffordshire's greatest landowner and most portentous figure, the Marquis of Stafford at Trentham Abbey. Trentham surely would keep the Potteries in order! Littleton's first colleague in the representation of the county was Lord Granville Leveson-Gower (the younger brother of the Marquis), before he became Viscount Granville and went over to diplomacy. But his Staffordshire was the gaiety of Tixall (now vanished, except for its Mary Queen of Scots gate tower, a national monument)—Tixall, where as Greville relates, 'I never remember so agreeable a party—'le bon goût, les ris, l'aimable liberté' (30 November 1818). Lord Gower, however, the Marquis's heir, was the obedient son of a strict father, and he might do something. For he writes from Lilleshall (*Salop*), 7 December 1828:

My father is very ready to patronise the Mechanicks' Institution in the Potteries. I should think if properly conducted such establishments must be useful. They are very generally in fashion now, it seems everywhere— one at Shrewsbury. It is a better fashion than the rage for joint-stock companies was. I go to Sandon tomorrow and thence to Yorkshire and Castle Howard.[1]

But it is all patronage from above, and will not take us into the heart of the Potteries. A better guide is the man who lodged at the Dodo, opposite the little ironmonger's shop, and gazed into the plated piece till it told him its secrets: 'and don't you remember how you alighted at Stoke—a picturesque heap of houses, kilns, smoke, wharfs, canals and rivers',[2] etc., etc. Yet if our model member was not pottery-minded, he was, like almost everyone in Staffordshire, canal-minded. He succeeded his uncle in the Chairmanship of the Staffs. and Worcester Canal Co. and retained this office till his death (1863). At first hostile to the railways, he soon realised the shortsightedness of this (with Huskisson at his elbow to open his eyes), and one of his last and most valuable services to the Midland Counties, as Lord Hatherton, was the passage through Parliament of the bills for the Birmingham and Oxford and the Birmingham, Dudley and Wolverhampton Railways.

[1] Hatherton Correspondence 1828-9.     [2] Dickens, Reprinted Pieces, *A Plated Article*.

Another local service was of a legal order. In conjunction with Mr William Smith, the member for Norwich, he commenced a movement against the old iniquitous law of 'extents in aid',[1] which had worked ruinous effects in the manufacturing districts. At first they could make no impression on Mr Vansittart and they therefore organised petitions to Parliament, the discussion on which ultimately produced a legislative remedy for the evil.

Let us now follow our county member to Parliament. Inexpert myself in Parliamentary practice, I will hide behind an extract from the *Times* obituary notice of 5 May 1863:

Lord Hatherton was a member of the 'Independent Country Party' chiefly composed of county members and landowners, representing some of the older boroughs. They were generally supporters of the Tory administration . . . but they kept a vigilant control over taxation and our public expenditure. They were frequent defenders of constitutional government, occasionally expelling a Ministry from office, and often preventing party from becoming faction. The conduct of the private business of the Lower House was also chiefly in their hands, for almost all private Bills were endorsed by county members and under their management. The business habits of Mr. Littleton, his local knowledge of the growing manufacturing interests of our Midland counties, his tact and good judgment soon gained him a high station in the Commons: indeed, he was long considered one of the best authorities on the forms and procedure of Parliament, and Mr. Littleton and Mr. Stuart Wortley (later Lord Wharncliffe) were in those days the leading and working representatives of our great staple English manufacturers.

Ireland then, as later, was the grave of political reputations, and Littleton, as Chief Secretary for Ireland, was involved in relations with Daniel O'Connell, which resulted in the resignation of Lord Melbourne's ministry in 1834. To the version promulgated by Lord Brougham in his old age, he had a complete answer.[2] But relative failure in Ireland obscured his high performance in the domestic field. Charles Kingsley, indeed, thought so highly of him that, on his death, he wrote to Lord

---

[1] Seizures for debt.
[2] Cf. Lord Hatherton's Memoir, edited by Henry Reeve 1872.

Hatherton's sister, 'I believe it better to have been your brother than Pascal or Wesley—perhaps'; for he admired in him the combination of social reform and healthful country life. And the great Charles Kingsley was a fine judge, his modern detractors notwithstanding.

# CHAPTER ELEVEN

# THE STAFFORDSHIRE OF HUSKISSON
## AND LITTLETON
*(continued)*

*A Tale of Two Bills*

THERE is at Teddesley a bound volume entitled *Correspondence with Rev. Mr. Leigh 1830-2* (Rev. William Leigh, The Parsonage, Bilston[1]); and on it I base this chapter. Sentences introduced by / signify a paraphrase.

House of Commons.                                          25 March 1830

My Dear Leigh,

I have received Bilston Petition—too late to present it this evening. I shall do so tomorrow and think I shall be able to put all right about Mr. Herries's[2] statement. He was quite wrong to read *part* of the letter, and the Papers misrepresented him by omitting part of what he did read. He admitted that the great staple manufacture of iron and several of its dependent branches were in a state of the greatest suffering. I will state fully all I know and think, on presenting your petition tomorrow.

29 March 1830

/Presented Bilston petition . . .

The letter Herries read was one of 7 or 8 of a very different complexion. But I was anxious to allay a storm and not oblige my Walsallonian correspondents to rejoin. . . . Herries quoted one letter only, because he knew the man to be reliable. . . . Hawkes, who took the bill down, was obliged to run off with it to Worcester, where Dudley's people were. —That's why you didn't see it. Mr. Walker, who is Forster's partner in the Chillington Works, has written me a very courteous letter about my statement as to the number of furnaces in and out of blast in Staffs. in the hands of Money-paying and Truck-paying Masters. In his last letter he says that some short time ago he offered to pay his men in money provided

---

[1] A town, 2½ miles S.E. of Wolverhampton, and a centre of the hardware and heavy iron trade. While endless notes could have been compiled on the persons mentioned in these letters, I have restricted myself to such as illumine the narrative.

[2] Now President of the Board of Trade.

they would agree to a reduction of only 5 % in the amount of their wages, and the men declined. Can you learn for me the truth about this?

Your mention of the Paragraph in the Wolverhampton Paper was very kind. Those scurvy dogs, the Reporters, were all dining at St. Patrick's Day Dinner 17 [*March*]. Hawkes offered one a sovereign to take a full note of what passed and very nearly got insulted for it. I suppose he did not come up to his price.

Teddesley, April 11, 1830

My plan is to send the Bill in the first instance to a Select Committee of Friends to the Principle, to arrange the machinery previously to the Committee of the House. At this former C^ee I mean to submit to consideration all the observations I may receive.

I shall propose on my own part

1. To do away with the appeal and make conviction by 2 or more magistrates *final*. A rich master will always appeal against a poor workman, whose utter destitution of money is the cause of his complaint. How can such an one support 3 months idleness and the expenses of an appeal?

*Associations* must be formed to support him if the appeal is allowed.

2. To make a 2nd offence a misdemeanour.

3. To make it penal *on a shopkeeper* to make an agreement with a master to tommy his men.

4. High Penalties. Not less than 30 nor more than 50 for a 1st offence.

I certainly think that the amount of wage not exceeding 1 year on the whole should be recoverable before a magistrate. Its omission is an oversight!! It is unnecessary to enforce payment of *wages at any fixed period*. In the 1st place it is impossible. Work done by the job can only be paid for when done. But my Bill putting an end to Tick at Shops kept by masters —the latter *must* pay in money.

You will perceive that necessity grows out of the Bill. Its whole scope is to engender necessity. The title of Peel's Act seems to limit it to Penalties. But I have not the Act before me.[1] I think the counsel who drew my bill imagined it had a wider range.

Husbandry servants were always exempt. They are always fed in part— but never *tommied*—They make no complaint.

I will attend to Mr. Banks' point about the shopkeeper's power to bring an action.

---

[1] 58 Geo. 3, c. 51—30 May 1818. It has the textile trades mainly in view. The provisions are crude. Penalties are to go 'half to the informer, half to the poor of the parish'. The Peel is Peel senior.

I can stop it in the same clause in which I shall make it penal for shop-keepers to agree with a master etc. . . .

Come and dine and bring Peel's Act with you.

L.

April 26, 1830

I am glad you petitioned about the Beer Duty,[1] for the mode in which the thing stands leaves the public to suppose the Staffs. M.P.s approve of the principle of the proposed change.

It is very true that a High Penalty of £100 with mitigation, might prove a serious check to a 2nd offence of 'Trucking', but the very circumstances you state of the angry feelings arising from the apprehension of a 2nd offence being made a 'misdemeanour' prove the value of such a provision. My only doubt is whether the House would agree to such a proposal. If I were sure of that, I should certainly propose it. I mean to be guided by the judgment of the S-C. I mean to adopt the sense of the majority in all parts of the Provisions, as the best means of carrying the subsequent stages of the Bill.

I fear I shall not get the Bill read a 2nd time on Fri. The Book is so full. I am to have an interview with Peel and Herries on the morning of that day, and hope to get them to fix some day for me. This will not pledge them as to *ulterior* support—tho' I am sure they feel the growing necessity of doing something and the policy of doing it now.

With respect to the question about defining wages, so as to include the value of *contract* work. I will try to have it done, but it is a difficult subject. The kind of case you refer to has arisen on the new canal now cutting.[2]

What are a workman's wages when he is engaged in a piece of contract work? The job is not finished.

Teddesley Jun 19, 1830

I return to town tomorrow for the scratch on Tuesday. If I am alive on Aug. 20 I will be in town again and meet you here and give you a day's shooting.

I thank you for the account of what you observe to be the spirit and disposition of the working classes in your neighbourhood. I am not afraid of squabbles or even fights about wages to any extent provided they do not occur simultaneously with *political* organisations such as Attwood's Political Unions—their co-existence now is a source of great danger. But how

[1] The legislation of 1830 created 'free trade' in beer by granting beer licences *ad lib*. Designed to combat spirits, it stimulated the demand for them by the increase of drinking facilities.

[2] This refers, presumably, to the Liverpool-Birmingham Canal (see above, p. 318).

can the Ministry begin quarrelling with the Unions? They must settle the battle of Reform first, and leave other matters to take their chance. They may and ought to put down truck, and now is the time to give a chance to the effectiveness of a measure which can never be made so perfect as to succeed infallibly without the moral aid of public feeling, which is at its height against the system and has alarmed the Govt. Lord Wharncliffe will bring in my Bill—and pass it thru' the Lords, while we are amusing ourselves with reform. We may take up the Bill afterwards when they have got the Reform Bill.

I should not wonder if the Tories were fools enough to resort to every kind of contrivance to delay and defeat my measure. The Public will not submit to be defeated by such means. Depend on it, if the thing is carried too far, there will be work for the Glaziers and Slaters in London. . . .

/Thank Ld. W. for 'fathering the Bill'.

June 20, 1830

My Dear Sir,

Tho' my letters are franked to the limit of my number,[1] I can't omit thanking you for your very friendly letter and taking my chance of getting a frank elsewhere.

I anticipate no stir in Staffs. All my Correspondents in my part of the Country give assurances of Tranquillity. If any row is commenced by friends of my own against my colleagues, it will resemble one of those Irish proceedings, in which houses are set fire to, to burn out an enemy, without regard to the friend who is in it.

. . . Should it occur, you and I would have some fun at Bilston. . . . My principal effort would be to prevent your friends playing Hell and Tommy with my Purse. A man with an Entailed Estate, however large, and a family nearly grown up, with a small power of settlement, would not be justified in risking the future.

My Truck Bill and Papers are at the H. of C. Heaven knows when I shall get the Bill on!

July 19, 1830

I will send you a Couple of Leveretts, if I can, and also a couple of young wild ducks and also a Pine apple.

[1] By 35 Geo. 3, c. 53 members were rationed to 10 out and 15 in, daily, the balance being charged to recipients. The privilege applied during or within 40 days of the session. Further, a member could send or receive printed Parliamentary proceedings and could receive petitions not exceeding 6 ozs. each—free. The privilege of franking was greatly abused in the eighteenth century. In 1784 franks totalled 800,000.

/As to entertainment at Teddesley on Nomination Day: 'I hope nothing
will be said about 'Tommy'. But if the subject is broached, the Trucksters
shall have the worst of it.

I am glad on my account that Scott seconds Wrottesley. I am glad that
he has so good a supporter, and much pleased at this symptom of liberality
in politics on the part of Scott.

I had thought of asking Scott to do me the office. But Mosley,[1] who is
my 1st violin, begged that Tremlow might be the 2nd, as he thought it
bad for me to employ artists who resided in parts of the county with
which I had least communication.

I suppose someone will do something on the Catholic Q. and shall be
disappointed if they don't.

P.S. I have now had a week's holiday and am tired of idleness.'

July 26, 1830

Conceive my surprise yesterday when Wrottesley, who accompanied
me to the Polling Place yesterday told me that he had forwarded a letter
from Sir C. Wolseley[2] to Mr. Whitwick begging his attendance at the day
of Election. Wolseley had sent it to Wrottesley not knowing Whitwick's
address. Wrottesley directed it with his own hand and forwarded it without explanation to Whitwick—so the latter, seeing the Handwriting of
the two parties will naturally think they are acting in concert. . . .

I think it prudent under the circumstances to be tolerably well attended
on Sat.

Aug. 12, 1830

/Thanks for support at late election. . . .

I am told that on the morning of the nomination someone when enquiring how I voted on Sir J. Graham's[3] motion relating to Fees, Salaries
Emoluments of P.C.'s etc., no one could tell him. He ran up to Wrottesley
or rather, stopped him as he was coming into town and asked him. The
fact was I did not vote, being at Lichfield with the Yeomanry. But *I* gave
Graham the terms of the motion he made, and was its remote author !!

You told me I was to be attacked about the General Mining Co. I have
long since ceased to be a member of it—to have any prospects in it, or

---

[1] Sir Oswald Mosley (1785-1871) of Rolleston, Staffs, and Ancoats, near Manchester. In 1845
he sold the Manor of Manchester for £200,000 to the Corporation, whose predecessors refused
to give £90,000 in 1815.

[2] Sir Charles Wolseley, seventh Bart. (1769-1846) the political reformer.

[3] Sir James Graham (1792-1861) at this stage a Whig.

interest myself about it. When I entered it, it was solely occupied with mining speculation in Brazil.

Aug. 28, 1830

It was at first Mr. Ward's proposal that you should be asked to be present at my meeting with him and some of the Iron Masters who truck their men. . . .

As to Fines in the Bill—a fixed fine is bad, but a fine at discretion of the Court good (because of the Truck-masters some are rich and some poor).

Nov. 11, 1830.

I had heard of your success in preventing a Political Union being formed at Bilston—and am not at all surprised to find the D's speech had subsequently caused you discomfiture,—never was greater folly. It will however have the effect of making the Country think and act for itself. What makes the Duke's conduct the more silly is that men's minds are attuned to *moderation* on the subject of reform. They were united in temperate views and would have thought Representation given to a few Great Towns, as many rotten boroughs extinguished, and a Reform of the Scotch franchises a great thing. Now we must fight for it. I suppose the Treasury will get up every man whom Place, Fee, Rewards, the Promise or Hope thereof can bring together.

Govt. gives out it will retire if beaten—well knowing it cannot be. I trust the country will take up the cause itself, if necessary.

Yours at Bilston is a very strong case. You were quiet and confiding, repudiating sedition, till the D's speech came down, and then the agitators walked in.

I have put off the Truck Bill till the 2nd Dec. for divers weighty reasons. Men will only think of Reform now. The debate will probably extend into the 18th my day (first selected)—more time is asked for by some Committees for Petitions.

Then the Govt. will take up the measure. Mr. Herries in the Commons, the D. of W. in the Lords, and the former wants a little time, as his hands are full at the moment.

I trust no one will blame me for getting the Govt. to introduce the measure. It is safer in their hands than mine. It will relieve me of no trouble, as I am pledged to conduct the correspondence with the Trades . . . and exert myself as much as if it had continued in my hands.

Don't mention at present that the Govt. mean to undertake the measure.

P.S. Is your Union affiliated with the B'ham one? Does it acknowledge it as chief? Is it subject to its council, and does it collect and transmit money?

Nov 24, 1830

The Dissolution of the late Govt. and the time that must elapse before all the new ministers can be re-elected in the H. of C. have rendered another postponement of the Truck Bill unavoidable. And as after consultation with the friends of the measure, Mr. Herries included, it is judged expedient that another meeting similar to that of last session should be held, for the purpose of waiting as a body on Lord Grey and the Board of Trade, we, (that is the members principally interested) have written to the County to request the different Districts, would send one or more delegates each to this place, to meet at my [town] house at 12 o'c on Wednesday the 1st Dec. and to wait on the Ministers the next day. It would certainly be extremely useful if you could attend on behalf of your neighbours to speak yr. opinion as a Magistrate.

The present Govt. being composed of a totally different set of men from the last, more than one of them, I know, entertaining doubts of the practicability of putting down the system, and consequently of the prudence of the attempt, I should feel that I was rashly risking the measure if I dispensed with the course of proceeding that was judged so advisable last session with a set of Ministers even more favourably disposed to our object, and from which we had such benefit in the result. I have reason to believe that, had the late Ministers staid in, they would have undertaken the Bill, as they will certainly support it now.

In asking you to come to town I know I am asking your C^ee to incur trouble and expense, but I am determined to risk anything rather than the measure.

I wish so well to the present Administration that I should sincerely rejoice to see them take the popularity of making it their own.

Teddesley, Ju 23, 1831

I don't see what right a poor parson has with the Gout. You should be Tommied for a few weeks. I trust your next account will give a better report of yourself.

Enclosed I return Ld. Dartmouth's 2 letters. The gallant Captn. Hawkes sent me an account last night of the confession of Watkin and the implications of several others. It is most satisfactory that the whole country should have witnessed the undefatigable determination of the Magistrates to detect the authors of the outrage. Nothing will so much deter others from the commission of similar offences as witnessing the inveteracy of pursuit.

P.S. Thanks for the O'Connell Papers. He passes thro' Bilston on his way to town, does he not? Catch him; and burn him alive.

Teddesley, Jan. 30, 1831

/Congratulations on the Petition.

I am truely glad it omitted to mention the Ballot. Reform and the mode of giving a Vote are quite distinct Qs. The Govt. has taken a hard task on itself, and to load themselves with the debateable Q. of Ballot would be highly imprudent. If B. be necessary, it will be obtained much more easily from a Reformed House than this.

/Thanks for the mention of himself in the Resolutions.

There is no part of the country I have endeavoured to serve with more delight than the neighbourhood of Bilston.

Downing St., Dec. 21, 1831

Sir, Lord Grey desires me to express his thanks to you for the confidence manifested in the intentions of the Govt. of which he is a part and trusts that his future conduct will merit a continue of it.

Lord Grey will have great pleasure in presenting the petition of the Inhabitants of Bilston to the House of Lords if you will be so good as to forward it to him.

Yours obed. servant

Charles Wood[1]

The Rev. W. Leigh.

Grosvenor Place
March 4, 1831

My Dear Leigh,

I long to know how you all feel about this Reform Plan. I am charmed with its comprehensiveness and its *perfect safety*. I think it a full satisfaction of the Govt. pledges, and I hope it will prove such to the popular expectation.

Pray hold another meeting to petition for the Bill. The Country must be roused from one end to the other if the Bill is rejected, for its only chance will be to get a Dissolution of Parlt. and try to do the business itself in that way.

It is all very well for Boro' Members, their Proprietors, and members

[1] 1800-85: later Viscount Halifax.

like Peel whose power depends on them, to cry out against excitement. 'Strike while the iron is hot': 'Make Hay while the Sun shines' are sound practical sayings—No great good was ever accomplished in Popular Assemblies, or at least no great changes were ever accomplished in their constitution, except by the aid of popular excitement.

I presented your Petition in a full house. But there were such hundreds presented, little was reported—I put a slight sketch of what was said in the Stafford Papers.

G.P. March 8, 1831

A County meeting before the 21st (when the Bill is to be read a 2nd time) would be very useful. It should be one of inhabitants as the subject interests others besides free-holders. The Marquis of Stafford, Lord Uxbridge and Sandon would have their names put to it. They told me so this morning. So would Lady Anson, St. Vincent, Lyttleton and Vernon no doubt. . . .Sir O. Mosley and half the Grand Jury would sign no doubt. To Sir Oswald I have written. Speak also to Sir T. Cotton Sheppard, to whom you might show this letter. I wrote to him this morning but omitted to mention the subject, as I had not then seen Ld. Stafford.

You should address the King and both houses, and Sir Oswald's your man to do the business.

The Boro' Proprietors are furious and prepared to fight like Wild Boars. Take their nominees out of the House, and we then have a very great majority.

P.S. Parish Returns will also be useful.

H. of C. March 9, 1831

Your indignation about the term 'Revolutionary' was so good that I slapped it all about in a little speech on a Petition to-day. *Loud* cheers.

Downing St. March 12, 1831

Sir,

I have had the honour of receiving your letter together with copies of the Bilston resolutions, addresses and petitions.

I beg to assure you of the sincere pleasure with which I have learnt that the measure brought forward by H.M.'s Ministers has met with the approbation of the Inhabitants of your Parish and to offer my best thanks for their expression of confidence in my colleagues and myself.

I shall have great pleasure in presenting the address to His Majesty and the Petitions to the House of Lords, which are referred to in your letter, and I have the honour to be,

Sir, Your obedient servant

Grey.

Rev. W. Leigh.

H. of C. March 14, 1831

/Reference your Requisition

Already I have asked and obtained Lord Stafford's, Lord Gower's, Lord Sandon's, Col. Walhouse's, Heeley's (Mayor of Walsall) signatures. Pray see the Requisition is *grammatically* worded. Look after Giffard.[1] In short organise every means you can of getting the fullest possible Requisition. It should be advertised in all the county papers before the Meeting—in the Lichfield on Fri (the Requisition should be sent to the Edr. on Thurs. evng. and he should be cautioned to keep room for it)—in the Pottery Mercury on Sat. and in the Stafford Paper on the same day. In the Wolverhampton Paper I have inserted a Para to save you trouble.

5 p.m. H. of C. 14 March 1831

In addition Ld. Anson and John Hodgetts, R. Foley have signed—and Wedgewood. Lord Uxbridge has given me authority to have his name added.

Lord Anson's name must stand after Ld. Stafford's.

Ask Mr. Ralph Bourne of Hilderstone and of Fenton in the Potteries for his name by all means—a stout Tory and a mighty man—a Reformer. I have written to Davenport of Longford also. Ask also the Ridgeways. And have some good Farmers and Yeomen. I have written to Sr. Oswald to Manchester, lest he should be there.

P.S. I showed Lord Stafford your rogueish letter, he said he would sign next to Wolseley, if it would do any good. The County never knew what a good fellow he is.

Pray let Lord Gower present the County Petition.

County Petition to the High Sheriff of the County of Stafford.

14 March 1831

requesting a meeting of the Gentry, Clergy, and Freeholders to suppprt the Reform Bill and thanking His Majesty for his gracious approbation of the Measure.

[1] In 1831 the head of the family in residence at Chillington was Thomas William Giffard.

The signatures include

Alex Hordern.[1]

Rich Fryer.

James Bradshaw.[2]

Stubbs Wightwick.

Jno. Davenport sends in his name

—do— Theo Price (who considers it equally anti-democratical and anti-revolutionary and adds 'I hope we are going thro' slowly yet surely with the Truck Bill. . . . I intend to stick close to it till it's 'lost or won't, tho' I do not fear the former')

—do— James Watt.[3]

19 March 1831

In case of the rejection of the Bill it will be the duty of every Parish to address the King to Dissolve the Parlt. and to insert such a wish in your address.

It would be *very useful* if 2 or 3 of the speakers were to remind the Freeholders present that they must not augur ill of the Govt. if it has fared badly, or shall still fare badly with the present H. of C. It was elected under the influence of the D. of W. and Peel. It is notoriously full of their friends—men obliged by 10 years of favor and full of a lively hope of favors still to be received—all the Boro' Members e.g. who are to be disfranchised came up and voted against the Govt. proposal to *lower the Duty* on foreign timber last night. Such is the fury of Party Spirit that they do not hesitate to make a whip to oppose the reduction of a tax—a thing the Govt. was not prepared to expect.

Parlt. must be dissolved, 'we must be born again', as the pious Wilkes said.

It will be my Province as your Senior Member to present the Petition, and you may be sure I will make the most of it.

I am not without hope we may get separate members for the Potteries. I was with Ld. Grey about it.

I think Lord Gower, as your old member and a zealous Reformer and the Representative of the Wealthiest family in Great Britain, would be the best person to present your petition.

---

[1] The owner of Oxley. Cf. p. 303.    [2] Cf. p. 22 *n.*

[3] This is James Watt II. He writes to Littleton from Aston Hall, 7 December 1832, 'I have for some time ceased to receive the assistance of my partners in the management of our large concern, and the death or superannuation of our principal agents has thrown details upon me which require my undivided attention' (Hatherton MS. Correspondence 1832).

H. of C. March 19, 1831

I wish you were not a clergyman, but an M.P. with 5 or 6000£ a year.

April 14, 1831.

I have got the Truck Bill thro' a C^ee quite unexpectedly as to the time; tho' not with respect to the duration of the Committee, as I was badgered by a dozen persons for exactly 6 hours in it.

/Will send a reprint of Bill, with amendments underlined.

Mr. Hunt[1] has twice told the House since Easter that he has visited various seats of our population during the Recess, and that he has addressed 200,000 and that he found them *to a man* against the Reform Bill.

He mentioned twice having been in Staffs. He named Darlaston. Now I don't believe the Darlaston freeholders nor even the D. workmen, not freeholders, will admit H.'s statement as regards them to be a correct one. I am exceedingly anxious to contradict it.

/Find out about it.

I have of Hunt a very bad opinion. Truth is not in him. I never knew such a Compound of Vanity, Ignorance and Impudence: one feels for one's self and 'poor human nature' when one sees and hears him.

G.P. 6 o'c.

Thank God we are prorogued and shall be dissolved either today or Tues. Words cannot describe what has passed in the Houses of Parlt. The Lords were so uproarious, that the Chancellor left the House, with the Seals—Lord Shaftesbury was voted into the Chair and a debate that would have disgraced a Bull Ring took place till the King arrived. In the H. of C. Sir R— Vivyan began with a violent attack on the Govt. and endeavoured to keep possession of the House till the Black Rod arrived. But he could not hold out. Sir Robert Peel, Sir F. Burdett then rose together. Amidst tremendous noise, Lord Althorp endeavoured to be heard, with a view to move Sir F. Burdett be heard. The Speaker rose. All spoke together, at the same time, amidst a deafening noise. Sir R. Peel using the most threatening gestures—the whole scene resembling an Irish row. Sir R. Peel at length was heard at the Speaker's urgent call. The guns at this moment announced the King's arrival at the H. of L. Each shot was answered by a loud cheer in the House. Sir R. Peel kept bellowing in vain.

---

[1] Henry Hunt, 'Orator Hunt', 1773-1835. M.P. for Preston 1830, he was one of the solitary farmers in the unreformed House of Commons, but in 1832 he was joined by Cobbett. The farming interest was so under-represented, because the yeomanry was thought of, not as an occupational but as a social class—the class below the gentry—the Robert Martins of Miss Austen's *Emma*.

Z

Black Rod at length came in. The Speaker walked forth, almost trampled under foot by his followers, and in the House of Lords the King made his speech, putting his intention to dissolve expressly on his determination to appeal to the People on the Question of Reform.

God Save the King.

The mob hissed Him in Parlt. St.

'The last Frank I ever used in the unreformed Parlt.'—E.J.L.

London, April 22 1831

Rev. W. Leigh, Parsonage, Bilston.

E. J. Littleton

{ FREE
22 Ap 22
1831

26 March 1831

What you state of Ld. Gower's Reception and Discharge of his Duty was so well suited to please Lord S and his mother that I have been unable to refrain from sending them your letter.

Did I tell you that Mr. Wood, Lord Grey's son in law and private secretary, asked me who wrote the Bilston Resolutions? He thought them so good that he told me he had sent them to Sir C. Wood, his father in Yorks as a model for them to follow in that County. Really the Public is much indebted to you in a variety of ways.

The Truck Bill is divided into 2—a Repeal Bill—and an Enabling Bill. Privy Council clause struck out and its machinery improved. . . . I fear it will be quite impossible to get the bill recommitted before Easter. But remember I am now as far advanced as I was in the last week of June last year.

Nothing shall be, as it never was, wanting on my part, to push the Bill on. There has not been a day I have not danced attendance on someone about it—the Lord Chancellor kept it a week.

H. of C. April 10, 1831

I have read the whole of the material part of your Letter to the House, and the yellow Hand-bill: and Hunt, who is furious, has not *contradicted* one word. He is fallen, depend upon it.

Dimchurch, April 25, 1831

I entirely adopt your suggestion of not having a cavalcade formed at Teddesley. It would divide inconveniently the friends of Reform. Wrottesley and I are completely in the wake of the Govt. and tho' it would not do for us to unite on the Road and go in together, it would be imprudent and inconvenient that our friends might be forced into any proceeding which might wear the air of personal preference.

/Wrottesley and I will go to Stafford early and meet the Freeholders in the Town—as at any other County Meeting.

/A good rally wanted 'for the immediate interests of our election and the reputation of the Great Cause.'. But no Procession.

April 26, 1831

No meeting here on Monday but we all meet at Stafford—Workmen in my House and Establishment in Town.

/No cavalcade: relations with Wrottesley delicate.

April 27, 1831

You will oblige *me* most by giving your personal presence wherever you can do a Tory most harm, or a Reformer most good. You are too good a man to employ on a Pageant (for such I hope the Staff. election will be).

Downing St. May 10, 1831

Lord Grey will have the greatest pleasure in presenting the address which was received this morning at the next levee.

Ch. Wood

H. of C. 7' o'c Thurs. May 21, 1831

Dissolution certainly . . . I believe tomorrow.

June 5, 1831

/Spring Rice as a member for Staffs?

I saw Clare today in a pair of new coloured pantaloons: a perfect Lothario and looking admirably. Quite stout—about Reform. What have you heard about Attwood's canvass at Walsall? It is an impudent thing. It is the game of Maurice O'Connell[1] but he'll not succeed. Mrs. L. is better.

House of Lords, June 23, 1831

I am told that the impression at Wolverhampton is against Clare. But depend on it. Hill has made him the victim and influences his silence. He is shamefully treated. There was a substantial consideration named by Hill for his resignation of the Office.

[1] Sir Maurice Charles Philip O'Connell, d. 1848.

June 24, 1831

Lord Wharncliffe brings in the Truck Bill early next week.

H. of C. July 26, 1831

I am sitting on the Committee of Privilege in the H. of C. sadly bored with a week's discussion.

/Offers a day's duck shooting at Penkridge. 'Hordern might drive you over'. They will shoot over Pillaton: and thence to the Pools at Teddesley.

'We march slowly in the Reform Bill. All sorts of unfair tricks are practised to clog and defeat it. Sir R. Peel affects to dislike it, but never tells his friends privately not to delay it—this is always his way—it gets him the character of a Jesuit. He wishes to upset the Bill and defeat the Govt. I pant, it is true, like a Hart for the Watery Brooks. But I think it no sacrifice—I have had the best constituents for 20 years a man ever had and hope to repay them by taking a share by unfailing presence in the H. of C. in the accomplishment of a measure which shall shut the door of the temple for ever to mere Dandies, young Lifeguardsmen, Jobbing Lawyers and Money Changers. No man can say what the Lords will do. They hardly dare *face* the Country. It is probable they will try to emasculate the Bill by altering its essential features. But we must fight it up to its original standard. There is not in the H. of L. a more foolishly violent man than our Lord Lieut. Indeed, Staffordshire shines in that class. If all the peers were like him, Lds. Dartmouth, Bagot and Bradford, men of Property in the Kingdom, would soon be knocked on the head.'

Aug. 3, 1831

I am writing in the Gallery of the H. of C. at 12 at night, amidst the uproar accompanying a noisy speech from Croker. We had a meeting at Lord Althorp's this morning—200 present—We agreed to waive all minute differences of opinion.

Aug. 31, 1831

Will send your letter to Ld. Melbourne. But it only is in the H. of C. that the clause you suggest can be inserted.

Aug 31, 1831

I send the Truck Bill that has passed the Lords a 2nd time yesterday without opposition, but with an undertaking entered into with the opponents of the Bill that they should have the opportunity of recording their dissent to the Principles by opposing the Speaker's leaving the Chair before going into Committee, which I got Lord Althorp to agree should sit on the 12 Sept.

Sorry to say that both Lord A and Mr. Poulett Thomson gave me notice they should move the reinsertion of the clause limiting the application of the Act to cases of masters employing more than 5 artificers. I think Mr. T. should be written to.

We killed in all 95 Black Game.

G.P. Sept. 13, 1831

I got Truck thro' a C^ee last night. I found the Bill had many new influential enemies—Paget (Leicestershire), Ld. G. Somerset (Monmouth).

It has made me rather vain to observe that the Parties I have had to fight on Truck are all my very best friends in the House.

Oct. 12, 1831

The best move of securing tranquillity will not be by old womanish Tory preachings about people not knowing where mobs may stop when once excited: but by men of Rank and Property and Station taking a lead on their own side . . .

I have not heard from anyone at Birmingham to-day how King Thomas [*Attwood*?] has taken King William's proclamation. Will the Unionists knock under now or after the Bill has passed, or will they wait for a fresh law giving Secretaries of State and Lords Lieutenant extraordinary powers?

Dec. 2, 1831

/Tied to Parlt.

March 5, 1832

Conceive the Impudence of Croker pretending to instruct the H. of C. in Statistics when he thought Bilston was a village. You will see he calls Wednesbury a City because it answers his purpose there.

/Not seen Brougham yet. . . . 'You must not be sanguine. The Truck Bill seems doing well everywhere. Magistrates don't hesitate about convicting when there is a fair common-sense presumption of influence. In the Potteries the practice has ceased. In Gloucestershire it is waging an unequal war with the Law, which I am told will put it down.

Thank heaven it is a Law and no longer a Bill, tho' I am now in for another as bad—the Boundary Bill.'

June 23, 1832

Thank God. The Boundary Bill is now out of my hands.


26 June, 1832

There is a Ball at Apsley House tonight where the King and Queen are to be. I suppose we shall all be hooted. The mob seems without any reason disposed to treat as an enemy every man who is clothed with authority or has a good coat on his back. The only cure is to go on steadily doing for the People all that ought to be done and that can be done in the way of removing Monopolies, Abuses and Burdens, and all will then come right. I am thoroughly satisfied that coute que coute we l'lords must alter the Corn Laws and reach by degrees an entirely Free Trade. Our possessions are not safe if we don't, and it is the real interest well understood of all classes. I am quite satisfied that even the Tenantry mistake the effect that would be produced by the change, and the Landlords still more.

When the last bill was passed, Huskisson said to me you will have 2 more changes—if Peace continues. In 2 or 3 years time you will pass a Law for a Free Trade under a 10s. duty and then, in a few years more, you will pass another to reduce that Duty yearly till it comes to nothing, and you will not feel the change by the increase of trade it will cause you and the consequent improvement in prices.

In these times the men who are willing to boast and bully and *pledge* themselves to changes which others approve of, but will not bind themselves to from *principle*, have a great advantage.

L.


The Truck Bill received the Royal Assent on 15th Oct. 1831 (1 and 2 Will. 4, c. 37): the Reform Bill on 7th June, 1832 (2 and 3, Will. 4, c. 45).

\*       \*       \*       \*

*Huskisson: Littleton: Disraeli*

Huskisson's contact with truck was incidental but significant. He was on the threshold of it when as Under-Secretary for War and the Colonies he had to deal with the abuses arising from the payment of surgeons by deductions from sailors' wages (September 1794). Again, in his fight for the restoration and maintenance of the gold standard, he bore in mind the need of an adequate medium of small notes and subsidiary coinage for wage payments, and he took steps to eliminate illicit tokens from the circulation of the country.[1] In 1826, as Treasurer of the Navy, he found himself in the heart of it:

The Treasurer having found great abuses and gross frauds to be practised by dealers from the system of yard notes given by such dealers to persons borne on the ordinary (sc. *warrant officers and servants employed on ships of war laid up in port*)—proposed to the Navy Board on the 23rd December 1825 to abolish the yard notes and to substitute a weekly payment of part of the wages due to such persons, so borne on the ordinary, instead of a quarterly payment, and thus to give the men an opportunity of providing for their families in future without the intervention of these dealers. The consideration of this proposition was, at the recommendation of the Navy Board to the Admiralty, postponed, and after a long correspondence, the Treasurer's proposition for abolishing yard notes was carried into effect, and a monthly payment of wages, instead of a weekly payment [*as desired by the Treasurer*], finally agreed upon.

From this background of professional experience and monetary knowledge he supported on 5 July 1830 Littleton's Labourers' Wages Bill:

Why was money invented at all, but that it should serve as an invariable standard, and a measure of value, in contracts between man and man, and to prevent the inconvenience which must follow from having that standard in articles perishable in their nature, and changeable in their value. The system of paying in goods and not in money, had arisen from the exercise of power, on the one side, over the necessity which existed on the other. The workman was obliged to submit, because he could not obtain employment on any other terms. The difficulty of the master was not caused by a want of a sufficient quantity of the circulating medium; but the effect of his being so paid to the workman had been to lower his wages twenty, and in some instances, twenty-five per cent.[2]

He then adverted to the known evils prevalent in Staffordshire and part of the textile districts. In Liverpool he was happy

---

[1] Cf. *Times* obituary notice of Lord Hatherton, 5 May 1863. 'Another benefit which Mr. Littleton years ago conferred on them was to persuade the Staffs. manufacturers to call in their base circulation of local copper tokens. His success induced Mr. Huskisson to pass the Act for terminating the circulation of alloyed silver coins.' The legislation in question was 57 Geo. 3, c. 46 (1817); and although at this time Huskisson officially was only First Commissioner of Woods and Forests, he was in fact behind every currency move of the period.

[2] Speeches, III, 624.

to say it was unknown (Liverpool was, however, interested in an adjacent problem—'the evil consequences arising from payments of wages at public houses,' against which, under the signature of Mr. Geo. Forwood and others, they petitioned in the same year).

It is possible that Huskisson and many of his hearers had read a newly published pamphlet—the Truck System, Dudley, 1830: endorsed by Littleton in the following terms: 'Mr. Littleton M.P. for Staffordshire strongly recommends the perusal of this pamplet to each member of the Legislature.' Its quality is indicated by the following extract:

In order to evade the law which forbids the payment of wages, some manufacturers (iron masters etc.) adopt the following trick. They pay the man in one room or office, and in the next, through which he is obliged to retire, is the clerk of the Tommy shop, who makes his demand, which, after the reckoning has been thrown off 4, 5 or more weeks, as is frequently done to force off goods, takes the whole or nearly of what he has just received. This game is very common. There is, moreover, a very convenient species of circulating medium in use, with some Tommy masters yclept 'Tommy notes'. A workman is in want of a few shillings, or some goods, between these *long reckonings*, and goes to the Clerk of the Works, who, instead of money, gives him a scrap of paper, bearing these or some such words, 'Let A.B. have goods to the amount of -s -d', signed C.D. These Tommy notes have in some instances a considerable local circulation. The man, instead of taking them immediately to the Tommy shop, frequently takes them to a public house for ale, or to a shoe-mender (the Tommy Master provides him with new shoes), or to his landlord for rent etc., when they are current at 15-20% discount. The persons so receiving them send them to the Tommy shop by wholesale, and thus many supply in a great measure their houses with necessaries.

In other cases, the goods are taken, and sold at about the above loss, and in this way the Tailor, Shoemaker, Publican etc. in the neighbourhood more particularly referred to is stocked with sugars, soap etc. often to excess.

The Truck Act of 1831 created no new offence *in principle*. It merely set out to make the existing law a reality by redefinition, better machinery and more appropriate penalties; and it followed the law-breaker into some, at least, of the crannies of evasion. The Act (as the extract from *Sybil* will later show) did not abolish the evil, but it made the first serious impression on it, and after the institution first of the factory and then of the mining inspectorate, the law was finally enforced to the full. But even that was only prevention. It remained for the workers themselves, organised in trade unions and co-operative stores, to make of their nominal earnings a cash reality.

The legislation consisted of two chapters both of Oct 15, 1831, c. 36 repealing previous Acts, and c. 37, the new Act, with its 27 clauses:

1. Contracts for hiring of artificers must be made in the current coin of the realm.

2. And must not contain any stipulations as to the manner in which the wages shall be expended.

3. All wages must be paid to the workmen in coin. Payment in goods declared illegal.

4. Artificers may recover wages if not paid in the current coin.

5. In an action brought for wages no set-off shall be allowed for goods supplied by the employer, or by any shop in which the employer is interested.

6. No employer shall have any action against his artificer for goods supplied to him on account of wages.

7. If the artificer or his wife or children became chargeable to the parish, the overseers may recover any wages earned within the 3 preceding months and not paid in cash.

8. Not to invalidate the payment of wages in bank notes, if the artificer consents.

9. Penalties on employers entering into illegal contracts (maximum sum of fines £100).

10. Penalties, how to be recovered.

11. Justices may compel the attendance of witnesses.

12. Power to levy penalties by distress.

13. A partner not to be liable in person for the offence of his co-partner, but the partnership property to be so liable.

14. How summonses are to be served.

15. Form of conviction.

16. Justices to return convictions to the Clerk of the Peace.

17. Convictions not to be quashed for want of form.

18. Application of penalties.

19. Specified trades to which the act is to apply:
    minerals: iron: textiles: glass and pottery: lace.

20. Domestics, including servants in husbandry, excluded.

21. No interested Justice to act.

22. County Magistrates to act when Town Magistrates disqualified under 21.

23. Particular exceptions allowed:—deductions for medicine and medical attention; for mining tools and animal provender; for victual consumed on the employer's premises.

24. Employers may advance money to artificers for certain purposes (friendly societies, savings banks, education).

25. Artificers are workmen in the trades enumerated in 19.

26. Act to begin 3 months after passing.

27. To extend over Great Britain.

Twelve years later, in the Report of the Midland Mining Commission of 1843 (on which Disraeli drew so liberally for his *Sybil*), Lord Hatherton looks back, writing on request to Mr Tancred, the investigating Commissioner, the following letter:

Grosvenor Place,
Feb. 2, 1843

My Dear Sir,

I have been so continually occupied since I saw you that I have never been able to give you the statement I promised you of the history of my Truck Act (1 & 2 Will 4, c. 37); and even now my time will not admit of my doing it at any length.

For some years previous to that time the system had been increasing in the manufacturing districts; and in South Staffordshire and the neighbouring parts of Worcestershire and Shropshire had become very general, not only among the smaller traders, but among the larger manufacturers; in the clothing districts it had become almost universal. The degree of hardship with which it was practised varied according to the necessities and characters of the masters. But a very general practice prevailed of allowing all the best workmen to run in debt at the truck shops, a habit encouraged by the masters as it kept the men bound to them when trade became good. Once caught in that trammel, the workman's life became one of slavery. When trade was bad, he was barely fed, and that was all. When trade became good, he found himself in bonds, precluded for ever from taking advantage of the improvement to lay up savings, for he was compelled to work on his master's terms. That policy was very commonly acted on by masters, and it was the part of the truck system which at that time had the most mischievous effect.

The laws against truck dated from the earliest times; they were very numerous and very complicated. The Magistracy was anxious for their 'repeal and consolidation'. 18 Acts or parts of Acts were repealed by the Truck Act, the earliest of which dates from the 4th of Edward IV. But these were not the only motives which induced me to undertake the task of their revisal. I had been long connected with a large manufacturing county in which almost every description of manufacture existed; and I saw clearly that if the system were not discredited and checked, it would go on increasing and become of necessity universal.

The large manufacturer, who paid in money when trade was bad, found himself beaten out of the field by those who could easily obtain 25 % advantage of him in the article of labour; the ordinary profit of a retail trader is 15 %. The truckmaster who employed 1000 workmen, who stored his truck shop from wholesale purveyors, contracted for three month's credit, then paid with a bill at 3 mos., which he perhaps got renewed, and was thus enabled by selling for labour or ready money to obtain a profit of full 10 % over the ordinary retail dealer. In many districts these latter people were ruined, and the class disappeared; for of necessity those who most disliked the system were forced to resort to it. In bad times all the orders or contracts were taken by the truck-paying manufacturer. I have been told of some great manufacturers who were among the first to begin paying in truck and who made immense fortunes through their truck shops alone in the worst of times. But then there was, and is, another evil inherent in the system; it admits of men entering into trade without any solid capital. There are many trades in which labour—extensive and perhaps expensive, yet labour alone—constitutes the principal outlay. In all such trades any men organising a truck system of payment may raise a year's capital without a shilling. There were many instances of this came to my knowledge.

All these arguments supported by facts, I hammered into the House of Commons for three years, and at last succeeded in carrying my Bill. It was opposed by most of the political economists, but not by all. Mr. Huskisson was staggered by the threats of the money-paying masters, that they must, in their own defence, resort to the system, if it were not checked, and he at length gave way, took my Bill and put it into the hands of Mr. Stephen, the present Under-Secretary, who repealed all the laws, and reduced all the enactments into the simple and comprehensive form in which they now appear. The language in which the Act is expressed has admitted much more frequent convictions than were obtained under the old law. Evasions are still practised but they are more easily exposed. One of the great evils affecting the workmen has been completely cured by the clause borrowed from a retail Spirits Act, which prohibits the master from recovering the value of anything he may have advanced his workman at his truck shop on the credit of his wages (Clause 6). This clause preserves to the workman his liberty, which he can now turn to account in good times. He may now leave his master at any moment. I know the workmen are very grateful for this provision. I know and appreciate all the general arguments against interference between master and man; but I am satisfied the law against payment for labour in trade otherwise than in money must be maintained. If the legislature shall cease to brand and stigmatise the system, and repeal the laws, the practice must become universal and that at once. The necessitous will fly to its advantages, and others must follow or lose their trade. No man can compete in manufactures in which labour constitutes the principal expense with those who can obtain in that article an advantage of 25%.

I think the penalties in cases of conviction, where evasive forms have been resorted to, ought to be increased.

If the law shall ever be broken down the retailers will disappear. The great seats of our manufactures will be occupied only by tyrant masters and dependent slaves; and then will begin a race among these masters who shall truck hardest, and get the greatest advantage of the others; and the peace of the country will be continually disturbed by servile insurrections.

I remain, My dear Sir,<br>Yours faithfully,<br>HATHERTON

Thomas Tancred, Esq.,
  —(Parliamentary Papers, 1843, XIII, *Midland Mining Commission*, pp. 102-3.)

The 'Mr. Stephen' of the letter was Sir James Stephen (1789-1859), permanent counsel to the Board of Trade and Colonial Office (1825 onwards) and Under-Secretary for the Colonies 1836-47. Joseph Hume was among the economists who supported the 'open' system.

Lord Hatherton's Act, as it came to be called—after his elevation in 1835—testifies to the indomitable energy of a county member who had such influence with both parties that he induced first his Tory opponents and then his Whig friends to assist its passage on to the statute book at a season of unparalleled political excitement over a totally different issue.

*Sybil or the Two Nations* was published in 1845; and I quote from the pocket edition introduced by the Earl of Iddesleigh with the words: 'a magnificent diagnosis of the country at a time when the country was very sick, but as Lord Beaconsfield perceived, not sick to death.'

Book III, Chapter I, pp. 214-17:

'The question is,' said Nixon, looking round with a magisterial air, 'what *is* wages? I say, 'tayn't sugar, 'tayn't tea, 'tayn't bacon. I don't think 'tis candles; but of this I be sure, 'tayn't waistcoats.'

Here there was a general groan.

'Comrades,' continued Nixon, 'you know what has happened; you know as how Juggins applied for his balance after his tommy-book was paid up, and that incarnate nigger Diggs has made him take two waistcoats. Now the question rises, what is a collier to do with waistcoats? Pawn 'em I s'pose to Diggs' son-in-law, next door to his father's shop, and sell the ticket for sixpence. Now, there's the question; keep to the question; the question is waistcoats and tommy; first waistcoats, and then tommy.'

'I have been making a pound a-week these two months past,' said another, 'but, as I'm a sinner saved, I have never seen the young Queen's picture yet.'

'And I have been obliged to pay the doctor for my poor wife in tommy,' said another. ' "Doctor," I said, says I, "I blush to do it, but all I have got is tommy, and what shall it be, bacon or cheese?" "Cheese at tenpence a pound," says he, "which I buy for my servants at sixpence! Never mind," says he, for he is a thorough Christian, "I'll take the tommy as I find it." '

'Juggins has got his rent to pay, and is afeard of the bums,' said Nixon; 'and he has got two waistcoats!'

'Besides,' said another, 'Diggs' tommy is only open once a-week, and if you're not there in time, you go over for another seven days. And it's such a distance, and he keeps a body there such a time; it's always a day's work for my poor woman; she can't do nothing after it, what with the waiting, and the standing, and the cussing of Master Joseph Diggs; for he do swear at the women, when they rush in for the first turn, most fearful.'

'They do say he's a shocking little dog.'

'Master Joseph is very violent, but there is no one like old Diggs for grabbing a bit of one's wages. He do so love it! And then he says you never need be at no loss for nothing; you can find everything under my roof. I should like to know who is to mend our shoes. Has Gaffer Diggs a cobbler's stall?'

'Or sell us a penn'orth of potatoes,' said another. 'Or a ha'porth of milk.'

'No; and so to get them one is obliged to go and sell some tommy, and much one gets for it. Bacon at ninepence a-pound at Diggs', which you may get at a huckster's for sixpence; and therefore the huckster can't be expected to give you more than fourpence-halfpenny, by which token the tommy in our field just cuts our wages atween the navel.'

'And that's as true as if you heard it in church, Master Waghorn.'

'This Diggs seems to be an oppressor of the people,' said a voice from a distant corner of the room.

Master Nixon looked around, smoked, puffed, and then said, 'I should think he wor; as bloody-a-hearted butty as ever jingled.'

'But what business has a butty to keep a shop?' enquired the stranger. 'The law touches him.'

'I should like to know who would touch the law,' said Nixon; 'not I for one. Them tommy-shops is very delicate things; they won't stand no handling, I can tell you that.'

'But he cannot force you to take goods,' said the stranger; 'he must pay you in current coin of the realm, if you demand it.'

'They only pay us once in five weeks,' said a collier; 'and how is a man to live meanwhile. And suppose we were to make shift for a month or five weeks, and have all our money coming, and have no tommy out of the shop, what would the butty say to me? He would say, "Do you want e'er a note this time?" and if I was to say, "No," then he would say, "You've no call to go down to work any more here." And that's what I call forsation.'

'Ay, ay,' said another collier; 'ask for the young Queen's picture, and you would soon have to put your shirt on, and go up the shaft.'

'It's them long reckonings that force us to the tommy-shops,' said another collier; 'and if a butty turns you away because you won't take no tommy, you're a marked man in every field about.'

'There's wuss things as tommy,' said a collier who had hitherto been silent, 'and that's these here butties. What's going on in the pit is known only to God Almighty and the colliers. I have been a consistent methodist for many years, strived to do well, and all the harm I have ever done to the butties was to tell them that their deeds would not stand on the day of judgment.'

'They are deeds of darkness surely; for many's the morn we work for nothing, by one excuse or another, and many's the good stint that they undermeasure. And many's the cup of their ale that you must drink before they will give you any work. If the Queen would do something for us poor men, it would be a blessed job.'

Huskisson: Littleton: Disraeli—the currency expert: the county member: the novelist—that in respect of one bill: the Colonial Secretary who lost office over East Retford: the all-but Speaker of the Reformed House: the Prime Minister who passed the Reform Act of 1867—that in respect of the other. Huskisson never forgot Staffordshire: Littleton lived for it: the heart of the widowed Disraeli found solace at Weston-under-Lizard with Selina, Countess of Bradford. Thus do politics and economics intertwine; and thus does a man of single purpose enlist in his cause the brain of the economist and the vision of the social seer. 'Weston's fair scenes' are still as fair as when Disraeli saw them. Teddesley Hall was never architecturally a notable home, but as the newly selected headquarters of the County Agricultural Executive Committee, it is assured of a further lease of rural status. Coal, however, is round the corner, and with taxation on the one hand and coal on the other, the future of Staffordshire's stately homes is somewhat grim.

# CHAPTER TWELVE

# THE LIVERPOOL OF HUSKISSON AND JOHN GLADSTONE

## Converging on Mersey-side

THE revolution in industry and transport: the integration of the mercantile community: the stresses and opportunities of naval war: new pathways of ocean commerce: new targets of economic policy: converged, like the climax and finale of Huskisson's life, on Mersey-side.

### (i) *The Revolution in Industry and Transport*

In whatever order we may list the reasons which localised the cotton industry in Lancashire—humid climate, pure water, proximity to a good port, abundant coal, the adjacence of a senior textile industry, it is certain that from the outset the port of Liverpool was crucial to it, inasmuch as the raw material of the industry came always from overseas. Industrial Lancashire, starting as an outlier of Yorkshire's old-established and naturally endowed woollen industry, turned from rough woollens to the manufacture of cotton brought in the first instance by Turkey merchants from Smyrna and other ports of Asia Minor. Later the raw material came from the West Indies: later, again, from the mainland of America: but always through the port of Liverpool, the only convenient port on the north-west coast. It would have been a miracle if the cotton industry had arisen in the Midlands or in the hinterland of an east coast port.

Eighteenth-century Liverpool, though it did not stage an industrial revolution, had important industrial activities—shipbuilding and ship repairing, sugar refining, tobacco manufacturing, rope-making, pottery and watchmaking, but these were in the main ancillary to its mercantile activities. From first to last it was a port town, not a factory town. The trade in naval stores was important, especially in wartime; and in the heyday of slaving there was a large trade in 'bugle', glass beads, from Venice and Leghorn for the West African coast.

As a port town it handled raw materials inwards, as well as finished goods outwards. Along with raw materials inwards, came foodstuffs. Along with finished goods outwards went ballast goods, such as salt and coal. Irish provisions, Cheshire salt and Lancashire coal were the foundation stock of its shipments. Problems of storage and trans-shipment were always present. As East Lancashire, led by Manchester, was occupied with improving its original assets of climate and water power, so Merseyside was occupied with improving its original asset of a river. In a sense the docks and transit sheds of Liverpool were its distinctive contribution to the Industrial Revolution.

Between Liverpool and its most profitable hinterlands— Manchester and Leeds to the east: Stafford and Birmingham to the south—were gaps (filled today by coal and chemicals) which it was essential to bridge by improved communications. This was the stimulus in turn to improved river navigation: to canals: to railways. In point of fact the leading personalities in the canal era came from Manchester and the Midlands; and in the railway era from Liverpool. But port and hinterland were at one throughout in desiring an improved inlet and outlet for their trade; and the speed of communication which the railways finally brought was valued in the first instance for the speed and regularity of the contacts which it established between merchant and manufacturer. For the revolutions in industry and transport were interdependent.

(ii) *The Integration of the Mercantile Community*

The earliest form of integration was municipal and inter-municipal trading privilege. The varying status of the freemen of Liverpool played an important part in its tangled local history. By the eighteenth century the significance was mainly political. It did not obstruct the economic expansion of the town, which an oligarchic council administered with honesty and efficiency. Under its government the town became possessed of a large corporate estate, which made Liverpool a cheap

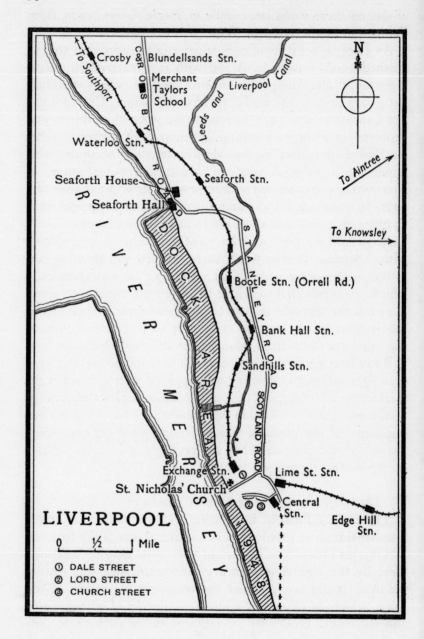

city in which to do business. New activities were entrusted, in the characteristic English fashion, to *ad hoc* authorities; and petty disputes over town rights were obscured by commercial affiliations based on the different branches of its trade. At the opening of the nineteenth century these affiliations crystallised into formal associations, which combined later to form the Liverpool Chamber of Commerce. The three senior associations were the West India Association, the American Chamber of Commerce (i.e. of Liverpool merchants, or American merchants domiciled in Liverpool, engaged in the American trade) and the Shipowners Association. And they were followed by other associations, professional or geographical: professional, such as the Cotton Brokers and Underwriters: geographical, such as the East India and China: the Brazil and River Plate: the Mexico and South American: the Newfoundland: the Mediterranean: the Baltic.

The Rules and Minutes of the American Chamber of Commerce have survived,[1] and are in the Liverpool Public Reference Library:

The objects of this Association are hereby declared to be, the redress of existing, and the prevention of future grievances which may effect this Branch of Trade generally: the establishment of regular and settled rules among the American Merchants in respect to the payment of freights and the rate of fees in the Customs etc. and at the public boards and offices in London: and in general the attainment of such objects as involve the general interests of the Trade, and which it might be difficult or impracticable for the separate and insulated exertions of individuals to effect.

Among topics between 1801 and 1830 may be mentioned—mode of paying landing waiters: support of shipowners in resisting 'all unlawful attempts made by the Journeymen Shipwrights to obtain by combination an advance of wages': request for a ruling from H.M.'s government on the Orders in Council (1811) and urging their repeal in the interest both of the port's trade and the national employment roll: approval of

[1] Cf. Transactions of the Historical Society of Lancashire and Cheshire, Vol. 85 (1933), W. O. Henderson, *American Chamber of Commerce in Liverpool.*

Mr Huskisson's liberal commercial measures (1825), with a list of commodities in which duties are 'still excessively high in proportion to the value of the goods': another strong protest against the wage demands of Journeymen Shipwrights which, if persisted in, will lead to 'the coppering and repairing of Vessels being transferred to other Ports'.

Thus important action generally involved an appeal to London; and so continuous was this want that the American Chamber of Commerce and other Associations maintained at Fludyer Street in Westminster a Liverpool Office. This office is first mentioned in 1812, and its secretary was John Backhouse, who became Canning's private secretary, and was eventually taken by him to the Foreign Office. In 1823 he was succeeded by William Wainewright, who held the office till his death in 1857. After 1857 the Liverpool Office was continued by Thomas Baines, the historian of Liverpool, as an information service at his own risk, with the merchants and mercantile associations of Liverpool as his patrons.

Wainewright, passing constantly between Liverpool and London, was, in effect, Huskisson's political agent. There was strong political feeling in Liverpool, but Huskisson, as the follower of Canning, had the support of the Tories because a good Tory, and the support of the Whigs because his measures were liberal ('Tory men and Whig measures'), and this delicate role was greatly facilitated by the fact that he could communicate with Liverpool through mercantile associations, on which both Tories and Whigs were represented. He was not at the mercy of the 'ultra's', and with liberal support he could take a strong line against, e.g., the illiberal programme of the West India merchants. When John Gladstone brought Canning to Liverpool in 1812 to share the representation with the sitting member, General Gascoyne, the Whigs sent Creevey and Brougham to the hustings against them. Creevey, for all his Sefton connexion (they say he was Lord Sefton's bastard), was a lightweight, but Brougham, on account of his fight against the Orders-in-Council, was *persona grata* with many. Yet he was not of the Liverpool type—too vulgar and too radical; and it was not so many years ago (1796) that Charles Jenkinson, Baron Hawkesbury, had taken, at the wish of Liverpool, the title of Earl of Liverpool, 'quartering the arms of this corporation with his lordship's own arms', in recognition of the services which he had rendered to the town in support of the African Slave Trade.

### (iii) *The Stresses and Opportunities of Naval War*

Great war imposes strains. It creates shortages of material and manpower. For many decades England had lived under the fear of a timber famine, in particular of Navy Oak. The Napoleonic war did not produce the iron steamship. For such ships, in their first form of paddle ships, were unsuited for fighting purposes. But it did compel the country to look for a new source of timber supply outside of enemy control: and that source was found in Canada. On it was erected a great trade in timber and timber ships across the North Atlantic. Other hemispheres were searched—the teak of Burma, the hard woods of Australia and New Zealand, but none of these grew into an ocean trade of bulk and continuity. Canadian timber, therefore, was the key commodity of Huskisson's policy of empire; and here Huskisson, the member for Liverpool, found himself at variance with Thomas Tooke, the Baltic merchant.

While Trafalgar gave supremacy at sea, it did not assure against commerce raiding, the losses from which were exceptionally heavy in the last ten years of the war (1805-15). To some extent this favoured Liverpool by comparison with more southerly ports, for the route by the North of Ireland was safer: but with the outbreak of the Second American War (1812-15) the comparative immunity ceased, and in any case it was outweighed by the damage done to the West Indian sugar trade, and by the strain imposed on naval manpower, which was subjected to the raids of the Press Gang. Mercantile Liverpool shed no tears when peace came in 1815.

Liverpool entered the French wars a slave-trader and emerged from them with no thoughts of reversion to its old staple. For one thing its zest for high reward from a ruthless activity had been slaked by the part it had taken, as a war effort, in privateering and blockade running. Many famous exploits were to the credit of the Liverpool Privateers: many fortunes were made from a share in cargoes which broke Napoleon's Continental Blockade. Though, from the standpoint of international morality, there may not have been much to choose between slaving and privateering, there was no comparison between them as a nursery of seamen. Common risks shared made a better school than common cruelties imposed.

### (iv) *New Pathways of Ocean Commerce*

'Oceans, not continents, made unities in the 18th century' it has been said. This continued to be true of the Atlantic Ocean in the nineteenth, but the pattern was different. The old roundabout trades persisted, as long as the sailing ship itself, being in part determined by the trade winds. But they were overshadowed by the emergence of regular sailings between terminal ports: one terminus on the European side, and the other on the American side. This direct to and fro service is termed in American parlance a shuttle service, and it was, for them, an extension to Europe of the shorter shuttle between America and the West Indies. We, when the age of steam came, spoke of it as the Atlantic Ferry; and perhaps the term 'herring pond', as jocularly applied to the North Atlantic, was indication of a growing familiarity with the once unknown. Today, however, after two World wars, it has the less pleasing title of Atlantic Graveyard.

In Huskisson's day the distinctive element in the new pattern was the increasing intimacy between New York and Liverpool. Liverpool became the terminus on the English side, because it was the best equipped and best situated port of export for the machine-made textiles of Lancashire and Yorkshire and the pottery and hardware of the Midlands. The enterprise of New York merchants made New York, against strong rivalry from ports to the north and south, the main receiving centre for this produce. As shewn by the historian of New York Port in two notable treatises, R. G. Albion, *Square Riggers on Schedule*

(1938) and *The Rise of New York Port, 1815-67* (1939), the first distinctive stroke was the opening in 1817 (which he terms *annus mirabilis*) of a regular service of sailing packets between New York and Liverpool for passengers and goods.

'In order to permit frequent and regular conveyances the subscribers have undertaken to establish a line of vessels between New York and Liverpool to leave from each place on a certain day in every month throughout the year'—the advertisement of October 1817 ran. The Black Ball line was followed by the Red Star, the Swallowtail and others. New York built its ships of the best materials, they were fast, commodious and commanded by captains of experience and activity, and they captured the cream of the Atlantic trade, conveying the majority of the cabin passengers, specie mail, fine freight and news between the United States and Europe. Not till the age of the steamship, heralded in 1838 and clinched in 1848 when the Cunard Line made New York its American terminus, was the shipping lead of New York challenged. The pull of New York was strengthened by the opening of coastal packet services, which brought cotton to New York from southern ports for re-export to Liverpool, and by the construction of the Erie Canal (opened in 1825) which took the imports of Europe inland and brought down to the Hudson River the growing produce of the interior. In 1821, of 54 million dollars of exports from the U.S.A., raw cotton accounted for 20 million, the unit of the Atlantic trade being the 400-lb. cotton bale. In 1825, of 38 million dollars of textiles entering the U.S.A., 24½ million came from the United Kingdom—nearly all of the imported cottons and woollens, and one half of the imported linens. Since then, as a port, though no longer as a shipbuilder, New York has gone on from strength to strength:

By 1860 New York was handling two-thirds of all the nations imports and one-third of its exports. . . . Although the decline of American shipping, already under way, would gravely affect the little ports down east after the Civil War, New York would still retain its commanding share of the nation's commerce, under whatever flag the cargoes might arrive or depart. World primacy still lay in the future; but in the meantime New

York waxed steadily greater in trade, wealth and population, thanks to the well-timed enterprize of its citizens in the decade following 1815.[1]

The merchants of Huskisson's day viewed the shipping ascendancy of America with some dismay, but they had no effective reply until Glasgow came forward with the steamship. Meanwhile, there were other growing trades, especially those with Canada, South America and the East, and the port of Liverpool had to build dock after dock in an effort to keep up with the ceaseless increase. In the 1840's a new form of mass traffic reached an apex—the emigration traffic. This, too, was mainly handled from Liverpool, whose relations with Ireland had always been close. Indeed, she had begun her commercial life by shipping soldiers and stores to Ireland, and her dock population was largely Irish.

## (v)  New Targets of Economic Policy

Liverpool was strong for free trade, but for free trade of a militant order. It was opposed to monopoly and hold-ups. The first great stroke was the opening of the Eastern trade in 1813 —the enjoyment by the north of the trade which had been monopolised by London; and this was consummated by the opening of the China trade in 1833. The next objective was the easement of the grain trade. The Corn Laws were not resented, as they were in Manchester, as an increased cost of production or hardship to the poor consumer, but as an obstruction to the orderly course of trade and in particular to the economies of storage; and this was where Canning and Huskisson made repeated efforts to help. A further objective was the defeat of the canal monopoly. It was in the name of resistance to a monopoly, which had a stranglehold on the flow of trade, that Mr Moss and his friends promoted the Liverpool and Manchester Railway. Similarly, the merchants disliked customs' restrictions which penalised legitimate trade:

The duty on tobacco we consider excessive both on account of its limiting the consumption, and of the injury done to the fair trader and to the

[1] R. G. Albion, *Rise of New York Port*, 386.

community at large, by fostering that extensive system of smuggling especially into Ireland, which is known to prevail in that article.[1]

But most of all did they resent the stoppage of trade by combinations of workmen. Listen to the American Chamber of Commerce in 1825:

Resolved unanimously:

That this meeting acknowledges the just principle which secures to every man, be his situation in life high or low, a free exercise of his proper calling, and the unrestricted right of estimating, as he may please, the value of his own labour; but it most unequivocally expresses its disapprobation of the conduct of those, who by threats, intimidation, or violence, prevent others from working on terms which they are willing to accept:

That it is with great concern that for several years past the members of the association have heard the Masters of Vessels consigned to them complain of the small quantity of daily work done by the Journeymen Shipwrights of this Port to Vessels while under repair, and of the insolence with which they were treated if they ventured to express their dissatisfaction thereat, the effect of which has been increased disinclination to have any repairs made in this Port that are not absolutely unavoidable:

That it is the opinion of this association that unless vessels can be repaired and coppered at this Port on more reasonable and moderate terms both as regards the rate of wages and the work to be done for those wages, there is great danger, of the coppering and repairing of vessels being transferred to other ports where they can be coppered and repaired more advantageously:

That although a short time has elapsed since the Journeymen Shipwrights struck work, yet many American vessels have already left this Port without being coppered or repaired. And this meeting believed that in wages to Ship Carpenters and others a sum of £1200-1500 per week is thus lost to the working classes of the Port:

That under present circumstances there appears to be only one alternative that the Journeymen Shipwrights do resume their work upon reasonable terms, both as to wages and the labour to be performed or that Shipwrights shall be invited to settle here from other ports, in which case the meeting has the fullest reliance on the protection which would be afforded by the Magistrates of the Borough against any threats intimidation or violence which might be offered.

[1] American Chamber of Commerce, 1825.

That these Resolutions be signed on behalf of the meeting by the President and published once in each of the Liverpool Papers.

It is significant that on the statute book, close to the legislation of 6 Geo. 4, 1825, relating to the Customs Consolidation of Deacon Hume, comes 6 Geo. 4, 1825, c. 129—to repeal the laws relating to the Combination of Workmen and to make other Provisions in lieu thereof. Huskisson, as President of the Board of Trade, had moved for the committee which produced the new law, denouncing in particular the hold-up tactics of the Seamen's Union.[1] He liked to hear of John Gladstone bringing the journeymen carpenters to their senses; and his Act of 1825 reversed in part the unrestricted liberalism of that of 1824, as Dicey, in his *Law and Opinion*, makes us clearly to see.

## The Economics of Salt

The economics of salt are a study in various sorts of 'tie-in', to use a not too graceful phrase: salt and transport: salt and coal: salt and the fisheries: salt and agriculture: salt and particular industries—textiles, pottery and chemicals.

In the history of the industry the landmarks are:

*c.* 1670 onwards. The extraction of rock salt and the tapping of brine on the rock bed in Worcestershire and Cheshire, the Cheshire deposits proving to be the largest.

1721. The incorporation of the Weaver Navigation (with supplementary legislation 1759-60) providing an improved waterway from the Cheshire centres of Northwich and Middlewich to the Mersey at Weston Point near Runcorn.

1823. The repeal of the Salt Excise.

## (i)  Salt and Transport

The magnitude of the salt trade in point of volume is indicated by a Liverpool Memorial of 1861, which claimed that at that time 'it exceeded the export of coal and iron together, being one-half of the loaded tonnage cleared at the Port of Liverpool, dependent on the management of the Weaver Navigation'.

---

[1] Huskisson Speeches, II, 375.

It dovetailed with returning cargoes. Early eighteenth-century Liverpool, argues a modern historian,[1] rose on rock salt. Return cargoes of Baltic and American timber began to prop up the cavities in the adjacent coalfields of South Lancs. and Staffs., for which the salt industry, through the fuel used in pan evaporation, was largely responsible. In the coastal trade salt moved from the salt works at Hale, on the Lancashire side of the Mersey Estuary, to the fisheries in Cornwall, and in return came china clay for the Liverpool pottery at Herculaneum, on the site of the later Herculaneum Dock. In the ocean trade salt provided ballast cargo for vessels going to the American South for cotton, or to the Baltic (which is almost a fresh-water sea) for timber.

It dovetailed with outgoing cargoes, providing in its day ideal ballast. The ballast sequence ran: sand; salt; salt and coal; coal with railway irons and heavy machinery. When through inferior sources of supply the Shields (Tyneside) salt industry fell away, many of its coasting ships had to go out in sand ballast. There was even a phase in the early emigration traffic from Liverpool when the emigrants were accommodated on tarpaulin spread over a cargo of salt.

Salt was ideal ballast, because it was in universal demand for a variety of uses at home and abroad: as a medicine, a food, a preservative of fish and meat, a flux in glass-making and metal smelting, a pottery glaze and, of course, as a chemical ingredient. Today in Cheshire, as in Germany, the chemical and allied industries with their gigantic international marketing and financial structure are fixed on the scenes of centuries of salt production. Professor Innis in his *History of the Fur Trade* has accustomed us to the view that the victory of the Hudson's Bay Company over the French fur traders was due in part to the earlier industrialisation of England. Their goods of barter, blankets, ammunition and kettles, were cheaper than those of the French. A similar superiority in the lowly commodity of common salt, based less on technique of manufacture than on

[1] E. Hughes, *Studies in Administration and Finance 1558-1825 with special reference to the history of Salt Taxation in England* (1934).

abundance of supply and shipping, reinforced the export trade of Huskisson's day, and was of importance right down to the present century in holding trade with India and the East.

## (ii) Salt and Coal

In the Mediterranean countries 'bay' or 'solar' salt, as it was called, was made in lagoons by evaporation under the influence of the sun: in England by boiling in salt pans, and as such it was a great consumer of fuel. By the close of the eighteenth century the use of wood for the purpose had been discontinued. At that time, of coal coming up the Weaver, one-tenth went to domestic uses, nine-tenths to the salt works.

As in the extraction of coal, so in the making of salt there was no drastic change in technique until the arrival of the vacuum process in very modern times. The open pan, with its rule-of-thumb methods, held its own. Nevertheless by degrees during the nineteenth century the amount of coal required to produce a ton of salt was almost halved.

On the river navigation of the Weaver and Mersey there was no such nursery of seamen as that which existed on the east coast, where 'admirals and statesmen looked more and more to the colliers, which sailed between Newcastle and London, to provide the navy with trained seamen always available to serve within a few days' notice'.[1] Salt, however, played its part at one remove by providing the outward staple of the Newfoundland Fishery. And there was a vigorous community of watermen, owning flats (barges), renting works, a thrifty, adaptable ambitious class of little undertakers, some few of whom became great names in the salt trade—and it would be interesting to follow the analogy further from the Newcastle Coal Vend to the Salt Union of 1888.

## (iii) Salt and the Fisheries

This, for Liverpool, is the story of the Newfoundland Trade, in which, by 1815, it had a clear and final lead over its old rivals of the West Country. Before the end of the eighteenth

---

[1] J. U. Nef., *Rise of the British Coal Industry* (1932), I, 238.

century the system by which the merchant went out and fished had been replaced by a division of functions. The resident planters and their servants caught the fish. The merchant maintained supplies at St. John's, Newfoundland, and the principal outports, and bought from the planters the fish and oil which he took to European and West Indian markets. The climate was severe, and the resident labour supply, largely immigrant Irish, moved out under sailing conditions rivalling those of the slaver's 'middle passage'; and St. John's was by no means an Arcadia, being an unplanned concentration of wooden houses, out-buildings, fishing-rooms and oil vats exposed to the constant menace of fire. But it had one great asset. Its strategic value was such that it could rely at any cost on the protection of the Royal Navy.

Like the Guinea trade, the Newfoundland trade was triangular: salt and other supplies from England to Newfoundland: cod to West Indies or Mediterranean: sugar and coffee or wine and fruit, as the case might be, to England. For supplies the West Country sent woollens, ropes, nets and twine. London sent fine goods and continental wares. Liverpool sent textiles and hardware and bulk cargoes of salt and coal. Ireland sent provisions and emigrants. The produce of the fisheries was codfish, train oil and seals. During the Napoleonic War the largest vessels in the trade belonged to Liverpool and Greenock. The leading West Country port in the trade was Poole. Another was Teignmouth, whence came John Job of Bulley and Job, who after some years of voyaging across the Atlantic settled at Liverpool, where his business still flourishes under the old name and guidance of his direct descendants.[1]

### (iv) Salt and Agriculture

Salt affected agriculture in two ways: first, as a preservative in the provision trade, second, as a raw material—for fertiliser and salt lick. The former use linked it with the animal husbandry of Ireland: where the shifts of English fiscal policy com-

---

[1] Cf. Chapter X by A. C. Wardle in *The Trade Winds: A Study of British Overseas Trade during the French Wars 1793-1815*, editor C. N. Parkinson (1947).

plicated the course of things. For the combined effect of Cattle
Laws, Navigation Laws and tariff restrictions was to stimulate
the Irish livestock industry without allowing it to become the
basis of a rounded economy. There was no ban on the export of
provisions to the colonies, or to England itself 'for necessary
provisions'. 'The Islands and Plantations of America', says a
writer of 1689, 'are in a manner wholly sustained by the vast
quantity of beef, pork, butter and other provisions of the production of Ireland.' In 1797, the year of the French raid on the
South of Ireland, as much as £1½ million of Navy foodstuffs
were stored in Cork alone. In the 1750's the prohibition against
the importation of live cattle and provisions was withdrawn,
and in the last quarter of the eighteenth century there was a big
rise in the provision trade with England, which took at the end
of the century some 60% of Irish provision exports.

For this industry Ireland had numerous advantages—excellent pasture, a strategic situation at the point of departure for
the Atlantic Ocean, and cheap bay salt, obtained from Spain
and Portugal on the last leg of their triangular trade. Furthermore, it was duty-free, whereas in England such salt, in order
to foster the native industry and yield revenue, was heavily
taxed. Under these conditions Cork maintained a population
in 1760 of 60,000, when that of Liverpool was under 40,000.
But it could not advance with Liverpool to Metropolitan stature. For under the Navigation Laws the colonial trade was confined to English shipping and Irish merchants could not engage
in the re-export trade of sugar and tobacco, which launched
Liverpool and Glasgow on their metropolitan career. The lack
of coal was some handicap, though South Wales was close at
hand, but the factory industry of sail-cloth making which was
beginning to develop was checked by hostile duties of English
origin in 1750, and a promising trade was lost to Holland.
After 1800 Ireland abandoned itself, with disastrous social consequences, to the three 'p's' of pigs, population and potatoes,
between which there was a nefarious 'tie-in'. For the potatoes
that fed the pigs fed Paddy and his family. He fed as the pig
did, and the pig lived with him, his co-equal in diet and dirt.

Till the potato crop failed, the calory value of the diet of potatoes and milk was high. But when it failed, there was disaster. There was, perhaps, an element of hopelessness in it. What remained but procreation? At any rate the redundant mass flowed over to Liverpool and Glasgow and thence by emigration to the New World, supplying both the Old World and the New with strong hefty men and women, with dockers, navvies, manual labourers and domestic servants, but also with grave social problems of slum life and political discontent.

### (v) Salt and Industry

This is a prelude to the nineteenth-century developments in chemicals and soap on or near Merseyside—at Northwich, Widnes and Port Sunlight. The potters with their demand for a salt glaze, the textile makers with their demand for bleaching and dyeing materials, set the pace of demand. But serious development was impossible while salt was an article of excise. In 1823 the Salt Excise was repealed; and James Muspratt (1793-1886), in the same year, set up in Liverpool the Le Blanc recovery process, the foundation of the modern alkali industry.

The fight for repeal was elaborately organised, and in the Board of Trade Minutes for 1817 there is a graphic account of the forces which were mobilised and the arguments used.

On 3 April 1817 the deputation, led by Lord Kenyon, presented their case, and at a series of meetings during the month every aspect of the case was studied. Lord Kenyon discoursed on the burden to the poor consumer: J. C. Curwen, M.P., on the need of it in agriculture: a Scotchman on its value to the kelp industry of the Western Highlands: chemists spoke of its use in the manufacture of muriatic acid and alkalis: the Secretary to the Association for the Relief of the Manufacturing Poor testified to the disposition of the lower orders to a fish diet. Calculations were made as to the probable increase of consumption if the duties were withdrawn.

Sir Thomas Bernard, the spearhead of the agitation, stressed the use of salt for manure in Cornwall, 'the improvements to be expected in the manufacturing process, if excise interference was withdrawn: the moral ill of tempting the lower orders to evade the duties.' A chemist contributed a paper stating that 'the consumption of soda for the purpose of washing linen instead of pearl ashes has of late increased and that it would probably be increased in a much greater degree if the duty on salt were repealed, and that a very considerable quantity would in such case be used in the manufacture of soap'—and so forth.

The enquiries of 1817-18 established clearly that the competition of foreign salt in the fisheries and Irish trade, against which English salters demanded protection, was a very small part of the problem and that the essential need was for new and extended uses of a commodity in ample supply. Eventually in 1822 the duties on native salt were reduced from 15/- to 2/- a ton: and on foreign salt to 2/3 a ton: and in 1823 they were repealed, bar the extra 3d. on foreign salt, which went the next year. This achievement was pre-Huskisson. But it ranged Liverpool on the side of the more comprehensive changes which at his instance were to come in the general field of industry and commerce.

### John Gladstone and his Circle

Mr Huskisson, surely, you know already. May I introduce now my fellow townsman, John Gladstone (1764-1851, baronet 1846), the man who brought Canning to Liverpool, and after Canning, Huskisson: the man who knew every detail of Liverpool's commercial and shipping life with an ear for everything and an opinion on everything: never happier than when giving evidence on port charges and the measurement of shipping tonnage: egotistical but not vain: fond of controversy, but too outspoken to be entrusted with political secrets: the distinguished father of a more distinguished son. One regrets that John Morley, with the vast task of Gladstone's life ahead of him, could find room only for the few notes supplied by his son. Samuel Smiles was at one time to have written a life, and while we may be grateful to have escaped this, the lack of one is a challenge to the economic historians of the University of Liverpool.

There is an admirable portrait of him in his old age by William Bradley of Manchester (1801-57), presented to the Walker Art Gallery in 1919 by Mr Arthur S. Gladstone. He has the erect carriage, firm mouth and fine forehead of his son —the likeness, indeed, is striking. The left hand rests on two folios and in the background is a sailing ship at sea.

He died worth over half a million, and it was in overseas trade, west and east, that he made his fortune. An immigrant Scot from Leith, he graduated in the firm of Corrie and Co., corn merchants of Liverpool. He managed the American side of this business with high success at a difficult time, and later became equally interested in cotton and sugar, freighting the first ship to clear for Calcutta from Liverpool and becoming the owner of a sugar plantation in Demerara, the produce of which he brought home in his own ships. He was a free trader with reservations. Like Pitt, Canning and Huskisson, he put imperial considerations first, and valued the East India trade not only for the new market it afforded, but also as an alternative source of supply of raw cotton that relieved the country of a dangerous dependence on America. These men, be it rememberd, had lived through Embargo and Non-Importation.

At the point where the Mersey approaches the open sea, he built Seaforth House (importing the name from Scotland), the scene of many a famous gathering. Here Canning stayed in the interval between Castlereagh's death and his appointment to the Foreign Office, when he was due to leave for India as Governor-General. The house is described in J. P. Neale's *Seats* of 1819, with an emphasis, which every guest repeated, on the magnificent view out to sea—'the broad estuary of Mersey, with numerous vessels which must all pass within from one to two miles of Seaforth House . . . an interesting diversified scene, particularly when a week or ten days of contrary wind has detained the shipping in Liverpool; on such occasion it frequently happens 150 or 200 of ships bound to foreign and coasting ports go to sea in one tide.'

The house no longer exists. The site was between Gordon and Elm Road, Seaforth, north-east of the present Dog Stadium. It is not to be confused with Seaforth Hall, the residence of the Muspratts, which was close by and has been demolished also.

John Gladstone was an admirable correspondent and kept Huskisson supplied not only with his own views, but with those of well-informed friends in Liverpool and of his Scottish *alter ego*, Kirkman Finlay (1773-1842), of James Finlay & Co. of Glasgow, who freighted the first ship to clear from the Clyde for India (1816, the *Duke of Buckinghamshire*, a ship of 600 tons, followed by the *George Canning* 1817). Three examples of this correspondence may be given:

1. *Gladstone to Canning*
   (*Abstract*) State of trade of Liverpool:

Seaforth, Jan. 27, 1818

Increase in past year. Import from foreign and empire sources up £3 million—cotton, flour, rice, wheat, etc. Total for 1817, £13 million. Export trade up also.

Stocks lower than they were. Money on real security to be had at 4%, as compared with 5% a year ago; and twice the tonnage now building. Arrivals from India since the opening of the trade:—

|            | 25 ships with cargoes worth |
|------------|------------------------------|
| 1815       | £45,000                      |
| 1816-7     | £310,000                     |
| 1817-8     | £520,000                     |
|            | £875,000                     |

Cleared for India 48 ships, all freighted with British produce. In 1817 the Indian Market was glutted and values fell, but should recover, with large sales at the lower price level.

Increase, 1816-7, in Irish coasting trades also.

The reports of the professional reporter—of William Jacob on agricultural conditions in Europe, for example—may be of great value, but they are never so arresting as facts from the men who have helped to bring them to pass.

## 2. *Kirkman Finlay to John Gladstone*

It is very cruel in Baring and some other persons who ought to know better to press the Government and mainly Mr. Huskisson with the attacks they do.

Can there be anything wider than the truth to assert that the distress of the silk trade is caused by the new law? It could never be a question of entire exclusion of foreign silk, for that you can never do, but it is purely whether the Government or the smuggler will get it all. Even at that rate they will get a great deal.

That the present Ministers have done more good to trade and manufactures by the new principles they have introduced and acted on than any Ministry which has preceded them, no rational man can deny. But the rational men are quiet and say little, while noise and nonsense get possession of the fools, who will in all kingdoms form an immense majority.

Forwarded by Gladstone to Huskisson, who replied thanking K. Finlay, 28 March 1826:

I have no doubt, when the report is made, that the good sense of Scotland will form a fair and impartial estimate of the advantages and inconveniences of the present system, and that Parliament will be able to come to a satisfactory result.

The history of James Finlay and Co. is in course of preparation by the firm and will have the pleasure of burying a second quite imaginary Kirkman Finlay of the D.N.B., 'who was neither killed in Greece nor born anywhere,' according to my informant.

## 3. *Swinton Holland to George Lyall* (reaching Huskisson as an enclosure from John Gladstone).

(*Abstract*):

Within the last 30 years the shipowners of London have changed their character. Merchant and Shipowner are become so quite distinct classes. In Liverpool they are still in many cases united—as also in Bristol and minor ports. Sometimes the shipowner will purchase a cargo, if none offers, to fill his own ship. In brief, United Kingdom tonnage is largely the property of owners with a local outlook, who will resist equality with the foreigner in matter of treatment. American tonnage is of this nature:—

(i) The Maritime States export ships for sale.

(ii) Boston and Salem trade with Asia, merchant and shipowner being one.

(iii) New York, in addition to owner-merchants, has a fine merchant
    service, carrying passengers, mail and a full cargo, sailing weekly
    for Liverpool. American ships are better found and quicker. 'I
    have never heard of a British vessel attempting to compete with
    one.'
(iv) Philadelphia has large vessels employed chiefly by their owners.
Under reciprocity we should be no worse off than we are, but we must
expect an increase of foreign produce imported in American ships. The
oriental trade may go to U.S.A., because we still think in terms of merchant men of war like the East India-men.

Huskisson did not live in a fool's paradise. He took a risk
over shipping reciprocity which in the end met with success,
because technical advantages of iron and steam came to the
help of English shipping.

Canning was not boasting when he wrote to Huskisson, 21
October 1822, 'the Government must not be surprised that,
whenever I leave Liverpool, my place should be in all probability supplied by a Whig or Radical.' For the liberal opposition contained notable men in their ranks, William Roscoe,
James Cropper, William Rathbone.[1] The issue which sharply
divided the two parties was the status of slavery in the West
Indies. John Gladstone, signing as Mercator, conducted a
lively correspondence on the subject with James Cropper in the
Liverpool press in 1823-4. And if Gladstone had the advantage
in facts, Cropper had the broad moral appeal, to which Liverpool had responded when sending William Roscoe to Westminster in the year of Slave Trade abolition. William Roscoe
(1753-1831) was a gracious and beloved figure. Artist, historian and botanist, the biographer of Lorenzo de' Medici, the
cataloguer of the Italian MSS. at Holkham, he unfortunately
entered into a banking partnership which brought him to bank-
ruptcy in 1820:

The last visit [writes Alexander Young of Harburn] which I
paid to Mr. Roscoe was shortly before his death; where, instead of finding

---

[1] William Rathbone IV, 1757-1809, imported in 1784 the first cotton from the American
mainland. William Rathbone V, 1787-1868, drafted the rules of the American Chamber of Commerce. Among the Quakers, son follows father, with the same name, as often as may be.

*WILLIAM HUSKISSON*

*from a contemporary portrait*

*SIR JOHN GLADSTONE*
*from the portrait by William Bradley*

his handsome villa of Allerton with a magnificent library and an excellent collection of pictures, one of them being a whole room full of paintings by Fuseli, I had some difficulty in finding out his place of residence in a small country cottage some miles from Liverpool, the door of which he opened himself. Though he seemed to be steeped to the eyes in poverty, his cheerfulness and good temper appeared to be entire. He was an eminent botanist and the Botanical Gardens of Liverpool was chiefly his work. I found him engaged in painting with his own hand some of the most magnificent flowers in point of size and colour which I had ever seen.[1]

The Liverpool banking community of the day was ably represented by Heywood, Leyland, and Ewart and Moss. One Heywood founded Arthur Heywood Sons & Co. of Liverpool (1773-1883), absorbed ultimately by the Bank of Liverpool: another Heywood founded the Manchester Bank. Both started as merchants, with an interest in the African and privateering trades: both ended as pure bankers. Robertson Gladstone, John's second son, married a Heywood and became a partner.

Thomas Leyland (1752-1827) got a lucky start from a lottery prize of £20,000 in 1776, and made great profits in the African and Mediterranean trades. Shrewd and calculating, he left £600,000. His bank eventually was amalgamated with the North and South Wales Bank Ltd.

John Moss's father was a timber merchant, and John Moss (1782-1858), in addition to founding a bank, (Ewart & Moss), promoted in turn the Liverpool and Manchester, and Grand Junction Railways. His bank was incorporated in the London Midland Bank Ltd. in 1897.

These banking houses enter in great detail into the Huskisson Correspondence because of a tiresome dog-fight as to who should have the remittance of the Customs and Excise from Liverpool to London. 'Nothing', wrote Huskisson to John Bolton, 6 October 1823, 'since my political connection with Liverpool has given me half so much pain as the misunderstanding or whatever it be that occasioned the discussion on this subject.'

Herries's ruling from the Treasury (4 October 1823) was:

[1] Herries MS. at Spottes. The visit was in 1826.

Of the three parties with whom that engagement was made, one alone (Ewart & Moss) was punctual and constantly efficient in the fulfilment of it. Of the two others, one has remitted scarcely any part of the Revenue and the other a very small proportion; while Messrs. Ewart and Moss have frequently effected the remittances which the other two had rejected.

Under the circumstances, these gentlemen have certainly no right to impute it to any undue preference of Messrs. Ewart and Moss, nor to any improper slight of their respective establishments, that the former were selected for the experiment directed to be made by the Board of Customs. It was a fair and proper distinction between those who had and those who had not taken an active part in the execution of the previous arrangement.

—(Huskisson Box—Liverpool Public Reference Library.)

### Huskisson's Services to Liverpool

County of Lancaster: Borough of Liverpool.

Parliament of 1820:

> George Canning
> General Isaac Gascoyne } 15 March 1820
>
> William Huskisson, *vice* George Canning, appointed one of the Principal Secretaries of State, 15 February 1823.

Parliament of 1826:

> William Huskisson
> General Isaac Gascoyne } 12 February 1826
>
> William Huskisson re-elected after appointment as one of the Principal Secretaries of State, 5 February 1828.

Parliament of 1830:

> William Huskisson
> General Isaac Gascoyne } 2 August 1830
>
> William Ewart, *vice* William Huskisson deceased, 30 November 1830.[1]

In a few pages, with a wealth of references which might be expanded into a book, Prof. Veitch sets out the nature of the services rendered by Huskisson to the Borough of Liverpool as one of its two members from 1823 to 1830:

[1] Detail from Parliamentary Papers—Members of Parliament, 1878, 62, Pt. II.

In commercial matters Huskisson was perpetually employed in the interests of Liverpool traders. He was kept busy about rum and cotton; he was importuned to get preference for coffee or rice grown in the British dominions; or asked to secure longer credit for traders paying duty on tobacco. One constitutent wrote to him in trouble about his West Indian business; another so that he might prod the Admiralty into greater activity against the West Indian pirates. On behalf of a Liverpool owner he contrived to wring the price of a ship out of a reluctant Treasury, and he stirred Peel to activity against the wreckers on the coast of Denbigh and Carnarvon. He got our Ambassador in Paris to protest to the French Ministry against the detention of *The Merchant's Friend*, a ship belonging to Finlay and Holt, and he supported an application to the Admiralty for 'a Vessel for the purpose of being converted into a Floating Chapel for the use of the Seamen in the Port'.[1]—and so on.

This record of miscellaneous service shows how he set himself to serve the commercial community of Liverpool without distinction of party. The Tories of the Canning Club, headed by John Gladstone and John Bolton, brought him to Liverpool and guaranteed, as they had done with Canning, that it should be at no financial cost to himself. He came with reluctance, but he came, partly to please Canning and partly because prominent Whigs assured him of their support also. At several of his elections there was a contest, but it was nominal only. He was trusted by both sides. In a dispute between the Dock Trustees and the Ratepayers, one correspondent wrote, 2 May 1825, 'If Mr. Huskisson will state his approval of those proposals, the merchants have so much respect for his opinion that they will accede to them.' He became an arbitrator, though sometimes he had to remind the parties that there must be reason on both sides:

I settled the business between the railway and the Sankey Canal yesterday in the Committee in a manner just I am sure to both parties, but I am afraid not quite to the liking of Mr. Carr. In fact there was no satisfying him because he wanted what is not fair and reasonable.

(1830. Liverpool Public Reference Library).

[1] G. S. Veitch, *Huskisson and Liverpool* (1929), 38-9.

There were certain friends who tried his patience hard, notably the railway enthusiast John Moss—'Moss is too much alive to every floating rumour that touches his interest, but I cannot always be inquisitive because he is fidgety, neither would it be for his advantage that I should' (1825), and again: 'If Moss were less fidgety he might have saved himself and me some trouble' (1829). But though they worried him, they came to love him. T. F. Dyson writes to Wainewright from Everton, 5 February 1829, that he has been made Chairman of the new 'Liverpool Brazil and River Plate Association'. 'I am rejoiced to hear from my friend Mr. Bolton that our highly esteemed member Mr. Huskisson is in perfect health, his meritorious conduct will, I feel persuaded, assure him a seat in Parliament by an overwhelming majority as long as he chooses to sit for Liverpool: the feeling towards him in the Town is everything we wish.'

The affectionate esteem which he had won for himself makes a poignant background to the tragedy of 15 September 1830. But perhaps the most satisfying picture is that which emerges, incidentally, from the MS. Autobiography of a Liverpool Merchant, compiled in 1843. It shows how Huskisson's career converged on Merseyside from his Treasury days onwards—not doing jobs for Liverpool, so much as associating Liverpool with his progressive economic policy. For example, in 1815, when Canning was in Portugal, the Rt. Hon. William Huskisson and General Gascoyne presented a memorial from the Liverpool Shipowners Association, recommending that measures be taken to equalise the duties levied on British and American shipping (Board of Trade Minutes, 6 May 1815). And as Professor Veitch so truly points out, the importance of Liverpool was that it had a corporate voice in an unreformed Parliament in which Manchester and Birmingham, as such, had no representation. What Liverpool said today, Manchester and Birmingham would be saying tomorrow. First came the merchant capitalist, then the industrial employer, conformably to the general law of our industrial evolution.

But before we come to the autobiography, let us remember

that there was another side of Liverpool's life, not glimpsed by those who, from a merchant's villa in Otterspool or Seaforth, looked out on the sea and the sunsets. Ramsay Muir closes his introduction to the *History of Municipal Government in Liverpool to 1835* with these grim lines:

The swarming vagrants in search of work, the rush of a growing commerce, had overwhelmed the powers of the town government to make the conditions of life even tolerable. . . .; the quiet and healthy little market town, with its picturesque tower and castle . . . has at a bound passed into a sordid, ugly home of serfs and their masters, each penned, according to the modern fashion, in its own separate quarters, each stunted and narrowed by the starving of human sympathy which this involved.

*Extracts from the Autobiography of Thomas Fletcher*
Autobiography of Thomas Fletcher of Liverpool, written in 1843, and privately printed for circulation in the family, 1893.[1]
Thos. Fletcher was a West India merchant. The Liverpool West India Association (he tells us) was modelled on the London Association, the parent merchants' association of Liverpool.

1803. Passing of the Warehousing Act:

Hitherto the Customs Duties on all goods imported had been paid by the merchants on landing the same; and as the customs on most articles had been much raised in consequence of the war, and more particularly on sugar, from which a very large revenue was obtained, it had been very burdensome and inconvenient to the merchants to raise money for the purpose. But by this Act goods were allowed to be warehoused for a time not exceeding 12 months, without payment of duty. . . . If sold for exportation no duty payable. . . . Best thing he (Pitt) ever did, the Union with Ireland excepted.
Act in 1st instance confined to London.

February 1805. T.F. on Deputation to London to get Liverpool's scattered warehouses (—'no prison docks') accepted:

We could not be admitted to see Mr. Pitt, who was in bad health, and in fact did not long survive; but we saw Mr. Huskisson and Mr. Sturges

[1] Fletcher's daughter married Henry Roscoe, father of Sir Henry Roscoe.

Bourne, Secretaries of the Treasury, who were very civil. This was the first time I saw Mr. H., then a young man. I was much pleased with his appearance and manners, and conceived that good opinion of him which I have never had occasion to change. The result was an intimation that certain of the existing warehouses which were within a reasonable distance of the Custom House and which the owners would put into such a state of security as the officers of the Customs might require, would be accepted, and the privileges of the warehousing Act extended to Liverpool; but in addition to the warehouses so admitted being put under the King's locks, bonds would be required from the importers for the amount of the duties on the goods deposited therein. This was in fact conceding everything that was desired, and the deputation returned with flying colours. But it would seem that some further power was tho't necessary by Government, for there was a bill brought into Parliament in June 1805, in furtherance of the warehousing of goods at the outports. Liverpool, however was declared to have that privilege in the course of the summer.

T.F. in retrospect deplores the scattered warehouses with their four-fold fire risk. Better to have adopted the London system, as the Dock Committee proposed, 'and now the original design is being acted upon; for the commerce of the port having continued to increase, an Act was passed May 31, 1841, for making a new dock with surrounding warehouses to the Westward of the Salthouse Dock, and sheds to the Westward of the Prince's Dock, which warehouses are to be made fireproof.'[1]

1806. T.F. succeeds Mr Bolton as Chairman of W.I. Association.

1808. Downing Street Deputation to the Prime Minister on West Indian War Distress:

After waiting in a small ante-room we were shown into a large library where he was seated at a writing table full of papers, and there were two or three other gentlemen with him, one of whom was Mr. Huskisson. Mr. Perceval was a small slender man of a pale complexion with an intelligent and pleasing expression of countenance.

[1] Acts Local 4 and 5 Vict., c. 30. An Act for enabling the Trustees of the Liverpool Docks to erect transit sheds on the West Quay of the Prince's Dock, to make a Wet Dock with Warehouses on the Quay, etc., 'and whereas the establishing of the said Warehouses under Regulations for landing, housing, depositing and shipping of Goods & Merchandize & the Erection of such Transit Sheds will facilitate the Business of the Port, furnish additional Security to Merchants and others and render the Collection of the public Revenue more safe and convenient', etc.

Mr. Perceval granted a committee which recommended the use of sugar for grain in distillation; and the coffee duty was reduced from 2/2d to 7d a lb. 'The lower duty in a short time brought more money into the Exchequer than the higher one.'

1818. Deputation concerning the mode of paying landing waiters:

Wm. Rathbone, D. Hodgson and T. Fletcher were all 'political opponents of Mr. Canning'. 'However, he received us with great civility, but being at that time confined with the gout and lying on the sofa, he said Mr. Huskisson would supply his place and do anything he could for us.'

They found no favour with Mr. Frewin (of the Customs), who, having been a landing waiter himself wanted the work to be 'well done, not quickly done'. But 'Mr. H. spoke in favour of our plan with his usual good sense and fluency of expression'. They got their way then, the pay to be partly by fee to encourage speed, and partly by salary, but now (1843) they have fixed salaries.

1823. The issue: the comparative duties on West and East India sugar. Cropper and Fletcher were on opposing sides. Cropper denounces the higher rate on East Indian sugar, claiming it to be the product of free labour. Fletcher presents the 'melioration' programme. Big meeting at Fife House:

In came the noble Earl [*Liverpool*] attended by Lord Holland and several ministers. He stepped across the room and opening an inner door said 'Come gentlemen'. Accordingly we followed into a very large dining room—the ministers on his right—Robinson, Bathurst, Canning, Huskisson: the deputation on his left—on the extreme left Mr. [*John*] Gladstone and myself.

In the course of a long debate, the ministers insisted on ultimate emancipation. Canning said that the colonial legislatures had promised amelioration and done nothing. Mr. Ellis [*Lord Seaford*] admitted this. Therefore Canning carried a motion for measures which 'will produce a progressive improvement in the characters of the slave population, such as may prepare them for equal rights and privileges, as enjoyed by others of H.M.'s subjects'.

1823. Another West India Deputation to Fife House (arranged by Mr Huskisson):

I sat next to Mr. H.

1823. Investigation into the Dock estate. Deputation to Huskisson, 'who was impressed by my statement of the case' and tried to persuade the Liverpool Council to concede a larger representation to ratepayers. But the Council declined, and their original offer was accepted.

1826-8. Fletcher is a Member of the Cheshire Whig Club: working for Catholic Emancipation and the repeal of the Test and Corporation Acts:

Our Petition was sent up by the 5th April (1827) to Mr. Huskisson for presentation but in consequence of his indisposition not presented till May 28.

Tho' Mr. Canning's friend did not object to either, it was clear they would not support repeal of the Test Acts, without Catholic Emancipation. This I know at least was Mr. H.'s opinion, as Canning's. The event, I think, proved them wrong. The Repeal of the Test Act moved by Lord J. Russell was carried against the Government Feb. 1828, against both Huskisson and Peel. Peel could have stopped it in the Lords, but did not.

In the 1830's Mr Fletcher took a house 'in Huskisson St. looking upon St. Bride's Church': and quite close to the cemetery where Huskisson lay.

## A Fortnight at Cheltenham Spa

1790-1820 saw the rise not only of Liverpool and other ports but of Cheltenham and other spaws.[1] For continental war forced invalid England to seek its cures at home. Huskisson went to Cheltenham for treatment in 1798, and Fletcher, his business in London finished, went there out of curiosity in 1820. Cheltenham, first the summer complement and then the year-round rival of Bath, celebrated the centenary of its Royal Old Wells in 1838. Twin-salt saline, sodium sulphate saline, alkaline saline, magnesium and calcium saline, drunk in tumblers or run into a bath (the real medicine being obedience to doctor's orders) would cure every ill but one; and if the maid got that,

---

[1] They had not, as yet, in England the 'ah' sound, and therefore sometimes spelled the continental word Spa as they pronounced it—'spaw'. Similarly they called Pa 'Paw'—cf. Kawbul for Cabul and Punjawb for Punjab. But I cannot imagine them saying Paw-paw for Papa.

you could send her round to Edward Jenner. The language of its approvers is the language of abundant ecstasy:

A most commodious purge for those that do not bear strong cathartics.

It restores a relaxed habit, whether from long residence in a hot climate (the benefit received by many just returned from the East-Indies in a debilitated state, and their recommendation of this water on the spot to their friends is the best proof of this assertion), free living, use of mercuries, or any other cause. In rheumatic, schrophulous, erisipelous, scorbutic, leprous cases, but especially in spermatic, and hemorrhoidal; in disorders of the urinary passage, which it cleanses, corroborates and frees from obstructions; and in those tormenting pains of the hips, and limber muscles, proceeding from a lodgment of hot scorbutic salts, it is sovereign, and not to be equalled. It gives quiet nights in nephritic and gouty complaints, when not under the fit.

This is but a slender extract from the *Tour to the Royal Spa at Cheltenham 1797*. One impious obstinate contended for a better way. 'Good punch at night, and copious gargles of good port by day, would cure any mortal disease in life,' said Lord Howth. But to the sober merchant of Liverpool it all seemed rather silly:

My business in London finished, I went down to Cheltenham to try the waters there. I was recommended to a house where only gentlemen were received and the company consisted of military men who had served in the E. Indies: to me not very congenial society. However, I stayed there for about 14 days. I drank the waters and bathed in a warm bath which agreed with me very well. The waters of this place are salt mixed with sulphur, and the effect much like those of Harrogate, tho' they have nothing of the unpleasant smell of the latter. . . .

Cheltenham consists chiefly of one long street, with a turnpike gate at some little distance from each end of it, between which it was the daily practice of the visitants to ride and drive. . . . It struck me as very ridiculous.

## With Mr Bolton at Storrs

Huskisson enjoyed his visits to Storrs, and Mrs Huskisson the potted char.

If Huskisson had a wiser friend in Liverpool (he could not have had a more faithful) than John Gladstone, it was the doyen of Liverpool commerce, the West India merchant prince, John Bolton, of Storrs Hall, Windermere, where Huskisson often

stayed and whence several of his letters are dated. Storrs
Hall is the Mervyn Hall of Scott's *Guy Mannering*, from the
window of which Julia Mannering listened to the flageolet of
her lover by moonlight. Though few remember the fact, unless
perhaps they have lunched by the Three-Shire Stone, where
Westmorland, Cumberland and Lancashire meet, a goodly portion of the Lake District is in Lancashire—Storrs Hall, in
Westmorland, looks out on Coniston Old Man and the Furness
Fells in Lancashire.

But being in Liverpool, how shall we get there? There was
no railway then from Oxenholme to Windermere, and there
never would have been, if Wordsworth could have had his way.
It is tempting to go by sea (along with the Bishop's books consigned to Dominie Sampson) to some Cumberland port, to
Whitehaven, from which came the Brocklebank of Liverpool's
Brocklebank Dock, commemorating its oldest surviving shipping line: or further along to Workington, where we should
call on J. C. Curwen at Workington Hall and then, if Parliament was not sitting, on the member for Cockermouth, Thomas
Wallace (not unknown to William Huskisson), to whom
Wordsworth dedicated the 1816 edition of his *Guide through
the District of the Lakes*. But I leave this route to Professor Pigou and the Buttermere fans, and as an economic historian I land you at Ulverston: not Ulpha Fell, most delectable
of walking centres, but Ulpha's Town—Ulverston, famous for
its slates and potatoes and Quaker meeting-house.

> The devil himself made lawyers and 'torneys
> And placed them in U'ston and Dalton-in-Furness.

Our objective is Backbarrow Fell, from which we can look right
down the Lake on to Storrs Hall and its little Temple; and we
shall reach it with the Industrial Revolution in our pocket. For
Isaac, John Wilkinson's father, was chief caster to the Backbarrow Iron Company, and John Wilkinson (1728-1808) built
at Castlehead, near Lindale (which is a little inland from
Grange-on-sands), a mansion which he roofed with copper
from his own mine. He was buried there in an iron coffin with

an iron monument above him. The legend is that at the bottom of Lindale Tarn is the iron boat, which he and his father built: the fact, less colourful, is that the great iron master, who lived here, floated on the River Severn the first iron-skinned boat.

But time presses. John Bolton, of course, would go to Windermere by post; and we know the route, stage by stage, because Celia Fiennes went there on horseback a century before—from Liverpool, with its new-built houses and very pretty Exchange; by Prescott; Wigan with its fine Cannel coal, 'burns as bright as a candle'; 'Preston a very good market town'; Garstang, where she ate of oaten Clap bread; Lancaster, 'old and much decay'd' (John Gladstone, for a while, was its M.P.); to Kendal; and thence to Bowness, six miles away, through narrow lanes among rich enclosures. Having lived myself for thirty years at Ferry View, with Storrs Hall to the left and Bowness to the right, and opposite to me the Ferry Hotel (the successor to that 'd——d cake house, the resort of walking gentlemen of all descriptions'), I need no further guidance from Celia Fiennes or Arthur Mervyn or William Wordsworth himself.

At Storrs, John Bolton had three notable neighbours, a bishop, a poet and an industrial magnate whose hobby was the improvement of agriculture—Richard Watson, Bishop of Llandaff (1737-1816) at Calgarth, and subsequently QUOD MORTALE FUIT in the parish church of Windermere at Bowness: John Wilson, 'Christopher North' (1785-1854), at Elleray, near the Windermere of the Railway Station: John Christian Curwen (1756-1828), at Belle Isle on the Lake itself. (Scott's Arthur Mervyn is a composite of Bolton and Curwen.)

Bishop Watson of Trinity, like William Wordsworth of St. John's and Samuel Taylor Coleridge of Jesus, links Cambridge with the Lakes. Wordsworth immortalised their scenery:

> To speak of you, ye mountains and ye lakes,
> And sounding cataracts, ye mists and winds
> That dwell among the hills where I was born.
>
> —(Prelude Book II)

But the attractions of Windermere were appreciated already.

Calgarth, which the Bishop improved by planting and water meadows, is a property on the lake front, just north of Bowness, and by his day its fringe was dotted with 'neat snug boxes, belonging to gentlemen of moderate fortune, that adorn the banks of its beautiful lake'. And these gentlemen, great and small, fighting a selfish fight that has meant everything to the Lake District, have defended it against the ravages of tourism: conserving in Wordsworth's phrase 'the natural blend of land and water' against everyone save the Manchester Corporation at Thirlmere and Hawes Water.

Bishop Watson was an ex-professor,[1] both of Chemistry and Divinity (there was no narrow specialisation in those days); and if he frowned on the slave trade, he made up for this by improving the manufacture of gunpowder. 'The quicker the conflict, the less the slaughter,' as his grateful sovereign assured him.

John Christian Curwen, the great coal and iron magnate, had a holiday retreat on Belle Isle (thousands, nay hundreds of thousands, have rowed or gone by launch around it since then). If not the first agriculturist in the kingdom, as was claimed for him in 1818, he was the first north of the Trent, second only to Coke of Holkham. Alexander Young of Harburn describes the 'annual exhibitions at Workington Hall, where nothing could exceed the kindness and hospitality with which his numerous guests were received and entertained. At one of these annual exhibitions I have seen more than 400 persons, for three days running, dining in his greenhouses disfurnished for that purpose, and entertained with a liberality that, as far as I could learn, was not eclipsed, if equalled, by similar exhibitions of agricultural patrons with greater names'.[2] The Annual Register of 1806 has an article on Mr Curwen's method of Feeding Cows during the wintertime, 'with a view to provide Poor

---

[1] Translated to Toronto, he would have made an admirable Professor of Actuarial Science and taken charge of our pensions. Faringdon Diary, VII, 96, 3 November 1815: 'We talked of Provident Institutions and of the excellence of the *Equitable Insurance Office*. He said that Dr. Watson, the late Bishop of Llandaff, had, at different times, insured to the amount of £5000, which Sum had accumulated to such an amount by the increasing profits of the Society, that at his death about £19,500 was paid to his family.'

[2] Spottes MS.—Memoir of J. C. Curwen.

Persons and Children with Milk at that time'; and we have heard him already at the Board of Trade campaigning for untaxed salt. After one of these gatherings, selected guests would accompany him to Windermere to meet the statesmen and the poets. Sir Walter Scott, Mr Bolton's guest at Storrs, has an honourable mention for the improved grasses of Mr Mervyn.

Christopher North, the first Newdigate prizeman of Oxford, was, as a poet, about on the level of William Hayley. As Blake to Hayley, so Wordsworth to the author of the *Isle of Palms* and *Noctes Ambrosianae*. But in physique he could give points to the poet of the extravert umbrella. He was a giant in strength, an adept at 'the fancy', ready to ride or walk any distance to see a main, a wrestler, and a patron of wrestling who launched the Grasmere Sports on their long career. From Windermere, when he lost his fortune through the peculation of a trustee, he went to Edinburgh to try his luck at the Scottish bar and failing there found his *métier* as a principal contributor to Blackwood's Magazine. In 1820, by a gross political job, in which he had the support of Sir Walter Scott and all the Tories, he was appointed Professor of Moral Philosophy at Edinburgh to succeed the great Dugald Stewart; and this is how he comes into the Huskisson Correspondence. For knowing no philosophy he got his friend Alexander Blair to write his lectures for him and left out the traditional appendage of political economy altogether. Therefore, in May 1825, certain Edinburgh Professors backed a proposal for a Regius Professorship of Political Economy at Edinburgh as 'forming an indispensable part in the education of every gentleman: it is a science, the magnitude and importance of which require the unhindered attention of a separate professor'. J. R. McCulloch was a candidate and wrote grovellingly to Huskisson (as the fashion was in those days), advocating his claims in letter after letter. But he was a Whig, and a letter to Huskisson from John Wilson of 'Elleray, Nr. Kendal', 1 June 1825, protested at the proposed encroachment on his rights as Professor of Moral Philosophy. 'It appears to me', wrote Canning to Huskisson, 11 June, 'that Mr. W. would have good cause of complaint if Mr. McC's project had been

2 C

encouraged'. And eventually on the ground that the Senatus of Edinburgh was not agreed, the Government took no action.

For this favour many thanks promptly rendered on a royal scale:

> In August the Right Hon. Secretary was at Storrs, the elegant mansion of Mr. Bolton. Scott and Lockhart came to Elleray on their return from Ireland, and after a few days with the Professor, joined Canning at Storrs, accompanied by the Wilsons, Wordsworth, and many other illustrious persons. On Monday, 22nd August, 1825, the lake of Windermere exhibited symptoms of gaiety that far surpassed anything witnessed there during many years. About thirty boats mustered in Bowness Bay under the command of Christopher North, and proceeded in a line to Storrs, where the ornate barge of the Boltons joined the party, the celebrities within being hailed with universal bursts of cheering. Churchbells rang joyously and cannon was enthusiastically fired as the flotilla swept triumphantly onward. In the course of an hour every boat on the lake had joined the regatta, and performed a variety of evolutions at the order of Wilson, who was at once dubbed 'Lord High Admiral of the Lakes'.[1]

This was the heyday of Lake society, with Wordsworth at the head, and around him Coleridge, Southey, De Quincey and others. It is beyond the province of the economic historian to assess their place in the history of literature, and I would not cause Wordsworth to stir in his Grasmere grave by importing into this section 'the idol proudly named the Wealth of Nations'. But there are notions of which even Dove Cottage need not disapprove, which are within the economic ambit. Here is one of them. Did not the Lake District in its Liverpool merchants, from John Bolton to Sir William Forwood, prove ideal conservers of a great invisible export of natural beauty, which the world would never tire of visiting? And here, finally, is another. In the Lakes, Oxford met Cambridge, and London met Edinburgh. During the French wars a visit to these parts took the place of the Continental Grand Tour. New joys and new values were engendered in which the gentlemen of Liverpool shared, one of which was healthy competition in sport. John Bolton willed Storrs to the Rev. Thos. Staniforth, and Thos. Stani-

---

[1] Elsie Swann, *Christopher North (John Wilson)* (1934), 199.

forth stroked Oxford in the first Oxford and Cambridge Boat Race of 1829. John Gladstone's son went to Oxford, as also did the son of John Moss, the first of a long line of rowing blues. Light Blue and Dark Blue. I trust that for once the order will be forgiven. For how should

> I slight my own beloved Cam, to range
> Where silver Isis leads my stripling feet?

Sussex, Thames-side, Staffordshire, Liverpool—you may have them all if you leave me Cambridge and the Lakes.

# INDEX

# INDEX

Coutts, John, and Company, and Coutts Bank, 112
Cowley, Lord. *See* Wellesley, Henry
Cowper-Temple, William Francis (later Baron Mount-Temple), 82, 254, 256
Creevy, T., 20, 24, 356
Crewe, growth of, 22, 59, 318
Croft, Rev. George, 311
Croker, J. W., 50, 53, 54, 76, 162, 166, 167 n.
Cropper, James, 29, 60, 251, 252-4, 372, 379
Crown Lands. *See* Woods and Forests
Crown Lands Act of 1851, 232
Cunard Line, 359
Cundy, Nicholas Wilcox, 251
Currie, W. W., 29
Curwen, John Christian, 44, 367, 382, 383, 384-5
Customs, 270 ff., 360; Out-Port Letter Books of, 18-19; Herries Consolidation of the laws, 113, 285-6, 291-6; Commission of Enquiry, 1818-1824, 114, 286-9; evasion of, 139-42; Scottish Customs, 268-70; language peculiar to, 274-6; Long Room, 275; Coast Guard, 275-6; Minutes, 284-5; transfers from Excise to Customs, 289. *See also* Corn Laws *and* Silk
Customs' Benevolent Fund, 282-3

Dalhousie, Lord, 132
Sir Hugh Dalrymple: account of Napoleon, 128-9; account of Wellington and Waterloo, 129-31
Darwin, Erasmus, 15
Davis, Robert Hart, 148
Davison, Alexander, 42
Dawkins, Henry, 210, 211
Declaratory Act, 291-6
Delamere, Lord, 6
Denison, J. E., 17, 150, 166
Denny, William, 18
Derby, Earl of, 24, 31, 32, 87, 88
Disraeli, Benjamin, 53, 122, 315; *Sybil*, 349-51

Dobie, Professor, 43
Dock Acts, 36
Dodgson, Charles Lutwidge. *See* Carroll, Lewis
Dover, 45 and n.
Drummond, James, 118
Dudley, Earl of. *See* Ward, John William
Dundas, Henry (Viscount Melville), 41, 62, 65, 66-70, 73, 135, 230
Dupin, Charles, 178-9
Dyott, General William, 313 n.
Dyson, T. F., 376

Earle, Hardman, 29
Eartham, 238 ff. *See also* Huskisson, letters to his wife; Huskisson, Emily, will of; *and* Hayley, William
Education, in Edinburgh, 43, 385; in Staffordshire, 306-13
Education Act of 1870, 82
Egerton, Lord Francis (Earl of Ellesmere). *See* Leveson-Gower, Lord Francis
Egerton, R., 6-7
Egerton, W., 6
Egerton, Sir Philip, 5
Eliot, John (later Lord Eliot), 44, 46
Eliot, William, 44
Ellenborough, Lord (later Earl of Ellenborough), 88, 93
Emigration: Committee of 1826-7, 85-6, 125; to Australia, 261-4; from Liverpool, 360, 363, 367
Enclosure, 211 ff., 225, 231, 233, 290
Enclosure Act, 209, 224
Erie Canal, 359
Esterhazy, Prince, 5, 9
Ewart, Joseph, 29
Excise. *See* Customs

Fagnani, Maria, 51-2
Farquhar, Sir Robert, 148
Farquhar, Sir Thomas, 108, 117
Farrer, T. N., 291
Fay, Charles, 20 n.
Fiennes, Celia, 47, 318, 383
Fife, Earl of, 193 and n., 208 n.